ICONS OF WOMEN'S SPORT

Recent Titles in
Greenwood Icons

Icons of Unbelief: Atheists, Agnostics, and Secularists
S.T. Joshi, Editor

Women Icons of Popular Music: The Rebels, Rockers, and Renegades
Carrie Havranek

Icons of Talk: The Media Mouths That Changed America
Donna L. Halper

Icons of African American Protest: Trailblazing Activists of the Civil
Rights Movement
Gladys L. Knight

Icons of American Architecture: From the Alamo to the World Trade Center
Donald Langmead

Icons of Invention: The Makers of the Modern World from Gutenberg
to Gates
John W. Klooster

Icons of Beauty: Art, Culture, and the Image of Women
Debra N. Mancoff and Lindsay J. Bosch

Icons of Mystery and Crime Detection: From Sleuths to Superheroes
Mitzi M. Brunsdale

Icons of Black America
Matthew C. Whitaker, Editor

Icons of American Cooking
Victor W. Geraci and Elizabeth S. Demers, Editors

Icons of African American Comedy
Eddie Tafoya

Icons of African American Literature: The Black Literary World
Yolanda Williams Page, Editor

ICONS OF WOMEN'S SPORT

Volume Two

Steven J. Overman
and Kelly Boyer Sagert

 GREENWOOD

AN IMPRINT OF ABC-CLIO, LLC
Santa Barbara, California • Denver, Colorado • Oxford, England

Library of Congress Cataloging-in-Publication Data

Overman, Steven J.
  Icons of women's sport / Steven J. Overman and Kelly Boyer Sagert.
    p. cm. — (Greenwood icons)
  Includes bibliographical references and index.
  ISBN 978-0-313-38548-3 (hardback) — ISBN 978-0-313-38549-0 (ebook)
  1. Women athletes—Biography. I. Sagert, Kelly Boyer. II. Title.
  GV697.A1.O987 2012
  796.092'2—dc23
  [B]
                                                    2011041561

ISBN: 978-0-313-38548-3
EISBN: 978-0-313-38549-0

16 15 14 13 12   1 2 3 4 5

This book is also available on the World Wide Web as an eBook.
Visit www.abc-clio.com for details.

Greenwood
An Imprint of ABC-CLIO, LLC

ABC-CLIO, LLC
130 Cremona Drive, P.O. Box 1911
Santa Barbara, California 93116-1911

This book is printed on acid-free paper ∞
Manufactured in the United States of America

Contents

Olga Korbut throws up her arms in joy after winning the Individual Women's Gymnastic event for Russia at the 1972 Summer Olympics in Munich, Germany. (AP Photo)

Olga Korbut (1955–)

Olga Korbut is a gymnast from the Soviet Union who, perhaps more than any other gymnast, raised interest in the sport in the United States and in other countries around the world. In fact, the five-fold increase of gymnastics participants in the United States in the 1970s was largely attributed to Korbut. Her radiant smile (often called "cheeky") and upbeat personality captured the hearts of fans in countries around the globe, with one television analyst stating that watching Korbut compete was like watching a kid play in the sun ("Olga's Crash Landing: Olympics Special," 2004, 14). One of her trademarks was her ponytails; she would pull her coarse brown hair back into two messy ponytails, tying them with brightly colored ribbons.

Prior to Korbut's debut, gymnastics often focused on elegance of movement; Korbut, however, introduced challenging acrobatic moves that changed the direction of the sport and helped to pave the way for gymnasts such as Romania's Nadia Comaneci and Mary Lou Retton from the United States.

In the 1972 Olympics Korbut won the gold medal for the balance beam and floor exercises, as well as another gold medal for being on the winning Soviet team. She also won a silver medal in 1972 on the uneven bars. In 1976 she earned a gold medal for being part of the first-place gymnastics team, and a silver medal for the balance beam. In 1988 Korbut, nicknamed "the Sparrow from Minsk," became the first person inducted into the International Gymnastics Hall of Fame.

After moving to the United States, Korbut has been involved in more than one controversial situation. These include accusations that her coach physically and sexually abused her, as well as a conviction for shoplifting and insinuations that she was involved in a counterfeiting scheme, although no formal charges were ever made against her for the latter.

CHILDHOOD

Olga Valentinovna Korbut was born on May 16, 1955 in Grodno (also called Hrodna), located in the Belarus Republic, which was part of the Soviet Union at the time of her birth. Grodno is located three hundred miles west of Moscow, close to the border of Poland; for most of its history, the town has been part of Poland, with Grodno serving as one of two seats of the Polish-Lithuanian parliament during the sixteenth century. In 1795 Russia seized and maintained control of Grodno until 1920, when it became part of Poland again. The Soviet Union's military occupied the region during the first part of World War II; in 1941 Germany occupied Grodno and maintained control until 1945, when it became part of the Soviet Union again. Thousands of Polish families were required to leave the town after the war, and Byelo-Russians, also called White Russians, moved into the region.

By the time Korbut was born, approximately 80,000 people lived in Grodno, with residents often working in tobacco factories, distilleries, and soap- and candle-making facilities. Korbut was the youngest of the four daughters of Valentin and Valentina Korbut; her sister Irina was born in 1946; Zemfira, in 1948; and Ludmilla, in 1953. Her father was wounded in World War II fighting against the Germans when he was just fifteen years old; hospitalized, he began studying engineering after his recovery, eventually working in that field after the war. Her mother, trained as a nurse, worked as a cook for a workers' collective. The two met when Valentin, as secretary of the Grodno Young Communist District Committee, helped to set up supply systems for the area, restore factories to working condition, and obtain blood for people who needed it. In this last capacity, he met the young nurse he was to marry. Eventually, he was unable to work and was awarded a war pension.

Olga was the smallest child in her class and she struggled with her grades, but she clearly possessed athletic ability. Her sister Ludmilla was a gymnast, and Olga was also interested in the sport. Her physical education teacher suggested that Korbut, who was prone to playful mischief, could make a good gymnast. Korbut began training in gymnastics when she was nine years old by successfully obtaining a spot in a sports school, where she would be schooled in academics and gymnastics. More than 700,000 youth participated in gymnastics in the Soviet Union, but only the most promising were able to attend one of the thirty-five schools with top quality gymnastics training.

Korbut began training in a program overseen by Renald Knysh, the senior instructor at the school, although he reportedly was not impressed with her when he first met her. According to the *Daily Mail*, Knysh told Korbut that if she could not do the splits, then she was not welcome back in his gym. Korbut tried to do the splits, broke her leg, and then returned to practice once the bone healed.

Knysh assigned her to the care of Yelena Volchetskaya, who had been on the gold-medal team in the 1964 Olympics in Tokyo, Japan, and Tamara Alexeyeva, the national champion on the vault. Female gymnasts in the Soviet Union were taught to incorporate ballet-like techniques into their routines, and the combination of highly disciplined athletes using the graceful moves of ballet created the powerhouse gymnastics legacy that existed throughout the modern Olympics era.

It was in 1952 that the four individual gymnastics events—vault, floor exercises, uneven bars, and balance beam—became part of the Olympic experience; the women's teams from the Soviet Union won team gold that year, and they repeated that accomplishment in 1956, 1960, 1964, and 1968. Whoever made the Soviet team in 1972 had huge shoes to fill.

In the vault event, an athlete runs approximately sixty feet down a padded or carpeted runway onto a springboard and, after placing her hands on the vault apparatus—which resembles a pommel horse without any handles—she performs a series of spinning and/or flipping acrobatic moves before landing on the other side.

On the balance beam, athletes perform a series of flips, twists, tumbles, and graceful dance moves on a beam that is 500 centimeters long, 125 centimeters above the ground, and 10 centimeters wide.

On the uneven bars, athletes perform a series of flips and maneuvers over a set of asymmetrical bars. The upper bar is 241 centimeters off the ground, and the lower is 161 centimeters off the ground. Each bar is 240 centimeters in length and 4 centimeters in diameter.

Most floor exercises are performed on spring floors where athletes perform a series of acrobatic and graceful movements; out of bounds areas are clearly marked. In this event—and the other three events—judges scored each gymnast based on her performance, with the elusive 10 being the top score. (The scoring system has since changed.)

KORBUT: COMPETITIVE GYMNASTICS

When Korbut turned twelve, Volchetskaya suggested that Knysh take a closer look at her; after he did, he decided to coach her personally. He was impressed with her ability and her confidence; he had some concerns about her headstrong nature and her conviction that she was ready to tackle any gymnastic move, no matter how difficult, but he decided to use that trait to their advantage. Sometimes, Olga would cry with frustration when she wanted to achieve a new skill which her body was not yet ready to accomplish.

Nevertheless, Knysh honed in on her strengths, one of which was an unusual suppleness of the spine, which permitted her to perform backward moves exceptionally well. These moves include the eponymous "Korbut loop" where she flung herself backward from the top of the two uneven bars and then caught the bar again. She suffered at least three concussions in a five-year period performing this move. Korbut later said that Knysh never praised her during their practices or competitions, but she trusted his gymnastics judgment completely.

Knysh's philosophy about gymnastics was not widely shared by other coaches and officials in the mid-1960s; he believed that whatever acrobatic moves could be performed on the floor could be performed on a gymnastic apparatus as well. According to author Michael Suponev, Knysh was "eternally brimming over with ideas. An inventor by temperament . . . [he] has accomplished a real revolution in gymnastics" (Suponev, 1976, 36). Suponev also describes Knysh as "kindhearted, shy" and "mercilessly demanding of himself and of others" (Suponev, 1976, 38).

With the help of Knysh's revolutionary style of coaching, Korbut entered the Belorussian junior championship competition in 1967. In 1968 she won the gold medal at the Spartakiade championships. The following year, she debuted a move known as the "Korbut flip," in which she stood on the high bar, performed a back flip in the open air, and then caught the bar; this was the first backward release move done on the uneven bars, and it is, to this day, considered one of the most difficult gymnastics moves to master.

Korbut incorporated the move in her first Soviet national championships, which was in 1969. Typically, a gymnast would need to be at least sixteen years old to compete in the nationals, but Larissa Latynina, the national women's team coach, advocated for fifteen-year-old Korbut to be an exception, possibly because she envisioned Korbut having the ability to compete in the 1972 Olympics, given enough high-level experience.

Korbut placed fifth overall in the national championships, placing higher on the uneven bars and balance beam than the women who had won medals in the 1968 Olympics had achieved. At this competition, some judges did not approve of her radical new move, the Korbut flip, most likely penalizing her for her originality. Korbut nevertheless continued to incorporate other unexpected and previously unperformed elements into gymnastic events.

In 1970 Korbut placed fourth in the national competition, winning on the vault, typically her weakest event. Korbut did not compete in the World Championships, held in Ljubljana, Yugoslavia, because her coaches felt that she was too young for this type of international attention. She was permitted to travel with the team, though, and to perform in an exhibition in front of the judges; during this competition, Korbut offended some teammates when she verbalized her belief that she belonged on the international team ahead of some who were granted a spot. After lying low for a few months because of an illness and an injury, Korbut then returned to active competition. In 1971 she placed fourth in the national Soviet championships once again.

During an event leading up to the Olympics, the U.S.S.R. All Union Cup, Korbut beat both of her Soviet rivals: Ludmilla Turischeva, who had clinched the World Championships in 1970 and the European Championships in 1971, and Tamara Lazakovich, who was the reigning European champion. After that stunning win, Korbut returned to Moscow, where she worked with Knysh and Latynina on her choreography for her Olympic floor exercises. She also consulted with a sports psychologist to prepare for the spotlight of Olympic competition. Initially, Korbut was to be the team alternate, but she replaced an injured teammate, thereby securing a spot on the team.

Five days before the team was to leave for Germany to compete in the Olympics, Korbut announced that the choreography for her floor exercises, called the Bumble Bee, was not right for her. This announcement came after several months wherein she and her coaches had worked hard on the routine. Korbut stated that bees were nasty and this was alien to her nature. Her coaches, her sports psychologist, and her doctor all attempted to persuade her that it was far too late to change her routine, but Korbut went to bed insisting that she was right. The two coaches stayed up all night, fretting about what to do. In the morning, they decided to present Korbut with a new routine, one that she had only seven days to learn.

Besides learning a new routine with just days to practice, Korbut also needed to be prepared for six events at the Olympics: the four individual events and two other competitions, one individual and one team, wherein each competitor received an overall score for the combined events. For each event there is a compulsory exercise, in which the movements are predetermined, and an optional exercise, in which the athletes have some freedom in creating routines, choosing levels of difficulty, and highlighting areas of expertise.

Four judges score each athlete's performance; the highest and lowest scores are thrown out and the middle two scores are averaged to come up with the athlete's score. The maximum number of points awarded for each event was 10.

1972 OLYMPICS

Before the Olympics began, controversy arose over whether or not to admit Rhodesia to the Games, with African countries insisting on a ban against the country because of its apartheid regime in which the minority (whites) ruled the majority (blacks). Ultimately, Rhodesia, as well as South Africa, was banned because of apartheid policies.

The Olympic Games took place in Munich, Germany, with the gymnastic events being held August 27 through September 6. This was the first time that the Summer Olympics had been held in Germany since 1936, when Adolf Hitler ruled the country.

When Korbut competed in 1972, she stood five feet, one inch tall and weighed ninety-four pounds. She and her five teammates—Lyubov Burda, Antonina Koshel, Tamara Lazakovich, Elvira Saadi, and Ludmilla Turischeva— were the latest representatives of a country that had dominated every women's gymnastics Olympic competition in modern history.

Between 600 and 800 million people watched the 1972 Olympics on television, and one of their earlier impressions was of Korbut perfectly executing a backward somersault on the balance beam. She also performed well on the vault, quickly earning the applause and admiration of spectators. After these two events, four athletes—Ludmilla Turischeva, Tamara Lazokovich, and Korbut from the Soviet Union, and Karin Janz from East Germany—rose to the top.

Korbut then performed on the uneven bars; although she had created an incredible routine, she slipped badly, actually coming off the bars. After returning to her seat, she began to cry, something not typical for a Soviet athlete. American gymnast Bart Conner, who won Olympic gold in 1984, had this to say about Korbut's tears: "We had the impression that every athlete from the Soviet Union was an unemotional machine. Then she came along, this vulnerable little girl. Everyone wanted to hug her" (Longman, 2001).

Judges awarded her a score of 7.50, causing the audience to jeer. Turischeva ended up winning the gold in combined exercises after Korbut's slip; that night, in the Olympic Village, she comforted Korbut, who appeared on television reassuring the world that she would not make any more blunders in the competition.

The next day, the athletes were to compete in the four individual events. In the compulsories for the beam, Korbut performed well, as did Turischeva and Lazakovich. In optionals, Korbut nailed her backward somersault, earning the gold medal in the balance beam event; Lazakovich earned the silver, and Janz, the bronze.

The vault was next; this was Korbut's weakest event, one that was difficult for her given her tiny stature. In the vault, Karin Janz from East Germany took the gold; Erika Zuchold, also from East Germany, the silver; and Turischeva, the bronze.

When it came time to perform on the uneven bars, the event in which Korbut ordinarily excelled but had slipped on the day before, she scored a 9.65 in her compulsories. She needed an extraordinary score on the uneven bars to medal; she performed an incredible routine, but only received a score of 9.80. The crowd was furious, cheering loudly for Korbut and jeering the judges; the spectators were soon standing up, stamping their feet on the wooden floor, making a racket. Olympic officials could not stop the protest; it took the actions of another gymnast, Angelica Hellman from East Germany, to calm the crowd. Hellman stood up, placed a finger on her lips to ask for silence, and began her uneven bars routine. She did not make a good landing and she began to cry, which effectively shamed the crowd into near silence.

Korbut's two scores for the uneven bars totaled 19.450 out of 20 points, behind Janz, who scored 19.675 and won the gold medal. Korbut tied with Erica Zuchold, but Korbut was awarded the silver medal on a legitimate technicality.

The last individual event was the floor exercises, with the Soviet Union's team expected to dominate. Korbut, Turischeva, Lazokovich, and Saadi all had the capability of performing outstanding floor routines. After the compulsories, Korbut was in second place behind Turischeva; Korbut then performed an incredible optional floor routine—one that she had only practiced for seven days—incorporating complicated backward somersaults and other rolls and dives, along with graceful and lighthearted dancing moves. Korbut scored a 9.90, earning the gold medal. Tursicheva clinched the silver, and Lazokovich the bronze. The Soviet Union also won team gold, adding to Korbut's medal total.

OLYMPIC TRAGEDY

Korbut clearly captivated the hearts of the audience worldwide, helping to kick off the Olympics on a thrilling high note. On September 6, 1972, however, perhaps the greatest tragedy in modern Olympic history took place. On that date, the Palestinian Black September guerilla group stormed the Olympic Village, killing two Israeli athletes and kidnapping nine others. The West German government offered to pay the guerillas for the release of the athletes, but they rebuffed the offer; the government then supplied the Palestinian group with three helicopters to transport them to the airport. A gun battle between police and the guerillas took place at the airport, and all nine hostages were killed by explosives planted in a helicopter by the Palestinian group. Four of the kidnappers also died, along with one police officer. It was questionable as to whether or not the Olympic Games would continue; the Israeli and Egyptian teams immediately withdrew. American swimmer Mark Spitz, who had won a record seven medals, was spirited away before closing ceremonies because he was Jewish and perhaps at risk.

As horrible as this tragedy was, it only served to further the adoration of Korbut. Perhaps the sheer ugliness and horror of the massacre created a hunger for uplifting Olympic stories—and Korbut fulfilled that purpose extremely well.

POST-1972 OLYMPICS

In 1972 ABC's Wide World of Sports chose Korbut as Athlete of the Year, and the British Broadcasting Company named her Sportswoman of the Year, the first Eastern Bloc athlete to ever receive the latter award; in the Soviet Union, she was named an Honored Master of Sport, the youngest person to receive that high honor. When *Life* magazine created a retrospective piece on the 1972 Olympics, Korbut was the only non-American to be included.

Perhaps even more important, after Korbut won the hearts of people around the world, girls throughout the United States and Europe wanted to become gymnasts. Korbut did much more than succeed in gymnastics; she popularized the sport. She would receive large amounts of fan mail, some of it simply addressed to "Olga, Moscow," requiring her to have a secretary to organize her mail. Korbut traveled around the Soviet Union after the Olympics, giving talks about and demonstrations of gymnastics. She became accustomed to journalists asking her questions and photographers taking her picture, but they tended to avoid her mother; it is said that Valentina Korbut used media occasions to ask why the family was not given a bigger house by the government after her daughter had won Olympic gold.

Korbut was not universally beloved, though. The International Gymnastics Federation expressed concern about the level of risk incorporated into her routines. Eleven months after Korbut's Olympic wins, they took their concern a step further, banning backward somersaults on the beam and the backward flik-flak move on the uneven bars. Reasons given included that they believed backward somersaults belonged on the floor, not on a beam; they also stated that gymnasts could become hurt if they tried these moves.

Korbut and Knysh responded furiously to these bans, seeing them as a personal attack, with Korbut saying, "If this ban is implemented, I see no place for me in the future of gymnastics" (Beecham, 1974, 116). It's possible that these bans went into effect because of rumors that Korbut had injured her spine by performing these advanced moves; these rumors probably arose because of Korbut's visit to the Tskatubo Spa two months after the Olympics. She was suffering from a backache and exhaustion at the time.

Afterward, Korbut returned to Grodno, where she began studying history in a teacher's college. She lived in her own apartment, paying her bills with the thirty-six rubles that the government paid her each week for her gymnastic accomplishments; this was the equivalent of $50.

While at the teacher's college, she followed a regular schedule, starting with breakfast at 7:30 AM. For that meal, she might consume up to two pints of ketchup, her favorite food; or she might have an egg, some meat, and a cup of coffee. She then practiced two hours of gymnastics before attending classes. Returning to her apartment around 4 PM, she would eat vegetable soup and perhaps meat for lunch. From 6 to 9 PM she practiced gymnastics again. For dinner, she typically ate fruit and drank tea before going to bed at 10:30 PM. She engaged in these activities six days a week; on Sundays, she enjoyed walking through nearby forests.

In March 1973 Korbut visited the United States, where Olga Korbut fan clubs had been established. She and the Soviet gymnastics team visited eight American cities—Houston, Buffalo, Los Angeles, Miami, Washington, Philadelphia, New York, and Chicago. People jammed into airports to catch a glimpse of Korbut, and the stadiums where she performed filled up and sold out. In Chicago, the day of her visit was dubbed "Olga Korbut Day," and she received the key to New York City. She received a similar welcome in Denmark, Germany, and England. Not surprisingly, the Associated Press also chose her as Athlete of the Year.

In August 1973 she competed in the World Student Games in Moscow, winning three gold medals and a bronze in the individual events, and the gold for the individual combined event. The following year, Korbut competed in the World Championships, winning five medals. In 1975 the Women's Sport Foundation named her Athlete of the Year and Mother of Gymnastics.

COLD WAR DIPLOMAT

The adoration of Korbut in the United States is especially remarkable considering the strained relationship between the Soviet Union and the United States during the Cold War era. The Cold War was a non-military battle between Communist countries and capitalist countries, which began after the close of World War II and lasted through 1991 when the Soviet Union collapsed. It was believed that if the United States and the Soviet Union clashed militarily, it would become a nuclear battle that could end the world as we knew it.

In the middle of this contentious era, tiny Olga Korbut bridged the gap and became well loved in both countries. When the U.S. president, Richard Nixon, was seeking re-election, he sought out an audience with Korbut; he informed her that she was very small—and she, in return, let him know that he was very big.

Perhaps the first television commercial ever filmed by an American producer in the Soviet Union starred Korbut. From May through October 1974, the Soviet Union planned to rent a booth at the World Fair, to be held in Spokane, Washington; their booth would feature sports teams, including their gymnastics team. Because of Korbut's good reputation worldwide, she became the spokesperson for the fair.

American producers had attempted to arrange to film a commercial to promote the World Fair with Korbut, but, for weeks, they received no response from the Soviets. The producers then received a telegram stating that they had three days to arrive in Moscow to film the commercial; Korbut was preparing to leave on a gymnastics tour, so time was of the essence. This seemingly impossible task was accomplished and revisions to the script approved, but stumbling blocks still existed. The Soviet cameramen warned the American producers that Korbut occasionally had "temperamental outbursts," there were compatibility issues with equipment, and Korbut was more than an hour late to the filming, causing the Americans to worry that she did not plan to show up. Just as frustration levels were reaching their peak, Korbut appeared in a full-length fox-fur coat, looking "absolutely smashing." Because the temperatures were 3 degrees Fahrenheit below zero, Korbut stayed in the car until it was time for her to be filmed.

The first time Korbut spoke her lines, which were in English, she did not deliver them correctly and appeared irritable. The second time, she made more mistakes and refused to look into the camera; she began to sob and went back to the car. The producers revised her lines so that all but one of them could be spoken in Russian; although she delivered the lines in a more satisfactory manner, the camera had frozen.

The film crew quickly wrapped up what needed to be done, using another camera, and then it was time to travel to another location. The sunlight was fading and the crew needed to hurry. At the second location, Korbut refused

COLD WAR ERA OLYMPIC TENSIONS

In 1952, the USSR (Soviet Union) began sending teams to the Olympic Games, sparking intense competition between Eastern Bloc nations, under the influence of the USSR, and western nations, particularly the United States. Wins by either side were often seen as validation that the country's ideology—whether capitalism or Communism—was best. Eastern Bloc athletes were typically subsidized by the state, meaning that both their living and training expenses were paid by the government. Perhaps the country of Germany best illustrates this era. After World War II had ended, Germany effectively became divided in half, into West Germany and East Germany, with the latter considered the Soviet Zone of Germany. A combined East/West team competed in the Olympics, leading some to believe that Olympic competition was so valued that it trumped political turmoil; in 1968, though, West Germany was considered the German team, with East Germany considered a separate territory that deserved its own team—and so two teams were sent from the divided country. In 1980, the United States boycotted the Games, which were held in Moscow, because the Soviet Union had invaded Afghanistan. Sixty-four other countries did not participate in those Games, most of them in support of the boycott. In 1984, the Soviet Union and thirteen other Eastern Bloc nations boycotted the Olympics, held in Los Angeles; a notable exception was Romania, which participated. It has been noted that nearly as many political writers as sports writers attended the 1984 Games. The reunification of Germany took place in 1990, with the Soviet Union collapsing the following year, thereby ending the Cold War era of Olympic competition.

to return to filming until after she ate sausage, which was not available at the filming site. The film crew traveled ten miles to a village, coming upon a restaurant—but it was closed. After banging on the door, a woman appeared, willing to serve Korbut sausage, chicken, and soup. By the time the gymnast finished eating, it was dusk, making filming more challenging, but Korbut was much more cooperative and upbeat and the filming was completed.

Although the text on her Web site about this time period in her life seems over the top (with prose that reads how "she did more to ease the tensions of the Cold War than all the politicians and diplomats of the day put together" [Olga Korbut Web site]), Korbut did bridge a wide and deep chasm, and, for that reason, it makes sense that in 1975 the United Nations selected her as the "Woman of the Year."

All was not so peaceful closer to home for Korbut, though. Some of Korbut's Soviet teammates resented the attention that she received after the 1972 Olympics. Ludmilla Turischeva, who went on to coach the Ukrainian women's gymnastics team, has called Korbut selfish, while Korbut has responded by saying that Turischeva had a lack of grace (McElvoy, 1999).

Korbut's lifestyle did more than irritate her teammates; it also took a toll on her. In 1974 Korbut was exhausted from her hectic lifestyle and she was smoking as a form of weight control, which put a further strain on her body. She, along with her teammates, continued to travel around the United States and Europe, putting on gymnastic exhibitions. Although the performances brought in a significant amount of money, each gymnast only received $20 per day, with the government claiming the rest; some gymnasts used their money to buy Western-style T-shirts.

It should be noted that Eastern Bloc athletes were extremely reliant upon their governments to provide for them. They typically attended less school than the average person in their country so that they could have more time to practice their sport; this gave them fewer options in a career outside of their sport. Because their governments had invested so much in their athletic development, it was expected that money raised by the athletes would largely belong to the state.

1976 OLYMPICS

In 1976 Korbut competed in her second Olympics for the Soviet Union, this time in Montreal, Canada. She was considered one of the three strong contenders for Olympic gold, along with teammate Turischeva and a young athlete from Romania, Nadia Comaneci. As the newcomer to the Olympics, Comaneci received a significant amount of attention from media; when a journalist pointed out that she seemed surly, Comaneci said that she came to the Olympics to do a job, not to smile, adding that she would leave the smiling to Korbut.

Although Korbut performed well, Comaneci gave extraordinary performances, including seven perfect 10s, the first perfect scores given at the Olympics. Whenever Comaneci completed a performance, television cameras would pan to Korbut to show her reactions; some written coverage of the competition seemed cruel and even unfair, with *Time* magazine pointing out Korbut's unkempt hair, her haggard face, and her churlish behavior (*Time*, "Olympics: The Games: Up in the Air," 1976).

It was the Soviets, though, that won the team gold; the team consisted of Maria Filatova, Svetlana Grozdova, Nellie Kim, Elvira Saadi, Ludmilla Turischeva, and, of course, Olga Korbut. Korbut also won a silver medal in the balance beam event; it was this performance that received the loudest cheering from spectators. This meant that Korbut had won four Olympic gold medals and two silver medals from the 1972 and 1976 Olympics.

POST-1976 OLYMPICS

In 1977 Korbut retired from competition and switched to coaching other athletes. In 1978 she married Leonid Bortkevich, the folk rock singer of a popular band, Pesniary; the following year, after first suffering a miscarriage, she gave birth to their only son, named Richard. In 1982 she was named to the International Women's Sports Hall of Fame; she was the first gymnast named to this organization and, since then, only eight other gymnasts have been inducted.

Four years later, Korbut's country was rocked with a tragedy of immense proportion. On April 25, 1986, a nuclear reactor in Chernobyl, located about 180 miles away from her home in Minsk, exploded; Korbut could see the radiation clouds from her house. It was later discovered that engineers were conducting an unauthorized test of one of the nuclear reactors, leading to an explosion so powerful that it blew off the top of the containment building, allowing radioactive material to enter the atmosphere. The subsequent fire caused even more radioactive material to be released. The international world did not learn of this disaster until Swedish scientists detected the radiation; the nuclear reactor was not sealed off until after eight tons of radioactive material had escaped.

Korbut began advocating for people affected by the explosion; she was quoted in a *Sports Illustrated* article written by Hank Hersch, stating that the government did not caution its citizens to stay indoors as the radiation escaped. After friends and family showed signs of illness from the radiation, Korbut began participating in fundraisers to provide relief to victims. On behalf of the Fred Hutchinson Cancer Research Center, she helped to raise $70,000 that was used for medical supplies. Korbut sent her son to live with friends in New Jersey to protect him against the effects of radiation.

Korbut was also quoted in *People*, sharing how terrifying the experience was for citizens. "When people began hearing bits of information, they felt panicky. They were afraid to drink the water, breathe the air, afraid of everything. We were all outdoors, because it was close to the [May Day] celebration, and we were planting gardens and enjoying the spring. If they had told us Chernobyl had exploded, we would have stayed inside and maybe avoided those early heavy doses of radiation" (*People*, "Olga Korbut's Deadly Foe," 1991).

Korbut also shared stories of people coming down with dreadful illnesses after being "perfectly healthy" prior to the disaster; no chemotherapy was available, she said, for the people who needed it to fight thyroid cancers, and produce and meat were challenging to find to nourish the sick or the still healthy.

In 1988 Korbut was featured in the news for a more uplifting reason: she was the first person inducted into the Gymnastics Hall of Fame, which was organized to recognize outstanding gymnasts who continued to participate in the international gymnastics community, in post-competition years. Not only was Korbut the first person chosen for this honor, but she was in fact the only member of the organization until 1993, when Romanian Nadia Comaneci joined her as an inductee. Since that time, more than seventy other gymnasts have been selected for induction.

UNITED STATES

In 1991 Korbut relocated to the United States, sharing with the American media that she also suffered from thyroid problems and stating that she believed that radiation poison caused her health problems. Korbut eventually found work in the United States as a gymnastics coach, and honors kept rolling in for the former Olympian. In 1994 *Sports Illustrated* named her as one of the top athletes of the past forty years. Two years later, she served as the official representative of Belarus at the Olympic Summer Games, which were held in Atlanta, Georgia. In 1999 the Italian news agency ACHA included Korbut in their list of the best sportswomen of the twentieth century.

That same year, though, Korbut revealed extremely disturbing news, saying that her coach, Knysh, had sexually abused her (McElvoy, 1999). Knysh denied these allegations, while Korbut remained steadfast in her story. The abuse, according to Korbut, started about a year before she competed in the 1972 Olympics, when she was just fifteen years old. He would begin by giving Korbut a massage, but the physical contact continued on from there; the first time they had sexual relations, Knysh had given her cheap cognac ahead of time. Korbut said that she eventually confided in one of her teammates, but not until four or five years later. Knysh, along with other Soviet coaches, saw young gymnasts as something more, Korbut told a Russian newspaper—as their concubines.

Korbut was torn in her feelings about Knysh; she recognized that he was the best coach available and she acknowledged that she would not have achieved all that she did in gymnastics if he had not coached her (*Daily Mail* 2004, 14). Korbut also alleged that Knysh regularly beat her and also tried to control her entire life, even suggesting at her retirement that they marry; Korbut said that she turned him down. According to Korbut, Knysh eventually turned his attention to younger gymnasts.

If Korbut's allegations are in fact true, then it has been suggested that the way in which the Soviet Union treated its athletes is partially to blame. Young athletes with potential were virtually separated from their parents' control and handed over to a coach. The coaches determined what the athletes could eat and decided what drugs could be given to them, perhaps even drugs to slow down the emergence of puberty; Korbut later said that she was not allowed to have her first menstrual period until she was twenty-one years old ("The Lost Olympians," 2004).

One journalist has interviewed former Eastern Bloc female athletes and their friends, asking if the authorities knew of the sexual exploitation of young females in these situations. The friend of an East German speed skating champion answered in the affirmative, saying that all that mattered was the number of medals being earned. This woman later refused to have her daughter trained for a sport; because she had married into an influential family, she had the power to refuse, while many other poorer families would not have a say in the matter.

Here is an example of the ways in which the Soviet government allegedly orchestrated the lives of their prime athletes. Korbut's rival, Ludmilla Turischeva, was married to Valery Borzov, the medal-winning sprinter; rumors suggested that the two were paired together by the Soviet government to create super-athletic children. In 1993, the same journalist asked the couple if there was any truth to the rumor; Turischeva answered in the affirmative in a deadpan voice. The couple did have a daughter, but she did not turn out to be a winning sprinter. Her father blamed that on laziness and the fact that this generation was not as motivated to win a medal for their state (McElvoy, 1999).

About one year after Korbut made her shocking statements about her coach, she and her husband divorced. She married Alex Voinich the following year and obtained work as a gymnastics instructor in Dunwoody, Georgia.

MORE CONTROVERSIES

Korbut has definitely not enjoyed a controversy-free life after her retirement from competition; she has said that she struggled significantly to cope with the effects of fame. In the United States, she has unsuccessfully attempted to open her own training gym; she has coached at other gyms, but she has gone from one to the next. One gymnasium owner, David Day of Gym Elite, severed his coaching ties with her because of her "excessive drinking" (Longman, 2001). Korbut also received harsh criticism from people who believed that she was too strict with her gymnastics students; she in turn has said that children in the United States are too lazy.

The publisher of *International Gymnast* magazine, Paul Ziert, cites the switch from the Soviet system to the U.S. lifestyle as a cause of her troubles. "'I think she's had a very troubled life. To me, it all basically stems from the mentality of athletes who came out of the former Soviet Union. They worked so hard when they were young with aspirations that, when they made it, life would be taken care of. Here, there's no free lunch."

Korbut's troubles continued. On January 31, 2002, Korbut was arrested for shoplifting $19.35 worth of figs, seasonings, tea, cheese, and chocolate syrup from a Publix supermarket in Norcross, Georgia, by concealing them in her purse. Her representative, Kay Weatherford, was quoted by the *Atlanta Journal-Constitution* as saying that Korbut had intended to get her wallet out of her car, but she accidentally took the food with her. Korbut was fined $333 on the misdemeanor charge and attended a court-ordered class on values.

That May, Korbut appeared on a *Celebrity Boxing* show, where she competed against Darva Conger, who competed on the 2000 reality show *Who Wants to Marry a Millionaire?* Conger was chosen to be the bride at the end of the show's season; a few days after marrying the star of the millionaire program, the couple announced that they were having their marriage annulled. Although *Time* magazine predicted that Korbut would win the boxing match against Conger, she did not; Conger won by unanimous decision (Katcher, 2002).

Shortly afterward, eviction proceedings were begun on an abandoned home that Korbut had once owned. She and her first husband, Leonid Bortkevich, had bought the home, located in an upscale neighborhood, for $160,000 in 1993; in the fall of 2000, the year of their divorce, Bortkevich refinanced the home for $240,000. By July 2001, he was listed as sole owner of the home; their son Richard occupied the home, and Bortkevich returned to Belarus. When the sheriff arrived at the property on December 5, 2002, to evict anyone living inside, approximately $35,000 in counterfeit $100 bills were found inside, along with several computers.

According to Sheriff's Deputy Tracy Lee, the house had been trashed. "Light fixtures had been removed, banisters had been unhinged from the stairs. A large oil painting of Ms. Korbut ended up on the curb until it was rescued by a neighbor" (Longman, 2002). In September 2002, Korbut's son Richard pleaded guilty to making $20,000 in counterfeit bills on his computer.

LEGACY

Although Korbut's reputation has suffered through more recent events in her life, she did achieve incredible feats, winning four Olympic gold medals and two silver medals and electrifying the audience; she transformed the sport of gymnastics from one rewarding elegance and style to one requiring acrobatic excellence. Moreover, she bridged the seemingly insurmountable gap between the United States and the Soviet Union, if only for a short while. People who watched Korbut in Munich would surely understand why her biographer highlighted "her magnificent skill, her innovations, her boldness, her simplicity and her personal charm" in his book (Suponev, 1976, 46–47).

FURTHER READING

Beecham, Justin. 1974. *Olga*. New York: Paddington Press.

Katcher, Paul. 2002. Ready to, um, Rumble. *Time*. May 21: http://www.time.com/time/sampler/article/0,8599,241136,00.html.

Longman, Jere. 2001. 30 Years of Hard Falls for Olga Korbut, After the Gold and Glory. *New York Times*, February 10. http://www.nytimes.com/2002/02/10/us/30-years-of-hard-falls-for-olga-korbut-after-the-gold-and-glory.html.

"The Lost Olympians." 2004. *The Independent*. August 8: http://www.independent.co.uk/sport/olympics/the-lost-olympians-555632.html.

McElvoy, Anne. 1999. Grin and bear it, Sex and drugs and forward rolls: the Olga Korbut story. *The Independent*, June 25.

Olga Korbut Official Site. 2011. www.olgakorbut.com.

"Olga Korbut 1972 Olympics EF BB." YouTube. http://www.youtube.com/watch?v=a2gNQcbicsA.

"Olga Korbut—1976 Olympic Uneven Bar Routine." YouTube. http://www.youtube.com/watch?v=YsiLsguqXBU.

"Olga's Crash Landing: Olympics Special." *The Daily Mail*, July 25, 2004, p. 14.

"Olympics: The Games: Up in the Air." 1976. *Time*. August 2: http://www.time.com/time/magazine/article/0,9171,914450,00.html.

Suponev, Michael. 1976. *Olga Korbut: A Biographical Portrait*. Moscow: Novosti Press Agency Publishing House.

Julie Krone smiles after riding Dance to Fit to a win April 18, 1999, at Lone Star Park in Grand Prairie, Texas. Krone rode three winners on her last day before retirement. (AP Photo/Bill Janscha)

Julie Krone (1963–)

Jockeys are among the most diminutive of athletes. The average female rider stands at five feet and weighs about one hundred pounds, while the horses weigh more than one thousand pounds. Julie Krone, at four feet, ten inches, was six inches shorter than the average thoroughbred measured at the withers, the highest point on the horse's back. Colonial Affair, the horse she rode to victory in the 1993 Belmont Stakes, stood at seventeen "hands" (nearly five feet, eight inches). Male jockeys aren't much bigger than the women. Racing legend Willie Shoemaker was an inch taller than Julie and weighed in at ninety-five pounds. Triple Crown winner Steve Cauthen, at five feet, two inches, was closer to the average. Photos of jockeys with their mounts portray a David and Goliath tandem.

While jockeys tend to be small, they assume outsized risks. Race horses run in dense packs at speeds over 35 mph. It is a scenario scripted for mishaps, and accidents occur routinely. Riders are shot into the air when the horse "props" suddenly, or they are somersaulted to the ground when their mount bolts into the rail or clips the heels of another horse. The typical jockey suffers career-interrupting injuries on the average of three times a year; broken bones are high on the list. Some jockeys have taken more than two hundred falls during their careers. By the time Julie Krone joined the ranks, most riders were wearing flack jackets, goggles, and high-tech helmets for protection. Despite the body armor, every racing season chronicles several catastrophic injuries to jockeys and a couple of deaths. Horse racing is unique among sports, in that an ambulance follows the contestants around the track.

Despite the risks, horse racing remains an enticing profession. It is renowned for its pageantry, tradition, and glory. The lavish festivities in Louisville during Kentucky Derby Week are a part of Americana dating back to the Gilded Age. The Derby at Churchill Downs holds an august status among sporting events, equal to tennis at Wimbledon or the Masters golf tournament in Augusta. Once dubbed the "Sport of Kings," horse racing has become a favorite pastime of the common people. It's one of the most popular spectator sports in the United States. Race tracks span the continent from Saratoga Springs in upstate New York, south to Tampa Bay Downs, and west to Santa Anita Park in California. No sport routinely offers richer purses or attracts more wagers. Why wouldn't a young horsewoman from rural Michigan want to be a part of this celebrated pastime?

CHILDHOOD

Julie Krone grew up riding horses. She was born Julieann Louise Krone in Benton Harbor, Michigan, July 24, 1963, and raised on a farm at nearby Eau Claire. She can't remember a time when she wasn't around horses. Her mother, Judi, was an accomplished rider and trainer who kept a stable. One day, when a prospective buyer was looking at a horse, Judi sat two-year-old Julie on its back to show how gentle the animal was. The horse wandered off with its tiny rider while the two adults were talking. From a distance, Judi observed the toddler grab hold of the reins and tug on them. The horse dutifully turned and came back. Julie learned to ride on a more appropriately sized Shetland pony named Dixie. Her parents always trusted her on the back of a horse. She was allowed to ride off miles from home at an early age. Julie and the horse always came back. The petite equestrian brought her horse into the house once when she couldn't manage to get the saddle on. Her father, Don Krone, crafted a pulley system on a tree in the yard so Julie could saddle the horse by herself.

Julie spent much of her childhood outdoors. When not on horseback, she was swimming, fishing in the creeks and ponds, or running through the woods with her older brother Donnie and the neighbor kids. There were always animals around; not just horses but dogs, cats, and farm animals. Julie graduated from her Shetland pony to a spirited half-Arab, half-Shetland called Filly. She would climb on Filly bareback and barefoot and ride off for hours at a time. Julie was never comfortable indoors for long and didn't particularly like school. Her talents weren't displayed in the classroom but at horse shows. She won her first ribbon at age five. Judi and Julie Krone traveled all over Michigan to compete at shows. Julie's bedroom walls were soon filled with ribbons for show jumping. She also won prizes for competitive trail riding. The young horsewoman seemed to have an innate talent. She developed an exceptional sensitivity and ability to communicate with horses that would serve her well in the future.

A PASSION FOR RIDING

Riding comprised most of Julie Krone's social life. She showed little interest in the more conventional activities that occupy girls her age. She was among the smallest of her schoolmates and was often left out of the popular cliques and social events. Like most teenaged girls, she wanted to be noticed by boys and felt slighted when she was rejected. Her earlier experiences with the opposite sex had been playing football and getting into scuffles with them. A friend, Lori, advised, "Love them, don't fight with them." Teachers didn't give Julie much notice either. One exception was her English teacher, Miss Shilling, who encouraged Julie to keep a journal and express herself through poetry. In one poem, Julie wrote, "Oh this class is such // a bore. I wish I could // get up and walk out the door" (Krone, 1995, 41). The only classes she seemed to enjoy were P.E. and art. An adult Krone speculated that she had suffered from a learning disorder. In truth, the teenager's mind was focused more on horses than school work or boys.

One teenage boy did catch her attention and influenced the course of her life. Julie Krone was watching on television when eighteen-year-old Steve

Cauthen won the 1978 Kentucky Derby on the great thoroughbred Affirmed. She headed to the bookstore, purchased the jockey's biography, and read it cover to cover. Julie worked at imitating Cauthen's riding style. Pictures of jockeys and race tracks soon covered the walls of her bedroom. That's when she announced that she was going to become a jockey. Her parents didn't discourage her. The Krones were a family of individualists, each pursuing his or her own passion. Julie's father, Don, was an art teacher and avid amateur photographer. He would seclude himself in his darkroom while wife Judi tended to her horses. Julie recalls the family rarely shared meals. She often ate with the dog. Her mother didn't believe in fences for children. There was no imposed bedtime; in fact, there were few rules at all. As a teen, she smoked pot and occasionally skipped school. She was a free spirit. After a circus proprietor observed her stunt riding, she came close to accepting his offer to join the circus. The family grew apart. When Julie turned fifteen, her parents divorced. She lived with her mother and visited her father on weekends.

Krone continued to pursue her passion. She and her mother signed up for a clinic offered by the noted dressage instructor Chuck Grant. Dressage (pronounced dress-ahhzh´) is a form of precision riding. Competitions are held for young riders as well as adults. Julie, on her Arabian, Ralph, quickly caught the instructor's attention with her exceptional riding ability. Grant invited Julie and Judi to lunch. Julie informed him that she wanted to become a jockey. He recommended that she read horse racing publications. Her mother purchased issues of *Turf and Sport Digest*, along with a copy of Willie Shoemaker's biography, *The Shoe*. But the book that really got Julie excited was *The Lady Is a Jock*, about the pioneering women jockeys. This was homework she didn't mind doing. The winter following the clinic, Julie helped her mother teach riding classes, as the two planned the next step in the young rider's quest to become a jockey.

During spring break of 1979, Judi Krone loaded her van, and mother and daughter set off for Louisville, Kentucky with the idea of working at Churchill Downs. Judi promptly got a job as a "hot-walker," an attendant who walks exercised horses to cool them off. Julie, appearing younger than her fifteen years, hung around the track looking for work. She impressed trainer Clarence Picou with her knowledge. He not only offered her a job during the break but agreed to hire her for the coming summer. The only problem was that Julie was too young to work full-time at a race track. Her resourceful mother altered Julie's birth certificate and drove her back to the Downs for the summer. Clarence put her to work as a workout rider and groom. Julie was not only young but still quite small. She had no problem on the back of a horse, but she had to stand on a bucket when washing them down. Clarence and his wife, Donna, were supportive. They provided Julie a room in their home. That made it easier for Judi Krone to leave her daughter by herself and head back to Michigan. Julie's stint as a workout rider proved an ideal way to learn the craft. She galloped horses almost every day. A lot of jockeys had started out exercising horses. Clarence assured her that her petite stature would be an advantage in breaking into the profession.

Julie returned Michigan for the fall semester of school with some reluctance. Back in the classroom, she couldn't wait for the school day to end so that she could practice her newly learned riding skills on Ralph. The following summer, Julie's education on horseback received another big boost. She lived with a family friend, Pat Sachen, and her husband who raced quarter horses. Julie got her start as a jockey riding for the couple at fairgrounds in Michigan, Ohio, and Illinois. For three months, she rode on the fair racing circuit. She rode both Arabians and quarter horses. In her first quarter horse race, she came in second. Julie won her first race on a horse named Hurricane Hatti. The summer ended much too soon for her.

Back in school her senior year, Julie felt a storm of hurricane proportions brewing inside of her. She was finding it more and more difficult to concentrate in the classroom. Her mind was elsewhere. The indifferent student talked her mother into letting her drop out, with a promise that she would return later to get her diploma. Julie wanted to move to Florida, live with her grandparents, and get a job at nearby Tampa Bay Downs. Her mother reluctantly consented. Don Krone, the schoolteacher, was not happy with their decision. In December 1980, mother and daughter drove to Tampa. Once settled, Julie headed for the track. Without a pass, she had to climb the fence to get in. Once inside, she caught the attention of horse trainer Jerry Pace. He exclaimed, "So, little girl, you wanna be a jockey, huh?" Julie responded, "No, I'm *gonna* be a jockey" (Callahan, 1990, 20). Pace sat the determined young rider on the back of a thoroughbred, watched her jog him around the track, and hired her on the spot. It took less than a week for Julie to get her apprentice jockey's license. Judi Krone headed back to Michigan, filled with reservations but supportive of her daughter's decision. She held few illusions about what Julie was up against.

THE BEGINNING OF A CAREER AS A JOCKEY

Julie Krone began her career as a jockey not long after women had been granted the opportunity to ride professionally at major race tracks. Previously, women jockeys were limited to riding at county fairgrounds, in steeplechases, and in quarter horse races. Lillian Jenkinson's experience was typical for the time. She rode hundreds of winners at "bush" tracks around the Midwest in the 1920s and 1930s. But no state would grant her a jockey's license. Penny Early had tried to race at Churchill Downs in the late 1960s, only to encounter boycotts. Then, in 1968, Kathy Kusner, a world-class dressage rider, became the first licensed woman jockey in the United States. The Maryland Racing Commission awarded her a license following a protracted legal battle.

Kusner broke her leg in a riding accident and was never able to race with the men. The following year, Sandy Schleiffers, who left a convent to ride professionally, became the first women accepted into the Jockeys' Guild. Two major events occurred in February of 1969: Diane Crump broke the gender barrier by riding in a race at Hialeah Park in Florida, and Barbara Jo Rubin became the first woman jockey to win a race at a U.S. thoroughbred track. The following year, Crump rode in the Kentucky Derby. These women were the trailblazers who cleared the way for Julie's generation.

In January of 1981, Krone got her big opportunity. She donned her racing silks and rode Tiny Star to a second place finish. She was on her way to becoming a tiny star in her own right. Her first win soon followed on Lord Farkle, a huge chestnut standing seventeen hands. There's a traditional celebration that follows an apprentice jockey's first win. It's referred to as "breaking your maiden." When Krone arrived back in the jockey's room, she was met by her fellow jockeys who covered her with a concoction of shaving cream, baby powder, peanut butter, and shoe polish. This was their way of saying, "Welcome to the club." Krone would make them proud; she won three of her next six races.

Apprentice jockeys are called "bug" jockeys in reference to the asterisks placed after their names resembling bugs. The handicapping system allows bug jockeys to carry less weight in their saddle packs than regular jockeys, while the favorites in each race carry the most weight. The weight handicap evens out the betting odds. It also helps bug jockeys find rides. By hanging around the track Krone was able to get a few mounts, but clearly she needed an agent. She found one through a former jockey, Julie Snellings, who worked at the track office. Snellings was partially paralyzed and confined to a wheelchair, the result of a horse falling on her in a 1977 race. The two Julies became best friends. Snellings introduced Krone to her former agent, Chick Lang Jr. Chick took the young jockey under his wing, even offering to let Krone stay with his family. It was tough finding mounts for a relatively unknown rider, let alone the rare female jockey. At first, Chick could only get Krone on long shots that had little chance of winning. Over a period of two months, she rode in fewer than four dozen races.

Jockeys move from track to track in order to work throughout the season. Race courses host meets that last from several days to a few weeks. For instance, Saratoga Race Track in New York currently schedules a thirty-six-day meet. When Julie Krone was breaking into the profession, tracks in the Northeast offered the best prospects. She had the opportunity to ride for the well-known trainer Bud Delp at Pimlico Race Course in Baltimore. The young jockey packed and headed north. Julie Snellings moved with her, and the two shared an apartment. By the end of the 1981 season, Krone was winning races consistently and acquiring a reputation as an up-and-coming rider. Clearly, she was the top female apprentice jockey on the racing circuit. The following

February, she became the state of Maryland's first woman jockey to win four races in one day. Krone had convinced the trainers that she could ride competitively. She always asserted that she didn't want to be the best *female* jockey in the world, she wanted to be the best jockey.

Thoroughbred horse racing is one of very few sports where men and women compete head to head. Regardless of gender, jockeys have to be superior athletes. They must command their mounts not while sitting in the saddle, but precariously perched over them. The only parts of the rider making contact are the hands on the reins and the feet in the stirrups. By the end of eight furlongs (one mile), this high-speed balancing act can turn the jockey's legs into rubber. On one occasion, Julie Krone dismounted in the winner's circle only to have her legs fold under her. Roughly two minutes are required to cover the distance around a track, but it takes stamina to repeat this feat seven or eight times a day. Moreover, horse racing features one of the longest seasons in sport. Meetings at various race tracks fill the monthly calendars and extend through most of the year. The indomitable Willie Shoemaker rode in more than 40,000 races over his forty-year career.

Krone was well aware that she was competing in a man's world. Despite her early success, many trainers and owners were reluctant to offer a ride to a female jockey. Krone was determined to minimize the "female" part of the equation and emphasize the "jockey." She made it a point to look and act like the male jockeys. She wore her hair short, wore no make-up, and didn't wear dresses around the track. The diminutive rider developed an extra firm handshake that impressed her male acquaintances. She also affected an exaggerated cockiness in the paddock and jockeys' quarters. On the track, Krone would resort to the same rough tactics the other jockeys employed—and suffered her share of penalties for rule infractions. The male jockeys granted her "no quarter." There were jockeys who didn't like being beaten by a woman. They colluded to box her in during races so she couldn't pass the other horses.

Krone got into several altercations with male jockeys early in her career. In 1986, during a race at Monmouth Park, Krone drifted into the path of Miguel Rujano's horse coming out of the gate. Krone straightened her mount and went on to win the race. When she dismounted, Rujano rode up to her and hit her in the face with his whip, drawing blood. Minutes later, at the scales for the post-race weigh-in, Julie ran over to Rujano, threw a punch at his head, and knocked him into a cooler. Back in the jockey's room, the fight continued. Rujano was suspended and Krone received a warning. Later on, she got into a fight with Yves Turcotte after he hit her horse across the face with his whip. She threw a saddle at him and shoved him. At the Meadowlands in 1989, Krone was suspended for fifteen days following an altercation with jockey Joey Bravo. She recalls that as a young jockey she had to act like a "tough guy" to hold her own. She felt she couldn't afford the luxury of behaving "like a woman."

Trying to be "one of the guys" had gotten Krone into another sort of trouble. When she was riding for Bud Delp, she ran with a crowd who were into drugs. In the winter of 1983, security personnel at Pimlico found a marijuana joint in her car on track property. Krone received a sixty-day suspension and was required to attend a drug recovery program (Smith, 1989, 84). It was a serious infraction that, if repeated, could cost her her jockey's license. The young horsewoman who grew up without reins had been taught a lesson in personal responsibility and maturity. Judi Krone was aware that her daughter had been using drugs and told Krone not to call her until she cleaned up her act. Beyond feelings of disappointing her family and colleagues, the worst part of the suspension was that she couldn't ride. Krone recalls standing outside the track fence and watching the horses run around the track. Chick Lang, her agent, stuck by her. He arranged a blood test. She passed and was allowed to gallop horses after thirty days. Krone beat the drug problem, had her license restored, and was back racing again. She completed her apprenticeship and became a journeyman jockey.

After her suspension in 1983, Julie Krone won a race at Belmont Park, famous home of the Belmont Stakes. This was a notable accomplishment in her budding career. Following the race, Kentucky Derby winner Angel Cordero personally congratulated her. But triumph was followed by misfortune. Back in Maryland, Krone was exercising a horse when it tripped over its leg wrappings and fell. She was thrown and landed on her back. As she lay on the track, she realized she couldn't move her legs. She thought about her wheelchair-bound roommate, Julie Snellings. Julie Krone had fractured a thoracic vertebra. Fortunately, the accident didn't injure her spinal cord. Her confinement would be temporary, in a back brace not a wheelchair. Krone's brother, Donnie, who had dropped out of automotive college to become an exercise rider, visited her at the hospital. She spent the next three months in physical therapy. Her desire to ride again as soon as possible provided the incentive to recover.

A recovered Julie Krone moved to New Jersey. It was a convenient location that allowed her to ride at Monmouth Park during the day and at the Atlantic City track in the evening. There she met Larry "Snake" Cooper, an agent who was able to get her more mounts. She also was introduced to John Forbes and began riding for his stable at Monmouth. John taught her a lot about riding and about personal responsibility. Krone put in long days, exercising horses as soon as the sun came up and often leaving the track near midnight. She might ride in a dozen races over the course of a day. More significantly, she kept winning. In fact, she "won the meet" at Atlantic City with the most wins of any jockey over the summer. She also had success at Monmouth Park, riding for horse owner Peter Shannon. Krone was frequently invited to the Shannons' home for dinner. She had been fortunate throughout her career to find mentors and supporters at the tracks where she rode. However, she continued to experience prejudice against women riders. It wasn't unusual to hear a fan yell, "Go home and wash the dishes," as she returned to the jockey's quarters after a race (Callahan, 1990, 35).

Krone could afford her own apartment. She had won 155 races in the last few years and taken in more than $1 million in prize money, of which she received ten percent, with a quarter of that going to her agent. That left her with $75,000. Fame accompanied modest fortune. Several articles on Julie Krone began to appear in the newspapers. The nineteen-year-old felt that she was on her way to a successful career. Krone was surprised to learn that her reputation extended across the Pacific. She and Patti "P. J." Cooksey, the leading female jockey in the United States, were invited to Japan to compete in an international challenge competition for women riders. The meet, sponsored by the Japanese National Association of Racing, would match the best women jockeys in the world. Upon her arrival in Japan, Krone came down with a high fever, a holdover from her recent injury. She was in and out of the hospital but still managed to win five races in the challenge series.

Over the next two years, Krone moved around a lot. She went into something of a slump. In the spring of 1986 she relocated to New Jersey to ride

BETTING ON THE HORSES

The sport of horse racing probably wouldn't exist without betting. After all, everyone is aware that one horse can run faster than another. But when you have a few dollars wagered on one of the contestants, it makes a difference which mount crosses the finish line first. Thus, the attraction.

Betting on the horses carries as far back as the chariot races at the Circus Maximus in Ancient Rome. Placing bets on horses is part of Anglo-American history, as well. Parimutuel betting pools at race tracks were an established practice in Britain and the United States by the 1920s. This system of pooling bets, with the track taking a cut (the "vig"), led to large crowds of spectators and big money wagered on races. The conventional system allowed bets on horses to win, place, or show (finish first, second, or third). This led to more exotic betting scheme such as "exactas," "quinellas," and "trifectas" where the bettor must correctly pick the order of finish for two or more horses.

Today, hundreds of millions of dollars are bet on horses at the tracks and at off-track betting parlors, where legal. There's also a thriving profession of "bookies" who take bets. Bookmaking is generally illegal in the United States, except for Nevada—arguably for good reason. Compulsive betting on the horses can become an addiction. Gamblers Anonymous, a support group for problem gamblers, provides help for individuals who can't control their impulse to bet on the horses.

at Garden State Park, near Philadelphia, and at Monmouth Park. She began riding for owner Glenn Lane and his partner Dennis Herd. Later that year, Krone received a call from her mother, who had moved to Florida. Judi told her daughter that she had been diagnosed with ovarian cancer and would have to undergo surgery and chemotherapy. Julie had always been close to her mother, but she had to set aside the disturbing news and concentrate on her career. She started winning races again. Krone phoned her mother on a regular basis and shared her successes with her. She even mailed videotapes of races for Judi to watch while she was undergoing radiation therapy. By the end of the 1986 racing season, Krone had accumulated $2 million in prize money and was looking forward to her two hundredth win.

GREAT SUCCESS AND SERIOUS INJURIES

In 1987 Julie Krone reached the peak of her success. She became the third rider in the history of Monmouth Park to win six races in one day. She finished the season winning more races than any other jockey at Monmouth by a wide margin. By the end of the year she had accumulated 324 wins, making her the sixth leading jockey in the United States. Krone set her sights on catching P. J. Cooksey, who now had more than 1,200 victories. In February of 1988, Krone reached 1,199 wins. She headed to Garden State Park looking for number 1,200. During the eighth race, her horse lurched to the side unexpectedly and she lost the reins. She finished second, hanging on to the horse's neck. The replay video showed that the leading jockey had grabbed her reins. Because of the foul, she was declared the winner. In March, Krone surpassed Cooksey in a late-afternoon race on a horse named Squawter. Her fellow jockeys were waiting in the winner's circle. When she dismounted, they showered her with champagne.

In the spring of 1988 Julie Krone rode in a match race against Willie Shoemaker, the winningest jockey in history. Willie was one of her heroes. She had read his biography as a teenager in Michigan. Krone drew the pole position on Don't Fool With Me. She won the eight-furlong race by a nose. Shoemaker was gracious in defeat. Krone went on to race in New York for most of the season. She escaped serious injury in an accident that occurred during a Memorial Day race at Belmont Park. Her mount ran into horses that had fallen, and the impact threw her into the rail. Two other jockeys suffered serious head and back injuries, but Krone was able to get back on her feet after the collision. She went on to capture the meet titles at Meadowlands and Monmouth Park. The highlight of the season was her opportunity to ride in the Breeders' Cup held at Churchill Downs. No woman had ever ridden in this event. The Breeders' Cup was the season-ending championship event, with seven races held on one day. The feature race offered a $3 million purse.

Krone was aboard Triple-Crown-winner Forty Niner. She didn't win, but she felt elated that her mother, whose cancer was in remission, was there to watch her. Krone finished the year as the fourth leading rider.

The following season, Julie continued to break records for women jockeys. She won five races in one day at a New York track. In February she was among a group of women athletes invited to the White House to be honored on National Women in Sports Day. She posed for a picture with President George H. W. Bush. Krone presented the president with a shoe from Kentucky-Derby-winner Winning Colors, and she received an award for her accomplishments. The recognition she received in Washington was followed by her appearance on the cover of the May 22 issue of *Sports Illustrated*.

In June of 1989 Krone returned to Monmouth Park to ride and then headed to the Meadowlands. During a race in November, Krone's mount was spooked by a shadow on the track and "propped." She fell forward onto the track, and the horse struck her left arm, breaking it in four places. She also suffered a dislocated shoulder. The battered jockey endured a painful ambulance ride to the hospital. Because she had eaten a meal just before the race—an indulgence that jockeys tend to forgo, for good reason—the doctors had to wait for over an hour before they could operate. Following a second surgery on the arm and eight months of recuperation, Krone returned to ride at Monmouth Park and got career win number 1,900. It was quite a comeback, given that doctors told her she might never be able to use her fractured arm again.

In 1990 Krone bought a farm in New Jersey. The barn had nineteen stalls. She kept several horses, including old friend Peter Rabbit, the horse her mother had bred for her. She also stabled the twelve-year-old bay Chicago, on whom she'd learned to jump fences as a youngster. The farm brought back memories of her childhood; it was a place to relax on the rare occasions when she could get away from the track. Krone maintained a full riding schedule. In October, she became the first woman jockey to reach two thousand career wins.

There still weren't many women riding on thoroughbred tracks. At a New York meet in the winter of 1990–91, Krone met fellow jockey Diane Nelson. The two became good friends. Nelson had grown up on Long Island and, like Krone, began riding at an early age. The pair were a study in contrasts: Nelson stood at five feet, six inches, tall for a jockey. While Krone played down her femininity, Nelson juggled her riding obligations with a modeling career. Nelson also swam and played softball, while Krone's entire focus was on riding. Her motto was, "Pick one thing, and stick with it." Nelson went on to become one of the few women jockeys with more than one thousand wins.

Krone returned to Japan in 1990 to ride in an international jockeys' competition, this time with the men. She had the opportunity to race with her childhood hero, veteran Steve Cauthen. Krone's father, Don, had made the trip with her, and he watched his daughter beat Cauthen in a turf race on an 1,800-meter track (approximately one mile and an eighth). Being congratulated by Cauthen in the jockey's room following the race was as big a thrill for Krone as finishing ahead of him on the track. Back in New York, Krone rode for trainer Bill Mott, who put her on some "stakes" horses. Stakes races are among the most prestigious and lucrative events in thoroughbred racing, deriving their name from the entry fee or "stake" that the owner pays. The pool of stakes, along with the contribution from the track owner, determines the prize money. Riding in stakes races required that Krone travel to different tracks on weekends. This opportunity contributed significantly to her education as a jockey. The mounts were true blue bloods with an array of temperaments. Krone had acquired a reputation for handling difficult horses.

Krone then met struggling trainer Clint Goodrich, who talked her into riding a young horse named Saint Ballardo. All of Goodrich's hopes, as well as his financial future, were "riding" on this horse. Saint Ballardo was intensely quirky. Krone relied upon her unique ability to communicate with animals. Indeed, she was the female "horse whisperer" among jockeys. It proved to be a taxing relationship. Snake Cooper, her skeptical agent, reluctantly agreed to let her ride Goodrich's horse in the 1992 Arlington Classic, a major stakes race. Krone and Saint Ballardo broke the Arlington track record. Soon after, Krone got the opportunity to ride in her first Kentucky Derby when the scheduled jockey was suspended. She didn't win, but it was quite a thrill to ride at the Downs where she had worked as a teenager.

The Kentucky Derby stands as one of three premier American thoroughbred races, known collectively as the Triple Crown. The triad begins with the Derby in early May, followed by the Preakness at Pimlico Race Course, and then the Belmont Stakes at Belmont Park. In June of 1993 Julie Krone became the first woman jockey to win a Triple Crown event with her victory in the Belmont Stakes riding Colonial Affair, a fourteen-to-one shot. The Stakes is a long race at a mile and a half, and the muddy track proved a challenge. Krone's mount broke fast out of the gate, but they were soon hemmed in on the rail. She recalls a flurry of dirt clods hitting her in the face. Then she spotted an opening and steered Colonial Affair to the outside. They made their final move on the backstretch, passing nine horses for the victory. The purse was over $400,000. Julie Krone had now won more than $50 million in prize money.

But again, success was a preview to tragedy. In August, riding at Saratoga Race Course, Julie Krone had the most serious accident of her career. In the third race riding Seattle Way, Krone was running with the pack coming into the home turn. Suddenly, Filberto Leon's horse bumped into Seattle Way, and the filly stumbled. Krone was thrown from the horse, landing on her ankle. Immediately, she was struck sharply in the chest by another horse. The blow sent her sprawling head over heels. Lying on the track, Krone recalls not being able to move her upper torso or her right foot. She saw that her left elbow was cut wide open with the bone exposed. The ankle was broken so badly that when she grabbed her boot the heel rotated to the front. The ambulance arrived, and paramedics took over. They initially attempted to cut the boot off her injured ankle but this caused her excruciating pain. Moreover, she was beginning to have breathing problems owing to the blow to her chest, later diagnosed as a coronary contusion (a bruised heart). The emergency crew wrapped an air cast around her leg, placed her on a stretcher, hooked her up to oxygen, and put her in the ambulance. Krone's valet, Tony, and two track officials rode with her to the local hospital.

Krone was given morphine at the hospital, but she continued to suffer terrible pain. Following emergency surgery, she was flown to Staten Island University Hospital where orthopedic surgeons repaired the broken bones in her lower leg. Metal plates were screwed onto the leg bones to hold them together while they healed. Her mother arrived at the hospital to be with her. Fortunately, Krone had been wearing a protective vest that kept her heart from being more seriously injured. After three weeks, with the surgery behind her, Krone was allowed to go home to her farm to recuperate. What came next was a regimen of agonizing physical therapy. Krone hobbled about painfully on a pair of crutches and fought episodes of depression. It would take eight months for her to recuperate. The following April she felt well enough to gallop horses for a friend, Scotty Schulhofer. The workouts exhausted her at first, but gradually her stamina returned. She wedged sponges into her boot to keep the metal screws in her leg from rubbing the skin raw. Then in late May at Belmont, Krone rode in her first race since the accident. She finished eighth. The following day she won a race, coming from behind at the three-eighths pole. In recognition of her accomplishments and courage, Julie Krone received ESPN Network's ESPY Award and was proclaimed the Best U.S. Female Athlete of 1994.

The following year was a time for ending and beginning relationships. Julie and longtime agent Snake Cooper parted. Then on August 26, Julie married six-foot-four-inch television sports producer Matt Muzikar. She and Muzikar had met several months earlier when he was assigned to interview her. On their wedding day, she was scheduled to ride in six races at Saratoga. This left her with less than two hours to arrive at the altar following her final race. But she made it. True to character, the newlyweds took a horse-drawn carriage to the wedding reception.

In January 1996 Krone had another serious accident at Florida's Gulfstream Park. This time she broke both hands. It would take six weeks to recover. The accident unnerved the veteran jockey, and she fought serious depression. She went into therapy with an acquaintance who was a psychiatrist and a horse owner. Dr. Tom Qualters diagnosed Krone with post-traumatic stress disorder and put her on antidepressants. With the therapy and medication, she was able to resume her career. Krone continued to ride winners over the next two seasons, finishing second in the standings at Monmouth Park in 1998. In her spare time, she served on the board of Special People United to Ride, or SPUR, an organization that teaches disabled children how to ride horses.

RETIREMENT AT THIRTY-FIVE

The thirty-five-year-old jockey decided to retire in the spring of 1999. Krone went out with a flourish, winning three races in one day at Dallas' Lone Star Park. At retirement, she ranked sixteenth in earnings on the all-time list of jockeys. Several factors had led to her decision. The accumulation of injuries over her career were taking their toll. She and Matt had divorced, and her mother was terminally ill and needed care. In December, Judi Krone died following her long battle with cancer. Julie had kept the promise she made to her mother when she was seventeen years old. Two years earlier, she completed correspondence courses and received her high school diploma.

In May of 2001 Krone married Jay Hovdey, an executive columnist for the *Daily Racing Form*, a daily broadsheet for bettors. She moved from New Jersey to Hovdey's home in Carlsbad, California. She worked as a cable TV commentator for several race tracks in the area. In her spare time, she enjoyed surfing at the nearby beach. For the first time in her life, she was riding something without four legs. Falling off a surfboard proved more forgiving than being thrown off a thoroughbred. But she missed racing.

Julie Krone came out of retirement in November 2002 to ride at West Coast tracks. She rode Debonair Joe, a fifty-to-one long shot, to victory in the Malibu Stakes at Santa Anita in December, but she fractured two bones in her back the following year and spent four months recovering. Following her return, she became the first woman jockey to win a Breeders' Cup race, but then she had another accident at Hollywood Park in December of 2003, fracturing several ribs. Krone attempted another brief comeback at Santa Anita in early 2004, but she quit riding for good in July. She reappeared briefly at Santa Anita in 2008 to take part in an "old timers" race with other retired jockeys.

A retired Julie Krone limits her time in the saddle to the horses she raises on her ranch at Oceanside. Late in her racing career, she began spending more time with her show horses, and she continues to keep busy as a riding instructor. She is an advocate of the Parelli Natural Horsemanship method that emphasizes the symbiotic relationship between humans and horses.

Julie Krone, the small but determined farm girl from Michigan, had to climb over the fence to get into Tampa Bay Downs to begin her career as an apprentice jockey. She retired two decades later as the most successful woman jockey in the history of American thoroughbred racing. In more than 20,000 starts, she won 3,704 races and some $90 million in prize money. She was the first woman jockey to be inducted into the thoroughbred racing Hall of Fame.

Krone also is a member of the Women's Sports Foundation. In 2004 the Foundation presented her with the Wilma Rudolph Courage Award in recognition of her perseverance and passion.

Julie Krone remains one of the most celebrated women athletes in the nation's history. She has received wide acclaim in the electronic and print media. During her career, she was a guest on *The Tonight Show* and *Late Night with David Letterman*. Stories about her appeared in *Newsweek* and *People* magazines. She is one of only eight jockeys to have appeared on the cover of *Sports Illustrated*. Hollywood writer-director Katherine Brooks is planning a film of Julie's life, to be called *The Boys' Club*.

FURTHER READING

Callahan, Dorothy. 1990. *Julie Krone: A Winning Jockey*. Minneapolis, MN: Dillon Press.

Davidson, Scooter T., and Valerie Anthony, eds. 1999. *Sport of Kings: America's Top Women Jockeys Tell Their Stories*. Syracuse, NY: Syracuse University Press.

"Julie Krone Biography." 2009. Jrank.org: Famous Sports Stars. http://sports.jrank.org/ pages/2644/Krone-Julie.html

Krone, Julie, with Nancy Ann Richardson. 1995. *Riding for My Life*. New York: Little, Brown & Co.

Miller, Mark. 2000. Julie Krone. *Salon*. Dec. 19: http://dir.salon.com/people/bc/2000/12/19/krone/print.html.

Nack, William. 1993. Bittersweet Victory. *Sports Illustrated* 78:23: http://sports illustrated.cnn.com/vault/article/magazine/MAG1138678/index.htm.

Nack, William. 1994. The Ride of Her Life. *Sports Illustrated* 80:23: http://sports illustrated.cnn.com/vault/article/magazine/MAG1005288/index.htm.

Smith, Gary. 1989. She Who Laughs Last. *Sports Illustrated* 70:84: http://sports illustrated.cnn.com/vault/article/magazine/MAG1068429/8/index.htm.

Lisa Leslie, while a member of the U.S. Olympic women's basketball team, shoots during practice in Stanford, California, July 2008. (AP Photo/Marcio Jose Sanchez)

Lisa Leslie (1972–)

Women have been playing basketball virtually since the game was invented. A few years after James Naismith hung peach baskets at each end of the YMCA school gym in Springfield, Massachusetts, women were playing a modified version of the game at several northeastern colleges. The popularity of the women's game spread across the country. The first women's intercollegiate contest took place between Stanford University and the University of California in 1896. By the opening decades of the twentieth century, high schools were fielding interscholastic girls' teams. The 1920s witnessed the rise of industrial leagues made up of company teams like the one Babe Didrikson played for in Dallas, Texas. The Amateur Athletic Union, or AAU, which had first opposed women's basketball, was sponsoring a national tournament in the mid-1920s. However, women's basketball—like women's sports in general—progressed in the shadow of the men's game over the next half century.

School teams for girls began to flourish in the late 1970s following the implementation of Title IX legislation. This mandate required educators to provide equal access to sports programs for students of both sexes. High schools and colleges added women's varsity basketball to the extracurriculum. The first national collegiate tournament was held in 1978 under the auspices of the Association for Intercollegiate Athletics for Women. The AIAW conceded control of women's sports to the National Collegiate Athletic Association in the early 1980s. The NCAA eventually expanded the national basketball tournament to sixty-four teams. Under their jurisdiction, women's rules moved closer to the men's, and the women's game became more physical. By the 1990s, basketball had become the most popular women's collegiate sport.

Professional women's basketball took off in Europe and then caught on in the United States after a couple of false starts. Lisa Leslie would play for professional teams on both sides of the Atlantic during the 1990s. Two decades earlier, women's basketball became an official Olympic sport. The Soviet team won the initial gold medal at the 1976 Montreal Games. Following the U.S. boycott of the 1980 Moscow Olympics, the American women won their first gold medal in basketball at the 1984 Los Angeles Games. That same year in the suburbs of L.A., twelve-year-old Lisa Leslie began playing the game. Little did she realize at the time that she would collect four Olympic gold medals.

Growing up in Southern California, Lisa Leslie wasn't particularly interested in basketball, despite her extraordinary height. As a young girl, she didn't watch basketball on TV or join in neighborhood pick-up games. By age twelve, she was over six feet tall and stood out among her schoolmates, both the boys and the girls. People were always walking up to her and asking, "You are so tall. Do you play basketball?" (Leslie, 2008, 23). Lisa became irritated by the persistent question and responded testily that she had no interest in the game. Finally, she decided to give basketball a try, if for no other reason than to bring an end to the interrogation. The local youth playground league didn't sponsor a girls' team, so Lisa joined the boys' team. At first, her male teammates tended to ignore her on the court, but they soon realized that no one could block her shots under the basket, and they began passing her the ball. Lisa's game skills began to improve. Her early success playing basketball with the guys would determine the course of her life. Fortunately, girls' basketball was coming into its own in the early 1980s.

CHILDHOOD

Lisa Deshaun Leslie was born in Gardena, California in 1972 and grew up in nearby Compton, a working-class suburb. Her father, Walter Leslie, left before Lisa was born. Christine Leslie raised her three daughters Dionne, Lisa, and Tiffany as a single parent. Christine got a job with the U.S. Postal Service delivering mail in Inglewood. The daily commute of a dozen miles meant getting up at 5:00 AM and arriving home late. But the working mom found time to spend with her daughters in the evening. She made sure that they finished their homework and provided them with the things they needed for a happy childhood. Lisa remembers her mother pouring a cement patio in back of the house and installing a tetherball pole. When Christine Leslie was at work, the girls were left with a babysitter, or Dionne, the oldest, watched after Lisa. It was a role that Lisa would assume later with her baby sister, Tiffany. The Leslie girls were latchkey kids who often had to look after themselves and each other while their mother was earning a living.

Lisa grew up fast in more than one sense. It was in her genes. Her mother was six feet, three inches and Lisa's father was reputed to be six feet, four inches. Both of her parents had been basketball players. Walter had played some semiprofessional ball. Christine knew what it was like to grow up as the tallest girl in the neighborhood and made it a point to reinforce her daughters' self-images. She sent the two older girls to a charm school run by a woman who had worked with professional models. Later on, as an adult, Lisa would do some professional modeling. This positive reinforcement helped to counter the teasing by schoolmates, who nicknamed Lisa "Olive Oyl" after the tall, skinny character in *Popeye* cartoons.

When Lisa turned nine, her mother quit her job with the post office to become a cross-country truck driver. She took out a loan and bought her own rig. This job paid much better, but it meant being on the road for a week at a time. Christine routinely traveled back and forth from California to the East Coast. She hired a live-in housekeeper to take care of the girls. Lisa and Dionne were assigned chores to do around the house, including taking care of their new half-sister, Tiffany. Lisa missed her mother's presence and recalls sitting for hours looking through the family photo album. During the summer, Christine would take the girls with her on the cross-country hauls. They spent their days together in the truck, shared a small bunk in the back of the

LATCHKEY KIDS

Lisa Leslie's mother was a single parent who worked hard to provide for her daughters. She got up early, arrived home late, and often was on the road. Her work obligations required that the older girls look after the younger ones when relatives or babysitters weren't available. The Leslie sisters were "latchkey kids," a growing phenomenon in American working-class families.

The label derives from a latchkey being hung around the oldest child's neck so he or she can unlock the door to the house after school. Positive consequences of being a latchkey kid include developing independence and self-reliance at a young age. Negative effects are most prevalent among children under age ten and those who are left alone more than three hours a day. These youngsters often become bored and lonely, if not fearful. Teenagers are susceptible to peer pressure, and may be more likely to experiment with drugs or become sexually promiscuous. Lisa Leslie recalls missing her mother when she was young. Fortunately, her aunt lived close by in case of an emergency. As a teenager, Lisa a found a healthy outlet in sports.

Some communities have set up organizations to check on latchkey kids. Automatic calling programs require someone in the household to answer the phone and acknowledge that they are OK. Cell phones make it easier for today's working parents to stay in contact with latchkey kids. Many communities try to offer after-school sports programs for children who would otherwise be latchkey kids. Cities, schools, organizations such as the YMCA, the Boys and Girls Clubs, and others have done so, but with the economic downturn, many of these programs have been cancelled or reduced in number.

cab at night, or stayed in inexpensive motels. The arrangement was less than ideal, but the two sisters got to see their mom, and the country: the Rocky Mountains, the Plains, and the large eastern cities. Before long, the girls had grown too big to go on trips and were busy with their own social activities.

When Lisa reached junior high school age, her sister Dionne left home. The two younger girls were sent to live with their aunt, J. C., in nearby Carson, California. The junior high in Carson had a girls' basketball team. Lisa decided to try out for the team as a way to fit in at her new school. She not only made the team but enjoyed a lot of playing time. When the coach divided the team into left handers and right handers for drills, Lisa, the only southpaw, made it a point to learn how to dribble and shoot with both hands. It was a skill that would serve her well. The team went undefeated in seven games.

When the brief junior high season ended, Lisa's education in basketball fell into the hands of her cousin Craig, who played on the high school team.

When Lisa finished her homework each afternoon, Craig took her to the gym at Victoria Park for a physical workout and to work on her game skills. Craig realized that his unusually tall cousin had a promising future in basketball, if she practiced diligently. Lisa recalls that Craig "wore her out" doing sit-ups, push-ups, and jumping rope. It was drudgery, but she stuck with it. He taught her how to pass effectively, to shoot hooks and jump shots. He played her one-on-one to improve her defensive skills. Once she learned the fundamentals, Craig took her to the local courts to compete in three-on-three games against the guys. Lisa got further encouragement from her Uncle Ed, who took her with him to the court at his church, where they played a physical brand of basketball. Lisa soon got used to being pushed, tripped, and knocked down. It was a hard lesson but proved good training for the future.

Meanwhile, Aunt J. C. was intent on teaching her niece to be feminine. She had Lisa walking around the house with a book balanced on her head and practicing proper etiquette. On Saturdays, a hairdresser came over to do Lisa's hair. Lisa's aunt told her that she had to make a decision: be a young lady or play basketball. Lisa put her hair in a ponytail and headed to the courts. Basketball had become a passion. Lisa switched schools midyear and began playing ball in a boys' league the following spring. She was the only girl, and at six feet, two inches, she was also the tallest player. Coach John Anderson took Lisa under his wing; he bought her her first pair of basketball shoes and took her home to have dinner with his family. Lisa had gotten used to playing ball without her own family in attendance to cheer her on. Her mother was usually on the road, and her aunt didn't think basketball was an appropriate activity for a young woman.

HIGH SCHOOL SUCCESSES

When Lisa completed junior high school, her mother relocated because of a job change. The two Leslie girls moved to Inglewood to live with their grandmother, and Lisa enrolled in Morningside High School. After bouncing around from school to school, she was getting used to being the new kid in class. Morningside had one of the best girls' basketball teams in the area. Coach Frank Scott recognized that Lisa was not only tall but had learned the basic skills of the game. Lisa found it a bit strange to be playing ball with the girls again. She became the team's starting center, the only freshman on the varsity squad. Lisa had the good fortune to play with forward Shaundra Greene, a high school All American. The team finished the season with a 27-3 record. Lisa was named California's Freshman of the Year. She continued to improve. In her sophomore year, she averaged twenty-one points per game, and the team finished the regular season at 33-1. The Monarchs qualified for the California 4-A state tournament. Lisa missed a last-second shot in the game against Freemont High, and they were eliminated. However, she had two more seasons to look forward to.

A few weeks after the end of basketball season, the U.S. national team came to California to play an exhibition game. As Lisa watched the game with her teammates, she set a goal for herself: to play basketball in the Olympics. She was already receiving a flurry of letters and phone calls from college coaches who were interested in recruiting her once she graduated. Lisa realized that a college scholarship would be a financial boon to her family. She dedicated herself to keeping her grades up and improving her game. She was an all-around student who participated in a range of extracurricular activities. She played on the volleyball and track teams and was elected class president three years in a row.

By her junior year, Lisa Leslie reached her full height of six feet, five inches. She became a triple threat: scoring, rebounding, and blocking shots. The Morningside Lady Monarchs were rated the number-one team in the state at the beginning of the season. The team gained more attention when Leslie became the first female high school player to dunk a basketball during a game. She was able to perform the feat even though her hands were too small to palm the ball. Her team went undefeated during the regular season. They then won the California state tournament in a rematch against Freemont, with Leslie scoring twenty-one points and bringing down fourteen rebounds.

More exciting news came in the wake of the state tournament championship. Lisa was invited to try out for the U.S. national junior team, made up largely of college players. This "feeder" team supported the U.S. women's Olympic basketball team. The better players would have the opportunity to try out for the Olympic team. Lisa had to compete against more experienced players. She not only made the team but the starting lineup. The California girl who had taken summer cross-country trips with her truck-driving mom was to become an international traveler. The U.S. team flew to Bilbao, Spain for the Junior World Championship. There they competed against international teams from as far away as Australia. The American women finished with a mediocre 3-4 record, but Lisa impressed the coaches and fans by leading the team with a thirteen-point scoring average. It was a remarkable performance for the youngest player on the squad.

When Lisa Leslie returned for her senior year at Morningside High School, she was rated the top girls' high school basketball player in the nation. The Lady Monarchs' schedule included tournaments against teams outside the state of California. The team got better as the season progressed, and they won their league championship without a defeat. Leslie averaged twenty-seven points a game, even though she routinely sat out much of the second half in games when the team built up a large lead. Although they normally didn't run up the score against other teams, Morningside had a tradition where, during one game, they would try to score as many points as possible.

Coach Frank Scott instructed his team in a game against weak South Torrance High to feed the ball to Lisa whenever they got possession, so that she could attempt to break Cheryl Miller's national high school record of 106 points in a game. Miller, who went on to play in the Olympics, was considered the best women's basketball player of all time. South Torrance's team had been decimated by injuries and had only six players in uniform when they played Morningside. Coach Scott put his players in a full court press the entire game, swarming all over their opponents each time they got the ball. When Morningside gained possession, they immediately passed the ball to Leslie. No one on South Torrance was tall enough to stop her from scoring, even when the entire team tried to guard her, front and back. At halftime, the score stood at 102-42 in favor of Morningside: a rout. Leslie had scored 101 points in one half of high school basketball!

Two of the South Torrance players had fouled out of the game going into the third quarter. With only four players left, their team decided to forfeit. In response, the officials called two technical fouls on South Torrance for not finishing the game. Leslie sank the four free throws, tying Miller's record. After the game, Leslie was mobbed by the media. Newspapers from all over the country carried the story, and it merited an article in *Sports Illustrated*. However, league officials nullified the final free throws, and the praise was short-lived. Many basketball fans considered Coach Scott's stunt to be an example of poor sportsmanship and a distortion of the game. Leslie and her coach both were widely criticized, although Scott received most of the blame. Lisa took the criticism in stride and moved on. In December of 1989 she received the Dial Award, given to the nation's outstanding high school athlete-scholar.

Morningside entered the California state high school tournament as the favorites with a 33-2 season. The other teams realized that they had to stop Lisa Leslie in order to win and began guarding her more aggressively. She became more physical in return and often got into foul trouble. Her talented teammates were able to compensate, and they made it to the championship game against Berkeley High. Leslie felt ill on game day, suspecting that she might be catching the chicken pox from her little sister, Tiffany. She played anyway. Despite carrying a fever, she scored an astounding thirty-five points, took down a dozen rebounds, and blocked seven shots. Morningside won the game by a margin of eleven points. An exhausted Leslie, suffering from dehydration, was taken directly from the Oakland Coliseum to the hospital, where they confirmed her suspicion that she had contracted chickenpox. She was at home in bed while her teammates celebrated the victory, but she recovered in time to go to the senior prom.

The following summer, Leslie was invited to try out for the USA World Championship team and flew to Florida for the tryouts. Again, she had to play against older, more experienced players, and didn't make the team. However, she was invited to accompany the USA junior team competing in a four-game tournament in Vancouver, Canada. The Canadians played a roughhouse game that included a personal skirmish between Leslie and the Canadian center. She recalled her initiation on the city courts of L.A., tussling with her cousin Craig and his buddies. It was a style of ball that Leslie would witness again in international competition.

COLLEGE BASKETBALL

Back in California, Leslie's focus turned to college. The highly recruited high school senior had lots of choices. After narrowing her preferences to a handful of schools, she began visiting college campuses. Notre Dame University was high on her list. The Southern California native arrived in South Bend, Indiana during a bone-chilling cold spell and decided to look elsewhere. Another school that had recruited Leslie was the University of Tennessee. She knew their highly successful coach, Pat Summitt, from USA Basketball. Leslie's high school team had recently played in a Christmas tournament in Shelbyville, Tennessee. During the tournament, she and her African American teammates were confronted with an unremitting display of racist behavior from white fans in the crowd; Leslie had never experienced this type of bigotry. She informed Coach Summitt that she had no desire to play ball in Tennessee.

This left two schools on her list, Long Beach State and the University of Southern California. Leslie had visited LBSU and was impressed, but her mom wanted her to attend nearby USC. There were other incentives. USC had hired Marianne Stanley as their new coach. Stanley previously had won three national championships and had already recruited some talented freshmen. Leslie settled on USC but had a problem qualifying academically. Despite having won the Dial Award, her score on the Scholastic Aptitude Test suggested that she hadn't picked up the necessary academic skills in high school. She prepped for the test, took it again, and scored a qualifying score on the third try. In May, Leslie announced that she would attend USC. She was required to attend summer school to make up for her marginal test score. It was an opportunity to familiarize herself with college life and meet some of her future teammates.

In the fall of 1990, Lisa Leslie began her first full semester at USC on a basketball scholarship. She found her college classes challenging. The freshman student-athlete had a full schedule with the demands of road games, practice sessions, and workouts beginning at 6:00 AM. USC played in the Pac 10 conference but also competed against top nonconference schools across the country. There were high expectations for the 1990–91 season under coach Stanley. The USC women hadn't won a national championship since 1984, when All-American forward Cheryl Miller led the team. Despite the team's celebrated history, Leslie soon discovered that women's basketball wasn't a major attraction at USC. Unlike high school, few of her college games would be sellouts. Football and men's basketball got most of the attention. Women's basketball received little press coverage, and the team often played before a few hundred fans. Significantly, Leslie's family members were often in the crowd. In Coach Stanley's first year at USC, the Lady Trojans had gone 9-18. This year's team, with Leslie playing at center, was determined to reclaim their past glory. They got better as the season progressed. The team finished third in the Pac 10 and qualified for the NCAA tournament. They were eliminated in the West Regional by Long Beach State. Leslie was voted National Freshman Player of the Year.

Leslie spent the following summer playing for the U.S. team at the World University Games in Sheffield, England. The team went 8-0 and won the gold medal. She was back at USC in the fall for her sophomore year. In her second season, USC won the Pac 10 championship and reached the quarterfinals in the NCAA tournament before being eliminated. Leslie had another outstanding year, averaging twenty points and eight rebounds per game. She was selected first-team All American. The summer following her sophomore year, she was invited to try out for the U.S. Olympic team preparing for the 1992 Barcelona Games. The nineteen-year-old didn't make the cut but gained valuable experience competing with accomplished players like Nancy Lieberman and Cheryl Miller. As a consolation, Leslie played on the national Jones Cup team that won the 1992 gold medal at the annual games in Taipei, Taiwan.

Leslie's third season at USC was a rebuilding year, as the team had lost several of their better players through graduation. The team struggled to come together in the early season. However, they finished second in the Pac 10 and again qualified for the NCAA tournament. USC was ousted by a powerful Texas Tech team with future professional basketball star Sheryl Swoopes. Leslie played on the U.S. national team the following summer. The team had won the bronze medal at the Barcelona Games and were setting their sights on winning the gold medal at the 1996 Atlanta Olympics. That summer's team won the world championship in Sao Paulo, beating Brazil on their home court. Leslie's improvement as a young player was duly noted. She was named USA Basketball Female Athlete of the Year.

Leslie's senior year at USC was embroiled in controversy. Coach Stanley had questioned the inequity between her salary and that of men's basketball coach George Raveling. Stanley felt that she had a verbal agreement with Athletic Director Mike Garret to remedy the inequity. When USC reneged on the salary offer, she took her case public. Just before the 1993 season opened, Stanley was fired. She filed a gender discrimination suit against the university. Leslie, as team captain, landed in the middle of the controversy when several of her teammates threatened to transfer to other schools. They liked their coach and resented the way she'd been treated. Leslie herself considered transferring, but she realized she would have to sit out a year before regaining her eligibility. So, she decided to stay at USC, as did most of her teammates.

Former USC star Cheryl Miller was hired as the new coach. Early on, the players struggled to adjust to Miller's approach to the game, which was quite different from what they were used to under Coach Stanley. But they came together as a team when the season opened, losing only once in their first eighteen games. They won the conference championship and again made it to the NCAA tournament, ranked number eight in the country. The 1994 NCAA women's tournament had expanded to sixty-four teams. This meant that the Lady Trojans would have to prevail in six straight games to win the championship. They came close, finally losing to nationally ranked Louisiana Tech by nine points in the quarterfinals. Leslie's college career was filled with individual honors, even though USC had failed to win a national championship as they had when Cheryl Miller was a player. Leslie received All-American honors for the third year in a row, and she received the Naismith Award given annually to college basketball's top male and female players.

PROFESSIONAL WOMEN'S BASKETBALL AND THE 1996 OLYMPICS

Women's basketball in the United States was focused on international competition during the summer of 1994, with the Olympic Games just two years away. Leslie participated in the Goodwill Games in St. Petersburg, Russia, and joined the national team at the World Championship Games held in Australia in June. The team played well but lost to Brazil in the semifinals and returned home with the bronze medal. For her part, Leslie had a good tournament, averaging more than ten points a game. Women's basketball was finally drawing the support it deserved, thanks to emerging corporate sponsorship. When the official U.S. team was selected the following May, the players were provided a stipend that allowed them to concentrate full-time on preparation for international competition. In effect, the American women were already competing against professional players from other countries.

Lisa Leslie wanted to continue playing basketball, but there were virtually no professional opportunities for women in the United States other than the struggling Women's Basketball Association. (The WBA disbanded in 1995 after three seasons.) Several foreign countries did sponsor professional leagues. Leslie was impressed with the Italian League, and decided to sign with Sicilgesso, a team based in Alcamo near Palermo, Sicily. The Italians played under international rules. Leslie appreciated that this experience would help her adjust to the Olympic game. The most significant variation was the splayed free-throw lane that stretched to nineteen feet under the basket. The European professionals also played a more physical game. Leslie would have to be aggressive to compete successfully. Sicilgesso had signed several non-Italian players, including a few Americans—notably former USC star Cynthia Cooper—who helped Leslie acclimate to the new milieu. Leslie made some Italian friends, as she picked up the language. The team provided an apartment and a bought her a Fiat with a modified driver's seat to accommodate her long legs. Typically, the team played once or twice a week, so she had ample opportunity to experience southern European culture. She especially enjoyed the tourist sights in Rome. The Italian fans, impressed with her height, dubbed her "Grande Liza!" The team had a so-so season, but Leslie was a sensation, scoring over twenty points a game. She decided to return to the United States at the end of the season. She was a bit homesick and was having problems with her knees. Back home, she rested her legs and looked forward to tryouts with the U.S. women's Olympic team.

Team tryouts commenced in May at the Olympic Training Center in Colorado Springs, perched six thousand feet above sea level. Tara VanDerveer, who had led Stanford University to NCAA championships in 1990 and 1992, was selected to coach the team. VanDerveer had seen Leslie play in college and had coached her on previous national teams. Leslie wasn't a shoo-in to make the team, as sixty top players were invited to try out, and only eleven would be selected. Leslie made the final cut, despite having exceeded the required time in the prerequisite two-mile run. That fall, the national team embarked on a fifty-two game tour. They went undefeated against the two dozen college teams they played. In early 1996 the national team headed to Russia and then on to China, where Lisa was matched against six-foot-eight-inch Zheng Haixia, known as the "Great Wall of China." She easily handled Zheng with her superior quickness, as the American team defeated the Chinese. The U.S. women were still undefeated when they returned home from Australia, but they nearly lost to the Russian team in Chicago. Leslie ended the tour with a seventeen-point average. The tour was a success in more than one sense. It had drawn a quarter of a million fans and raised awareness of women's basketball in the United States. All eyes were on the upcoming Olympics.

The Atlanta Olympics commenced in July 1996. President Bill Clinton inaugurated the Games, and the great boxing champion Muhammad Ali lit the Olympic Flame. The U.S. women's team won their first two games against Cuba and Ukraine. The next game against Zaire at the Georgia Dome drew the largest American crowd ever for a women's basketball game. The team advanced to the medal round, and in the opening game, Leslie scored thirty-five points in a win against Japan. It was a U.S. single-game Olympic scoring record. Fortunately, Leslie was in her hotel room when the bomb exploded in Centennial Park on the evening of July 27, killing one person and injuring dozens. Olympic security got even tighter after the bombing, but the Atlanta Games continued without further incident.

The American women's team made it to the finals for a rematch with the undefeated Brazilian team that had beaten them in the World Championship.

Brazil had two outstanding players in Silva Paula and Hortencia Oliveira. Early in the game, Brazil's center got into foul trouble, and Leslie picked up the pace for the Americans. They pulled away in the second half, winning 111-87. Leslie finished with twenty-nine points. More than 30,000 fans were at the awards ceremony when Leslie and her teammates received their gold medals. Among the crowd were Lisa's mother and her new husband, Tom.

BECOMING A SPORTS CELEBRITY

Lisa Leslie experienced what it's like to be an American sports celebrity. She had signed a commercial contract with Nike, and her picture was featured in their booth displays at the Olympic Games. Her image also appeared on the covers of several magazines. Given her now familiar face and conspicuous height, Leslie found it nearly impossible to blend in when out in public. A trip to McDonald's for a snack resulted in being inundated by autograph hounds and fans asking her to pose for pictures. At times, she required a police escort just to make it back to her hotel.

Following the Olympics, Leslie was compelled to think about her future and whether she wanted to continue playing basketball. Two new professional leagues were in the planning stages: the American Basketball League, and the Women's National Basketball Association. The WNBA was affiliated with the men's National Basketball Association. Both leagues would recruit her.

Leslie had another career option. Her recent appearances in television commercials and on magazine covers caught the attention of the modeling industry. She had signed a contract with Wilhelmina Models, a prestigious New York agency, prior to the Atlanta Games. Leslie decided to take a temporary break from basketball and pursue a modeling career. She didn't have a portfolio other than having taken part in a fashion show when she was in high school. However, her tall, slim figure was what the modeling agencies were looking for. She arrived in New York City and began scheduling photo shoots. Her modeling career took off. She did spreads for *Vogue*, *Elle*, and *Sports Illustrated for Women*. She even got to work with famous photographer Annie Leibovitz. Leslie did an ad for American Express that appeared on a billboard in Los Angeles. The unspoken message in the ad was, "Hometown girl makes good." Leslie learned that modeling was even more "cut-throat" than basketball. It was a novel experience, she recalled, to be judged solely on your looks rather than your physical skills.

Leslie found her brief stint as a model gratifying, but she wanted to keep playing basketball. She passed on the opportunity to play overseas and turned down an offer from the American Basketball League, which began its initial season in the fall of 1996. Although the ABL had signed a number of highly touted players, Leslie was convinced that the WNBA stood on more secure financial footing, and she waited for the opportunity to sign with them. When the WNBA offered her a contract to play for the Los Angeles Sparks, she couldn't resist the opportunity to play in front of her hometown fans. The new league decided on a summer schedule to begin in June 1997.

PLAYING FOR THE WNBA

Lisa Leslie joined Sheryl Swoopes and Rebecca Lobo as the first players to sign with the Women's National Basketball Association. The three did several promotions for the league, including one filmed by Hollywood director Spike Lee. Meanwhile, Leslie continued to do commercials for Nike. Playing for the Los Angeles Sparks meant that Leslie could live at home during the summers and be with her family. The Sparks' home court would be the Great Western Forum in Inglewood, where the NBA's Lakers played. The team's challenge would be to fill the seats in the huge arena. The WNBA had acquired several corporate sponsors, including Nike. The mood remained optimistic when 14,000 fans arrived at the Forum for the Sparks' opening game. Leslie had planned a surprise for the crowd; however, she missed her attempt to dunk the ball in the home opener—a feat that would've drawn needed attention to the new league. Nevertheless, she finished the game with an impressive sixteen points and fourteen rebounds in a losing effort against the New York Liberty.

Leslie's personal statistics weren't enough to ensure success. The high-scoring center needed help on the court. Los Angeles lost eight of their first thirteen games. China's Zheng Haixia joined the team, but they endured a mediocre season. The good news was the Sparks averaged some 10,000 fans per game. Leslie, for her part, played well over the summer and was named to the All-WNBA first team. She was on her way to becoming a dominant player in the league. Her intuition about the two professional leagues proved accurate; the ABL folded after two seasons.

In October 1998 Morningside High School honored Lisa by naming their new Sports Complex after the former high school All American. This tribute was tempered by news from home that Lisa's mother, Christine, was diagnosed with two lumps in her breast and would have to undergo surgery. Leslie became a spokesperson for the National Breast Cancer Foundation. She and her mother did a public service announcement for the Foundation that played on television and on the jumbo screens at sports arenas across the country. Cancer remained a specter in Leslie's life. Her stepfather, Tom, would succumb to liver cancer in January 2001.

Meanwhile, the WNBA had expanded to include a dozen teams for the opening of the 1999 season. Leslie started at center for the Western Conference team in the All-Star game and was awarded the most valuable player trophy. The Sparks finally made it to the Western Conference finals with a

20-12 record, amidst a "musical chairs" of coaching changes. They were eliminated by the Houston Comets and didn't make it to the league finals. When the WNBA season ended in August, Leslie joined the national team preparing for the 2000 Olympic Games in Sydney, Australia. The team had six players returning from the 1996 gold medal team. They completed a successful pre-Olympic tour in late March with an impressive 38-2 record.

Leslie had a busy year. After playing the pre-Olympic tour over the winter, she headed back to L.A. for the start of the WNBA. Under new coach Michael Cooper, the Sparks had their most successful season. Cooper worked closely with his star center to improve her game. Leslie's personal trainer had her on the running track and in the weight room. Leslie even enrolled in a yoga class to help her channel her combative energy. The Sparks made it to the Conference finals but were eliminated again by the rival Comets. League play ended in August. The following month, the Summer Olympic Games commenced in Sydney. The American women blitzed through their early round opponents and defeated the Australians for the championship. Christine Leslie was there to watch her daughter receive her second gold medal. Leslie hung her medal around her mother's neck, proclaiming that she had won it for her.

In 2001 the Los Angeles Sparks acquired their own arena, the Staples Center in downtown L.A. The team won the Western Conference championship and then the WNBA title, beating the Charlotte Sting before a packed house. Leslie was named the league's most valuable player. The following season she was the first WNBA player to score three thousand career points. A week after setting this record, Leslie became the first women's professional player to dunk the ball in a game. The feat was front-page news across the country and was featured on ESPN highlights. Leslie also continued her education, as time allowed. The USC graduate completed a Master of Business Administration (MBA) degree at the University of Phoenix. Leslie's business acumen was paying off. Endorsement deals with Nike, American Express, and Sears, along with her WNBA salary, brought her total earnings to over $1 million.

In 2004 the WNBA suspended play during August so that their players on the U.S. women's team could get ready for the Olympic Games. The national team played a tune-up game against a squad of WNBA All-Stars at Radio City Music Hall in New York City before heading to Athens, Greece. The American women dominated the competition at the Summer Games and made it to the finals against a tough Australian team for the gold medal. The U.S. won the game 74-63, their twenty-fifth Olympic win in a row. Leslie finished the game as Team USA's all-time leading scorer and rebounder.

Leslie had a disappointing 2005 season in the WNBA. She realized that she needed to work on her skills during the off season. She signed a contract to play for Spartak, a Moscow-based team in the Russian Basketball Federation. She hadn't played professional ball overseas since 1995 in Italy, but she had been in Russia previously in 1994 for the Goodwill Games. Her new husband,

Michael Lockwood, a six-foot-six-inch former Air Force Academy basketball player and UPS pilot, agreed to accompany her. The couple, who had been married in the Hawaiian Islands, packed their thermal underwear and headed to Moscow in January. Spartak set the couple up in a nice, warm, two-story house. Leslie found some familiar faces from the WNBA on the team. The twice-a-day practices helped Leslie improve her shooting. Again, the rules were different from those in the United States, and the Federation teams played a very physical game. In their free time, Leslie and Michael haunted the Internet cafes and studied their Russian vocabulary books. In the 2006 Euro Cup finals in March, Spartak defeated the French team for the championship, with Leslie scoring twenty and pulling down fourteen rebounds.

Leslie returned to the States for the 2006 WNBA season. Los Angeles Sparks club president Johnny Buss had a surprise waiting. The team dedicated the Staples Center basketball court to her. At the ceremony, the Sparks revealed a stencil on the floor reading, "Lisa Leslie Court." Lisa was stunned; athletes usually have to be retired before receiving such honors. The Sparks lost the 2006 championship game to Sacramento, but Leslie again was voted MVP. All the hard work with Spartak had paid off. She then received another honor. The University of Southern California retired her and Cheryl Miller's jersey numbers in a halftime ceremony at the new Galen Center.

A BABY AND ANOTHER GOLD MEDAL

Following the 2006 season, the Sparks were sold by the Buss family to two Los Angeles businesswomen. Leslie informed the new owners that she was expecting a baby and would sit out the 2007 season. In June she gave birth to daughter Lauren, who joined Michael's two daughters from a previous marriage in their melded family. They were a long-distance family as well, with Michael based in Miami and Lisa in California. The couple made plans to build a house in Southern California.

Lisa shed the thirty-five pounds she had gained during her pregnancy and was back playing in the WNBA in 2008 and again on the Olympic team. She won her fourth gold medal at the Beijing Olympic Games in August, as the American women easily defeated the Australian team in the championship game, 92-65. Leslie had taken her previous gold medals to China as an inspiration. Ignoring Olympic protocol, she wore all four medals at the Awards Ceremony amidst some criticism, particularly by the Australians.

Lisa Leslie retired from the WNBA following the 2009 season. It had been a rough year. She badly sprained her knee in June and missed eleven regular season games, as well as the All-Star Game. She had been playing basketball for twenty-four years beginning in junior high school. Over her career, she received numerous honors. During her twelve years as center with the Sparks,

Leslie collected three MVP awards, was twice voted defensive player of the year, and was elected to the WNBA All-Decade Team. Leslie had been a member of two title-winning teams in Los Angeles. She ended her professional career with more than 6,000 points and 3,300 rebounds. She was truly an American sports icon. In 2001 the Women's Sports Foundation presented Lisa Leslie with the Flo Hyman Memorial Award. The annual award recognizes the recipient's athletic performance and charitable activism.

The thirty-seven-year old retiree planned to remain active in civic and charitable causes. She founded the Lisa Leslie Basketball Academy and a basketball camp for young girls. She continues to support Right to Play, an international humanitarian organization that sponsors community sport in twenty-three nations. She also does some public speaking. Lisa coauthored an autobiography with Los Angeles–based sports journalist and broadcaster Larry Burnett that was published in 2008. She has worked as an analyst and commentator for ESPN Network and NBA TV, and planned to do some college basketball broadcasting in 2009. Leslie had a few minor roles in TV sitcoms and looks forward to doing more acting. For fun, she and Michael take winter vacations at Tahoe, California, where she enjoys snowboarding. In her quieter moments, she reads romance novels. The international sports star and world traveler settled into life with her family in Southern California where she had grown up and made her first appearance on a basketball court.

FURTHER READING

Christopher, Matt. 1998. *On the Court with . . . Lisa Leslie*. New York: Little, Brown & Co.

Heyman, Brian. 2009. Lisa Leslie, the Face of the W.N.B.A., Prepares for Life. *New York Times*, Aug. 22: http://www.nytimes.com/2009/08/23/sports/basketball/23leslie.html.

King, Melissa. 2002. Lisa Leslie as a Work in Progress. *Sports Illustrated Women* 4:3: 86–90.

Leslie, Lisa, with Larry Burnett. 2008. *Don't Let the Lipstick Fool You*. New York: Kensington Books.

Peter, Josh. 2009. "Day in the life of Lisa Leslie." Yahoo! Sports. http://sports.yahoo.com/wnba/news?slug=jo-leslie072108.

Smith, Shelley. 1990. She Was Truckin'. *Sports Illustrated*, Feb. 19: http://sportsillustrated.cnn.com/vault/article/magazine/MAG1135992/2/index.htm.

Taylor, Phil. 1991. A Model Role Model. *Sports Illustrated*, Nov. 25: http://sportsillustrated.cnn.com/vault/article/magazine/MAG1140202/index.htm.

Nancy Lopez chips her way onto the 18th green during the first round of the LPGA Ping Banner Health tournament in March 2002, in Phoenix. (AP Photo/Roy Dabner)

Nancy Lopez (1957–)

Women's sports made significant gains in the 1970s; however, tennis drew most of the media attention. Women's professional golf continued to struggle. The game wasn't receiving the public recognition or financial support that it needed to thrive. Part of the problem was structural. The Ladies Professional Golf Association, founded in 1950 by a group of women golfers that included Babe Didrikson, still operated as a player-run organization. In 1975 the Association transformed itself into a business with a commissioner and corporate support. A year later, Judy Rankin became the first golfer to win more than $100,000 in prize money on the LPGA Tour. But women's golf still lacked an essential ingredient to reach its full potential: a superstar with the charisma of Babe.

In 1978 a twenty-one-year-old from New Mexico put women's golf on the national map. Nancy Lopez's prodigious drives, precise putts, photogenic smile, and outgoing personality were just what the sport needed. In her official rookie year she won nine LPGA titles, including a string of five consecutive wins, and collected $189,000 in prize money. It was the most successful rookie season in the history of American golf. Her success put her on the cover of *Sports Illustrated*, a rare honor for a woman athlete. Lopez was named LPGA Player of the Year and voted Associated Press Female Athlete of the Year. Women's golf began attracting money and fans. The following year, the annual LPGA Tour prize money exceeded $4 million. By the early 1980s, women's golf tournaments were being broadcast on national television. Nancy Lopez did for women's golf what Arnold Palmer had done for men's golf in the late 1950s. Her gallery of fans, dubbed "Nancy's Navy," emulated "Arnie's Army." Crowds at LPGA tournaments tripled in size.

CHILDHOOD

Nancy Marie Lopez was born on January 6, 1957 in Torrance, California, the youngest daughter of Domingo and Marina Lopez. Domingo's family had migrated from Mexico to Texas, and then to New Mexico. While married and living in California, Nancy's father turned down an offer to play minor league baseball. Instead, he enrolled in an automobile repair course. The family moved back to New Mexico, where the couple had met. Domingo opened a body shop in the town of Roswell. This is where Nancy grew up. She had no brothers and her only sister, Delma, was twelve years older. Delma married at sixteen and moved to California. Nancy was raised as an only child. The family resided in a modest two-bedroom house that Domingo remodeled and enlarged over time. For recreation, the former ballplayer took up golf and soon was playing a 3-handicap (three strokes over par). Marina joined him on the links when her doctor recommended that she get more exercise. Instead of hiring a babysitter, the couple allowed young Nancy to tag along as they golfed.

Roswell sits on the high plains of eastern New Mexico, two hundred miles southeast of Albuquerque, the state capital, and a hundred miles west of the Texas line. It's a center of irrigated farming and ranching; like most towns in the area, it is engaged in petroleum production. The town of 35,000 had a large Hispanic population that resided on the south side, while the Anglos lived in north Roswell. The Lopez family played golf on the nine-hole municipal course on the west side. They couldn't afford the annual fees to play the Country Club course, even if they'd been allowed to join, which was unlikely. Hispanics in the Southwest continued to face discrimination, subtle and not so subtle. Nancy grew up with Anglo friends, but there were still social barriers in the 1970s as to dating and marriage, as well as club membership.

When Nancy was eight years old, her father handed her a 4-wood out of Marina's bag and allowed her to hit a ball as she followed her parents around the municipal course. Nancy hit drives down the fairway onto the greens and putted until she got the ball in the cup. One day, she hit a ball clear over her parents' heads. Nancy's father realized that he had a golfing prodigy "in the rough." He began working with Nancy to correct minor faults in her swing. Domingo Lopez was a confirmed pragmatist when it came to technique. He allowed his daughter to develop her own natural swing. The results spoke for themselves. Within a few months of serious practice, Nancy was a better golfer than her mother. Marina graciously relinquished her set of Patty Berg clubs so that Nancy could practice with her father. Nancy was tall for her age, so her mother's clubs didn't have to be cut down. But her hands were small, so she started out using an interlocking grip and never changed.

Nancy's father would be her only coach during her formative years. The Lopezes couldn't afford lessons from a golf pro. Green fees on the municipal course were about all they could handle on their modest income. Domingo and Marina made the necessary sacrifices, setting aside $100 a month so that their daughter could travel and play in amateur tournaments. Domingo dug up the backyard and filled it with sand so Nancy could practice hitting out of the homemade sand trap. It wasn't long before she was ready to compete against New Mexico's best young golfers. But Nancy Lopez had to be sponsored by a country club in order to play in several of the area tournaments. The odds that the local country club set would support a young Mexican-American golfer were not encouraging. Fortunately, a club near Albuquerque recognized her promising talent and agreed to make her an honorary member.

Golf, like tennis, had always been a country club sport. Both activities were distinct from baseball or basketball, whose future stars might develop their skills on the sandlots or urban blacktop. Few professional golfers got their start on municipal courses. Nancy Lopez was the exception, the equivalent of tennis' Arthur Ashe, who developed his game on the public courts of segregated Richmond, Virginia. For Nancy, playing Roswell's municipal golf course had advantages beyond the affordable green fees. Its rough terrain and minimally maintained fairways taught her how to excel under adverse conditions. In contrast, playing the manicured private courses was like "taking a mulligan"—being given an extra shot at the green. No matter where you played golf in New Mexico, the dust was blowing in your face. At the same time, the winds of change were altering the ethnic tenor of the Southwest. Back in the 1950s, Mexican-American golfer Lee Trevino had to sneak into Dallas' private golf courses to learn the game. Two decades later, a young Nancy Lopez was invited to play in tournaments at country clubs in her home state.

When Nancy was nine, her father entered her in the Pee Wee golf tournament in Alamogordo, a hundred miles west of Roswell. It was a three-day tournament for girls under age twelve. Nancy shot a couple of 62s and won the tournament by a huge margin. Her victory initiated a family tradition: Domingo would buy his daughter a Barbie doll each time she won a tournament. Nancy was on her way to accumulating a large collection of dolls. The following year, she won the New Mexico Girls' Championship, and by age eleven she was routinely beating her father on the links. She won the New Mexico Women's (not Girls') State Amateur Tournament at age twelve. Still shy of junior high school, she claimed the Roswell City Championship. When Nancy became state amateur champion, the mayor of Roswell granted her free golfing privileges on the local military school's course, a great improvement over the municipal facility. Nancy Lopez was a teenage phenomenon. At age fifteen, she made four holes-in-one, two in the same month. One was sunk with a 4-wood on a 220-yard par 3 in a downpour. Domingo recognized that his protégée had the talent to pursue golf as a career.

TRYING TO FIND PRACTICE SITES

Like most athletic girls of the time, Nancy Lopez faced the common barriers to competition. Her high school didn't have a girls' golf team, and the golf coach refused to let her try out for the boys' team. Title IX legislation, ensuring girls equal access to school sports, had just been signed into law by President Richard Nixon. Nancy's father, no stranger to discrimination, was prepared to file a lawsuit against the school. The school board capitulated. Nancy not only became a member of her high school golf team, but she led them to the New Mexico State Championship two years in a row in 1973 and 1974. Significantly, Nancy hit from the men's tees just like her teammates and routinely out-drove her opponents by fifty yards. (Note: ladies' tees are set in front of the men's tees at a distance based on the length of the hole.) While in high school, she won the Western Women's Amateur three times and the U.S. Girls' Junior Championship twice. At age sixteen, Nancy was rated the top women's amateur golfer in the country.

From early on, Nancy Lopez hit the ball with an unorthodox swing, although it incorporated all the fundamentals. Her father would offer occasional suggestions and make minor corrections, but he was reluctant to tamper with what he saw as a natural swing. His advice on follow-through was characteristic: Domingo advised his daughter that the ball doesn't care what you do after it has left the tee. Lopez hit the ball with a very slow tempo, especially on the backswing, but she still generated enough club speed on the downswing to drive the ball 260 yards. Unlike most right-handed golfers, she kept her left heel on the ground during the backswing and didn't turn her hips as much as most women golfers do. She also had a slight hitch when addressing the ball. In all, it was a far-from-picture-perfect swing, but it proved highly effective. What Lopez's father did emphasize was practice, practice, practice. She never forgot that lesson.

COLLEGE GOLF TAKES A BACKSEAT TO THE LPGA

Nancy looked forward to playing collegiate golf and continuing her education. Her father told her that he couldn't afford to send her to college without a scholarship. Nancy's first choice was Arizona State University, but the Sun Devils offered golf scholarships to men, not women. The University of Tulsa in Oklahoma fielded a women's golf team, and they offered her a half scholarship. Lopez told the university that this wouldn't be enough financial support for her to attend. Tulsa didn't want to lose the promising prospect and ultimately provided her a full scholarship, the first ever to a woman golfer. The high school senior entered the U.S. Women's Open, where she finished an amazing second. As an amateur, she couldn't accept any prize money, but she was awarded a golf scholarship worth $10,000. This meant that she could afford to go to college anywhere she wanted. Lopez honored her commitment to Tulsa and enrolled as a freshman in the fall of 1975.

Nancy had been a "B" student in high school, with math as her strongest subject. She took a major in engineering at Tulsa. Her obligations to the golf team, especially the extensive travel schedule, clashed with the academic demands of this rigorous field of study. Typically, the team was on the road every second or third week, traveling as far as Florida to play in tournaments. Lopez missed classes and struggled to maintain a "C" average her freshman year. Her initial season on the college golf course proved more rewarding. She was named Female Athlete of the Year at Tulsa and earned All-American honors after winning the women's collegiate championship. Coming back as a sophomore, she switched her academic major to business administration, but continued to struggle academically. Golf was taking too much time away from her studies. She decided to drop out of college and become a professional golfer. Nancy Lopez qualified for the LPGA and joined the Tour in 1977. The talented young golfer from a working-class family was intent on earning a living playing the game she loved. If successful, she would enjoy many of the comforts of life that her sacrificing parents couldn't afford.

Nancy's father had made a modest but adequate income in his auto body business. He was a good provider and, if the truth be told, occasionally indulged his talented daughter. Nancy was a self-admitted "car nut." When she turned fifteen and obtained her driver's license, she was playing in golf tournaments around the state. Her mother had been driving her to these events. That's when Domingo bought Lopez her first automobile, a brand-new canary-yellow Ford Gran Torino with silver rims. Later, when she was on the professional tour, Domingo bought her a sporty maroon Chevrolet Monte Carlo with an FM stereo. Lopez installed a CB radio, the popular hobby that preceded the cell phone era. While on the road with her caddy traveling to tournaments, she would chat with other CB operators under the "handle" Jive Cookie. Domingo was proud of his successful daughter. He advised her that she would have to buy the next car on her own. As things turned out, she didn't. Sponsors provided Lopez with cars once she became a tour celebrity. The young golfer signed a contract to do commercials for a Ford Agency in Albuquerque, and they would hand her the keys to a new Thunderbird or the equivalent.

LIFE ON THE LPGA TOUR

Some one hundred women were playing the LPGA Tour when Nancy Lopez joined. The active members were required to enter a minimum number of tournaments and place in the money. Otherwise, they lost their eligibility to play on the tour. Competition was intense, and the young golfer from Roswell had her work cut out for her. Moreover, it took money to make money in professional golf. Travel expenses, room and board, caddy fees, and equipment all added up. The total could easily reach several hundred dollars a week. There were other pressures. The LPGA had its cliques and harbored intense rivalries. At first, Lopez didn't fit in with the veteran golfers and became something of a loner. But the novice golfer survived her initial season. She played in a few tournaments in 1977, but not enough to qualify as a rookie. Then in September, she suffered a heartbreaking loss. Her mother died following surgery for appendicitis. She consoled her father, while he encouraged Lopez to pursue her budding career. Domingo Lopez had lost his wife, but he was proud of his successful daughter who had learned the game with her mother's clubs.

Nancy Lopez returned to the LPGA Tour in 1978, her official rookie season and one that became legendary for its accomplishments. She won her first professional tournament, the 72-hole Bent Tree Classic in Florida. It was an emotional four days in the wake of her mother's death. She was in tears at the award ceremony as she dedicated the victory to the memory of her mother. The win gave her new confidence. Lopez had always played an aggressive style of golf, and now she began going for the "birdies" (holing out a stroke under par). She won her next tournament in California, along with the $15,000 prize. She caught the attention of the golfing world and the sports media. Lopez continued to play well but didn't win another tournament until May, when she won the Greater Baltimore Classic at 7 under par. She had a three-tournament winning streak when she took a week off to prepare for the LPGA Championship in Ohio. The tournament would take place on the challenging Jack Nicklaus Course, long in yardage and dotted with sand traps and water hazards. On the second day of the tournament Lopez finished with a score of 65 that included two "eagles" (two stokes under par) and four birdies. She went on to win the tournament by a resounding six strokes.

The rookie had become a celebrity. Nancy Lopez was flooded with requests from the media and entertainment industry. She was invited to appear on the television show *Good Morning America* and the *Dinah Shore Show*. She appeared on the covers of *Time* and *Newsweek*. *Sports Illustrated* did a feature story on her. *Golf Digest* hired her as a "playing editor." Then she was invited to play an exhibition match with entertainer Bob Hope and former U.S. president Gerald Ford. Back on the professional circuit, Lopez opened with a par 72 at the Banker's Trust Classic in Rochester, New York. This round was followed by a horrible second day that included hitting a spectator with an errant drive—a mishap the former president could empathize with. Fortunately, the fan wasn't badly injured. Lopez went on to win, shooting a 69 on the final day. The twenty-two-year-old had won five tournaments in a row.

Lopez's remarkable winning streak finally ended in Hershey, Pennsylvania, at the Lady Keystone Open. The loss took some of the intense media pressure off the rookie and gave her a breather. Lopez then won the Rolex International Mixed Doubles Championship, held in Japan, partnering with Mexican golfer Ernesto Acosta. Her score of 68 won her the women's individual honors at the tournament. She finished the season by winning the prestigious Colgate European Open in England by three strokes, and then the Far East Women's Invitational in Malaysia. Her nine wins were the most on an LPGA Tour since 1966, when Kathy Whitworth won ten. The prize money reached nearly $200,000, the most ever for a rookie in the LPGA, or the PGA. Domingo Lopez would no longer have to set aside money to support his daughter's golfing career. The honors poured in. Nancy Lopez was voted LPGA Rookie of the Year, and Player of the Year, won the Vare Trophy for lowest average score on the Tour, and was named Associated Press Female Athlete of the Year.

The young golfer's celebrity led to more product endorsement contracts and commercial ventures. These sources of income matched her tour winnings. Like most successful athletes, Lopez retained an agent to handle her financial affairs. She signed with International Management Group, an agency that represented a number of high profile clients including Arnold Palmer and Billie Jean King. IMG invested her money, handled her taxes, and managed publicity. Her personal agent, Peter Johnson, negotiated the endorsement offers that came her way. She signed a profitable contract with the Florida Citrus Commission to promote Florida orange juice. Other endorsements followed. She did a television commercial for Colgate toothpaste and represented a Florida real estate developer. Following her rookie year, Lopez signed with Fila, the (then) Italian-based company that specialized in golf and tennis clothing for women. As their representative, she wore their apparel on the golf course.

By the late 1970s, equipment manufacturers, following the lead of sportswear manufacturers, began addressing the special needs of women golfers. Companies marketed lighter clubs with shorter shafts. Generally, golf clubs offer an array of design features, including a range in shaft tension from flexible to stiff. Clubs also come in a variety of "swing weights"—the weight ratio from the grip to the club head. Nancy Lopez liked to play with long, fairly heavy clubs with medium shaft flexibility. She preferred conventional steel shafts to the new graphite models. Like many golfers, Lopez hit drives with a glove on her left hand, but she putted without a glove. Early in her career, she played with clubs manufactured by Ram.

The LPGA rules allowed golfers to carry fourteen clubs in their bags. This limit imposed some strategic tradeoffs between woods and irons, along with the obligatory putter. Lopez was very deliberate in choosing a club on the fairways. (On one occasion, she was penalized two strokes for slow play.) Having competed in golf tournaments since her preteen years, she had a store of experience to draw upon when choosing which club to use in a given situation. For instance, she knew that hitting a 150-yard shot with a 7-iron usually put her on the green. Nancy Lopez began her professional career before the technological revolution in golf equipment. The innovations in club design allow contemporary weekend golfers to hit the ball farther and with more control. Arguably, golf is a different game than when Nancy Lopez joined the LPGA Tour.

Travel on the tour also was different in the 1970s and 80s. Young professionals getting their start usually traveled to events by automobile. The LPGA sponsored some three dozen tournaments, and the season ran from January to late fall. The tour began in the West, moved to the South, then to the Midwest, and closed in the Northeast. Players had to compete in a minimal number of tournaments to remain competitive. Thus, a great deal of golfers' time was spent on the road, living in motel rooms, shuttling from city to city. Occasionally, two women on the tour put rivalry aside and shared accommodations to save money. But more often, professional golfers roomed by themselves. All in all, a golfer's life could be solitary, despite the public attention at the tournaments. Nancy Lopez developed a few casual friendships with other

GOLF'S TECHNOLOGICAL REVOLUTION

Innovations in golf club design have changed the game dramatically. Today's golfers can choose from "woods" composed of steel, carbon fiber, or titanium. Graphite drivers add fifty yards to tee shots. Club designers apply the physics concept "moment of inertia," or MOL, to club heads to the effect that they are approaching the size of grapefruits. The layered composition and redesigned surface of golf balls have further increased flight distance. GPS range finders that calculate distance to the target are being marketed to amateur golfers. It's a different game than when Nancy Lopez played.

Other technological advances include inventive grooves on golf iron faces that create backspin. Balls that land long on the green back up several yards toward the cup rather than roll onto the apron. New, longer-shafted putters allow golfers to employ a pendulum effect that greatly reduces putting errors.

High-tech equipment is employed to analyze and correct the golfer's swing. Hand-held video cameras have become passé. Today's golf instructors utilize a device known as a computerized launch monitor. Radar signals produce 3-D images of the golfer. Even the soles of golf shoes are going high-tech—at a time when golfers are walking less.

Golf carts, which have been around since the 1950s, changed the game dramatically. Few weekend golfers walk eighteen holes any more, calling to mind Mark Twain's comment that "Golf is a good walk ruined." Professional golf tours disallow carts except for physically disabled golfers. Meanwhile, caddies seem to be carrying larger and larger bags filled with gear.

golfers. Future Hall-of-Fame member Donna Caponi, who was the same age as Lopez's older sister Delma, became a close friend and mentor to her. However, the only person she saw on a regular basis was her caddy, Roscoe Jones.

Caddies make an important contribution to a professional golfer's success. They are expected to comprehend all the fine points of the game and give their golfer appropriate advice and feedback, as well as taking care of the clubs and equipment during a tournament. A good caddy has to get the yardage down precisely on the course, and hand the golfer the preferred club. Roscoe Jones was recommended to Lopez by a mutual friend. Lopez paid him a flat fee plus 10% of the prize money when she won a tournament. They had more than a business relationship. Roscoe became her traveling companion. The two often ate meals together on the road. He continued to caddy for Lopez into the 1983 season.

Nancy Lopez met someone else during her rookie year who would become a big part of her life. At a tournament in Hershey, Pennsylvania, in late

June, Nancy and Roscoe were interviewed by local sportscaster Tim Melton, a handsome six-foot-three-inch bachelor. Nancy and Tim were attracted to each other. Subsequently, they occasionally ran into each other on the golf circuit and soon began dating. Melton proposed in the fall of 1978, and the couple were married the following January on Lopez's twenty-second birthday. Following a brief honeymoon in Hawaii, Lopez returned to the LPGA Tour. Tim's and Nancy's careers framed their relationship, often separating them. The couple had an apartment in Pennsylvania, where Tim worked for a Harrisburg TV station, and kept a condominium in Palm Coast, Florida. They moved to Cincinnati in 1979 when Tim took a job there with the CBS-TV affiliate. A couple of years later, they were living in Houston.

The 1979 season proved another sensational success for Lopez. She won eight tournaments. To put this accomplishment in perspective, Jack Nicklaus, regarded by many as the greatest golfer of the twentieth century, maintained that a professional golfer who won 20% of the time would surely be the world's best. Lopez had beaten these odds and then some. In two years, she had entered forty-four tournaments and won seventeen. (Tiger Woods would win seven tournaments his first three years on the PGA Tour.) Lopez was again voted Professional Golfer of the Year and won her second Vare Trophy. She went on to finish in the top ten in seventeen tournaments in 1980 and 1981, winning three each year. Her marriage, however, was struggling. The couple was apart much of the time. Tim couldn't always travel with her and wanted to be together. She felt the pressure from him to be home more often. Lopez dealt with stress by eating and began to gain weight. Her golf game suffered. At home with Tim, discussions led to arguments and finally to a separation.

Nancy Lopez turned to an acquaintance she had met through Melton for emotional support. Major league baseball player Ray Knight had been good friends with Tim while the two were in Cincinnati. Lopez had first met Ray in the Reds' clubhouse, and then ran into him again in Japan on a goodwill tour the end of her rookie year. Coincidentally, Ray was traded to the Houston Astros in 1982 when Tim and Nancy were living there. Ray's marriage had recently ended in divorce. Lopez and Ray became close friends, consoling each other about their marital problems. Lopez filed for divorce from Tim Melton in May 1982. Following the divorce, she and Ray saw more of each other over the next several months, began dating, and were married in October. The couple settled in Ray's hometown of Albany, Georgia. The newlywed athletes faced the familiar problem of careers that kept them apart. Lopez cut back on her schedule and attended Ray's ballgames on occasion. Ray made it a point to get to some of her tournaments when he could. A year after they were married, she gave birth to a daughter, Ashley Marie. She always said that she didn't want to grow old playing golf, but to have a family. The young golfer would find it challenging to balance a career, marriage, and motherhood.

TWILIGHT OF A GREAT CAREER

Nancy Lopez played in fewer tournaments in 1983, and managed to win a couple. She passed the million-dollar mark in prize winnings, despite spending much of her time at home taking care of her daughter. She played the 1984 Tour with her daughter in tow. The golfing mother won two tournaments that season. The following year proved her best year since 1979. She sank a phenomenal twenty-five birdies at the 1985 Henredon Classic. She played until she was five months pregnant, winning a total of five tournaments, including the LPGA championship by eight strokes. She led the tour in winnings, and again won the Vare Trophy for her 70.73 stroke average. However, she would play in only four events during 1986 Tour, when she gave birth to her second daughter, Erinn.

The following season was one of ups and downs. Lopez won the 1987 Saratoga but finished out of the money at the next tournament. She took a month off to be with her family. However, she ended up seventh on the money list that year and was inducted into the LPGA Hall of Fame at age thirty, the youngest golfer to be so honored. She then received another singular honor, being named Golfer of the Decade by *Golf Magazine*. At season's end, Lopez had passed the $2 million mark in earnings. She went on to play in some twenty tournaments in 1988 and 1989, winning only three each year and maintaining a 71 stroke average. In 1989 she took in close to half a million dollars in prize money, her best year.

During the decade of the 1990s, Nancy Lopez struggled to balance her golf career with family obligations. She gave birth to her third daughter, Torri, in 1991. Ashley was now in school, and Erinn would soon follow. Lopez cut back on Tour appearances to be with Ray and the children. She played in just eleven tournaments in 1991, winning one. She came back in 1992 to compete in twenty-one tournaments, winning back-to-back playoffs and tying her career low of sixty-four in the final round of the Rail Charity Classic. Lopez played in eighteen tournaments each of the next two years, but claimed only one title. She won a final tournament in 1997, her last year to surpass $200,000 in prize money. Ray had ended his playing career in 1988. He went on to manage the Cincinnati Reds in 1996. Later, he would work as a game analyst for ESPN and pregame show host for Mid-Atlantic Sports Network.

Lopez decided to put off retirement, although the LPGA was becoming more competitive. A bevy of talented young golfers like twenty-three-year-old Rookie of the Year Annika Sorenstam had joined the Tour. In 1996 Lopez, now thirty-nine and overweight, realized that she had to get back in shape to stay in the money. It was time to give up the junk food and get back on the treadmill. Lopez had suffered a recurring weight problem over the course of her collegiate and professional careers. The skinny girl growing up in New Mexico, who had run on the high school track team, recalled weighing 165 pounds when she played golf in college. Lopez felt her ideal playing weight (at five feet, four and one-half inches) was about 130 pounds. She realized that the excess weight was hampering her swing, so she hired a trainer, changed her diet, and began working out six days a week. She lost forty pounds, and the workouts helped her endurance playing the 72-hole, four-day tournaments. Lopez entered eighteen tournaments on the 1996 Tour, finishing in the top ten five times; but she picked up no wins. She got her forty-eighth tournament win at the 1997 Chick-Fil-A Championship, an event that she would later host. It would be her last victory on the LPGA Tour.

The U.S. Women's Open remained the proverbial "one that got away" for Nancy Lopez. She entered the 1997 Open at Pumpkin Ridge Golf Club in Portland, Oregon, with the goal of adding this elusive title to her golfing ré-sumé. She shot in the 60s the first three rounds, placing her in contention. Significantly, her gallery of fans was still there, cheering her on. The finish would prove dramatic. She was within one stroke of the leader, Alison Nicho-las, going into the final hole. Lopez missed a fifteen-foot putt by an inch on the eighteenth, ending her bid for a playoff. As a consolation, she was the first golfer in LPGA history to shoot in the 60s all four rounds of the tournament. Her nine-under-par was her best ever in the Women's Open, but she fell a stroke short. Lopez had thought about retiring at the end of the 1997 season, but her performance at Pumpkin Ridge convinced her to keep playing.

As a wife and mother, Nancy was finding it more difficult to schedule enough practice time. She played in nineteen tournaments in 1998, but fin-ished in the top ten only twice. She lost in a four-way sudden-death playoff at the Sara Lee Classic, then struggled at the Women's U.S. Open, shooting an 83 on the second day and missing the "cut." Ray was there to console her. The highlight of her year was receiving the Bob Jones Award from the United States Golf Association. The award, named for the great champion of the 1920s, is given for outstanding sportsmanship. She played in a limited num-ber of tournaments the following year owing to knee surgery. Her best finish was a tie for twelfth.

The veteran cut back her tour schedule to about a dozen tournaments an-nually over the next four years. She began to devote more time to charitable causes and commercial ventures. Lopez worked with handicapped children and made fundraising appearances. She continued to play in charity golf tour-naments, including the annual Celebrity Professional-Amateur that raised money for breast cancer research. Lopez hosted the annual Chick-fil-A Char-ity Championship, and she worked with young women golfers at tournament clinics. The enterprising golfer also had an interest in golf equipment. She had worked briefly for Arnold Palmer Golf Co., designing clubs for women, and then founded Nancy Lopez Golf in 1997. NLG marketed golf clubs and equipment for women, and later, a line of golf apparel. Business income be-came more of a necessity as her golf earnings slumped. Lopez estimated that it cost nearly a $1,000 a week to play on the Tour, taking into account travel expenses, meals, and lodging. Her 2001 tour earnings of a little over $12,000 barely met expenses.

In April 2002 Lopez's father died of heart failure. He had been her golf coach and number-one fan. Domingo, who played golf into his sixties, made it a point to attend his daughter's tournaments when he could. The two had remained close over the years. A month earlier, Lopez had announced that she would play in only fourteen events as part of the Nancy Lopez Farewell Tour. She recorded her third hole-in-one as a professional at the Jamie Farr Kroger Classic, but failed to make the "cut" in her final U.S. Open in July. Her gallery of loyal fans was there to applaud her twenty-five-year career as she played the final hole.

Following retirement in 2002, Lopez and husband Ray joined a campaign to promote heart health, working with GlaxoSmithKline, the British pharmaceutical company. Heart disease ran in her family, and Ray had had heart problems. The couple embarked on a multicity "Back in Full Swing" tour with the purpose of promoting a healthy lifestyle that emphasized diet and exercise. Ray talked about his having suffered a heart attack the previous year, and Lopez spoke about her parents' problems with heart disease. GSK was marketing a beta-blocker drug, Coreg, that Lopez's father had taken for his heart condition.

In 2003 seventy-four-year-old Arnold Palmer joined Lopez for nine holes of golf to celebrate the grand opening of the Torri Pines Course at the Nancy Lopez Country Club south of Ocala, Florida. Lopez entered a few LPGA tournaments over the following years. She made the "cut" in only one tournament, in 2004. Her career accomplishments were acknowledged when she was appointed captain of the 2005 U.S. Solheim Cup Team. The Solheim Cup, like the men's Ryder Cup, is a match-play tournament between select American and European teams. Lopez had played on the initial Cup team in 1990. By convention, a recently retired professional is chosen as team captain. Under Lopez's leadership, the U.S. women retook the Cup from the Europeans at Crooked Stick Golf Course in Carmel, Indiana. In 2007 Nancy Lopez was named captain of the PING U.S. Junior Cup Team, a competition for amateur girls. The Americans bested the Europeans 14-10 in match play. Lopez would captain the Junior Cup Team again in 2009.

In 2006 Nancy Lopez took part in the Legends Tour for professional women golfers over age forty-five. This tour was the counterpart to the Senior PGA Championship Tour for men. She played in the Hy-Vee Classic, in June, finishing a disappointing twenty-ninth. Lopez put herself on another diet and exercise program, lost thirty pounds, and attempted a comeback in 2007. But she didn't have much success, now shooting in the low 80s. She suffered an embarrassing last-place finish at the Ginn Open, while playing with a broken toe. Like so many veteran athletes, she kept putting off the decision to retire from the game she loved. She was criticized by some golf analysts for playing too long, but her fans still loved her. She always found time to pause and sign autographs or pose for photos, no matter how her golf game was going.

RETIREMENT

In 2008, after playing in only three LPGA tournaments, Lopez retired to the six-hundred-acre farm outside Ray's hometown of Albany, Georgia. It was a great place to relax, go fishing, and to do some home cooking, one of her passions. The retired professional didn't give up golf entirely. She continues to play in charity tournaments and on the Senior Tour. Lopez also does occasional television commentary. She remains involved in design and marketing for Nancy Lopez Golf, recently purchased by Ontario-based Tournament Sports Marketing. She fulfills her interest in developing young golfers at her golf school near Ocala, Florida.

Looking back on her career, Nancy Lopez can lay claim to one of the great success stories in women's sport. She is widely considered the best golfer on the women's professional tour from the late 1970s to the late 1980s. Her nine tournament wins as a rookie is unparalleled in the history of golf. At one point during her rookie year, she played forty-one straight holes without a bogey (shooting par or better). Lopez was the sole woman golfer to appear on a cover of *Sports Illustrated* for more than two decades. She finished her twenty-six-year professional career having won forty-eight tournaments, including three LPGA Championships. She finished second in the U.S. Women's Open Championship four times, including a tie finish in 1975. Her career golf earnings topped $4 million. For several years, she was the top earning woman in American sports.

Nancy Lopez's career accomplishments have been widely acknowledged by the sporting community. She is the only golfer to win the LPGA Rookie of the Year, Player of the Year, and the Vare Trophy for lowest tour average in the same season. She was the youngest golfer ever to be inducted into the LPGA Hall of Fame. In 1992 she won the Flo Hyman Memorial Award, conferred by the Women's Sports Foundation. Further honors were bestowed by the community where she grew up. Her home town of Roswell named an elementary school after her. In like manner, the veteran golfer has lent her name to recognize the accomplishments of others. The Nancy Lopez Award was established in 2000. The annual award is presented to the world's top amateur woman golfer.

In the final assessment, few athletes have had a greater effect on their sport than Nancy Lopez. Her unique achievements and winning personality transformed women's professional golf. The LPGA Tour was still battling the conventional prejudices regarding women athletes in the late 1970s. Lopez's photogenic, feminine image was exactly what was needed to attract spon-sors, fans, and television coverage to the sport. At the same time, her visible ethnicity broadened the parameters of acceptance within this country-club sport. Like Tiger Woods, Nancy Lopez was a minority golfer whose father had played a prominent role in her development. She never forgot her father's advice that golf should be fun. Her vivacious personality was a testament to this approach to the game. Few golfers have been more popular with the fans. She always had time for her fans and rarely turned down interviews. Nancy Lopez demonstrated a remarkable ability to balance the roles as daughter, mother, wife, and celebrity athlete. This is part of her legacy.

FURTHER READING

Davies, Patricia. 2002. Lopez brings glittering career to end. *Times Online*, Oct. 15: http://www.timesonline.co.uk/tol/sport/golf/article 171027.

Deford, Frank. 1978. Nancy with the Laughing Face. *Sports Illustrated*, July 10: http://sportsillustrated.cnn.com/vault/article/magazine/MAG1093843/index.htm.

Jenkins, Sally. 1997. Nancy Lopez. *Golf Digest*, August, 48:8.

Lopez, Nancy, with Peter Schwed. 1979. *The Education of a Woman Golfer*. New York: Simon & Schuster.

"Nancy Lopez, 1957–." 2009. Jrank.org. Famous Sports Stars. http://biography.jrank.org/pages/3136/Lopez-Nancy-1957-Golfer.html

Newman, Bruce. 1986. The Very Model of a Modern Marriage. *Sports Illustrated*, Aug. 4: http://sportsillustrated.cnn.com/vault/article/magazine/MAG1065086/index.htm.

Sharp, Anne Wallace. 2008. *Nancy Lopez: Golf Hall of Famer*. Farmington Hills, MI: Lucent Books.

Newly named executive director of the World Sports Foundation Donna Lopiano, right, at a news conference in 1992. Race car driver and president of the WSF, Lynn St. James, is on the left. (AP Photo/David A. Cantor)

Donna Lopiano (1946–)

Physically active girls have been branded "tomboys" as far back as the reign of England's first Queen Elizabeth in the sixteenth century, who was something of a tomboy herself. Writings from the Victorian Era, three centuries later, describe a tomboy as a "woman who trespassed against the delicacy of her sex," a reference to those who were frolicsome, romping, or rude. Skipping rope, climbing trees, and jumping up and down were singled out as inappropriate activities for young women.

Strictures on female conduct relaxed over time. For twentieth-century girls growing up in a working class or rural environment, the label "tomboy" might single them out as distinctive but wasn't necessarily viewed as disparaging. All the same, girls often were teased for engaging in rough-and-tumble activities or for playing boys' games. Once beyond puberty, athletic young women were viewed more critically as appearing "mannish." They were discouraged from participating in organized sports by their families. Over the course of the century, women's sporting events became more popular, and family members routinely were found among the crowd of spectators. Parents came to realize that athletic daughters went on to assume successful roles as adults. Notably, four out of five women executives in Fortune 500 companies described themselves as tomboys growing up.

Donna Lopiano, a four-sport athlete who went on to head the Women's Sports Foundation, was a self-described tomboy. As a girl, she never felt the label to be a putdown but simply descriptive. It meant that she'd rather get a baseball glove than a doll for Christmas. She was given her first glove by her parents following Confirmation in the Catholic Church. She grew up in the post–World War II era. Norms governing feminine behavior were undergoing change. Women of her parents' generation had left their war-time jobs and returned to full-time domestic life. Donna's mother had worked in a factory during the war and went on to launch a successful family business with her husband, while raising a family.

CHILDHOOD

Donna Lopiano was born September 11, 1946 in Stamford, Connecticut, the eldest of three children. When she was seven her parents, Thomas and Josephine Lopiano, opened a restaurant. Her mother ran the busy kitchen. Neither of her parents, who grew up in the Great Depression, had graduated from high school. But they made it clear to their children that education was a priority. They also supported Donna's athletic aspirations. Josephine Lopiano had played basketball in the seventh and eighth grades. She always found time to play catch with her athletic daughter. Donna got her height from her mother, a definite advantage on the pitching mound. Thomas Lopiano took his daughter to Yankees baseball games in New York City. Donna recalls that from the age of five she dreamed that someday she would pitch for the Yankees.

Donna began playing sports in the 1950s, when gender discrimination was the rule. However, no such prejudice prevailed in her neighborhood. She was one of two girls among more than a dozen boys and was treated like one of the guys. Donna not only played stickball and baseball, but also football. She was tall for her age, bigger than most of the boys. She would tuck her long hair under her helmet and stand in at quarterback in pick-up games. But baseball clearly was her best sport. By age eleven, she had developed into an all-around player with exceptional pitching skills. That was when she decided to accompany the boys to the local Little League field for team tryouts. Donna was ecstatic when she made the cut, only to be told by a player's father, brandishing a Little League rulebook, that girls weren't allowed on the team. The talented young pitcher suffered an unforgettable lesson in the unfairness of sexism. She recalls crying for months following the incident. She was so devastated that she couldn't go to the ballpark to watch her friends play on the team that had barred her. It proved to be a pivotal event in her life. The dugout dad's edict would generate a future adversary of male-only athletics. Indeed, Donna Lopiano would become one of the foremost advocates for gender equality in American sport.

Donna's parents were the children of Italian immigrants. They had experienced ethnic prejudice and could empathize with their daughter's exposure to gender discrimination. When Donna was rejected by the Little League team, the Lopianos tried to shift her interest to horseback riding; but she was a ballplayer, not an equestrian. Over the next several years, her father made repeated efforts to contact some of the industrial league softball teams in the area, entreating them to give his talented daughter a tryout. But no offers came her way. A breakthrough occurred when Donna was just shy of her sixteenth birthday. By chance, a friend of her father who was a scout for the Pittsburgh Pirates came into her family's restaurant. He knew the coach of the Raybestos Brakettes, one of the premier women's softball teams in the nation. The Brakettes, located in nearby Stratford, Connecticut, were sponsored by Raymark Industries, a manufacturer of auto brakes. The scout, Sal Cagginello, reluctantly agreed to take Donna to Stratford for a tryout. It didn't take long for Donna to impress Sal and the Brakettes' coach with her talent. She was offered a starting position at second base and went on to play in the national championship softball tournament at age sixteen. She would play softball with the Brakettes over the next ten summers.

Most of Donna's early athletic experience was playing ball outside school programs. This was an era before women's interscholastic sports were widely promoted. There were no state high school championships for women in Connecticut at the time. So Donna played on club teams. Her two strongest sports were softball and basketball, but she also played volleyball and field hockey.

She played field hockey on teams in the Long Island Field Hockey Association and a league in Massachusetts, since there were no competitive field hockey teams in her home state. She also played AAU basketball, and volleyball on teams affiliated with the U.S. Volleyball Association (now USA Volleyball). She competed in national tournaments in these sports. Donna wasn't allowed to play on her high school softball team unless she gave up playing for the Brakettes. Such were the rules governing eligibility. She played on her high school's basketball team instead. But softball remained her forte.

SOFTBALL

The sport of softball began as a modification of baseball. Forms of the game date back to the final decades of the nineteenth century. Firefighters in Minneapolis were playing the game with a twelve-inch ball in 1895. During the twentieth century, softball developed into a popular amateur sport for men, women, and youngsters of both sexes, although softball has always been more popular with women than men. Today, over 90 percent of youth softball teams are girls' teams. The Amateur Softball Association (ASA) formed in 1933 and began holding tournaments in the late 1930s. The sport grew rapidly over the next several decades. In the post–World War II era, softball spread to other nations, but it was still largely an American game. By the early 1960s, when Donna Lopiano began playing with the Brakettes, more than 15,000 adult softball teams flourished from coast to coast.

Two types of softball emerged. Slow-pitch evolved as the recreational game. It was featured at the 1933 Chicago World's Fair and quickly caught on to become the most popular form of softball. In 1953 slow-pitch was recognized by the American Softball Association. Fast-pitch, which gained popularity in the 1940s, evolved into the more competitive game. While most American boys and men played baseball, athletic women—routinely barred from playing on baseball teams—gravitated to the game of fast-pitch. High school and college softball teams formed here and there, and semipro industrial leagues flourished. By the early 1940s, more than two hundred corporations were sponsoring softball teams, many of them for women. The Raybestos Brakettes organized as an amateur fast-pitch team in 1947. Intercollegiate competition developed more slowly. Donna Lopiano had graduated from college by the time the short-lived Association for Intercollegiate Athletics for Women (AIAW) began sponsoring national fast-pitch tournaments in the early 1970s. The National Collegiate Athletic Association (NCAA) assumed the sponsorship of intercollegiate championships, including softball, in 1982. In 1996 softball became an Olympic sport, again too late for Lopiano's generation. She and her teammates competed in national ASA championships and in international tournaments sponsored by the International Softball Federation (ISF).

The first ISF Women's World Championship was held in Melbourne, Australia in 1965. The tournament attracted teams from five nations, with the Raybestos Brakettes representing the United States. The Brakettes were the ASA women's national champions and the favorite in the ISF tournament. However, the host team proved to be surprisingly competitive. Following a 3-1 opening loss to the Australians, the Brakettes met them in a rematch in the semifinals of the tournament. The Aussies won again, shutting out the Americans 7-0. The U.S. team redeemed itself and—under the modified double-elimination format—advanced to the final round. With Donna Lopiano pitching, the Brakettes defeated Japan 6-0 and gained the opportunity to play the Australians in the title match. Lopiano took the mound again in what became a pitching duel. The championship game went for five scoreless innings. Then, in the sixth, the leadoff batter for the Australians reached second base. Lopiano unleashed a wild pitch that carried over the catcher's head. The teams were playing on a converted soccer field with no backstop behind home plate. The ball rolled unimpeded with the catcher in pursuit. The runner on second rounded third base and scored the winning run. The American team had to settle for the silver medal.

Despite Lopiano's personal disappointment in the outcome of the tournament, it had been an exciting experience for the teenager to travel halfway around the world to play the game she loved. The excursion didn't end with the medal ceremony. The Brakettes left Australia for a whirlwind tour that covered ten countries in thirty-seven days. The players and coaches held instructional clinics in various countries and took on the role of sports ambassadors, promoting the game around the world. The hope was that more than five nations would send teams to the next world championship tournament in 1970, to be hosted by Japan.

Upon graduating from high school, Lopiano formulated plans for continuing her education and began considering a career. There were virtually no opportunities for women in the 1960s to play professional ball. Fortunately, she had other options. Lopiano always had been a good student. As a girl, she cultivated a love of books that rivaled her love of sports. She recalls regular visits to the public library and immersing herself in the *Encyclopaedia Britannica* at an early age. Lopiano's parents made a point of complimenting her on finishing books and rewarded good grades in school. They reinforced her academic achievements just as they supported her accomplishments on the playing fields.

She continued to play for the Brakettes. In 1966 she was voted the Amateur Softball Association's most valuable player. Lopiano realized early on that her dream of pitching for the Yankees was just that—a dream. Instead, she settled for being a fan. The talented athlete shifted her career goal to becoming a physical education teacher and coach. Her high school P.E. teacher, Mary Jane Hagan, had been a mentor and a role model.

Lopiano enrolled at Connecticut State College (now Southern Connecticut State University), where she played basketball, volleyball, and ran track and field. But this was an era before national women's collegiate tournaments in most sports—golf being the exception. Not until the 1970s were national collegiate championships for women held in a range of sports. For the most part, college women participated in intramural and extramural sports. Nor were there any athletic scholarships for women at the time. Lopiano was fortunate that her parents could afford to help her with tuition. She had her own automobile, and she could afford to buy the necessary equipment to play ball in the amateur leagues. Lopiano received her bachelor's degree in physical education in 1968. She completed a master's degree in physical education at the University of Southern California the following year. She stayed another year in Los Angeles to begin coursework for her Ph.D. While there, she played on teams in California's open amateur leagues.

Lopiano continued playing ball upon completing her education. Summers meant playing for the Brakettes. She led her team in batting in 1970 and 1972, and hit a team record eight home runs in one season. She had the highest batting average (.429) in the 1972 Women's Fast-Pitch National Tournament, when she again was voted the Amateur Softball Association's MVP. Her achievements on the mound included pitching a no-hitter. During her years with the Brakettes, she won 183 games and lost only 18. In the process, Lopiano struck out more than 1,600 batters. Over her ten-year pitching career, she played on six national championship teams. She was a nine-time softball All American, playing four different positions. Overall, the multisport athlete had played in twenty-five national championships in softball, volleyball, basketball, and field hockey.

WORKING IN SPORTS AFTER SOFTBALL

In 1970 Lopiano took a position on the physical education faculty at Brooklyn College, a campus of the City University of New York. She coached softball, basketball, and volleyball, and volunteered as the assistant athletic director in order to gain administrative experience. Lopiano had developed a reputation for being a workaholic; she was out of bed before the sun came up and occasionally put in eighteen-hour days. On top of her duties as a coach, administrator, and faculty member, she found time to complete her doctoral dissertation for her Ph.D. from the University of Southern California.

The 1970s were an eventful decade for women's sports, with the founding of the Association for Intercollegiate Athletics for Women in 1971 (an organization that Lopiano would later head), and passage of Title IX legislation in 1972. This legislative act required American colleges and high schools to provide sports opportunities for young women equal to those accorded male

THE TITLE IX REVOLUTION

Title IX of the 1972 Educational Amendments was passed by Congress and signed into law by President Richard Nixon. It was by far the most significant legislation to address gender inequity in sports. The provision outlawing sex discrimination in education stated, "No person in the United States, on the basis of sex, [shall] be excluded from participation in, denied the benefits of, or be subjected to discrimination under any education program or activity receiving federal financial assistance." This federal directive applied to athletic programs.

Schools and colleges receiving federal assistance were required to provide equal opportunities, financial support, and facilities for girl's and women's sports. The legislation had a dramatic impact on the number of high school and college women who would participate in sports over the next two decades. In 1971, only one in twenty-seven girls played high school varsity sports. By the mid-1990s, the figure had risen to one in three. The number of women playing on college teams would increase by a factor of ten. Where separate women's teams didn't exist, women were allowed to try out for the men's team. Today, more than a thousand girls are playing high school football.

Women's athletic budgets increased significantly, but often didn't attain parity. A great deal of "foot dragging" occurred when it came to implementing Title IX provisions. Some of the strongest opposition came initially from the NCAA. Women coaches and athletes filed numerous complaints with the U.S. Office of Civil Rights and instigated lawsuits when denied equal opportunity in school and college programs. Women coaches also sued their employers, demanding equal pay to what male coaches were receiving in co-equal sports.

students. Progressive women's voices were finding an audience, and advocates for girls' and women's sport were among them.

Donna Lopiano, always the avid reader, would soon discover feminist literature. The 1973 publication of Germaine Greer's book, *The Female Eunuch*, arguing for a sexual liberation movement, caused a national sensation. That same year an article appeared in the newly established *Ms.* magazine titled, "Closing the Muscle Gap." *Sports Illustrated* published a three-part series on sexism and sport. Lopiano had experienced both subtle and not-so-subtle discrimination as a ballplayer and as an educator. The combination of life experiences and emerging feminism would transform her into an activist for women's sports. Her girlhood confrontation with discrimination on the baseball field had left its mark.

Little League Baseball was exempt from Title IX legislation since it was a privately-funded organization. Little League had been sponsoring organized teams for boys going back to the pre–World War II era. Thousands of teams formed in every state in the nation, and eventually in dozens of foreign countries. Little League continued to ban girls from playing on teams until 1974. The rule was revised following a lawsuit filed by the National Organization of Women in New Jersey Superior Court on behalf of twelve-year-old Maria Pepe. Unlike Donna Lopiano, Maria was invited to join the local Little League team in her hometown of Hoboken, New Jersey. She played in three games before Little League headquarters threatened to suspend the team's charter if she continued playing. She was dropped from the team. Maria's parents sued. Following the court's ruling in her favor, the twelve-year-old baseball player became something of a national celebrity. She was honored by the New York Yankees, who made her an honorary "Yankee for a Day." The broader consequences of the court ruling were dramatic. Within a couple of years, some 30,000 girls were playing Little League baseball. In contrast, Donna Lopiano's generation of girls was restricted to the softball fields.

DIRECTOR OF WOMEN'S ATHLETICS AT THE UNIVERSITY OF TEXAS

Donna Lopiano left Brooklyn College in 1975 to accept the new position of director of women's athletics at the University of Texas. She was the first full-time women's director on the Austin campus. Texas Athletic Director Darrell Royal felt that women's athletics should have their own budget in the post–Title IX milieu, where wrangling over finances had become increasingly contentious. Texas was one of very few colleges at the time to create a stand-alone women's athletic department. The job offer wasn't a shoo-in. University president Lorene Rogers, a native Texan, initially was concerned that Lopiano's East Coast directness would be a poor fit with the more genteel southwestern decorum, but the search committee convinced Rogers to support the Connecticut Yankee. Despite a few early missteps, the twenty-nine-year-old Lopiano stayed on to build the Texas women's program into one of the strongest in the nation. The athletic department would eventually support eight women's sports—all of them ranked in the top ten in NCAA Division I at one time or another during her tenure. However, there were a few bumps in the road along the way.

Two weeks into her tenure in Austin, Lopiano came close to being fired after she testified before a congressional committee against a proposed amendment to Title IX legislation that would exempt college football from the provisions covering gender discrimination. The amendment, named for Texas senator John Tower, had the support of Lopiano's boss, Darrell Royal, who was the head football coach. More than a few coaches and alumni wanted her out.

Cooler heads among the university's administrators saved her job. She was advised to pay a courtesy call to Senator Tower, which she did. But Lopiano never compromised her principles in fighting for the rights of women athletes. It took her Texas colleagues some time to get used to her brashness. She quickly acquired a reputation for firing coaches who didn't meet her standards. At the same time, she advised more than one women's coach that her only recourse was to sue for discrimination. Indeed, several universities had been sued in the wake of Title IX. Following a lawsuit in 1993 (the year after Lopiano left her position as women's A.D.) the University of Texas added softball, soccer, and rowing as women's varsity sports. The rowing crew named one of its shells after Lopiano.

Donna Lopiano may not have always been the easiest person to work for, or with, but she proved to be the consummate administrator. She built a comprehensive full-time staff for the women's program that eventually included positions in event management, fundraising, finance, ticket sales, and publicity. This, too, was exceptional for women's college programs at the time. The sports-minded university and its alumni came to appreciate her outstanding accomplishments. She was afforded a generous budget that allowed her to hire some of the best coaches in the country and to purchase first-rate equipment. Lopiano supplemented the department budget and enhanced public relations with a variety of fundraisers, including an annual silent auction of memorabilia and a tennis-golf gala.

The results spoke for themselves. Under Lopiano's leadership, University of Texas women's teams won eighteen national championships in basketball, cross country, indoor and outdoor track, swimming, and volleyball, plus numerous Southwest Conference championships. The women's basketball team, a perennial powerhouse, actually outdrew the men's team over a couple of seasons. In 1986 President Ronald Reagan invited the undefeated Lady Longhorns to the White House to acknowledge their outstanding success. While Lopiano was athletic director, the women's program produced more than three hundred All Americans and fourteen Olympians.

When Lopiano ended her tenure at the University of Texas in 1992, the women's program had a budget of more than $4 million. It had been less than $100,000 when she arrived. Arguably, she had built the best—and best-funded—women's college athletic program in the nation. However, she was quick to note the men's program at UT Austin was receiving $12 million at the time. Women's sports at the university weren't just about money and winning, however. Lopiano stressed academics and held her coaches to high standards for their athletes. Over 90 percent of the Lady Longhorns who exhausted their eligibility graduated under her watch. This was at a time when the graduation rates of male athletes had become an embarrassment to the NCAA. (Congress began requiring colleges to publish their graduation rates in the 1970s.)

THE WOMEN'S SPORTS FOUNDATION

Lopiano left Texas to assume the position of CEO of the Women's Sports Foundation. She had previously served on the Foundation's board. This wasn't her first job as head of a national women's sports organization. She had been president of the Association for Intercollegiate Athletics for Women in 1981–82 during the AIAW's anti-trust battle with the National Collegiate Athletic Association for control of women's athletics. It was a David and Goliath battle, with Goliath prevailing. AIAW, which had governed women's collegiate athletics since 1971, folded in June of 1983. Subsequently, the NCAA took complete charge of women's sports in the major colleges. (The rival National Association of Intercollegiate Athletics, representing small colleges, had begun sponsoring intercollegiate championships for women in 1980.) The upside of the change in governance was that the NCAA provided more money to financially strapped women's programs. Later on, Lopiano would work with the NCAA in rewriting their rule book and would serve as a consultant to the association. Her extensive involvement in the politics of sports governance served her well in her new position.

Lopiano arrived at the Women's Sports Foundation as it was completing its second decade as a nonprofit organization. Tennis star Billie Jean King and a small group of athletes, including champion swimmer and Olympic medalist Donna de Verona, had founded the WSF in 1974 as an educational organization to promote girls' and women's sports. The Foundation maintained a speakers' bureau, provided sports camp scholarships to financially needy girls, and served as a clearinghouse on women's sports issues—as it still does. In 1980 the Foundation established the International Women's Sports Hall of Fame to honor women athletes and coaches who made history. At the initial fundraising banquet, nine athletes were inducted into the Hall, including Babe Didrikson, Gertrude Ederle, Althea Gibson, Wilma Rudolph, and Billie Jean King.

The Foundation was equally active on the political front. Its members had been instrumental in the passage of the Amateur Sports Act of 1978. This legislation was pivotal in annulling the powerful Amateur Athletic Union, an organization infamous among women athletes for its record of gender bias. The AAU had controlled a wide range of amateur sports for most of the twentieth century. The act also assured that women would be accorded fair representation on the United States Olympic Committee and national sports governing bodies. Over the next dozen years, a woman would serve as president of the National Collegiate Athletic Association, the National Association of Intercollegiate Athletics, the National Federation of State High School Associations, the United States Tennis Association, and as vice president of the International Olympic Committee.

The year that Lopiano assumed her executive duties at the WSF, the U.S. Supreme Court ruled that women were entitled to monetary damages under the provisions of Title IX. Women coaches at the high school and college levels continued to experience discrimination in pay, and school athletic budgets still favored men's football and basketball. Gradually, women were gaining access to the necessary financial resources to build viable sports programs and pursue careers as well-paid coaches. But the battle over funding would carry into the following decades.

Donna Lopiano came to the Women's Sports Foundation with significant management experience in marketing and fundraising. She was successful in establishing a new national headquarters on Long Island, and she was able to cultivate a number of commercial sponsors including Nike, Reebok, Gillette, and Merrill Lynch. Sponsorship income tripled during her first five years as CEO. An increasing number of companies that marketed athletic equipment and clothing, or advertised their products during sports events, had begun to appreciate the advantages of establishing ties with women's sports organizations. Lopiano saw the opportunity to create a mutually beneficial relationship between these moneyed interests and the growing phenomenon of women's sport.

Lopiano established a relationship with ESPN, the television sports network, advising network executives on editorial coverage of women's sports. She encouraged them to consider a separate women's sports network. Women's sports programming on television would increase somewhat by the end of the twentieth century as women's golf, tennis, and basketball received more coverage, but the level of coverage failed to come close to that afforded men's sports. Women's sports never attained a segment of programming greater than 8 percent of total sports coverage on American television. A women's sports network remains a dream.

Lopiano emerged as a high profile advocate for girls' and women's sports during George W. Bush's presidency. Growing resistance within the men's athletic sector threatened to compromise Title IX legislation. A battle over Title IX had been waged previously during the Reagan administration after a U.S. Supreme Court decision weakened some of the law's provisions. In the interim, several men's non-revenue sports on college campuses had been eliminated to meet budgetary constraints, while football, the most expensive sport by far, had to make do with less money. College athletic directors had been lobbying to exempt football from the law's provisions for some time. In late 2002 the Bush administration responded to these overtures by forming a fifteen-member Commission on Athletic Opportunity, charged with examining Title IX and proposing changes. At the same time, the executive branch was being pressured by the WSF and other women's advocacy groups not to tamper with Title IX. Donna Lopiano publicly denounced the Bush commission as a sham and urged it to disband. The commission continued to meet and issued a final report with twenty-three recommendations for changes in Title IX legislation. Notably, two commission members, Julie Foudy, president of the WSF, and WSF founder Donna DeVarona, refused to sign the report. With a national election looming in 2004, President Bush eventually rejected the controversial commission's recommendations to change the law.

Under Lopiano's leadership, the Women's Sports Foundation began funding GoGirlGo, an initiative to motivate sedentary girls in third grade through high school to become more active in sports. The program, initiated in 2004, encouraged a healthy lifestyle that would improve girls' self-image and lower obesity rates. Studies reported that a third of American schoolgirls were overweight, and nearly one in five, obese. Some 75 percent of young women in high school reported that they were unhappy with their bodies. The Foundation appreciated that physical activity, along with diet, is a crucial element in combating poor self-image and obesity. There remained a large segment of young women who didn't participate in athletic activities. Following Title IX legislation, many girls' and women's programs began to mirror the male model by focusing on high-profile, elitist athletics. In the typical American school, the majority of girls didn't participate in varsity sports. They were relegated to the role of spectators. Intramural sports and school recreation programs lagged in funding. At the same time, surprisingly few high school students were enrolled in daily physical education classes. The Women's Sports Foundation eventually raised some $3 million to fund new physical activity initiatives for underserved girls.

The struggle for equal rights in sport proved to be an ongoing battle. The status of women's coaches became a growing concern within the Foundation. In 1972 when Title IX was passed, 90 percent of women's teams were coached by women. By 2007, the thirty-fifth anniversary of the law, 58 percent of women's collegiate teams were coached by men. When the Women's National Basketball Association began play in 1997, seven of the eight coaches were women. Ten years later, the majority of WNBA coaches were men. A similar phenomenon was occurring among sports administrators. As late as 2004, less than 9 percent of NCAA Division I programs were under a female athletic director. A WSF survey found that there were more women college presidents than athletic directors. Gender discrimination replicated racial discrimination in sport. Women, like African Americans, found access to the playing fields much easier than entrée into the coaching and executive ranks.

REMAINING ACTIVE IN THE NATIONAL SPORTS SCENE

Donna Lopiano spent fifteen years as CEO of the Women's Sports Foundation. When she stepped down in 2007, the Foundation established the Dr. Donna Lopiano Leadership Fund in her honor. WSF initiated a $2 million fundraising campaign in her name, directed at research and advocacy. Lopiano didn't retire when she left the Foundation. She remains active on the national sports scene. In 2008 she founded Sports Management Resources, a consulting firm that advises school and college athletic departments. She currently serves as president. She began teaching a course in amateur athletics at the University of Massachusetts Isenberg School of Management in the spring semester of 2009.

Donna Lopiano also has been active in promoting women's sports abroad. She was invited to coach the Italian women's softball team and spent the summer in Italy recruiting players and training the national team. The Italian team won the European championship and qualified for the world championship for the first time. She recently traveled to the Middle East to develop sports programs for Muslim women that are consistent with their culture. She convinced the country of Qatar to add a girls' program at its national sports academy. The ASPIRE Sports Academy, which opened in 2005, now offers programs for girls 6–14 years old. Qatar is one of the more progressive Islamic nations when it comes to women's rights. It has become a regional powerhouse in sports like basketball and volleyball. The country's ASPIRE Zone, the so-called Sports City, features some of the finest athletic facilities in the area.

In 2009 the International Baseball Federation (IBAF) selected Lopiano to chair the women's baseball committee. The IBAF proposed that women's baseball be included in the 2016 Summer Olympic Games to be held in Rio de Janeiro, Brazil. The American Women's Baseball Federation has sponsored regional and national tournaments since 1992. The first women's national team competed in the 2004 World Cup of Baseball, held in Edmonton, Alberta in Canada.

Lopiano serves on numerous national panels, appears frequently at symposiums, and tours the country delivering as many as three speeches a week. She coauthored two books on women athletes and a baseball/softball playbook with former Mississippi State University coach Ron Polk. She has written numerous articles on women's sport for newspapers and journals. Lopiano believes that we must introduce girls to sports and fitness activities at an early age, and that we must encourage girls and boys to play together in matched competition. She emphasizes the need for adequately financed community organizations that promote sports and recreational activities for both sexes.

Donna Lopiano was listed as one of "The 100 Most Influential People in Sports" by *Sporting News,* the century-old sports magazine. Fox Network named her one of the ten most powerful women in sports. She has been recognized for her advocacy for gender equity in sports by the National Collegiate Athletic Association and the International Olympic Committee. In 2001 Lopiano received the U.S. Sports Academy Distinguished Service Award. She received the Award of Excellence from the Sports Lawyers Association in 2008.

Lopiano has been inducted into the National Softball Hall of Fame, the National Sports Hall of Fame, and the National Italian American Sports Hall of Fame. The Institute for International Sport inducted her into its Hall of Fame and designated her an International Scholar-Athlete. She has been awarded several honorary doctoral degrees, including one from her alma mater, Southern Connecticut State University.

Lopiano has maintained a busy professional life, but it's not "all work and no play." She enjoyed playing golf in her leisure, although arthritis in her hip made it difficult for her to play. She eventually underwent hip surgery and still gets on the links occasionally. She took up kayaking and enjoys paddling along streams in the New England countryside. She also walks outdoors and rides an exercise bike indoors to stay in shape. She lives with her sister in the family home in Easton, Connecticut.

Donna Lopiano stands out as one of the foremost advocates for women's sports in the nation's recent history. She testified before three Congressional committees on Title IX and on gender equity issues. She served as a consultant to the Office of Civil Rights Title IX Task Force and was an expert witness in twenty-eight court cases. She has served as a consultant on gender equity to schools, colleges, and state education agencies and continues to appear as an expert witness in court cases.

Because of the concerted efforts of Donna Lopiano, Billie Jean King, and other advocates for gender equity, girls and women are enjoying increasing opportunities to participate in sports. Today, young girls join basketball, soccer, and softball leagues at the same rate as boys. By 2009, more than three million American girls were participating in high school sports. Thousands of high schools across the country were sponsoring girls' teams in basketball, volleyball, track and field, cross country, fast-pitch softball, soccer, golf, tennis, and several other sports, according to the National Federation of State High School Associations. On the college level, the NCAA sanctions twenty-one women's sports, and there are currently some thirty Olympic sports for women. Over 40 percent of the athletes participating in the 2008 Beijing Summer Games were women. At the 1948 Olympic Games in London, one woman participated for every ten male athletes. This is a huge improvement over the course of Donna Lopiano's lifetime. Women's professional sports also have made significant advances. The Women's National Basketball Association is now in its thirteenth year, and the Ladies Professional Golf Association has enjoyed increasing popularity among television viewers and is attracting more sponsors.

The advantages of girls participating in sports are manifest. They reach beyond the direct benefits of physical fitness and improved social skills. Girls who play sports are less likely to use drugs or to become pregnant, and they are more likely to remain physically active and stay healthy in later life. In regard to the latter, Donna Lopiano serves as a model for retired athletes.

FURTHER READING

Donna Lopiano. 2004. *Sport Marketing Quarterly* 13:126–28.

"Donna Lopiano." 2010. Women's Sports Foundation. http://www.womenssports foundation.org/Content/Athletes/L/Lopiano-Donna.aspx.

Lopiano, Donna. 1995. "Growing Up with Gender Discrimination in Sports." In *Sport in Society: Equal Opportunity or Business as Usual*, ed. Richard E. Lapchick, 83–95. Thousand Oaks, CA: Sage Publications.

Salter, David. 1996. *Crashing the Old Boys' Network: The Tragedies and Triumphs of Girls and Women in Sports*. Westport, CT: Praeger Publishers.

Show, Jon. 2010. Donna Lopiano. *Sports Business Journal*, March 22: 26–30.

Thompson, Helen. 1994. A whole new ball game. *Texas Monthly* 22:3: http:// www .texasmonthly.com/1994-03-01/index.php.

Wolff, Alexander. 1990. Prima Donna. *Sports Illustrated*, Dec. 17: http://sports illustrated.cnn.com/vault/article/magazine/MAG1136053/index.htm.

Shirley Muldowney at a race in May 1975. (AP Photo)

Shirley Muldowney
(1940–)

Within the wide world of sports, we find a distinct subset of activities in which humans and machines compete as units. The sport of cycling is an obvious example. Less familiar are the regattas with high-tech yachts characterized as "racing machines." Sailboats share the aquatic arena with powerboats: racing machines propelled by internal combustion engines. The twentieth century introduced motor sports to the world. From the early 1900s, men and women raced on the land, on the sea, and in the air. Former motorcycle and bicycle racer Glen Curtiss was named "Champion Air Racer in the World" after defeating French aviator Louis Blériot in a 1909 race. Famed aviator Amelia Earhart, prior to flying across oceans, had joined the cadre of women pilots competing in air races in the 1920s.

Back on terra firma, auto racing rapidly became the most popular motor sport. Currently, the combined forms of auto racing make up the fastest growing sport in the United States. Popular series include Indy Car, Formula One, NASCAR, and drag racing. American women were racing automobiles before they won the right to vote. The Women's Motoring Club, founded by Mrs. Alice Huyler Ramsey, sponsored an all-women auto race from New York to Pennsylvania and back in 1909. Denise McCluggage was the most celebrated female auto racer of the post–World War II era, driving Ferraris and Porsches to victory. McCluggage elevated women drivers from the status of novelty to serious competitor. A generation later, Janet Guthrie broke the gender barrier at the Indianapolis 500 auto race. That was in 1977, the same year that Shirley Muldowney became the first woman to win drag racing's prestigious Winston World Championship. Muldowney's quest to compete in the male bastion of drag racing began on the streets of Schenectady, New York, two decades earlier.

CHILDHOOD

Shirley Muldowney (née Roque) was born on June 19, 1940 in Burlington, Vermont. Her parents moved to Schenectady when she was five years old. The move was made under less than ideal circumstances. The family of four crowded into a small apartment in a four-story walkup where Shirley shared a bedroom with her older sister, Linda. Mae Roque was a working mom and the force that held the family together. Shirley's father, Belgium, nicknamed "Tex Rock," was a country and western musician who earned his living as a cab driver. Shirley has mixed feelings about her father. She fondly remembers sitting on her dad's lap, "steering" the family car down country roads. But the former prize fighter spent more time at the local clubs than at home with his family. He was known for his temper and rough behavior. Shirley's mother had to bail him out of jail more than once. Shirley inherited traits from both parents. She had her mother's determination and work ethic, and her father's pugnacity.

As a girl, Shirley was a loner. She didn't like school, and she didn't get along with the other kids. Her father, the brawler, instructed her on how to deal with bullies. He suggested "parting their hair" with a club. Shirley preferred the company of animals. She would hitchhike to a horse barn on the edge of town for companionship. She spent the summers with her aunt and uncle on their dairy farm in Vermont. Shirley helped with the cows and worked in the garden. And she loved to fish in the rural Vermont streams. Back in Schenectady, life was more problematic. As a teenager, Shirley's toughness turned into rebellion. She dropped out of school and found work as a lunch counter waitress and car hop. This was when she met Jack Muldowney, a young mechanic who shared her budding interest in fast cars, and who would shape the course of her life.

The late 1950s was an era when customized "hot rods" defined adolescent culture, like a scene lifted from the popular Hollywood film *Rebel Without a Cause*, starring James Dean. Drag racing became a passion for Jack and Shirley. She would sneak out of the house at night to meet up with her boyfriend and cruise the streets. The two got married when Shirley turned sixteen. The couple purchased an old Ford that Jack fitted with a Cadillac engine. They would work at their jobs during the day and join the street-racing scene after dark. Early in the marriage, Jack took a job with an auto dealership in upstate New York. The couple relocated to a small town in the Adirondacks and settled into an apartment above a garage. Their son, John, was born a year and a half into their marriage. Shortly after, the Muldowneys moved back to Schenectady, and Shirley took a job at a downtown dairy.

Jack taught Shirley how to drive and soon realized that his wife had a natural talent for racing. Shirley recalls how it all started one night on Route 50, while she was driving their 1951 Mercury. An Oldsmobile pulled alongside, and the driver challenged them. She pushed the accelerator to the floor and didn't let up until the speedometer topped 100 mph. Jack, sitting next to her, was both taken aback and impressed. He installed multiple carburetors on the Merc's engine, and the two of them would drive around looking for challengers. At first, Jack did most of the driving. They routinely raced a rich kid from Albany whose father had bought him a fuel-injected Corvette. This was when they had traded up to a red 1958 Chevrolet Impala fitted with three two-barrel carburetors on its 348-cubic-inch engine. Jack would let Shirley take the wheel, and she routinely "smoked" the competition. Needless to say, the local guys didn't like being beaten by a girl. Shirley Muldowney became a rebel with a cause.

After some success on the streets and a couple of run-ins with the police, the young street racers decided to try their luck at the local tracks. On weekends they headed to the drag strips at Glens Falls and Fonda Speedway. That's where Shirley first drove in an organized drag race. They raced a variety of cars during these early years, including a split-window Corvette. The pair regularly took home trophies, but they were violating the norms of the era:

women didn't drag race. Muldowney's intrusion into the male terrain didn't make her popular with her peers. She recalls having few girlfriends. That was fine with her. The independent-minded teenager realized she wasn't cut out to be a housewife. Jack let Shirley do most of the driving, while he prepared the cars for racing. It proved to be a winning combination.

Shirley's success on the drag strips garnered a lot of attention, positive and negative. Someone came up with the nickname "Cha-Cha," and it stuck. At first, the moniker was daubed on the sides of her cars with white shoe polish, and then it was painted on. Drag racing impresario Tommy Ivo advised her to never let go of the eye-catching nickname and to continue painting her vehicles pink. The color pink became her trademark, but she eventually dropped "Cha-Cha" because of its sexist connotations. Muldowney wanted to be recognized for her driving ability, not her gender. At the same time, driving pink cars and wearing pink boots and racing helmets was her way of "rubbing it in." Muldowney drove a 426-cubic-inch Plymouth in a match race against Vermont driver Charlie Lendrum. The "battle of the sexes" drew a big crowd to the local track. Muldowney won the event and set a new time record for Super Stocks. Match races brought in modest prize money. Drag racers routinely booked these contests to enhance their income.

Much of the local and regional racing at the time was in "Sportsman Car" classes. This included everything from regular street cars with license plates to Super Stocks to home-built dragsters. Stock class cars, or "stockers," had to retain most of the original manufacturer's equipment. The Super Stock class in which Jack and Shirley raced featured cars with numerous modifications to the engines and suspension systems, but body modifications weren't allowed. The Modified Stock rules permitted car owners to drop a huge V8 engine into a subcompact car. The various classes employed a system of handicapping based on elapsed time (ET) to ensure fair competition. For example, a Super Stock clocking an ET of 10.5 seconds in a quarter-mile currently races in SS/D class. This scheme provided an enticing format that attracted scores of local mechanics and drivers to the tracks.

NEEDING PERMISSION TO RACE A CAR IF YOU ARE FEMALE

In the 1960s the big auto manufacturers in Detroit were spending lots of money promoting Super Stocks. Companies like Chrysler sent race teams to tracks around the country and sponsored individual drivers. Shirley Muldowney wanted to be part of the Detroit scene; however, they weren't interested in a woman driver. She took a job at a newspaper in Albany, New York to earn enough money to race. In order to get the job, she implied that she had a high school diploma. The school dropout realized that she would have to produce a certificate at some point, so she signed up for a correspondence course and earned a G.E.D. This fulfilled the job requirement and a promise made to her dad to finish school. As for drag racing, the couple was on their own. Jack built a B/Gas dragster with a Chevy engine. It was in this homemade vehicle that Muldowney obtained her Top Gas license in 1965. However, when National Hot Rod Association officials realized she was a woman, they disallowed the license. The association explained in a letter that women weren't allowed to drive dragsters, only stock cars. Muldowney convinced the Albany paper where she worked to run a story implying that the NHRA discriminated against women. NHRA Director Wally Parks didn't want the negative publicity and gave Muldowney permission to race, but only in local events. The impasse continued for a couple of years before she was allowed to enter national competition.

Muldowney had her first racing mishap in the B/Gas dragster. The brakes failed during a run, and the dragster rolled clear through the shutdown area and into the woods. Fortunately she wasn't hurt, and Jack could repair the damage. A couple of years later, the couple scraped together enough money to buy their first professional chassis from California car-builder Don Long. Shirley recalls that she and Jack were the envy of everyone in the Tri-City area when the rail job made its appearance. Despite their success, racing dragsters was a financial struggle for the young couple. Shirley worked two jobs and looked after young John, while Jack ran a service station and plowed driveways in the winters to meet expenses. In late 1969 they purchased a dual-engine dragster from Long. Shirley clocked 198 mph at Indianapolis in the new vehicle and just missed qualifying it for the 1970 U.S. Nationals in the Top Gas class.

The development of drag racing as a sport mirrored Shirley Muldowney's early racing career. It began with impromptu duels on city streets and progressed to organized events at drag strips. Drag racing was based on a simple premise: two drivers raced from a standing start over a short distance—usually a quarter-mile—and the car reaching the finish line first was declared the winner. The sport got its name from drivers "dragging" their engines through the lower gears before upshifting. Drag racing first became popular in California following World War II and then spread across the North American continent. The earliest off-street venues were dry lake beds and abandoned airstrips. Drag race enthusiasts formed local car clubs that set rules and sponsored events. At first, the racers competed in factory-stock street vehicles, but soon they were "souping up" cars with aftermarket parts. The hobby attracted a national following when *Hot Rod Magazine* began publication in 1948.

National sanctioning bodies formed in the 1950s. The National Hot Rod Association organized in California in 1951, and five years later the American Hot Rod Association, or AHRA, became active in the Midwest and eastern United States. The NHRA introduced the stopwatch, which facilitated recording of elapsed times, and established organized classes for competition. The introduction of overhead-valve V8 engines transformed drag racing in the early 1950s. The sport continued to grow during the following decades. After the NHRA lifted the ban on nitro fuel in 1963, multi-engine dragsters gave way to the single-engine "rail jobs." That year, a California company developed the "Christmas Tree," drag racing's iconic light pole that signals the starts. The prize money got a big boost in the mid-1970s when R. J. Reynolds Tobacco Co. began sponsoring the Winston Points Championships in the now-dominant NHRA and fledgling International Hot Rod Association, or IHRA, prevalent in the southeastern states. Both amateurs and professionals participated in drag racing across the United States and Canada. The premier professional classes were Top Gas dragsters and Funny Cars. These were the events in which Shirley Muldowney would make her mark. By this time, the sport was drawing a large number of fans to regional and national events.

Drag racing has to be experienced live to appreciate the spectacle. Television can't do it justice. Being on the scene bumping elbows with the raucous crowd of spectators on race day engages all the senses: the deafening roar of powerful racing engines and squeal of spinning tires; the smell and taste of burning rubber and exotic fuels; the searing heat radiating from the pits and track surface; the panorama of brightly painted racing cars spouting orange-white flames from their exhausts; the spectacular burst of parachutes at the end of runs. Nothing can top the tension and excitement of one-on-one competition punctuated with the sporadic shock of an exploding engine or an out-of-control vehicle crashing into the barriers. In addition to the main event, there's the sideshow of exhibition cars and motorcycles performing wheelstands down the strip, along with the jet-powered "weenie-roasters," so named for their tendency to blow up on occasion. It's no wonder that these events draw thousands of fans.

But for all of the attractions, drag racing can prove exhausting and expensive for the drivers and crews. Nomadic racing teams tour the North American continent from Southern California to Ontario, Canada to compete in the numerous weekend racing events. They travel in caravans, driving trucks and pulling large trailers. The crews endure all the usual inconveniences and expenses of being on the road. Upon arrival at their destinations, the crews spend countless hours tuning the temperamental racing vehicles. High performance auto parts are expensive, as are racing tires, which last about a week. The pricey nitro-methane fuel that propels Funny Cars and dragsters is consumed in gallons per mile, not miles per gallon. The toll adds up over a racing season. This was the life that the young Muldowneys had adopted. Racing on the tour excited Shirley, but it was beginning to wear on Jack.

FUNNY CARS, FIRES, FANS, AND TOP FUEL RACING

Top Gas dragsters were on the decline in the early 1970s. Funny Cars were becoming the popular attraction. Shirley and Jack bought an old converted

Mustang from fellow driver and car builder Conrad "Connie" Kalitta. Shirley wanted to continue racing on the "nitro" circuit. Jack, however, was looking forward to settling down and running a service station. The married racing partners reached an impasse. Shirley decided to leave Jack. One night, she loaded the Funny Car onto the trailer and headed to Michigan, the hub of the Midwest racing circuit. In 1972 the Muldowneys divorced. Despite the breakup, the two would remain on good terms. Shirley continued to race under her married name, by which she was known. She and Jack Muldowney had accumulated more than two hundred wins in their fifteen years together. Now in Michigan, Shirley Muldowney began driving for Kalitta's Funny Car team. She won her first Funny Car title at the IHRA Nationals in Rockingham, North Carolina: the first woman ever to win a Pro class national event.

Funny Cars, or "floppers," first appeared as exhibition cars in the 1960s before becoming an NHRA sanctioned class in 1970. The prototype vehicle's altered wheel base and jacked-up rear end on a production car body looked odd, or "funny"; thus, the name. However, this configuration was soon to change. Stock bodies were discarded for one-piece flip-up fiberglass shells hinged at the rear. The combination of a 7,500-horsepower engine on a frame half as long as a dragster makes it difficult to hold these cars on the track. The driver is constantly fighting the butterfly-wing steering wheel to keep the nose pointed straight. It doesn't sound like a venture that a petite five-foot-four-inch woman should attempt, but Shirley Muldowney mastered the art of driving these monsters. Kalitta acted as Muldowney's agent. He put pressure on track owners to book Muldowney in this class. Connie would tell them that if they booked him, they had to book her as well. Later on, she would become the main attraction.

Muldowney continued to drive Funny Cars through 1973, mostly on the match race circuit. The enclosed vehicles were notorious for catching on fire, and Muldowney endured several fires while competing in this class. While the silver fire suits protected drivers' bodies, their upper extremities remained vulnerable. At a race in Indianapolis, the engine exploded on Muldowney's car, and fire engulfed the cockpit. She climbed out with her helmet aflame and her goggles completely burned off. Her eyelids were singed shut, and she suffered bad burns around her eyes. Fourteen-year-old son John was in the pits to witness his mother's accident. She was fortunate not to have suffered more severe injuries. A week later, she was racing in Toronto with bandages on her burns. Muldowney was one of the early drivers to install Plexiglas windows in the firewall so that she could see if the engine caught fire. Today's cars have built-in fire-extinguishing systems with a nozzle pointed at the driver.

Given Shirley's encounters with vehicle fires, it seems counterintuitive that she was one of the drivers who performed "fire burnouts" on the strips. Drag racers normally do burnouts, a procedure in which they spin their rear tires down the track (or in the staging area) prior to a run to increase traction. For a fire burnout, they poured gasoline rather than water on the track surface and then spun their tires a short distance down the strip amidst flames. The racing fans loved the spectacle, but the sanctioning bodies quickly outlawed the dangerous stunt. On one occasion at a Michigan track, Muldowney's engine almost died during a fire burnout that sucked up all the oxygen. Luckily, the engine kept running. She could have been "roasted like marshmallow" inside her fire suit.

Together with Connie Kalitta, Shirley began a marketing relationship with Chrysler Corporation in 1973. Pictures from the era feature the Plymouth logo on her vehicles. Chrysler would send Muldowney to auto shows and promotional events in return for promoting her racing team. By the 1970s, it was getting prohibitively expensive to race in the Pro classes without a sponsor. Providentially, television began covering drag racing events, and this attracted more sponsors. Muldowney was able to connect with several sponsors over the years. Cologne manufacturer English Leather, along with Chrysler, provided her enough money to compete at the top level.

Connie had a Top Fuel dragster built for Shirley. She began competing in this class after obtaining her Top Fuel license at the Cayuga drag strip in Toronto in 1973. She clocked the second-fastest pass at the 1974 U.S. Nationals and was voted to the prestigious "All-American Team" by the American Auto Racing Writers and Broadcasters Association. Two years later, she got her first national Top Fuel win at the 1976 Springnationals in Columbus, Ohio. Shirley's mother, Mae, was there to watch her, while son John was now a regular member of her pit crew. She went on to post the best ET (5.77) and top speed (249.3 mph) of the racing season. This feat foreshadowed one of the defining events of her racing career. In 1977 Muldowney became the first woman to win the NHRA Top Fuel championship. She would win the title again in 1980 and 1982. As Shirley's popularity grew, she and Connie gained a following competing at tracks around the country, billed as the "Bounty Hunter" and "Bounty Huntress." By now, she was the main draw.

Muldowney and Connie had a tempestuous relationship over the previous six years, in which they mixed business with romance. She broke away from Connie at the end of 1977 and hired future husband Rahn Tobler as her crew chief. There were hard feelings between the two for quite a while; Connie became a fierce rival on the track. At the 1980 World Finals in Pomona, California, Muldowney beat Connie in the second round of competition and went on to win the event. The following year at San Antonio, with 10,000 fans looking on, Muldowney beat drag racing legend Don "Big Daddy" Garlits for the AHRA World Championship. Garlits was famous in racing circles, in part for building and driving the first rear-engine dragster. The innovation came after he suffered a serious accident in 1970. The new design greatly improved the safety of dragsters and changed the course of Top Fuel racing. When a front-engine dragster's engine blew, the flying parts often flew into the cockpit. With the rear-engine design, the explosion occurred behind the driver.

Don and Muldowney competed in a series of match races, billed as the "King and Queen of Drag Racing." Garlits piloted his all-black "slingshot," and she her trademark pink dragster.

At Columbus in 1982, Muldowney was pitted against Lucille Lee in the finals. It was the first time that the two women drivers met in a Top Fuel championship. Shirley beat Lucy off the line and clocked the lowest ET of the day to win. Lucy came back to beat Shirley in the final run at Bakersfield, California later that year. Shirley Muldowney also competed in match races with Canadian driver Aggi Hendriks in her jet dragster. There weren't a lot of women in the sport at the time. Drag racing, like other forms of auto racing, was reluctant to admit female drivers. The NHRA granted a license to Barbara Hamilton in 1964. Two years later, Shirley Shahan, a California-based driver, became the first woman to win a major NHRA title at the Winternationals. Shirley Muldowney fought to obtain her NHRA license in 1965, the same year Paula Murphy and husband Dick Landy began drag racing. It was Paula who later convinced Shirley to move to Funny Cars. Paula and Muldowney raced Funny Cars for a season, only to have the sanctioning bodies pull their licenses. The officials felt that it was too dangerous for women to be driving these hard-to-handle vehicles. With the intervention of racing sponsors like STP, the two women were reinstated.

Early on, the women received a lot of hostility from the fans and from male drivers. Muldowney recalls fans throwing soft drink cans at her pit crew on one occasion when she beat a male driver. Drag racing venues allow more interaction between drivers and fans than at Indy Car or NASCAR tracks. Fans are allowed to walk through the pit areas as long as they stay behind the temporary barriers. It's not unusual for spectators to talk to the drivers and pit crews between runs. Most fans are well behaved, but there are always the exceptions. Muldowney singled out the IHRA tracks that allowed beer to be served as the worst situations.

Muldowney gradually won over the fans with her impressive racing skills. When she took the trophy at the U.S. Nationals at Indianapolis in 1982, the crowd went wild. In the finals, she and Connie Kalitta ran the fastest side-by-side race in NHRA history. Shirley Muldowney became the first woman to win at Indianapolis. She would go on to beat Connie some fifteen times. Her success in a male-dominated sport was beginning to garner attention beyond the world of drag racing. 20th Century Fox studios planned a film of her life and began shooting in 1982. *Heart Like a Wheel* was released in 1983. It didn't do well at the box office, but the critics liked it. *Sports Illustrated* writer Frank Deford called the feature a "good car movie," normally a Hollywood oxymoron. Shirley had mixed feelings about how the film portrayed her, but she felt that it was good for the sport of drag racing.

Just when Muldowney's racing success was reaching unprecedented heights, she suffered a serious accident that almost ended her career and could have ended her life. The accident occurred during a Top Fuel qualifying run at the Molson Le Grand Nationals in Montreal, in July of 1984. She recalls getting a good jump at the start of the run and everything going well until the car crossed the timing lights. That's when one of the dragster's front tires began losing its inner tube. The tube coiled around the axle at 250 mph. Muldowney took her hand off the steering wheel to pull the parachutes. When she put her hand back on the wheel, the car jerked to the left, hit a culvert at the edge of the track, and crashed into an embankment head on. The twenty-six-foot-long dragster came around hard, causing the steering wheel to sever her thumb. The disintegrating vehicle tumbled across the landscape and finally came to rest some three hundred feet from the track. Muldowney was still inside the roll cage that had broken off from the dragster. She was initially stunned from the impact, and then regained consciousness in terrible pain. The track safety team got to her and administered first aid while waiting for the ambulance to arrive. Muldowney's thumb was hanging by a piece of skin. Damage to her legs was extensive; the open wounds were caked with gravel and mud. Confusion reigned for several minutes. Her crew chief sought someone who could translate French to accompany them in the ambulance. The ambulance then got stuck in the muddy parking lot. It took forty-five minutes to reach the hospital. The doctors X-rayed Muldowney and put her in a bed to recover from the shock. She would remain there for seven weeks, heavily medicated on pain killers. Stainless steel braces held her limbs together. The specter of amputation haunted her. Shirley's fans responded en masse. The Canadian hospital's switchboard had difficulty handling all the phone calls, while some five hundred flower arrangements arrived.

After Shirley was in the hospital for nearly two months, Connie Kalitta flew to Montreal in his private plane and took her back to the States. These were tough times, and her track rival and former partner proved a true friend. Muldowney was out of a job, with expenses mounting. Indeed, it was uncertain whether she would walk again, let alone race. She continued to undergo treatment in Detroit. Doctors operated on her leg, replacing the fixators with a cast. Muldowney was informed that they would have to fuse her left ankle—which meant saying goodbye to the sixty pairs of high heels in her closet. One leg would be slightly shorter than the other. Following the accident, fellow driver Don Prudhomme's wife, Lynn, held a fundraiser for Shirley and went on to organize the Drag Racing Association of Women. DRAW was created to provide financial and emotional support to men and women injured in racing accidents. The Association continues to function and has provided more than $3 million in aid to date.

Muldowney spent the next couple of years in therapy recuperating from her extensive injuries. She received hundreds of get-well cards and letters from fans. It was a struggle for her to write thank-you notes with three broken fingers on her right hand, but she managed with pen in fist. Muldowney

HEART LIKE A WHEEL

This 1983 film produced by 20th Century Fox stars actress Bonnie Bedelia as Shirley Muldowney and Beau Bridges as her racing partner and rival, Connie Kalitta. Country and Western artist Hoyt Axton plays Shirley's father, "Tex Rock." The narrative follows Shirley's life from her teen years and marriage to mechanic Jack Muldowney through her drag racing career in the 1960s and 1970s. The racing scenes were filmed at the Beeline Dragway near Phoenix, Arizona, where Shirley had raced.

Heart Like a Wheel wasn't really a "hot rod movie," as advertised, but more a story about a determined young woman fighting the system. The plot includes both the triumphs and tragedies of Shirley's career: her breakup with Jack, the 1973 crash of her funny car and her painful recovery from serious burns, and her first National Hot Rod Association World Championship in 1977. Her tempestuous relationship with Connie Kalitta provides a major subplot. The film concludes with Muldowney's victory over Kalitta for the NHRA championship in 1980. (The film title, *Heart Like a Wheel*, is the title of a song by Kate and Anna McGarrigle, which was first popularized by Linda Ronstadt in 1974.)

Hollywood has produced several movies about auto racing over the years—comedies like *The Cannonball Run* with Burt Reynolds (1981), or the parody Talladega Nights, The Legend of Ricky Bobby (2006, with Will Ferrell), and dramas like *Grand Prix* (1966) starring James Garner—but *Heart Like a Wheel* stands alone in its portrayal of a courageous woman competing in the sport of racing.

eventually underwent five surgeries at Detroit Receiving Hospital, plus skin and bone grafts. She credits Dr. Terry Trammell for putting her back together. All through this trying period, her singular goal was to return to racing. She finally made her return in January 1986, at Phoenix's Firebird Raceway. The Phoenix, a mythical bird that arises from the ashes to be reborn, was a fitting symbol for her return. Muldowney walked with the aid of a cane when she arrived at the track. The other drivers welcomed her back. Connie Kalitta was among them.

Since Muldowney's accident in Montreal, an important safety feature had been implemented. Dragsters were now fitted with tubeless front tires developed by Goodyear. There would be no repeat of the incident in Montreal. But one consequence of the accident remained. When Shirley climbed back into the cockpit for the first time, she realized she couldn't reach the clutch pedal with her fused ankle. John Muldowney worked on the problem into the night, designing a modified clutch pedal for his mother. His adaptation would be the one she relied on until her retirement. Shirley also changed the paint scheme on her dragsters from the trademark pink to pearlescent purple. On race day, a record crowd of 20,000 fans showed up at Phoenix to witness Shirley's return. She received a standing ovation when she was introduced to the crowd.

THE COMEBACK DRIVER BECOMES THE FIRST LADY OF DRAG RACING

The following February at the Winternationals in Los Angeles, Shirley and company drew a crowd of 48,000. She made a qualifying run of 5.47 seconds, the fastest in her career. Then she blew an engine in a first-round run with Don Garlits. Connie Kalitta went on to win the event, but Muldowney was back. She was named the "Comeback Driver of the Year" by the American Auto Racing Writers & Broadcasters Association. Muldowney's successful return resonated beyond racing circles. The news media chronicled her gutsy recuperation. Muldowney was invited to appear on *The Tonight Show* with Johnny Carson. Johnny came on stage in racing overalls covered with mock sponsor stickers and challenged her to a drag race in golf carts. She let him win.

Shirley Muldowney and Rahn Tobler were married in 1988, but the racing team was struggling. They retained the services of Don Garlits to help them with their Top Fuel dragster that had been performing poorly. The fifty-seven-year-old veteran Garlits signed on as a special adviser, another instance of former rivals burying the hatchet. His input seemed to make a difference. Muldowney became the first woman to crack the five-second barrier in 1989, reaching a speed of 284 mph on the run. She went on to win the NHRA Nationals in Phoenix, beating 1987 Top Fuel champion Darrell Gwynn in the finals. This would be Shirley's last NHRA National title. Then Gwynn was seriously injured at a track in England on Easter Sunday, 1990. Muldowney had raced against Darrell many times and considered him a good friend. She flew to England to visit him in the hospital with $500 collected from fellow drivers. The veteran drag racer knew firsthand what it was like to be hospitalized with serious injuries and medical bills piling up.

Shirley drove for Larry Minor in 1990 and then shifted her focus to the match race tour, where contestants are guaranteed a fee. She drew large crowds and long lines of autograph seekers at these events. Despite the occasional win, Muldowney's career was on the down slope. She suffered a spate of mechanical problems and had trouble getting sponsors. She got into a major disagreement with Petromoly Oil in 1991, which she accused of reneging on a $4 million deal. They ended up in arbitration, with Muldowney having to absorb the legal fees. This was an era when the costs of maintaining high-tech dragsters (now fitted with on-board computers) could easily reach $1 million. Drivers faced a conundrum: they had to win races to attract sponsors, and they had to attract sponsors in order to race competitively. Drag racing had become more and more dependent upon commercial revenue. Photos of the era portray vehicle surfaces and drivers' suits covered with dozens of sponsor logos. The sanctioning bodies also were becoming dependent on sponsors' money. The AHRA died out in the mid-1980s owing to lack of sponsorship. It was a sign of the times.

Shirley Muldowney was based in California in 1993 when the opportunity arose to accompany a group of drag racers on tour in Japan. The racing vehicles were loaded onto a ship at the Long Beach docks and made the two-week transit across the Pacific. The equipment and personnel arrived safely in Japan on time, but the event was postponed owing to rain. The delay afforded Muldowney and her crew a rare opportunity to be tourists. They took in the city of Tokyo and visited Mount Fuji. Then it was back to racing at the Fuji International Speedway. At 5:20 in the evening on a track with no lights, Muldowney made a run of 5.85 seconds, hitting a top speed of 285 mph. It was a Japanese record. She returned to her home base in Northridge, California, just in time to experience the record 6.7 magnitude earthquake. Muldowney and her crew decided to close the West Coast shop and move back to Michigan.

Muldowney raced on the IHRA circuit through 1996, winning three national events and finishing second in Top Fuel point standings. She returned to race at an NHRA event in Dallas in 1997 after being away since 1990. NHRA was sponsoring two dozen events a year, and it required a lot of money to compete at the top level. On New Year's Eve, 1999 promoters of an automotive exposition in West Palm Beach, Florida, set up a match race between Muldowney and Don Garlits, billed as the Millennium Drag Race. The run was scheduled for midnight. Muldowney won the race and the $10,000 prize. It was a welcome addition to the struggling racing team's coffers.

Muldowney calculated that she could afford to run in only a couple of NHRA races on the 2001 circuit. The team obtained sponsor support from Action Collectibles, the marketer of auto racing souvenirs. Muldowney posted a career-best 4.64-second pass, reaching a speed of 320 mph during the Mac Tools U.S. Nationals at Clermont, Indiana. In 2002 Muldowney competed in five national events sponsored by Mac Tools and Action Performance Companies. The following year, she ran in six NHRA events, and then decided to retire from racing. On her Last Pass Tour at the NHRA Nationals in Joliet, Illinois, she clocked a career-best ET of 4.58 at a speed of 327.6 mph. She was invited to serve as grand marshal at her final racing event, the Automobile Club of Southern California NHRA Finals in late 2003. Shirley insists that she never grew tired of driving dragsters, but the sport had changed a great deal. The business side of drag racing and the politics of competing on the tour eventually wore her down. She regretted that the sport had become less personal. Moreover, it took a huge amount of money to compete in drag racing in the new millennium.

The racing community, however, was magnanimous in showing its appreciation of Muldowney's legacy. At the NHRA Awards Ceremonies in November, she received the Don Prudhomme Award for her contributions to the sport. Notably, the two Shirleys, Muldowney and Shahan—who had retired in 1972—opened the doors to a younger generation of women drag racers. Subsequently, some forty women have stood in the winner's circle at NHRA national events. Shirley Muldowney remained active in the sport following her retirement. She mentored Top Fuel driver Hillary Will, who began drag racing in Michigan in the late 1990s and later drove for Kalitta Motorsports. Shirley has given thought to forming her own racing team with a woman in the cockpit of a Top Fuel dragster and raised some money to finance the project.

A retired Shirley Muldowney lives on five acres near Ann Arbor, Michigan. She worked for a while as sponsor representative for Kalitta Motorsports. After Rahn and Shirley split up, he began working for Connie Kalitta's racing team. She filed for divorce in late 2006. She continues to enjoy the quiet life with her dogs and cats. She now drives a red Cadillac, which offers substantially more interior room than her quarter-mile rides. She remains close to son John, who builds car chassis. She follows the career of current Top Fuel driver Doug Herbert. She occasionally attends races and NHRA ceremonial events, and even makes a run down the strip now and then to the delight of fans.

Shirley Muldowney has been dubbed "The First Lady of Drag Racing." She never saw a contradiction between being a woman and being a drag racer. She wore makeup and jewelry, and dressed attractively. While always conscious of her femininity, she could be less than ladylike if that's what it took to compete. Shirley's father had taught her how to handle bullies. Some of the "good ol' boys" at the tracks were less than gentlemen at times. One of them hung a water-filled condom on her trailer in the pits. A young Shirley had to "throw elbows" and verbal jabs to hold her own among resentful male drivers. The fiery competitor was described as opinionated, feisty, outspoken, and sharp-tongued. If Muldowney had the fastest mouth in the pits—and there was no shortage of competition—she also had the fastest foot in the cockpit of a dragster. The former street racer was known for her split-second reaction time. When the bottom light on the Christmas Tree turned green, invariably Muldowney was the first one across the line. Often as not, she was the first to pull the parachute at the end of the strip.

Muldowney was a pioneer in breaking gender barriers: the first woman to receive a license to drive dragsters, the first woman to break the five-second barrier, and the first woman to win the prestigious Winston World Championship, along with an AHRA World Championship. She prefers to be remembered as a driver, not a "woman driver." Indeed, her accomplishments stand on their own, irrespective of gender. Shirley Muldowney has been one of the most successful drag racers in history. During a career that stretched over three and a half decades, she won a total of eighteen NHRA national events and several more under IHRA and AHRA sanctions. Currently, she ranks twelfth in Top Fuel wins in the NHRA. In the interim, she won three NHRA Top Fuel world championships. Muldowney was inducted into the International Motorsports Hall of Fame and the Motorsports Hall of Fame of America. She is a recipient of the U.S. Sports Academy Babe Didriksen Zaharias Courage Award. Shirley Muldowney is unique among women athletes of the twentieth century: she made her mark competing one-on-one against male opponents. In doing so, she shattered one of the more obdurate gender barriers in sport.

FURTHER READING

Lowe, Jaimie. 2005. Shirley Muldowney (interview). *Sports Illustrated* 103:2: http://sportsillustrated.cnn.com/vault/article/web/COM1039848/index.htm.

McGuire, Bill. 2009. In Their Own Words: Shirley Muldowney: The Queen of Drag Racing Speaks. *Hot Rod Magazine*, April: http://www.hotrod.com/whereitbegan/hrdp_0904_shirley_muldowney_interview/index.html.

Miller, Timothy. 2009. *Drag Racing: The World's Fastest Sport*. Buffalo, New York: Firefly Books.

"Mondays with Murray: Shirley Muldowney." 2008. NHRA Dragster Insider. http://topfuel.nhra.com/blog/dragster-insider/2008/08/18/31696/.

Moses, Sam. 1986. Fiery Return of a Leadfoot Lady. *Sports Illustrated*, Feb. 10: http://sportsillustrated.cnn.com/vault/article/magazine/MAG1064485/index.htm.

Muldowney, Shirley, with Bill Stevens. 2005. *Shirley Muldowney's Tales from the Track*. Champaign, IL: Sports Publishing.

"Shirley Muldowney Biography." 2010. Jrank.org: Famous Sports Stars. http://sports.jrank.org/pages/3362/Muldowney-Shirley.html.

Martina Navratilova reacts after winning (with India's Leander Paes) a mixed doubles quarterfinal match at the French Open tennis tournament, 2005, in Paris. (AP Photo/Lionel Cironneau)

Martina Navratilova (1956–)

Martina Navratilova made her debut in professional tennis during an era of revolutionary social, cultural, and political change. The teenage tennis player defected from her native Czechoslovakia and became an American resident just as the feminist movement was redefining gender roles and fighting for equal treatment of women in the workplace. Concurrently, the U.S. Congress and federal courts were transforming women's status on the playing courts. In 1975, the year Navratilova defected, Title IX was implemented. This amendment of the Equal Opportunity in Education Act would dramatically advance girls' and women's opportunities to participate in school and college sports. Women's professional sports were experiencing their own significant breakthroughs, and tennis was at the forefront.

The 1970s were the infancy of tennis' Open Era, which allowed professionals to compete with amateurs in the major tournaments. The founding of World Championship Tennis in 1968 had generated the first big-money tournaments for the men, but the prize money for women remained meager in comparison. This gap diminished when Wimbledon champion Billie Jean King and a group of entrepreneurs organized the Virginia Slims Circuit in 1970. Tennis' economic transformation was prelude to a cultural revolution. Following the formation of the Women's Tennis Association, or WTA, in 1973, women players found it more accepted to be athletic without having their femininity questioned. While the double standard for sexual behavior was fading, the lesbian stigma still haunted women's sports. The contemporaneous gay rights movement led to increased awareness. Bisexuality and homosexuality were redefined as sexual orientations rather than mental disorders. However, this didn't mean that the typical sports fan was willing to accept openly gay athletes.

Meanwhile, the Cold War between the Soviet Bloc and the West set the tone for international politics and sport. The "Iron Curtain" was both a metaphor and a physical barrier. Martina Navratilova joined a steady stream of defectors who poured out of Eastern European countries like Hungary and Czechoslovakia. Some tunneled under walls or scaled barriers, while others, like Navratilova, asked for asylum while abroad. The Cold War carried over into the sports arenas. Olympic medals and tournament trophies became symbols of superiority for competing political systems. The ideological standoff between East and West culminated with the U.S. boycott of the 1980 Olympic Games in Moscow, followed by the Soviet boycott of the 1984 Los Angeles Games. International politics and the cultural revolution would frame Martina Navratilova's personal life and her iconic tennis career.

CHILDHOOD

Martina Subertova was born October 18, 1956, in Prague, Czechoslovakia (now the Czech Republic). Her mother, Jana, married Mirek Subert, a restaurant manager from Prague who became a ski instructor at the Martinovka Ski Lodge in the Krkonose Mountains. The couple named their first daughter after the lodge. With the customary patronymic, she was Martina Subertova. Jana was an independent woman who came from a prosperous family. Her parents had owned a large estate that was divided up following World War II in accordance with the government's policy. The couple was provided a one-room apartment in the small town of Revnice, southwest of Prague. The family resented what the government had done. Czechoslovakia was a client state of the Soviet Union, controlled by the national Communist Party, the KPC. The Party assigned living quarters, ran the educational system, and directed the national sports program. There was little personal or political freedom.

Jana and Mirek were both athletic and encouraged their young daughter's athleticism. They put her on skis soon after she learned to walk. However, the couple separated when Martina was three years old. She and her mother moved in with Jana's parents. The four of them shared the small apartment. It was a difficult period. Martina's eccentric grandfather was not easy to live with. They had no car and little money. Martina sporadically visited her father at the ski lodge, but the visits became less frequent over time. Mirek died when Martina was seven, but she was not told for almost four years. Only later, when Martina was an adult, did she learn that he had taken his own life.

Despite the hardship, Jana proved a good and caring mother. After working in a factory all day, she would come home and cook for her daughter. When time allowed, Jana took Martina with her to the ski slopes and tennis courts. On one trip when Martina was four, Jana met the man who became her second husband. Mirek Navratil would entertain young Martina while her mother was on the tennis courts. His devoted attention to the daughter soon extended to the mother. Mirek and Jana married in 1961 and moved in with her family. Two years later, Martina's sister, Jana, was born. By good fortune, a downstairs apartment became available, so the growing Navratil family had more room. Martina's stepfather adopted her, and she took the feminine version of his name, Navratilova.

Mirek worked as a factory economist, and like Jana demonstrated a streak of independence. His refusal to join the KPC likely deterred his professional advancement. Mirek couldn't afford an automobile. He drove to work and back on a motorcycle. Jana and Mirek both loved recreational sports. The couple swam and skied, and they encouraged Martina to play sports. Jana provided a model for the future tennis prodigy, and Mirek became her first coach. Martina, the skinny tomboy, loved outdoor activities and basked in her parents' attention. Communist ideology encouraged Czech women to participate equally with men in work and in recreation. Martina played ice hockey and soccer with both girls and boys. She revealed an independent spirit like her parents that prompted her to challenge the system. This characteristic repeatedly put her at odds with the autocratic Czech sports bureaucracy as she got older.

About the time Martina started school, she discovered her real love. Tennis was a popular sport in Czechoslovakia, and Martina enjoyed a couple of advantages. The clay tennis court from her grandparents' old estate was still playable, and her maternal grandmother, Agnes Semanska, had been a highly ranked amateur player in her youth. Agnes provided her young granddaughter with a hand-me-down racket. When Martina's parents played tennis at the municipal club, they took Martina along. By age six, she was hitting balls off the wall with a two-handed grip. Mirek recognized his stepdaughter's talent and took her on the courts to teach her the game. The lessons became a daily routine; the two would hit together all year until the snow interrupted them. Martina also had access to tennis courts across from her school, and she developed rapidly as a competitive player. When she turned eight, Mirek took her to her first tournament on the back of his motorcycle. She had the opportunity to see the great left-handed Australian Rod Laver play in Prague. Laver became Martina's role model. The budding southpaw wanted to be a champion just like him.

Organized competition was controlled by the Czech Tennis Federation, which operated regional tennis centers with paid coaches. Lessons were free, and the Federation supplemented the travel expenses of players who competed in tournaments. It was through this system that Martina met coach George Parma, a former Davis Cup Champion. Martina took lessons with Parma on weekends while she stayed with her grandmother Subertova in Prague. It was on the city's indoor courts that Parma taught Martina her trademark "serve and volley" style. This was an unconventional tactic for women players of the era. By the time Martina reached the age of ten, everyone who saw her play recognized her exceptional talent. Martina's parents made the necessary sacrifices to support her tennis career. They often would forego vacations to transport their daughter to important tournaments.

In early 1968 Czechoslovakia went through a period of political unrest and repression. What came to be known as "Prague Spring" was an attempt by Czechs to liberalize the political system. Their efforts were forcefully suppressed by the Soviet Union, which occupied Czechoslovakia, a nation of 14 million people, with more than a half million troops, and crushed the democratic movement. In many ways the system became more repressive. The resentment among the Czechs was passionate. Martina and her parents were able to avoid much of the political unrest in their rural home in Revnice, but one consequence of the invasion directly affected Martina's tennis career. Among the thousands of Czechs who defected to the West was her coach, George Parma. He continued to mail her tennis lessons from his new home in the United States, but it wasn't the same as having him on the court. Fortunately, the new political climate didn't alter the national tennis program. The Czech Tennis Federation maintained its tradition of producing top-level players, and Martina continued to win tournaments. She immersed herself in the sport.

WINNING CHAMPIONSHIPS OUTSIDE CZECHOSLOVAKIA

In 1969 Martina Navratilova traveled with her stepfather to a tennis tournament in West Germany. This was her first trip abroad and to a Western capitalist nation. She was fascinated by all the available consumer luxuries that were lacking in Czechoslovakia. Although the youngest player on the Czech team, she won several medals and received mention in the German newspapers. Her international success didn't go unnoticed back home. The fifteen-year-old was invited to play with Prague's prestigious Sparta Sports Club. This meant access to a first-rate facility and matches against other top national players. She accompanied the club team to the Soviet Union for a tournament, and then competed in the Czech National Championship, upsetting the club's top player, Renata Tomanova. Navratilova was a phenomenon on the courts, but otherwise a typical teenager. She attended high school, went to the movies, window shopped with friends, and dated. She became involved with a young man studying at the university, her first serious romance.

Martina's travels would make her more aware of the larger world outside Eastern Europe. She'd been exposed to images of American culture through Hollywood movies that played in Czech theaters. These impressions were reinforced through her subsequent tours to the West. In 1973 Navratilova traveled to the United States for the first time, accompanied by an older tennis partner who doubled as her chaperon. In spite of her minder, Navratilova openly flouted team rules by fraternizing with players from other countries. She played in eight tournaments sponsored by the United States Tennis Association, or USTA. It was an eye-opening opportunity for the sixteen-year-old. She had taken a semester of English in high school and could understand a smidgeon of the language. The Czech Tennis Federation provided spending money during the six-week tour, and Navratilova spent it liberally. Team officials were concerned that their young tennis prodigy was becoming "Americanized."

Indeed, Martina Navratilova had become infatuated with American culture. Notably, she indulged in fast food, and her trim figure quickly filled out. Teammates were astonished by her appetite for hamburgers. On the courts, Navratilova was duly impressed with American tennis players Billie Jean King and Chris Evert. Three weeks into the tour, she played her first match against Evert in Akron, Ohio, losing 7-6, 6-3. It was an inauspicious debut to what would become one of the great rivalries in women's tennis. Despite the loss, Navratilova impressed everyone with her raw athletic talent. Her success on the American tour prompted the Czech Federation to send her to the 1974 French Open, one of tennis' four Grand Slam tournaments. The young Czech made it all the way to the quarterfinals in Paris. Chris Evert won the tournament, defeating the U.S.S.R.'s Olga Morozova. The "Cold War" on the courts kept tennis on the front page.

Navratilova returned to the United States on a second tour later that same year, winning her first professional title in Orlando. She then traveled to California and rendezvoused with her old coach, George Parma, and some other Czech exiles. While on the West Coast, she also met Fred Barman, a Hollywood agent, whose daughter played on the tour. Fred's influence led Navratilova to question the Czech Tennis Federation policy of appropriating the prize money that its players won. Because of Navratilova's importance to the Czech team, she was able to convince the Federation to let her keep 80% of her tour earnings. The money allowed her parents to purchase a much-needed automobile. This wouldn't be the last sparring match between the CTF and the headstrong teenager. Martina had taken to the more socially permissive climate in the United States and chafed at the control the federation wielded over its athletes. Back home, she developed a growing ambivalence about the restraints that were imposed upon her life by the Czech bureaucracy. For the first time, Navratilova thought seriously about doing what her former coach had done: defect to the West.

DEFECTING TO THE UNITED STATES

Czech Tennis Federation officials had taken note of Navratilova's assertiveness and freewheeling behavior while on tours. She often ignored the obligatory team schedule and went her own way. The issue came to a head in 1975, when the Federation denied her permission to play in the U.S. Open. Martina was taken aback. She eventually gathered enough support within the tennis community to get the decision reversed, but the tension escalated. Back in Revnice, Navratilova confided to her stepfather Mirek that she was considering defecting when she reached American soil. He told her that he would support her. Navratilova hadn't finalized her decision when she left her native country for the U.S. tour, but she realized that the goodbyes to her unsuspecting mother and grandparents might be for good. It was a wrenching decision for a young woman a few weeks shy of her nineteenth birthday.

By the time Navratilova reached the United States, she had made up her mind. She called Fred Barman, now her business manager, and asked him to find an immigration lawyer to assist her. She kept her plans under wraps, worried that Czech officials might try to intervene. Within a couple of days, the story was leaked to the news media. Navratilova held a Saturday morning press conference at Forest Hills, New York, the site of the U.S. Open, and announced her decision. She told reporters that she had defected because she wanted control over her tennis career and her earnings. She took into account that most professional tournaments were held in the United States. Years later, Navratilova admitted that there was another, private reason for leaving her native country. She realized that she was attracted to women. Homosexuality was still considered a form of mental illness in Czechoslovakia, and homosexuals could be confined to an institution. She wanted freedom in her personal life as well as control of her career.

Martina moved in with the Barman family in L.A. and received her green card, the permanent resident certificate. She would have to wait five years to apply for American citizenship but was free to play professional tennis. The mid-1970s proved an opportune moment for women tennis players. Through the efforts of Billie Jean King, the women's professional tennis circuit attracted financial backing from American corporations like the Philip Morris Tobacco Company, manufacturer of Virginia Slims cigarettes. For the first time, women could earn significant tournament prize money. Martina, Chris Evert, and the other young players joining the tour were the beneficiaries of this revolutionary development in women's tennis.

THE CHAMPIONSHIP CAREER CONTINUES FROM THE UNITED STATES

The Czech expatriate didn't wait long to take advantage of her change of venue. She won both singles and doubles tournaments on the tour, including her first win over Chris Evert. Then paired with Evert in doubles, she won her initial Grand Slam title at the French Open. Navratilova was voted the most improved player of 1975, and *Tennis* magazine ranked her number four on the women's circuit. She signed a lucrative contract to play in the new World Team Tennis league in 1976, and she proved a resounding success as a member of the Cleveland Nets. Off the courts, Navratilova's English improved rapidly—if with a pronounced accent—and she readily adapted to the American lifestyle. Her image, however, provoked the prevailing gender prejudice. She appeared muscular for a woman, and she was aggressive, emotive, and often brash on the courts. One opponent commented that Martina must have a chromosomal screw loose somewhere. Martina and Chris Evert—who personified the "girl next door"—were paired as opposites by the press. But more to the point, Navratilova's game improved to where she was routinely meeting Evert in tournament finals. While their highly publicized rivalry on the courts became intense and their images were diametrical, the two would remain good friends.

Martina pursued her life off the courts at a time when gay women athletes kept their sexual orientation private. Despite her forthright temperament, she remained "in the closet" for the time being. Other aspects of her lifestyle proved more visible. Navratilova rapidly became prosperous and acquired a reputation for spending money on luxuries. She acquired the American penchant for status symbols, such as Gucci handbags and a Mercedes sports car with a personalized tag that proclaimed X–CZECH. A *New York Times* story referred to her as a "walking delegate for conspicuous consumption." Indeed, Navratilova consumed American junk food to the detriment of her game. These indulgences may have been a way to compensate, as the former Czech found herself on her own without family. Navratilova was able to maintain telephone contact with her parents in Czechoslovakia, but clearly she missed them. The tennis scene was familiar, but the tournament schedule could be exhausting. She became known for crying jags when she didn't play well. The good life in the United States was subverted by a gnawing loneliness.

Navratilova's life continued to have its ups and downs. She didn't win one WTA tournament in the first ten months of 1976. The intense competitor became known for her emotionally distraught behavior on the courts. She would bang her racket on the ground, berate herself, scream at the officials, and beseech the heavens when her game wasn't going well. In the spring of that year during the filming of the television show *Superstars*, Martina met thirty-two-year-old golfer Sandra Haynie. Haynie would provide her with much needed emotional support. Navratilova left Los Angeles for Dallas to be with Haynie. They bought a house and moved in. Navratilova's partner got her off junk food and onto a training schedule. Over the next two years, a more settled Navratilova, some fifteen pounds lighter, would dominate the tennis circuit. She won three dozen straight matches on the 1978 Virginia Slims Women's tour, then won the French Open, and bested Chris Evert for the Wimbledon championship. Navratilova displaced Evert as the Women's Tennis Association number-one-rated player in the world.

In September, after losing in the semifinals of the U.S. Open to Pam Shriver, Navratilova's relationship with Haynie ended abruptly. Earlier in February, Martina had met author Rita Mae Brown, an openly gay writer and political activist. The two began seeing each other in the summer of 1979. Their pairing was a classic instance of "opposites attract": a thirty-four-year-old radical intellectual and a young, rather unsophisticated jock. Brown frequented museums and the theater and had little interest in spectator sports. The two women did share a taste for life's comforts. They purchased a twenty-room Virginia mansion with a swimming pool, tennis courts, and a five-car garage for Navratilova's growing fleet of automobiles. However, the relationship developed tensions as time went on. Rita could be dismissive of Navratilova's commitment to tennis, remarking that it was "only a game." But clearly it was more than that to Navratilova. Eventually, Rita grew tired of accompanying her partner on the road. She devoted more of her time to her own career as a writer.

Another major change took place in Navratilova's personal life. Her mother received permission to attend the 1979 tournament at Wimbledon in the U.K., and the two women were able to visit after nearly four years of separation. Then the Czech government allowed Navratilova's parents and younger sister, Jana, to emigrate to the United States. Navratilova settled her family in Dallas and provided financial support. At the time, her parents weren't aware of her sexual orientation. When they found out about Rita Mae Brown, the tension escalated. Navratilova's relationship with her family was sporadic at best. She was shuttling from tournament to tournament and juggling her off-time between her partner and her family. Jana and Mirek resented Rita's role in their daughter's life. Mirek was particularly upset about Martina's homosexuality and was finding that he could not adjust to his new country. In July of 1980, just eight months after arriving in the United States, Mirek and Jana decided they would return to Czechoslovakia. Navratilova asked if her teenage sister could stay with her, but her parents refused. Following her family's departure, Navratilova obtained her U.S. citizenship and lived openly with Brown. The tennis celebrity's relationship with a high-profile lesbian pushed her sexual orientation into the forefront of public dialogue. In a news story, she admitted to a sexual relationship with Brown.

Navratilova again was struggling on the courts. Her inconsistent performance caused her to blow important matches. She didn't make it to the finals at Wimbledon in 1980 or 1981, and her world ranking dropped to number two. It was at this juncture that Navratilova met someone who would alter her life and transform her tennis game. During the 1981 tournament on Amelia Island, Florida, TV commentator Bud Collins introduced her to Nancy Lieberman, the nation's premier women's basketball player. There was an instant attraction between the two. Unlike Rita Mae Brown, Lieberman was appreciative of Navratilova's commitment to her sport, although she knew little about tennis. Lieberman accompanied her to the French Open and to Wimbledon, although Navratilova was still living with Brown. Martina and Nancy denied that they were romantically involved, but reporters kept prying into the relationship. Brown became suspicious. Shortly before Martina left for Wimbledon, she and Rita Mae had a melodramatic quarrel at the Virginia mansion that ended their relationship. Brown, feeling jilted, threatened to create a scandal in the press.

Notably, Billie Jean King at the time was being sued for "palimony" by her former traveling secretary, Marilyn Barnett. The married King called a press conference and admitted that she and Barnett had had a lesbian affair, calling it a mistake. At this time, virtually no gay celebrities of her status had been "outed." Meanwhile, Martina was telling the press that she was bisexual; she liked men. She lightened her hair, pulled it back with a ribbon, and wore more feminine outfits on the tennis courts. Appearances aside, it was Navratilova's game that would change most dramatically under Lieberman's influence.

Nancy Lieberman, the consummate athlete, was taken aback by Navratilova's rather casual approach to conditioning. She became Navratilova's

GAY WOMEN ATHLETES "COMING OUT"

Women's sports in the United States have been plagued by a perceived stigma of lesbianism almost from the beginning. Masculinity and femininity were viewed as a polarity; a woman who appeared masculine in any way was suspected of being a lesbian. Women who enjoyed competitive sports only reinforced the suspicions about their sexuality. Some women athletes wore ribbons in their hair while competing as if to prove their femininity, and thus their heterosexuality.

There are lesbian athletes, just as there are gay male athletes (somewhere between 5 percent and 9 percent of the American population identify as homosexual, according to various surveys). But gay athletes remained "in the closet" until recently. The gay rights march in Washington in 1979 was a sign of the changing mores. But homophobia persisted in the mainstream press and among the public. A palimony lawsuit "outed" tennis champion Billie Jean King in 1981. By the mid-1980s, Martina Navratilova's sexuality had become public knowledge. The Women's Tennis Association, fearing a loss of sponsors, warned other players against "coming out."

By the last decade of the twentieth century, there was more acceptance of lesbian athletes in tennis and other sports. Gay athletes in the new millennium are more likely to "come out" than be "outed." In 2005, high-profile WNBA star Sheryl Swoopes announced that she was a lesbian. By then, a growing number of sports fans seemed to accept an athlete's sexuality as a private matter. Public attention is directed at their performance in the arena.

partner and trainer. Lieberman put the struggling tennis star on a regimen of running and weight training, in addition to daily practice sessions on the courts. Their immediate goal was to win the elusive U.S. Open title. A fit and trim Navratilova arrived at the tournament with renewed confidence. While she had won over the fans with her impressive effort, her mental game still lacked discipline. Her loss to Tracy Austin in the finals left her in tears. Seated among the crowd was a controversial figure who would join Lieberman as one of several advisers on what was to become "Team Navratilova." Dr. Renée Richards, a six-foot-one-inch transgendered tennis player had competed on the women's circuit through 1981, following a court decision overruling the WTA's objections. Watching from the stands, Richards detected serious flaws in Navratilova's court tactics. The two were introduced following the finals match, and Richards offered her services as coach. Navratilova hired her. While Lieberman supervised Navratilova's conditioning, Richards worked on her strokes and strategy. Their student transformed her physique and her mental game. The results were impressive. In 1982 Navratilova won fifteen of eighteen tournaments, losing just three singles matches during the entire tour. The U.S. Open eluded her once more, as she played with a viral infection, but she reclaimed her number-one ranking. And she took in well over $1 million in prize money, a tour record.

Nutritionist Robert Haas joined Team Navratilova. He immediately changed Navratilova's diet, but his rather unorthodox "nutritional engineering" provoked controversy. The team became a classic case of "too many cooks." Richards resigned after the 1983 French Open to return to her medical practice. Following her departure, Navratilova hired former pro tennis player Mike Estep as a coach. He convinced her to pursue an even more aggressive strategy on the courts, armed with the recently introduced graphite racket. (Navratilova already had the fastest serve among women players using a wooden racket.) Estep's protégée had a stellar year, winning eighty-six out of eighty-seven matches. The U.S. Open remained the elusive target going into the 1984 tour. Navratilova not only prevailed at Flushing Meadows but also won the French Open, beating Chris Evert 6-3, 6-1, and Wimbledon for the fourth time. She put together an incredible eleven-month, seventy-four-match winning streak. Martina was featured on the cover of *Sports Illustrated*, and Associated Press voted her Female Athlete of the Year.

While Martina Navratilova's tennis career was on a more even keel, her personal life remained turbulent. Lieberman had been instrumental in turning Navratilova's game around, but Navratilova eventually grew tired of her "drill sergeant" persona. Their relationship ended in April 1984. Navratilova's tendency was to jump into successive relationships with little pause. By chance, she had run into a previous acquaintance from Texas who would become her next "significant other." Judy Nelson, a former beauty queen, was married and the mother of two boys when she first met Navratilova at a tournament in Fort Worth two years earlier. Following Navratilova's breakup with Lieberman, Judy invited her to say at the Nelson home. Judy's husband became aware of the two women's physical relationship, and the Nelsons separated. One son moved in with his mother and her new partner; the other stayed with his father. Judy Nelson accompanied Navratilova on the tennis tour.

In November, less than a year into their relationship, Martina and Judy decided to "get married." They flew to Australia and formalized their bond at a church, absent a minister. It was, of course, an arrangement without legal status in the United States. But it became very public. Unlike the Billie Jean King affair, which made the headlines after the fact, Martina had to acknowledge a current relationship with a partner of the same sex. While she accepted being labeled "gay," her openness had consequences. The tabloids sensationalized celebrity homosexuality, commercial sponsors remained wary of offering endorsement contracts to gay athletes, and some sports fans withdrew their support.

Team Navratilova continued to expand, adding a masseuse and osteopath to the existing staff of trainer, coach, publicists, agents, and managers. The collection of aides and assistants accompanied Navratilova on tour along with partner Judy, her son, and a menagerie of pets. Their luggage included a surfeit of personal items: elaborate wardrobes, Navratilova's health food, and special pet food, along with the Xerox and fax machines for the business staff. The entourage resembled a traveling circus with its own caravan. Navratilova had to rent two houses at Wimbledon to accommodate her retainers. There was nothing humdrum about the couple's life. In addition to the demanding tennis schedule, Navratilova had various personal and professional commitments that meant additional travel. During the rare breaks, Navratilova and Judy retreated to their seven-thousand-square-foot house in Aspen, Colorado. The accommodations were reminiscent of the previous mansion in Virginia. The one-hundred-acre property accommodated a lap pool, horse stables, and a seven-car garage.

Despite her rather frenetic personal life and escalating professional obligations, Navratilova continued to compete successfully over the next several years. However, 1986 proved a tough year: she parted with Coach Mike Estep and played the minimal twelve tournaments amidst repeated bouts with the flu. Despite the setbacks, Navratilova won her seventh Wimbledon championship after losing to Chris Evert in the French Open. This tournament would be the last major win in Evert's career. She would retire three years later, a couple of months shy of her thirty-fifth birthday. Navratilova versus Evert had been the preeminent rivalry in women's tennis since the mid-1970s. They had competed against each other on eighty occasions and swapped the number-one ranking several times. Amidst their long rivalry, the two remained on good terms and were occasional doubles partners.

MAINTAINING EXCELLENCE IN TENNIS AT THE RIPE AGE OF THIRTY AND BEYOND

Few athletes compete in world-class tennis long into their thirties. The women's circuit in the late 1980s was brimming with young talent like Steffi Graf and Gabriella Sabatini. Thirty-year-old Navratilova began the 1987 tour with six straight losses. She again changed coaches, hired a new trainer, and switched rackets. She recommitted to a rigorous training regimen that included a daily ninety minutes of two-on-two basketball. The physically fit veteran found her redemption at the 1988 Wimbledon tournament, beating nineteen-year-old Graf for the championship. But it was tough competing against aggressive young women a decade or more her junior. After losing in the quarterfinals of the 1989 U.S. Open, Navratilova again reorganized her support team, even hiring a sports psychologist to advise her.

Martina missed her family in Czechoslovakia. The Czech government continued to deny her a visa, as retribution for her defection. However, the bureaucratic standoff didn't keep Navratilova from accompanying the U.S. women's team to the 1986 Federation Cup tournament in Prague. The government had little choice but to allow her entry into the country as a member of the American team. The reception from Czech tennis fans was overwhelming. They had followed her career on German television and greeted her enthusiastically when she arrived, in defiance of authorities who tried to mute the impact of her appearance. Navratilova was able to visit her family briefly, while constantly tailed by Czech police. The U.S. team won the tournament, and it was Navratilova who accepted the trophy at the closing ceremony. But she had to leave Prague as soon as the tournament ended. Four years later, following Czechoslovakia's "Velvet Revolution" ending Communist rule, Navratilova would return to her homeland under radically different circumstances. President Václav Havel invited her to speak to a huge crowd at an election rally at Wenceslas Square in 1990. It was an overpowering experience for the repatriated tennis player.

The image of Navratilova on the cover of the July 1990 *Sports Illustrated* reveals a trim, muscular thirty-three-year-old standing at five feet, seven inches, with a well-chiseled face. The now-blond Martina wasn't inclined to alter her image to suit the conventional model of femininity. She had drawn critical attention by competing in shorts, a sartorial statement that challenged the traditional decorum of the women's circuit. Navratilova's radical image and lifestyle weren't an issue in the clubhouses. She was liked by the other players on the circuit. Meanwhile, Navratilova's personal life continued on its roller coaster track. Her relationship with Judy Nelson went through a rough period following the couple's move to Aspen. There were tensions over a business venture and finally a confrontation over Navratilova's dalliance with a ski instructor. True to character, she abruptly ended the relationship with Nelson. The breakup became messy and public—with the tabloids styling it a "love match." The couple worked through the details of their separation. Nelson hired a lawyer and filed a palimony lawsuit over the financial agreement, which was settled out of court. Navratilova consulted a psychotherapist.

The thirty-six-year-old was back playing on the tour in 1992 with a reconstructed knee, but she struggled and won only one tournament. In September she took on forty-year-old Jimmy Conners in what was billed as the third "Battle of the Sexes" at Caesar's Palace in Las Vegas. It was a restaging of the 1973 match between Billie Jean King and Bobby Riggs. Conners was given only one serve per point, and Navratilova was allowed to hit into the doubles court. She lost, 7-5, 6-2. The rematch seemed something of an anachronism, coming two decades after the original duel—a publicity stunt. As it turned out, Navratilova needed the publicity. There were to be no Grand Slam titles in the near future. She continued to play singles through 1994. A couple of months before her thirty-eighth birthday, Navratilova reached the Wimbledon finals only to lose in three sets to the young Spaniard Conchita Martinez. Soon after, she retired from full-time singles competition.

Navratilova maintained her ranch home in Aspen where she skied, snowboarded, and rode her motorcycle. She had chosen to reside in Colorado partly because she found fellow residents to be progressive and tolerant. In 1992 the state legislature had passed Amendment 2, which repealed gay rights laws that had been implemented in Aspen and other localities. Navratilova joined in a lawsuit against the state brought by the American Civil Liberties Union, claiming that the amendment violated the constitutional rights of gay men and lesbians. The lawsuit was decided in the favor of the plaintiffs. Navratilova had been active in the gay rights movement, but she became less so following her retirement. She still lent her name and money to gay and lesbian causes. In 2000 she was the recipient of the National Equality Award from the Human Rights Campaign, the nation's largest gay and lesbian activist/lobbying group. She also supported various charities concerned with animal rights and underprivileged children. A more relaxed but still active Navratilova earned a pilot's license, took a trip to Africa to shoot wildlife photographs, and took part in the 1997 dedication ceremony for the U.S. Open's new 23,000-seat Arthur Ashe Stadium.

Navratilova returned to the tennis tour in 2000 to compete mostly in doubles events. In 2003 she and partner Leander Paes won the mixed doubles titles at both the Australian Open and Wimbledon. This made her the oldest-ever Grand Slam champion at age forty-six. Navratilova then defeated Catalina Castano in straight sets at the first round of Wimbledon in 2004, to become the oldest woman to win a singles match in the Open era. The match took place thirty-one years after her Wimbledon debut. In August Navratilova competed in the doubles competition at the 2004 Olympics in Athens, where she and Lisa Raymond lost in the quarterfinals. In July 2006 Navratilova made her final appearance at Wimbledon, a couple of months shy of her fiftieth birthday. She and partner Liezel Huber lost in the quarterfinals to China's Yan Zi and Zheng Jie. In mixed doubles competition, Martina and Mark Knowles were eliminated in the third round. She capped her career by winning the mixed doubles title at the 2006 U.S. Open with Bob Bryan. Martina then retired for the second time.

Martina Navratilova's career belies conventional wisdom about aging athletes, having played on the international circuit for over three decades. She carried women's tennis to a higher level in the 1980s with her athleticism. Her rigorous approach to training and conditioning initiated under the tutelage of Nancy Lieberman had a profound influence on the women's game, as did her powerful serve and volley style. Navratilova was born the year that Babe Didrikson died, and it was she who picked up the mantle of the aggressive woman competitor who defied traditional views of femininity in the public arena. Her physique, personality, and mannerisms eclipsed the country-club image of women on the tennis courts, as Babe had on the golf links. And like Babe, she demonstrated that women could make a living as professional athletes. Navratilova is estimated to have made more than $20 million during her tennis career.

Billie Jean King, the symbol of women's professional tennis, was Martina's doubles partner at the 1979 U.S. Open and briefly her coach in the early 1990s. King referred to the iconoclastic Czech American as the greatest singles, doubles, and mixed doubles player to ever compete on the women's circuit. Navratilova had won fifty-nine Grand Slam titles in these three forms of competition. She and doubles partner Pam Shriver won all four Grand Slam titles in 1984. Navratilova held the longest winning streak in tennis at seventy-four straight matches. Over her career, she won a total of 168 singles titles and 178 doubles titles. She held the WTA ranking as the number-one women's player in the world seven times, beginning in 1978 at age twenty-two.

One cannot write about Martina Navratilova's career without acknowledging Chris Evert. Their eighty-match rivalry, beginning in 1973 and running sixteen years, defined women's tennis during an era of dramatic cultural change. The two women, with antipodal personalities and images—one hyperemotional and androgynous; the other reserved and feminine—were much alike in their relentless competitiveness on the courts. Martina was dubbed "Navrat the Brat," while Chris's nom de guerre was "The Ice Maiden." They shared the spotlight on the tennis courts and the invasive scrutiny into their personal lives and relationships amidst the rise of the tabloid press. Through it all, they remained friends.

Navratilova's life off the courts often drew as much attention as her play on the courts. Her ultimate openness about personal relationships made it easier for other prominent women to be candid about their sexual orientation. She was one of the first well-known athletes, male or female, to publicly acknowledge her homosexuality without apology. Despite Navratilova's comfort with her sexuality, her life reflected an inherent restiveness. Sportswriter Johnette Howard observed, "She went through a steady stream of coaches, gurus, girlfriends, homes, reincarnations, and allegiances to various causes" (Howard, 2005, 165). Her motives remain unclear: did any of this make her happier, more admired, stronger and freer as a person, or convey a sense of belonging? Navratilova often frustrated her friends. She appeared loyal and determined, yet she was apt to terminate personal and political commitments with a dispatch that opened her to charges of shallowness. Clearly, she had a big heart, adopting animals and causes with equal abandon. She's reported to have kept as many as fifteen dogs and a dozen cats as pets.

No one questions Navratilova's lifelong devotion to tennis. She served three terms as president of the Woman's Tennis Association and eleven years on the Board of Directors. She has been widely recognized for her achievements as a competitor. She was inducted into the International Women's Sports Hall of Fame in 1984. In 1987 the Women's Sports Foundation awarded Navratilova the first Flo Hyman Award for the advancement of women's sports. (Hyman was an American volleyball player who died unexpectedly at age thirty-one from an aortic rupture.) Navratilova was inducted into the International Tennis Hall of Fame in 2000. In 2006 she was installed into the USTA's Court of Champions at the National Tennis Center in New York. The outdoor pavilion, established in 2003, displays the names of inductees on bronze plaques.

Navratilova has remained in the public eye during her retirement. In 2007 she and John McEnroe were hired by the Tennis Channel as lead analysts. The Tennis Channel released a retrospective of her life and career in 2009, and ESPN produced a film about the Navratilova/Chris Evert court rivalry. Navratilova appeared on several popular television shows including *Saturday Night Live* and *I'm a Celebrity . . . Get Me Out of Here!* She would provide more grist for the tabloids in 2009 when her seven-year relationship with former tennis player "Toni" Layton Lambert ended amidst threats by Layton to file a palimony suit.

Navratilova maintains homes in Sarasota and in Aspen. She is seriously committed to personal fitness. She works out at a local fitness center when in Florida and skis the slopes of Colorado. She enjoys a variety of outdoor sports, including mountain biking, kayaking, and snowboarding. She refers to herself as a "pesco-vegetarian," one who eats fish, vegetables, fruit, and grains. Navratilova has written several books, including three coauthored murder mysteries and a coauthored tennis instruction book. In 2007 she published a health and fitness book, *Shape Yourself*. She also has written a tennis column for *USA Today*. Martina Navratilova holds dual American and Czech citizenships. She has announced plans to open a tennis academy in the Czech Republic. In early 2010 Martina was diagnosed with non-invasive breast cancer. The health-conscious fifty-three-year-old remained positive about undergoing a lumpectomy and radiation therapy. The early prognosis for recovery has been encouraging. She continued to be active. In December she was hospitalized briefly for altitude sickness in Kenya following an attempt to climb Mount Kilimanjaro.

FURTHER READING

Blue, Adrianne. 1995. *Martina: The Lives and Times of Martina Navratilova*. Secaucus, NJ: Carol Publishing Corp.

DeSimone, Donnie. 2006. "Act II of Navratilova's career ends with a win." ESPN.com. http://sports.espn.go.com/sports/tennis/usopen06/news/story?id=2578105.

Howard, Johnette. 2005. *The Rivals: Chris Evert vs. Martina Navratilova: Their Epic Duels and Extraordinary Friendship*. New York: Broadway Books.

Navratilova, Martina, and George Vecsey. 1986. *Martina*. New York: Fawcett Books.
Wallace, Hannah. 2009. Martina after 50. *Sarasota Magazine* 31:5: 68–75.
Wolff, Alexander. 1994. Martina Navratilova. *Sports Illustrated*, Sept. 19: http://sports
    illustrated.cnn.com/vault/article/magazine/MAG1005679/index.htm.
Zwerman, Gilda. 1995. *Martina Navratilova*. New York: Chelsea House.

Danica Patrick in the pits during a qualifying session, 2009, ahead of the IndyCar Series' Indy Japan 300 auto race in Motegi, Japan. (AP Photo/Shuji Kajiyama, File)

Danica Patrick (1982–)

On rare occasions, an athlete appears on the scene who exemplifies his or her sport through a combination of personal charisma and performance in the arena of competition. The irrepressible Babe Ruth was the symbol of baseball in the Roaring Twenties, just as the brash Babe Didrikson defined women's golf in the late 1930s and 1940s. Joe Louis' name was emblematic of the sport of boxing in the World War II era. In the 1980s, the duo of Larry Bird and Earvin "Magic" Johnson, billed as the "Bird and Magic Show," resurrected professional basketball. Eldrick "Tiger" Woods emerged as the iconic image of professional golf in the new millennium.

An individual athlete may attain preeminence as the result of breaching a cultural barrier, as when Jackie Robinson broke the "color line" in professional baseball in the late 1940s. Sport's gender barriers have proved to be even more obdurate. Danica Patrick wasn't the first woman to compete in motor sports, but her appearance in the field at the Indianapolis 500 in 2005 triggered a tidal wave of public fervor dubbed "Danicamania." Five years later, in the midst of an economic recession, the captivating IndyCar jockey would jump-start the sputtering NASCAR fan base by banging fenders with the good ol' boys on the stock car circuit. She has become the most renowned personality in American auto racing.

CHILDHOOD

Danica Sue Patrick was born in Beloit, Wisconsin on March 25, 1982. Her family relocated to the small town of Roscoe, Illinois, near the city of Rockford, and this is where she grew up. Danica's mother, Bev, and father, TJ, met at a snowmobile race. TJ also competed in midget car racing and motocross. Racing was a Patrick family tradition. Danica spent her early years watching her father work on race cars. She was the quintessential "chip off the old block." She inherited TJ's determination and his competitiveness. She didn't like to lose, whether it was playing cards, backyard tetherball, or running footraces against the neighborhood kids. She was the girl who didn't let the boys win. Danica was assertive, aggressive, and a little mouthy. More than one rival would accuse her of carrying a chip on her shoulder.

As a youngster, Danica played on the school volleyball and basketball teams, and she was a cheerleader. But racing go-karts took priority over extracurricular activities. She was kicked off the cheerleading squad because she missed too many practices. She missed her senior prom and the homecoming dance because she preferred to spend her weekends racing. TJ Patrick invariably was on the sidelines rooting for his daughter at the ball court and race track. He was both cheerleader and critic. Even when Danica won, he went over all her mistakes, pointing out how she could improve. Whatever TJ said came out unfiltered. His sharp tone hurt his daughter's feelings on more than one occasion. Bev Patrick was the calming presence. Danica referred to her mother as the referee of the household.

TJ bought Danica and her younger sister, Brooke, their first go-karts when Danica was nine. On a cold spring day the two girls took the karts for an initial spin around the makeshift oval in the parking lot of the family business. Danica's trial run ended with a bang. The kart's brakes failed, and she crashed into a concrete wall at 25 mph. Young Danica bounced off the steering wheel and hit the ground helmet first with her overcoat on fire. An alarmed TJ rushed to the scene and was relieved to find his daughter hadn't been seriously hurt. The budding kart racer was undeterred. She couldn't wait to get back on the kart.

The following year, TJ entered the two girls in local kart races. Danica found herself racing against much older guys and struggled at first to keep up, but she was a quick learner. By the end of the summer, the former midget racer's daughter had made her presence known on the track. While Brooke eventually lost interest in kart racing, Danica had discovered her passion. Often she was the only girl on the track. Danica overcompensated. Her aggressive tactics and dominance intimidated more than a few of the guys. In one race, she ran over the go-kart of a boy who wouldn't get out of her way. Fortunately, neither driver was injured. TJ made his hardnosed daughter apologize following the incident.

Soon the Patrick family was driving to neighboring states to promote Danica's racing career. She recalls spending hours in the family car on weekends traveling to and from races. At times, Danica's racing put a strain on the family budget. In addition to travel expenses, kart racing required a steady supply of engine parts, tires, fuel, racing suits, and helmets. Her parents weren't wealthy; they ran a glass company, at first out of their garage, and then expanded to an office and warehouse. Bev Patrick did the accounting, while TJ managed the company. Somehow her parents found the money. Racing became the central focus of Patrick's family life.

Go-kart racing isn't for the fainthearted. Occasional collisions with other karts were part of the competition. Danica's aggressive driving style was a contributing factor in her case. She recalls a dramatic accident at a national race in North Carolina when she was twelve. After getting pushed off the track by another driver, she came back to catch up with him late in the race. Into the final turn, she opened up the throttle and drove right over him, flipping the kart, and landing on top of him. The victim was future IndyCar rival Sam Hornish Jr. TJ Patrick reached the scene of the accident before the ambulance arrived. He reminded his prodigy that she wasn't invincible.

Karting has produced some of the biggest names in racing. The most talented youngsters move up through the ranks. Danica began racing in the Junior Sportsman Stock class, made up of drivers from eight to twelve years old. The karts were equipped with 5 hp engines, similar to those found on lawn mowers.

GO-KART RACING: A RISKY ACTIVITY FOR CHILDREN

Young Danica Patrick's first experience at the wheel of a go-kart ended in a crash. She had a few other minor accidents during her karting career, but suffered no serious injuries. Not all go-kart drivers are this fortunate. A report by the Consumer Product Safety Commission in 2000 found that in the previous year over 12,000 youngsters under age fifteen were treated in hospital emergency rooms for go-kart related injuries. A great majority of those treated were drivers. Fifty children died from karting accidents during that year. Notably, some go-karts exceed speeds of 75 mph.

Children often begin racing go-karts while still in the primary grades. A few kindergartners can be found on the tracks. Winston Cup champion Jeff Gordon was racing quarter midgets (a step up from go-karts) at age five. NASCAR Sprint two-time champ Tony Stewart began racing go-karts at age seven. Danica was a couple years older when she began racing.

The World Karting Association is the largest sanctioning body for kart racing in North America. They sponsor races for drivers as young as eight years old. The WKA emphasizes safety in its governing rules. Drivers wear protective racing suits, helmets with face shields and gloves. While go-karts are built with safety bumpers, most don't have roll cages. Despite their low center of gravity, go-karts have been known to flip over.

Danica was outfitted in a purple-and-green racing suit with her name written across the chest. By mid-season of her rookie year, she was setting records. She then moved up to the Junior Sportsman Series for drivers aged twelve and older, and then to the Senior level. The boys in this class were bigger, stronger, and just as aggressive as Danica. But she yielded ground to no one.

TJ Patrick's interest in, and knowledge of, racing boosted Danica's early success. She responded well to her father's mentoring. He served as coach, crew chief, engineer, sponsor, and manager. TJ also was in charge of publicity. He made a point of notifying the local press of his daughter's accomplishments. The newspapers had plenty of material for write-ups. Danica set the track record in her age group at Sugar River Raceway in Wisconsin and shattered two records in one day at Raceway Park in Michigan.

Two organizations govern karting, the World Karting Association and the International Karting Federation. Danica raced mostly in WKA-sponsored events in the Midwest. The season ran from April to late October, during which time she might enter a dozen races. Successes in local races led to appearances at regional events, and ultimately national events. Drivers qualify for advanced levels by accumulating points based on performance. Danica competed successfully at the highest levels. She became a kart-racing phenomenon, winning the 1994 WKA Grand National Championship in the Yamaha Sportsman class for novices. She added other titles the following two seasons. Danica won the WKA Championships in both the Yamaha Lite and HPV (100 cc. engine) classes. By age sixteen, she had won three World Karting Association championships and was more than ready to move up to open-wheel racing. Danica had found her calling. Her goal was to become a champion race car driver.

When Danica was growing up, her family made an annual ritual of watching the Indianapolis 500 on television. In 1992 Danica met Lyn St. James, who was in the field of drivers for that year's race. St. James was only the second woman to qualify in the long history of the Indianapolis 500. Danica had found a role model. She would watch the race and say to herself, "That's what I'm going to do someday" (Patrick, 2006, 30). Lyn saw in Danica the potential to become a champion and invited her to enroll in the St. James' Driver Development Program when she was fourteen. In 1997 Danica and her family attended the Indianapolis 500 for the first time. St. James invited the Patricks to watch the event from her private box.

During the following year's race at Indianapolis, Lyn introduced Danica to John Mecom III, son of John Mecom Jr., heir to the Texas oil fortune. The Mecom Racing Team had sponsored 1966 Indianapolis 500 winner Graham Hill. Mecom suggested that Danica might benefit from racing on the Formula circuit in England. Formula racing is a prestigious sport in the U.K. It's the ideal place for young drivers to hone their skills on the entry-level circuit. Successful drivers graduate to Formula One, the pinnacle of open-wheel racing. Very few women had ever driven Formula One cars, but that didn't dampen sixteen-year-old Danica's aspirations. She jumped at the opportunity to compete in the Formula series.

LEARNING RACING SKILLS IN ENGLAND

With permission from her parents, Danica Patrick dropped out of high school and headed to England to polish her racing skills. She received financial support from the Mecoms, who had contacted Patrick's father and offered her the opportunity to test a Formula Vauxhall Car while there. TJ Patrick gave his daughter a send-off lecture on what she could gain from this experience, and what she would lose if she fouled up. It was a heavy responsibility for a teenager away from home for the first time. TJ and Bev Patrick made the necessary financial sacrifices to support their daughter's racing apprenticeship.

The teen years are an age for exploration and Patrick, now on her own, was exposed to the array of vices and distractions that tempt young adults, including alcohol and drugs. She explained to her new friends in England that as a race driver she was subject to random drug tests. It was her way of saying "No" to recreational drugs. But the pressure to fit in with the crowd led to her drinking on a routine basis. It seemed natural to go to a pub with the guys and have a few ales during the week. And there were parties on weekends where everyone drank. Eventually, her team managers found out that she was partying late and considered letting her go—although she wasn't doing anything different from the male drivers. Patrick was allowed to remain in the program, but she felt that she was getting minimal support and guidance. She compared the experience to boot camp. The teenager felt lonely and isolated. Her parents were running the family business and couldn't come to England to visit her. It was a harsh lesson in independence.

Patrick's first race in England was on a damp track during the winter of 1998. John Mecom was there to watch her. She was running eleventh until she hit a barrier and totaled the car. The competition on the junior formula circuit proved challenging, and she was the only woman in the program. But she improved over time. When she did finish ahead of the guys, the team manager would chide them by saying, "You're being beat by a girl." It didn't enhance her popularity. There was little doubt in her mind that she was perceived as a threat to the male ego (Patrick, 2006, 78).

Following the end of the racing season in England, Patrick came home for a few months. One item on her parents' agenda was that she complete a General Education Diploma (GED), since she'd dropped out of high school. They understood that if Patrick didn't make it as a professional driver, her job choices would be limited without a high school diploma or the equivalent. Patrick took a part-time job at the mall for the holidays and began studying for the GED. The drinking and partying habits she acquired across the Atlantic didn't go over well with her parents. She was grounded for a month. Then the other shoe dropped. The Mecoms called her parents and told them they would no longer support Patrick, because of her undisciplined lifestyle in England. Patrick was getting a double dose of tough love. She made the most difficult phone call of her life to convince the Mecoms to reconsider. In the end, Mecom agreed to sponsor her for the upcoming season, but he required that she live with a British family and show up for dinner each evening. Ford Motor Company kicked in to help with the expenses. A chastened Patrick headed back to England.

Danica Patrick had some early success on the track. She finished second at the Formula Ford Festival for entry-level drivers while with the Haywood Racing Team. This was the best-ever finish by an American racer. But she still felt that she was neither getting the best cars to drive nor the credit that was owed to her. She ended the season ranked ninth in the Formula Vauxhall Championship Series. This was an important step toward moving up to Formula One racing. Meanwhile, life away from the track felt a bit constrained. Danica's sister Brooke came to England for a brief visit. It was during this period that Danica met her first boyfriend. When they broke up, the loneliness returned. Her experiences with men in England were confusing. Off the track, she was a pal or a drinking buddy, while on the track she was perceived as a threat to the other drivers' masculinity.

Danica spent three years in England through age nineteen. It proved to be a challenge for the novice formula racer. She didn't get the coaching or the equipment she deserved. As the lone female driver among ambitious men, she often wasn't taken seriously, even though she placed second in the Formula Ford Festival. Eventually the sponsors' money dried up, and her family had nearly exhausted their resources financing her racing career abroad.

Danica returned to the States looking to move on to the next stage of her career. She didn't have a sponsor and struggled to find a ride in the Formula Atlantic Series that featured the type of road racing in which she competed while in England. Danica and her father made their presence known on the racing circuit, attending races and talking to car owners. She was given the opportunity to test a U.S. Auto Club midget racer, her first experience on an oval track since kart racing. But the U.S. economy was tight in 2002. It was difficult for young drivers to break into the racing circuit. In auto racing, the quality of the car and the team that backs the driver are at least as important as the driver's skill. Moreover, racing had become a prohibitively expensive sport that required substantial financial backing. This wasn't go-kart racing. The Patricks didn't have the resources to go it alone.

FORMULA ONE RACING

Danica Patrick's ambition was to move up to Formula One racing. While in England in 2000, she had been introduced to car owner and Indianapolis 500 winner Bobby Rahal. They met through representatives of Ford Motor Company, one of Patrick's sponsors. At the time, Rahal was managing the Factory Ford Team competing in the Indy Racing League. Rahal was preparing to take a managerial position with the Jaguar Formula One team. He was impressed with Patrick's mental discipline and determination and let her test-drive a Jaguar Formula Three car, as Ford had showed little interest in sponsoring Patrick at this level.

In 2002 Patrick began driving for the Rahal Racing Team. Late-night television host David Letterman, who had grown up in Indianapolis and was a friend of Rahal's, was a minor partner in Rahal Racing. They had put together a highly competitive organization. (In 2004 the team's name was changed to Rahal Letterman Racing.) The racing team employed more than sixty individuals, including executives, managers, engineers, and mechanics. Rahal Racing offered a welcome show of support for Patrick following her disappointing experience in England. Bobby Rahal realized that his talented young driver needed time on the track to develop the necessary skills to be competitive. The team decided to sponsor Patrick in the North American–based Toyota

Atlantic Series, the top "feeder" series for young drivers interested in Formula racing, and then in the Barber Dodge Pro Series.

Danica Patrick's performance in the 2002 Toyota Pro/Celebrity Race in Long Beach, California was a turning point in her professional career. She took the checkered flag before a crowd of 100,000 fans: the first woman to win this event. The field included Sarah Fisher, another promising driver who set the lap speed record for women at the Indianapolis 500 that same year. Women drivers were making their presence felt on the North American racing circuit. In 2002 Patrick won the Gorsline Human Performance International Development Scholarship, given to the top upcoming driver. The award was presented at the annual American Auto Racing Writers and Broadcasters banquet by the Gorsline Company. CEO John Gorsline had pioneered motor sport insurance, including medical and disability insurance for drivers. The scholarship allowed Patrick to participate in the HPI (Human Performance International) driver enhancement program.

During the 2003 season, Patrick won one pole position and consistently placed in the top three finishers. The following year, she finished third in the driver point standings. Rahal was impressed with her performance in Toyota Atlantic races, and following the 2004 season he moved her up to IndyCar, the series of open-wheel racing sanctioned by the Indy Racing League (IRL). Patrick was running in eleventh place in the IRL race at Homestead Miami Speedway when she was involved in a multicar accident that took her out of the race. She gradually improved as the season progressed, winning three pole positions during her first year of IRL racing.

Patrick began to capture the attention of the media as the rare woman driver in a sport dominated by men. She was gaining recognition from her fellow drivers as well. Racing legend A. J. Foyt commented, "I don't care if you're a boy or girl, you have to take your hat off to her" (Indy-Tech Publishing, 2006, 13). However, a few male drivers carped about the five-foot-two-inch, one-hundred-pound Patrick having an unfair weight advantage over the men. Someone went to the trouble of calculating that every ten pounds of driver body weight translated into one-tenth of a mile per hour advantage. Patrick pointed out that the men had a strength advantage. She compensated by training rigorously to get in shape.

THE CELEBRITY ATHLETE

This was the era of celebrity athletes. Patrick realized that media exposure would boost her career. She agreed to do a photo shoot with *FHM*, the men's lifestyle magazine known for its annual listing of the world's sexiest women. The provocative photos of a scantily-clad Patrick sprawled on an automobile that appeared in the April 2003 issue created a buzz among race fans, as well as the wider public. The photos also generated criticism from feminists and comments from other sportswomen, including former IndyCar driver Janet Guthrie, who called the images distasteful. In her defense, Patrick pointed out that racing sponsors routinely hired sexy women to sell their products to men. She claimed that she was simply using her femininity to advance her career. Rahal, who savored the publicity for his racing team, had encouraged her to do the photo shoot.

Patrick's relationship with men's magazines and marketing campaigns continued to generate controversy. She declined *Playboy* magazine's offer to do a photo spread but sat for an interview with the magazine in 2007. In 2008 she appeared in the 2008 *Sports Illustrated* swimsuit issue. She also did a series of racy commercials for Go Daddy, a web hosting company. These included a "most-watched" commercial shown during Superbowl XLIII. The following year, one of her three Go Daddy Superbowl ads was banned by CBS censors. The head of IMG, the sports marketing company that represented Patrick, praised Go Daddy for an ad campaign that, in his view, exploited Patrick's attractiveness with a sense of humor.

Adjusting to the incongruent demands of the media and the race track was a Jekyll-and-Hyde experience. Patrick had always considered herself a tomboy. She dressed to highlight her femininity off the track, but played down her gender among fellow drivers. Her father taught her to employ a strong handshake when meeting people and to look them in the eyes. In the pits and on the track, she just wanted to be one of the guys. She maintained that her goal wasn't to be the first female to win, but simply to win.

Regardless of gender and media demands, auto racing is a full-time job. Drivers usually arrive at the track several days before a race. During race week they attend drivers' meetings, where they are given a map of the track that includes information on the pits, medical facilities, protocol, and the rules to be enforced. They also attend press conferences, but still must find time to practice in order to qualify. It's during practice sessions that drivers familiarize themselves with the layout: every track, every turn is different.

Driving in a race is distinct from a qualifying run; it's about more than pure speed. Winning requires an evolving strategy that takes into account the weather, the car's performance, tire pressure, and fuel level. When it's time to climb into the cockpit on race day, drivers go through an obligatory mental checklist of required items: ear plugs, gloves, helmet, radio headset, and more. Patrick, like many drivers, cultivated her own superstitious rituals. She might wear the same T-shirt that brought her previous success or carry a lucky charm. As starting time approaches, the driver must put on a game face and focus. Racing requires intense mental concentration. It's a continual learning process. The typical rookie logs more than thirty starts before he or she wins a race.

The public tends to underestimate the physical demands of racing as well. Driving a race car at high speed over several hours requires not only endurance but upper body strength. The exertion is constant, except for brief pit stops. During acceleration and cornering, the driver fights G-forces equivalent to those experienced by a jet pilot. The shorter the oval, the more rigorous the effort. Regardless of the distance around the track, there are a lot of left turns to navigate in dense traffic. It's not easy for a petite woman to maneuver an 1,800-pound racing machine at speeds exceeding 200 mph. Patrick continued to do weight training and yoga throughout her career to stay in shape. She also spent time in the gym on the treadmill and elliptical machine.

In addition to the physical effort of racing, the driver has to deal with the discomforts of the cockpit. The array of safety belts, straps, and harnesses that engird the torso make it difficult to move about freely. The driver's peripheral vision is severely limited as a result. It's not only cramped, but the close quarters are uncomfortably hot. The racing helmet, balaclava (head sock), and fireproof suit encapsulate heat coming off the engine. Drivers have to avoid becoming dehydrated during a race. An opening through the front of the helmet accommodates a water tube that can be activated, but the water itself is hot by the time it reaches the driver's mouth. In open-wheel racing, the driver's helmet is covered with rip-off plastic eye shields that protect the driver's face from the cascade of debris, such as rubber from tires, that flies off the surface of the track. Drivers experience invariable discomfort and occasional pain during a race.

IndyCar racing includes international venues. Patrick made her first visit to Japan in April 2005 to race at Motegi's mile-and-a-half oval. She did exceptionally well in the qualifications, losing the pole position to former go-kart rival Sam Hornish by a split second. Starting from the front row, she took the lead early on but had to conserve fuel late in the race and ended up finishing fourth. Patrick came back to the United States to prepare for her first Indianapolis 500 with renewed confidence. Only three women had ever raced at Indianapolis.

THE INDY 500

Danica Patrick cites the 2005 Indianapolis 500 as the greatest moment in her racing career. The race was her fifth in the IRL series. She realized she didn't have as much experience as the other drivers. The 500 is a month-long affair of car preparation, practice laps, and qualifying runs. Patrick posted the fastest lap at 227.86 mph on the first day and qualified to start on the inside of the second row, the best position among six rookies in the field. Her performance in the race was even more surprising: 300,000 fans cheered as Patrick took the lead in her No. 16 car. It was the first time in the long history of the race that a woman held the lead. She went on to lead for nineteen laps, surviving a fender bender with Thomas Enge's car on lap 154. As the two-hundred-lap race wound down, Patrick's team calculated that she needed to conserve fuel, and she backed off the throttle. Three cars passed her. After the race, her team discovered that she still had 2.5 gallons of fuel left. She might have won. Still, her fourth-place finish was the highest ever for a female driver. The previous best finish was by Janet Guthrie, who drove a mediocre car to a ninth-place finish in the 1978 race.

Danica appeared on the cover of *Sports Illustrated* the following week, the first Indy 500 driver to grace the magazine's cover in two decades. Her success brought a new set of fans to the sport. The Indianapolis track office received a deluge of mail addressed simply: Danica Patrick, Indianapolis Motor Speedway, Indianapolis, Indiana. Patrick received more publicity when she auctioned off the damaged front wing of her No. 16 car on eBay. The internet event generated a bidding frenzy. The winning bid was over $42,000. Patrick autographed the now famous part and donated the money to her favorite charity, Best Buddies Indiana, an organization that assists individuals with developmental disabilities.

The media rage continued through the entire 2005 racing season. Patrick spent much of her time between weekend races doing interviews, autograph sessions and photo shoots, and appearing on television talk shows to promote her racing team and IndyCar racing. Meanwhile, her agent, Lynn Roach, fielded a bevy of fresh commercial endorsements and marketing opportunities. The role of racing celebrity meant being on the road constantly. The phenomenon billed as "Danicamania" did indeed become manic at times. The celebrated rookie had to learn to say "no" to the unending requests for her time. The media circus was so intense that she had very little private life.

Patrick won the pole position at the IndyCar race at Kansas Speedway in early July. The final race of the 2005 season was the Toyota 400 held at Fontana, California in October. Patrick qualified for fourth position in what was her seventeenth IRL race. Her father was in his usual place behind the wall of her pit, visibly proud of his daughter's accomplishments during her rookie year. Patrick led briefly but finished sixteenth after coming into contact with Jaques Lazier's car late in the race and spinning out. Following the accident, an enraged Patrick went looking for Lazier to give him a piece of her mind. Track officials intervened and redirected her to the ambulance, the routine protocol following accidents. Lazier ended up in the same ambulance, whereupon Patrick unloaded on him. The tirade reputedly included a shove. Fortunately her feelings were the only thing seriously hurt. She walked away from the crash with a badly bruised elbow. Patrick had acquired a reputation for being aggressive on the track and off.

Her rookie season was a resounding success. She broke several IRL records, including most pole positions (three) won by a rookie. She became the first woman driver to qualify high and place consistently in the IndyCar series. But she still hadn't seen the checkered flag.

The successful rookie driver took a break from racing and media obligations to get married in late November of 2005. She had met the groom, Paul Hospenthal, following her return from England, while undergoing physical therapy for a hip injury sustained during one of her yoga classes. Paul was her therapist. Following a small ceremony in Phoenix, the couple honeymooned in Fiji in the South Pacific. Paul, who is seventeen years older than Danica, had spent much of his career working with top athletes. He took on the assignment of managing his athletic wife's training program, which now included "extreme yoga." Patrick would work out in 100-degree temperatures to prepare herself for the intense heat in the cockpit during races.

The following January, Patrick was invited to drive in the 24 Hours of Daytona, the prestigious sports car endurance race. Top drivers from all over the world compete in this event. Her racing team included Tony Stewart, the 2005 NASCAR champion, and past Daytona winner Rob Dyson. Patrick would drive a closed-cockpit Daytona Prototype car, an adjustment from open-wheel racing. Her loyal fans showed up to cheer her on. The 3.5-mile track combines an oval with a road course. Unlike most auto races, the Daytona event is won by the team that drives their car the greatest distance in the fixed time frame, rather than recording the fastest time over a fixed distance. Overhead track lights are installed to accommodate racing at night. Patrick's team didn't win the event, but she cherished the opportunity to race with some of the sport's premiere drivers.

Danica Patrick continued to compete in IndyCar events in 2006. Danica-mania was flourishing, and her celebrity status was good for racing. Attendance at IRL events was up about 9 percent. When Patrick arrived in Indianapolis in early May, she was surprised to discover a nineteen-foot-square banner bearing her image draped over the main gate of the speedway. She finished eighth in her second Indianapolis 500, and went on to finish fourth at Milwaukee and Nashville. She ended the season in ninth place in the Series point standings. Patrick left the Rahal Letterman Racing team at the end of the 2006 season. In July of that year she had signed a contract to race for the Andretti Green Racing team. Andretti Green had a reputation for effective teamwork and included some of the top IndyCar drivers. Marco Andretti finished second in the 2006 Indianapolis 500, and teammate Tony Kanaan had finished second the previous year. Patrick looked forward to racing with these top-name drivers.

In her first race in 2007 at Homestead Raceway in Florida, Patrick crashed into the pit wall and finished fourteenth. At Indianapolis she finished eighth. She ran as high as second before the mid-race rain delay. Patrick had another verbal confrontation with a fellow driver at Milwaukee after her and Dan Wheldon's cars came into contact. She was able to stay in the race and finished eighth. She had her best race at Belle Isle in Detroit, avoiding a wreck to finish second, her career high in the IndyCar Series. Patrick became the first woman in history to win an IndyCar race at the Indy Japan 300 in Motegi in

April of 2008. She finished 5.8 seconds ahead of Brazilian driver Helio Castroneves, who ran out of fuel on the last lap.

Patrick was fifth in the season point standings going into the Indianapolis 500 in May. Expectations were high for her and for this year's race. The rejuvenated 500 was getting some much-needed attention. The event had lost much of its luster over the last dozen years, following the breakup of the competing CART and IRL series. In the interim, many of the top drivers had passed over the race. In 2008 drivers from both series (now known as Champ Car and IndyCar) would be competing in the event. The projected attendance of 275,000 was the largest since the series rift in open-wheel racing. Publicity for the event got an additional boost when Patrick made her second appearance on the cover of *Sports Illustrated* a week before the race.

The month of preparation at Indianapolis commenced with a near tragedy. On a practice day in early May, Patrick's car struck a pit crew member. The victim suffered a fractured skull and lacerations but eventually recovered. It was one of those unfortunate incidents that occurs on occasion in the hectic pit area. Patrick regained her composure to hold the pole position temporarily during qualifying, and started in the middle of the second row. She was involved in another accident during the race. Driver Brian Briscoe clipped the right corner of her car when the two were coming out of the pits late in the race. Patrick spun around and hit the wall. Both cars were eliminated. A visibly upset Patrick got out of her car and headed toward Briscoe to confront him—a scenario not without precedent. She was intercepted by the head of track security before she reached Briscoe.

Patrick returned to Indianapolis in 2009, driving for Andretti Green. She finished an impressive third in a race marred by eight crashes. It was her best finish in five starts at Indianapolis. The following week she took fifth place in the race at Milwaukee. Andretti Green Racing added Boost Mobile (a brand of Sprint Nextel), along with Motorola, to her car sponsors. She ended the season fifth in driver points, her highest IndyCar finish to date. Estimates were that she had made $7 million in 2008 in racing prizes and endorsements. While Patrick was enjoying notable financial success on the IndyCar circuit, she yearned to test her skills in other racing formats. She had considered racing Formula One, but when Honda pulled out of the series owing to the current economic recession, nothing further developed. Instead, Patrick would test her skills behind the wheel of a stock car, the nation's most popular form of auto racing.

STOCK CAR RACING

In early 2009 Patrick drove in the ARCA (Automobile Racing Club of America) test session at Daytona International Speedway to prepare for her debut in the series. She posted the nineteenth-fastest time among some sixty drivers. It was an impressive beginning for her, maneuvering a 3,600-pound stock car (twice the weight of an IndyCar). The ARCA circuit drew a mix of professional and amateur drivers, as well as a contingent of younger drivers, in what served a development program for NASCAR. A surprising number of camera crews showed up for the practice event in Daytona to cover Patrick's initial appearance on the circuit.

In February 2010 Patrick drove in her first ARCA series race at Daytona. It was a bumpy start. She was squeezed onto the infield, spun the car, recovered, and then repeatedly banged fenders with the other drivers. This style of racing was a lot different from open-wheel format. She made a late charge to finish sixth in her GoDaddy.com No. 7 Chevy. There was little doubt about her potential to succeed in stock car racing. Patrick raced in NASCAR's Nationwide Series for JR Motorsports, co-owned by drivers Rick Hendrick and Dale Earnhardt Jr. She owned a stake in the team. The Nationwide Series is NASCAR's lower-level circuit with races often held the day before Sprint Cup races at the same venue. In Patrick's first Nationwide race at Daytona, she was involved in a fifteen-car accident and was knocked out of the race. She finished in the back of the pack in her next four races. Her twenty-fourth place finish in her fifth Nationwide Series race at Chicagoland Speedway in July was her best of the season.

Despite her mediocre performance on the track, Patrick's presence on the circuit was beneficial to NASCAR. Dozens of reporters swarmed around her on media day and the fans seemed to like her. NASCAR claimed a fan base of 75 million, twice that of IndyCar racing. It drew an American television audience second only to football. But the economic recession had put a dent in race attendance. Some 40 percent of NASCAR fans are women. They are attracted to drivers for their personalities as much as their performance on the track. The women identified with Patrick. She continued to be the top sponsor draw in American motor sports. The benefits were reciprocal. The successful IndyCar driver appreciated that racing on the NASCAR circuit would mean more exposure for her.

The skills and strategies required to compete in NASCAR are distinct from open-wheel racing. It takes novice drivers time to make the adjustment to the bigger, wider cars. Patrick commented on the apprehension that came with learning how the cars change in handling over a fuel run and the differences in tire wear as laps accumulate. Moreover, the closed-cockpit cars move around more and there's a lot of routine bumping. Novice drivers also must learn to "draft": to move into a lead car's slipstream to reduce wind resistance. It's a crucial skill that successful stock car drivers must master. Patrick wasn't the only open-wheel driver to make a recent switch to NASCAR. Sam Hornish Jr. and Dario Franchetti attempted it, and both struggled to adjust to the different style of racing. It took Hornish more than forty starts in Sprint Cup races before he finished in the top ten.

Danica Patrick wasn't the first woman to race in NASCAR. Louise Smith, known as "The First Lady of Racing," drove in top level stock car events in the 1940s. She won some three dozen races in various formats. More recently, Chrissy Wallace, born into a racing family, made history as the first woman to win at North Carolina's Hickory Motor Speedway in 2007. Wallace shifted to the Craftsman Truck Series in 2008. There were no women competing in NASCAR's Sprint Cup or Nationwide Series when Patrick made her debut. She was looking for her first NASCAR win, as this book was being written.

Patrick returned to the IndyCar circuit in mid-March 2010. Her sixth-place finish at Indianapolis in May was the highest among four women in the field, including Sarah Fisher in her ninth 500, Switzerland's Simona de Silvestro, and Brazilian driver Ana "Bia" Figueiredo. (Fisher would retire at the end of the 2010 season.) Patrick held the lead briefly at the Firestone 550K in Fort Worth, Texas, in early June. She finished second behind Australia's Ryan Briscoe, her best performance of the season. She raced at the Mid-Ohio Sports Car Course in August and finished a disappointing twenty-first. She then finished fifth in the Japan 300, took second at Homestead-Miami in October, and finished tenth in the Indy 500. Despite these showings, it had proved to be a demanding and somewhat disappointing season.

In addition to her IndyCar and NASCAR obligations, Patrick stays active as a media celebrity. She has hosted several television shows, was a guest on late-night TV shows (including two appearances on David Letterman's show on CBS), acted in an episode of *CSI*, the dramatic TV series, and did TV commercials for Secret deodorant and Honda. She also appeared in a music video driving a Pagani Roadster sports car. She even made a couple of corporate training videos. She continues to do commercials for Go Daddy, a relationship that goes back to 2006. Currently, she is represented by IMG Talent Agency, whose clients have included golfer Tiger Woods and tennis star Roger Federer.

Danica and husband Paul reside in a 9,000-square-foot home in Scottsdale, Arizona, overlooking Camelback Mountain. The property includes a gymnasium and a seven-car garage that houses a Mercedes-Benz ML 63 SUV and a $200,000 Lamborghini Galliardo sports car. Patrick has a reputation among the locals for driving too fast off the track and has been ticketed on a couple of occasions. On a slower pace, she and Paul enjoy cooking together and sampling fine wine. The couple like to vacation when time allows. They purchased a motor home to travel to races and for recreational jaunts. Until recently, Patrick's parents accompanied her as she traveled the racing circuit, but they no longer are active in her professional career. Paul advises Danica on endorsements and mediates deals with agents. He has adjusted to the status of "racing spouse" and the occasional ribbing he gets from male drivers at the tracks.

Danica Patrick amassed a notable record of accomplishments reaching back to her early years as a champion kart racer, and she received numerous accolades over her career. She was named Rookie of the Year at the 2005 Indianapolis 500 and in her initial IndyCar season. *USA Today* voted her Female

Athlete of the Year in 2005, and she was a finalist for the Sportswoman of the Year award bestowed by the Women's Sport Foundation. In 2006 she received the March of Dimes Sportswoman of the Year award. Patrick became the first woman driver to win an IndyCar race at the Indy Japan 300 in 2008. Her consistent performance at the Indianapolis 500 is unparalleled among women drivers. She is the only race car driver on the list of the 100 Leading Women in the North American Automotive Industry, compiled by the trade journal *Automotive News*.

Danica was the rare child athlete who beat the long odds to find success in the professional ranks. She had a lot of support along the way. TJ Patrick groomed his daughter to become a successful racer. She was fortunate to cultivate other mentors and patrons, like Bobby Rahal, who recognized her potential early on. Patrick demonstrated the combination of natural talent, desire, and dedication required to race at the highest levels. She joined a handful of women who breached the pit walls of race tracks to compete in the male-dominated sport.

The self-proclaimed tomboy cultivated a façade of toughness to compensate for her gender and small physique. While exuding the masculine traits of competitiveness and combativeness on the track, she had few qualms about capitalizing on her femininity in the media. Patrick's decision to exploit her sexuality for publicity and commercial gain has generated considerable criticism. She symbolizes the female sports celebrity whose sex appeal often overshadows accomplishments in the arena of competition. At the same time, male racing fans argue that the media attention Patrick receives isn't warranted by her less-than-dominant performance on the race tracks. The controversy exemplifies the contested terrain for women competing in men's sports.

Patrick always found a way to deal with the criticism that accompanied her unconventional career and her public life. The aspiring racing champion marched to the beat of her own drummer. She knew she had the support of the men who counted: her father, husband, and racing team. And she won the respect of her fellow drivers. Danica Patrick has risen above the fray to set the standard for women in auto racing.

FURTHER READING

Anderson, Kelli. 2005. Decent Exposure. *Sports Illustrated*. June 6: http://sports illustrated.cnn.com/vault/article/magazine/MAG1105382/index.htm.

Anderson, Lars. 2008. Forget the Hype. *Sports Illustrated* 108:20: http://images. si .com/vault/article/magazine/MAG1137271/index.htm.

Beech, Mark. 2009. For Patrick, NASCAR would bring endorsements, not wins. *Sports Illustrated*. April 23: http://sportsillustrated.cnn.com/2009/writers/mark _beech/04/23 /Danica/index.html.

Boyer, Peter. 2010. Changing Lanes. *The New Yorker*. May 31: 53–61.

Clarke, Liz. 2010. Racecar driver Danica Patrick stands out in a man's sport by playing up her sex appeal. *The Washington Post*. Feb. 6: http://www.washingtonpost.com/wp-dyn/content/article/2010/02/05/AR2010020503610.html.

Indy-Tech Publishing editorial staff. 2006. *Danica Patrick*. Ripon, WI: Sam's Technical Publishing.

Patrick, Danica, with Laura Morton. 2006. *Danica—Crossing the Line*. New York: Simon & Schuster.

Ryan, Nate. 2010. Juggling full plate tests Patrick's perseverance. *USA Today*. July 15: http://www.usatoday.com/sports/motor/irl/2010-07-14-danica-patrick-interview_N.htm.

Mary Lou Retton performing on the beam at the 1984 Olympics in Los Angeles. (AP Photo)

Mary Lou Retton (1968–)

In the 1984 Olympics held in Los Angeles, California, Mary Lou Retton performed two perfect routines on the vault, earning a score of 10 on both attempts. She became the first woman from the United States to win a gold medal in gymnastics, winning the all-around competition. She also won two silver medals—in team competition and in the vault—and bronze medals in the uneven bars event and floor exercise.

Retton became the first woman to win three American Cups (1983, 1984, and 1985); the only American to win the prestigious Chunichi Cup (1983); and the only woman to win two United States Gymnastics Federation American Classics (1983 and 1984). She also won the all-around title at both the 1984 national championships and the Olympic trials.

Retton's athletic style helped to further fuel the evolution in women's gymnastics from a graceful sport that rewarded elegant ballet-like moves to one requiring strength and speed. This change began the previous decade with gymnasts such as Olga Korbut from the Soviet Union and Nadia Comaneci from Romania, and it continued with Retton's powerful routines. Retton earned the nickname of "America's Sweetheart" because of her positive attitude, vivacious personality, and exuberant smile; another nickname given during the Olympics was "America's Pixie Hot Rod," and journalists have called her both a "piston-driven pixie" and a "spunky young spark plug."

Her working-class background was also frequently emphasized in articles about her, citing it as the source of her down-to-earth nature and her strong sense of determination.

CHILDHOOD

Mary Lou Retton was born on January 24, 1968, in the working-class town of Fairmont, West Virginia, where a large percentage of the 25,000 residents earned a living in the coal mines; Retton's paternal great-grandfather and grandfather had both worked in the mines. Coal mining was dirty, dangerous work; on December 6, 1907, the country's worst mining disaster occurred in nearby Monongah. Explosions ripped through two of the Fairmont Coal Company's mines, killing 362 men and boys; the earth shook as far as eight miles away, "shattering buildings and pavement, hurling people and horses violently to the ground, and knocking streetcars off their rails" (United States Department of Labor).

Retton's grandfather did not want his son Ronnie—Mary Lou's father—to work in the treacherous mines; instead, Ronnie attended college to broaden his opportunities. He was athletic, playing basketball for the West Virginia University team that, led by Jerry West, came in second place in the NCAA championships in 1959. After college graduation, Ronnie signed with the New York Yankees baseball team, where he played in their farm system for five years. He was playing minor league ball in Auburn, New York in 1960 when he married Lois Jean; when they exited the church after their wedding, they ran under a double row of bats and Lois cut their wedding cake at home plate.

After five years of baseball, Ronnie left professional sports behind to create a business in which he repaired transportation cables on coal mining sites. Retton and his wife had five children in just seven years: Ronnie, Shari, Donnie, Jerry, and Mary Lou. All five children became involved in athletics, and Retton remembered how, as the youngest child, she became especially daring because she did not want her older siblings to be able to outdo her.

At the age of four, Retton began participating in dance lessons at Monica's Dance Studio, including ballet, tap dancing, and jazz, and learning acrobatic moves. The next year, she added gymnastics classes to her schedule, which were offered at West Virginia University. Retton learned the basics of gymnastics quickly, so when she was seven, her mother transferred her to the Aerial-Port Gymnastics Center. At Aerial-Port, Retton began to learn the skills needed to compete in gymnastics. Retton often slept in her gymnast attire because she was excited about the next day's class.

Although interest in gymnastics was growing in the United States, the sport was not yet hugely popular in America. As a point of contrast, in 1961, 800,000 people actively participated in gymnastics in the Soviet Union, and the sport was a mandatory part of school. That same year, only eleven women in the United States competed in the all-around national championships. In 1964 no known school or college in the United States owned an Olympic-sized exercise mat, which is forty feet square in size. That tide slowly started to change and interest in gymnastics started to increase after Cathy Rigby won a silver medal on the balance beam in the world championships in 1976, the first time that an American woman had placed in an international gymnastics competition. It would take another eight years, though, for an American female to win an Olympic medal.

Retton competed in her first tournament in 1976 in Parkersburg, West Virginia. With 10 being the perfect score, Retton scored only a 1, in part because she fell off the beam a couple of times and partly because her coach needed to spot her throughout her routine, which caused judges to deduct points from her score. In her autobiography, Retton shared how she thought she had actually scored a perfect ten; she remembered when Romanian gymnastics superstar Nadia Comaneci scored a perfect 10 in the Olympics, but the scoreboard did not have the capability of showing a score higher than a 9.95, so it simply displayed a 1. Retton said that, as she shouted with glee about her own 1, thinking it was a 10, someone at the competition had to explain to her that it really was just a 1.

To compete in meets, Retton needed to perform in all four events; the vault and the floor exercises were easiest for her and suited her more explosive style and her compact, muscular body. She enjoyed the uneven bars but disliked the balance beam. Athletes competed for wins in each event and the best gymnast overall would place first in the "all-around" category.

In the vault event, an athlete runs approximately sixty feet down a padded or carpeted runway onto a springboard and, after placing her hands on the vault apparatus—which resembles a pommel horse without any handles—she performs a series of spinning and/or flipping acrobatic moves before landing on the other side.

On the balance beam, athletes perform a series of flips, twists, tumbles, and graceful dance moves on a beam that is 500 centimeters long, 125 centimeters above the ground, and 10 centimeters wide.

On the uneven bars, athletes perform a series of flips and maneuvers over a set of asymmetrical bars. The upper bar is 241 centimeters off the ground; the lower is 161 centimeters above ground. Each bar is 240 centimeters in length and 4 centimeters in diameter.

Most floor exercises are performed on spring floors where athletes perform a series of acrobatic and graceful movements; out of bounds areas are clearly marked. In this event—and in the other three events—judges score each gymnast based on her performance, with the elusive 10 being the top score in Retton's era.

PRE-TEEN AND TEEN YEARS

Throughout elementary school, Retton also participated in other sports and activities, including swimming, racing, cheerleading, baseball, and more. When she was eleven years old, she competed in a national track event where she finished second in the 50-yard dash—and, after receiving a dismal score of 1 in her first gymnastics meet, she did make a spectacular comeback later to win the West Virginia beginners' title, which was considered a Class III win.

Because she did so well in Class III competitions, she skipped Class II and went directly to Class I; Gary Rafaloski, who coached at Aerial-Port, began putting Retton through longer, more challenging workouts. At the age of twelve she competed in the 1980 Class I nationals, where she was younger than many other competitors and where she competed against girls she had only read about in *International Gymnast*. Despite her nervousness, Retton performed well, winning the vault event, placing second in the floor exercise, and ending up seventh overall.

When she competed in the Capital Cup in Washington D.C., coaches began noticing Retton; she got her name on the front page of the *Washington Post* sports section, which was a source of excitement for her. Retton then needed to decide if she would pursue junior elite status, where the competition became extremely intense. At that level, she would compete against gymnasts from the Soviet Union, Romania, East Germany, and other countries where the athletes had been training for high-level competition since kindergarten.

Later that year, she won the West Virginia state gymnastics title, earning a spot on the US Junior National Team, and she made the decision to keep moving up the competition ladder. Retton traveled to Canada, where she competed in her first international meet, despite having a concussion from banging her head earlier in the week. There, she won the all-around title; when she landed in the Pittsburgh airport, heading home, the airport paged her to let her know that the U.S. Olympic Committee wanted her to travel immediately to Syracuse to compete in the National Sports Festival. This competition served as a venue for potential Olympic athletes. Retton complied and she sprained her wrist at the competition, nevertheless finishing second and appearing on national television for the first time. Boxer Sugar Ray Leonard signed Retton's splint, and heavyweight boxer Larry Holmes sent her a photo with a note of congratulations.

Over the next two years, she competed in the United States, Canada, and beyond, winning multiple events. In 1981 she traveled to Japan to compete; in 1982 she competed in Peking, China; and, that year, she also finished first in every event in the South African Cup.

While competing in Las Vegas in 1982, Retton introduced herself to gymnastics coach Bela Karolyi, who had become known worldwide as the man who had coached Romanian gymnast Nadia Comaneci, who was the first athlete to achieve a perfect score of ten at the Olympics in 1976. Karolyi had a reputation as a harsh coach in Communist Romania, but he appeared to be somewhat mellower after defecting to the United States; either his actions or attitude in Romania had been exaggerated, or he was more relaxed in America. In either case, Karolyi invited Retton to train at his center, located in Houston, Texas. Although Retton's mother was reluctant for her daughter to leave home at the age of fourteen, the Rettons ultimately left the decision up to her; she accepted, moving to Houston and living with a family whose daughter Paige also trained with Karolyi.

Retton initially struggled with understanding Karolyi's heavy accent, and she became frustrated when he kept telling her no, she was not performing a move as she should. She was startled to be put on a diet, where she went from about one hundred pounds to ninety-four, and she became sore from the workouts, which were significantly more intense than what she was used to in West Virginia. Just as Retton began to feel comfortable with her new home and training gym, she fell and injured her mouth when ABC was at the gym taping the practices. When Karolyi yelled at Retton for making what he called a scene in front of television cameras, Retton considered returning home to West Virginia and even called her parents to say that she was leaving Texas. After recognizing that Karolyi often covered up his own fears by acting angry and realizing that she had the best shot to become an Olympic athlete by staying right where she was, Retton decided to stay in his training program.

Retton, who was already a good gymnast, improved rapidly under Karolyi's tutelage. After just two weeks of training with him, Retton competed in the

American Classic, where she scored a perfect 10 on the vault and won the all-around. After two months of training with Karolyi, Retton competed against the best gymnasts in the United States, outperforming them at the Caesar's Palace Invitational, where she won the vault final and the all-around. At this point in Retton's training, she was looking toward making the Olympic team; this would be especially challenging in 1984 because, in 1980, the United States had boycotted the Olympics and some athletes who might have already retired continued to compete in an attempt to make up for opportunities lost in 1980. Therefore, Retton had more competition for the Olympic team than what might have been expected.

In 1983 Retton traveled to the American Cup as an alternate; it was important that she compete, to give her the name recognition that she needed to have an edge in the Olympics. In order for that to happen, either Dianne Durham or Juliana McNamara would need to withdraw from the competition. Durham was ranked as the number-one gymnast in the country; she had been the junior national champion in both 1981 and 1982. McNamara, who was ranked number two in the nation, had won the 1980 U.S. all-around title and had earned a spot on the Olympic team, pre-boycott. In the 1981 world championships, she secured the bronze medal in the uneven bars.

Shortly before the American Cup began, Retton's teammate Dianne Durham hurt her hip and needed to withdraw from the competition, giving Retton her opportunity to shine. She was going to compete against Russia's Natalia Yurchenko, who would win the all-around in the world championships later that year; Romania's Lavinia Agache, who would go on to win three world medals; and McNamara, the American who had won the American Cup the previous two years.

On the first day of competition, Retton scored five- to six-tenths more than any other competitor, a meet record. Retton won the vault event and the floor exercises, and she tied for first (with McNamara) on the uneven bars, winning the all-around by three-tenths of a point. Even though McNamara's scores were higher than what she had earned in both 1981 and 1982—when she won the American Cup—she lost to Retton in 1983. *International Gymnasts* featured Retton on the cover, providing her with some of the name recognition that she wanted and needed.

By this time, Retton was putting in long workouts at the gym, sometimes as long as four hours each—and sometimes twice a day. She stopped attending traditional school and registered for a correspondence school run by the University of Missouri. She became so exhausted by her long and intense days that she once slept through a tornado; she had to be carried out of the house, which was then badly damaged by the storm.

Retton continued to improve and to tackle increasingly difficult moves and routines. At the American Classic II in May 1983, Retton performed a more challenging variation of the Tsukahara vault, which involved a one-and-a-half somersault with a double twist. Because the move is so difficult, there was a potential to earn 10.2 points with it; although Retton did not stick the landing perfectly, she still earned a 10 and was the first woman in the world to perform this move. Retton then competed in the Championships of the U.S.A., held in Chicago, Illinois, where she finished a disappointing third.

Although her performance at the national championships was discouraging, a third-place finish nevertheless opened doors for Retton to compete in major international competitions. Her next competition was at the McDonald's Invitational in Los Angeles, a precursor to the Olympic trials. Her wrist bothered her, but she wrapped it up and competed through the pain. She won the floor exercises, the uneven bars, and the vault event; she then had her wrist examined; it was broken.

Although doctors wanted her to wear a cast for eight to twelve weeks, she had it removed after four. It was still too late for her to compete in the world championships, and the American team was badly beaten by the Russians, the Romanians, and the East Germans. That December, Retton competed in the prestigious Chunichi Cup in Japan, a competition that no American had ever won. In the international gymnastic world, three tournaments are considered the biggest: the American Cup, the world championships, and the Chunichi Cup.

At the Chunichi Cup, Retton would need to compete against Maxi Gnauck from East Germany, the reigning world champion on uneven bars; Boriana Stoyanova from Bulgaria, the world champion on the vault; and Yelena Shushunova from Russia. Durham and Retton were representing the United States.

During the first day of competition, Retton won the vault and placed fourth on floor exercises, ending up just fifteen-hundredths of a point behind the coleaders, Gnauck and Shushunova. On the second day she outperformed all of the gymnasts, becoming the first American to ever win the all-around title in this competition.

In February 1984, Durham—who was Retton's main competition at Karolyi's gym—left for a new coach, a startling move so close to Olympic competition; her family apparently felt that she was not getting enough individual attention with the Karolyis. Meanwhile, McNamara switched to Bela Karolyi as a coach, providing Retton with new head-to-head competition in her home gym. Plus, Retton learned much about the uneven bars from McNamara, and McNamara learned much about the vault and floor exercises from Retton.

Retton began practicing routines designed for Olympic competition; Geza Pozsar, who had served as Karolyi's choreographer in Romania—and who had been Nadia Comaneci's choreographer—helped to create those routines.

She then returned to the American Cup in 1984 to defend her title. The Russian and East German teams did not send their athletes, citing security concerns as their reason. International athletes who did compete included Laura Cutina from Romania, who would place fifth overall in the 1984 Olympics;

Hana Ricna from Czechslovakia, who had won the silver medal on the beam in the world championships; Zhou Quirui from China, who would be part of the bronze-winning team in the Olympics; and Elke Heine from West Germany, who would end up in the Olympic all-around finals. Representing the United States were Retton, who had won the 1983 American Cup, and Mc-Namara, who had already won the American Cup twice.

On the first day of the competition, Retton scored a 10 on her floor routine. The following day, she scored a 9.95 on bars; a 9.8 on the balance beam; a 9.75 on floor exercises; and a 10 on vault. Overall, she scored 39.50 out of 40.00 possible points, successfully defending her title. From the fall of 1983 through when she would compete in the Olympics, Retton had won fourteen all-around titles in a row.

As she prepared for the Championships of the U.S.A., Retton stopped taking her correspondence courses so that she could focus solely on her routines. At night, she sometimes dreamed of falling during her routines; other times, she dreamed of doing them perfectly.

To qualify for Olympic trials, an American athlete needs to finish in the top twenty in the Championships of the U.S.A.; forty percent of the score earned there carries over from the championships to the Olympic trials. Retton was not in the best physical shape when the championships rolled around; she had torn a plantar fascia in one of her feet and it hurt to walk. Because this competition was so important, she simply got a cortisone shot, taped up her foot, and competed.

In the compulsory part of the competition, Retton scored a 9.9 on the vault. In the optional part, where she had more freedom to structure her routines, she earned a perfect 10 on the vault; a 9.85 on floor exercises; and a 9.8 on the uneven bars. Her lowest score was on the balance beam—9.4—but she still won the all-around title, in addition to a first-place finish on the floor exercises and vault, and a third-place finish on the balance beam.

At the Olympic trials Retton still struggled with foot pain, but she nevertheless was still two-tenths of a point in the lead after compulsories. In the optionals she scored a 9.85 on vault and floor exercises; a 9.75 on the uneven bars; and a 9.60 on the balance beam. Retton was in the lead at the end of the trials, so she, along with Julianne McNamara, Michelle Dusserre, and Pam Bileck, was assured a spot on the U.S. Olympic team, with two more gymnasts to be added to the team before the Olympics began.

Retton had also been suffering from knee pain during the Olympic trials, which worried her. Karolyi tried to brush it off as unimportant but, shortly afterward, she could not even walk on it. A surgeon gave her the news that she did not want to hear: pieces of cartilage had broken off from her knee, and one piece got stuck in the joint. She needed to have the cartilage surgically removed. Retton was told just six weeks before the Olympic competition. Although she feared that she would not heal in time for the Olympics, the surgery was necessary. So, she used her down time after her operation to visualize performing perfect routines and winning medals. Just two days after her surgery, she was in the gym, icing her knee before and after each workout. Within two weeks, she was practicing her full routines again, including her tumbles. Mary Lou Retton was going to the the Olympics.

1984 OLYMPICS

The 1984 Olympics were being held in Los Angeles, California, the first time that the Games took place in the United States in fifty-two years. Just a couple of months before the Games were set to begin, the Soviet Union announced that its athletes were boycotting them. A statement from May 8, 1984 said that the Soviets believed that "extremist groups in America were planning to make conditions unbearable for Soviet athletes and that American organizers were not planning to provide the Soviet team with sufficient security." Moreover, the Soviets stated that as many as one hundred other countries would boycott the Games along with them, which would effectively destroy the competition.

To understand the history behind this decision, one needs to look back to December 1979, when the Soviet Union invaded Afghanistan, with which it shares a border. When a pro-Communist leader was overthrown in Afghanistan, the Soviet Union invaded to provide support to the Communist factions in the country. The United States, in turn, condemned the actions of the Soviets and demanded international censure.

Because the 1980 Olympics were to be held in Moscow, the United States decided to boycott the Games, and sixty other countries followed suit. Thus, when the Soviet Union announced a boycott of the 1984 Olympics, it was thought by many that this was a retaliatory move in response to the 1980 U.S.-led boycott. Sixteen other countries joined the 1984 boycott, including East Germany and Cuba. Interestingly enough, this was the first time that China had sent an Olympic team since 1932—and, in a decision that shocked people around the world, Romania decided to ignore the pressure put upon them by the Soviet Union to boycott, and they sent their athletes to the United States, including a world-class gymnastics team. All told, 140 countries participated in these Olympics, the largest number to date.

Although Retton was clearly affected by these political decisions, a situation closer to home most likely had more of her attention. Because Karolyi was not part of the official Olympic coaching team for the United States, he could not coach Retton during the actual Games. He managed to get certified to move the gymnastics equipment though, so Retton could approach him to ask for guidance; perhaps his most valuable input was on the strengths and weaknesses of the Romanian gymnastics team, because four of the five girls representing Romania in the gymnastics events were coached by Karolyi before he defected.

Despite all of the political maneuvering, the Games commenced. The gymnastics competition in 1984 began with compulsories, where each athlete needed to perform the same routines, which were typically simpler than what were performed in the optional portion of competition. In compulsories, each team sent the weakest competitor on a particular apparatus first, and the strongest last. The Americans chose to place Retton last on the vault, floor exercises, and uneven bars, with McNamara going last on the balance beam. After compulsories, Ecaterina Szabo and Lavinia Agache, both from Romania, were in first place overall, with Retton five-tenths of a point behind.

On the second day, athletes performed their optional routines; they had had more freedom in creating them. Overall, the Romanians were beating the Americans by forty-five-hundredths of one point; the night before, the American men had beaten the world championship Chinese team for the gold, so the American women's team was feeling the momentum and excitement fueled by the men's win. In optionals, Retton earned a 9.9 on the uneven bars, with Szabo and McNamara each getting a 10; this was the first perfect score earned by an American woman in Olympic history. Retton got a 9.75 on the balance beam; a 9.9 on the floor exercises; and a 10 on the vault. The Romanians won the team gold, and the United States, the silver; this was the first team medal won by an American gymnastics team since the bronze in 1948.

Retton was the only gymnast who qualified for the individual finals in all four events, and she was well prepared to compete for Olympic medals. Although the top thirty-six finishers had the opportunity to compete, it seemed likely that the competition for the gold would occur between Retton and Szabo.

Entering the competition, Retton had a small lead—fifteen-hundredths of one point. Szabo started out with a perfect 10 performance on the beam, with Retton earning 9.85 on the uneven bars. Szabo then earned a 9.95 on the floor exercise, which was performed to a series of patriotic American songs, and Retton earned a 9.80 on the balance beam. Karolyi was frustrated over the score, which he thought was too low. Retton had started out with a lead of fifteen-hundredths of one point, and now Szabo was winning by the same amount. But Szabo's best events were already performed, while Retton's were still ahead of her.

Szabo then performed two vaults and the better of her two scores counted; she earned a 9.9 and a 9.8, giving Retton an opportunity to gain ground. Retton then performed an incredible floor exercise routine; when she saw the score of 10, she pumped both arms into the air and shouted, "Yes!" She ran to Karolyi, who hugged her and lifted her off the ground; the gym came alive with spectators shouting, "USA . . . USA!" Szabo was now in the lead by just five-hundreds of one point. Simona Pauca of Romania had already won the bronze, and Szabo and Retton each had one more performance to go, to determine who earned the silver and who clinched the gold.

Szabo earned a 9.9 on the uneven bars, which meant that Retton needed a 9.95 to tie for the gold and a 10 to win it solo; her last event was the vault, her strongest. The *Washington Times* later reported that, before Retton performed her vault, Karolyi whispered to her, "I know you can do it. The best you can vault. Now or never." According to the article, Retton just smiled and said, "Okay."

Retton performed her Tsukahara vault perfectly, a move that only she knew how to make; *Sports Illustrated* would call this performance the "vault without fault," and it earned Retton a perfect score of 10. At this point, there was no reason why Retton needed to perform her second vault—but she did, scoring yet another perfect 10.

Retton earned the gold medal in the all-around, the first time this was accomplished by an American woman. She also won the silver medal in the vault and bronze medals in floor exercise and uneven bars. Her five medals were the most won by an American athlete in the 1984 Olympics, and she was the youngest gymnast to win medals at these Games.

After the Olympics, Retton's picture appeared on multiple magazine covers, including *Time*, *Newsweek*, *Sports Illustrated*, and *Seventeen*. She became the Associated Press' 1984 Female Athlete of the Year, while *Sports Illustrated* chose her as the 1984 Sportsman of the Year. Wheaties signed Retton to appear on their cereal boxes, the first female athlete to do so; Wheaties boxes often featured the pictures of top-level athletes to emphasize the cereal's slogan that it is the "breakfast of champions." By 1999, it was estimated that Retton had earned close to $12 million in sponsorship deals alone.

Retton appeared on the Tonight Show; fit President Ronald Reagan for his Olympic team blazer; presented an Emmy award; received sponsorships from McDonald's, Vidal Sassoon, Dobie leisure wear, and Pony athletic shoes; appeared in the Macy's Day parade; and performed with Bob Hope in his Christmas special.

POST-OLYMPICS

Although Retton could have retired after the Olympics, she wanted to compete in the American Cup in 1985, to become the only athlete to win the all-around in that competition three times; she succeeded. In 1985 Retton became the first gymnast inducted into the U.S. Olympic Hall of Fame; she was the youngest inductee to date. In the fall of 1986 she announced her retirement from full-time gymnastics but returned to the 1988 Olympic Games as a commentator for NBC. In 1986 she and Karolyi cowrote her autobiography,

FIRST FEMALE OLYMPIC CEREAL BOX CHAMPION

In 1958, Wheaties cereal boxes featured a photo of Bob Richards, a pole vaulter; he was not the first athlete displayed on Wheaties boxes, but he was the first Olympic gold medalist. This is also when the athletes became featured more prominently on the fronts of the boxes, rather than on the backs or sides. Receiving a gold medal, though, is not enough to qualify someone to appear on the boxes of this "Breakfast of Champions." It is also important to have a wholesome, All-American image. Bob Richards was a minister, which helped, (as did the fact that he was the first director of the Wheaties Sports Federation!). In 1964, Wheaties featured runner Lt. Billy Mills, an Oglala Lakota (Sioux) from the Pine Ridge Indian Reservation; and, in 1976, decathlon athlete Bruce Jenner appeared on the boxes. It was not until 1984 that a female Olympian received this honor—and that was Mary Lou Retton. After Retton was chosen, it opened the doors for other female Olympic athletes, as well, including Amy Van Dyken, Stacy Dragila, Brooke Bennett, and Laura Wilkinson, and this quirky only-in-America tradition continues to this day.

Mary Lou: Creating an Olympic Champion, in which both the athlete and the coach shared parts of the journey to Olympic gold.

On December 29, 1990, Retton married former University of Texas quarterback Shannon Kelley, a man that she had met while taking classes at the university after retiring from gymnastics competition. The couple has four daughters: Shayla Rae (April 12, 1995), McKenna Lane (April 15, 1997), Skyla Brae (August 9, 2000), and Emma Jean (June 20, 2002).

In 1993 she entered the International Women's Sports Hall of Fame. That same year, the Sports Marketing Group conducted a study to identify the most-loved American athletes and Retton topped the list.

In 1994 the United States Olympic Committee (USOC) created the Mary Lou Retton Award, to be given for athletic excellence. The following year, she received the Flo Hyman Award from the Women's Sports Foundation; this is awarded to an athlete who has the same dignity, spirit, and commitment to excellence as Hyman, who captained the U.S. women's volleyball team that captured the silver medal in 1984. The Volleyball Hall of Fame site states that Hyman was the "most famous volleyball player of the time, not just here in the United States, but also worldwide."

Retton covered the Olympics for *USA Today* at both the 1992 and 1996 Olympics; in 1996, she also served as an on-air reporter for Gannett Broadcasting NBC affiliates, and she co-hosted the television series *Road to Olympic*

Gold. Bela Karolyi served as the head coach for the U.S. Olympic gymnastics team in 1996; in 1997, he was inducted into the International Gymnastics Hall of Fame.

In 2000 Retton published a book, *Gateways to Happiness*, in which she shared her philosophies of life. In 2001 she and her husband created a show for PBS titled *Mary Lou's Flip Flop Shop*; the target audience was preschoolers and the show encouraged physical activity. That was also the year that she was inducted into the World Sports Humanitarian Hall of Fame.

In 2005 Retton successfully had surgery for hip dysplasia, a hereditary disease where there is an abnormal formation of the hip joint. Her father had had the surgery as well, although he was in his sixties when he needed the operation and his daughter was only in her thirties. Retton shared her hip replacement story publicly; that same year, she also revealed that she had an overactive bladder and participated in a Life Beyond the Bathroom campaign to help others get the medical attention that they needed.

Retton gives motivational presentations in the United States, with one article stating that she receives $20,000 per presentation. She has also hosted the syndicated program *American Sportswomen*. She travels the globe as a fitness ambassador, discussing the importance of nutrition and exercise. Retton has served as the national chairperson of the Board of Governors of the Children's Miracle Network and on the President's Council on Physical Fitness. She also appeared in the films *Scrooged* and *Naked Gun 33 1/3*.

After living in Houston, Texas for twenty-eight years, Retton and her family moved to her hometown of Fairmont, West Virginia in 2009, when her husband accepted a job with Fairmont State University. He had been an investment banker in Texas, but he longed to coach; the university in Fairmont offered him a job as athletic association director and quarterback coach. He secretly had a home built for them in Fairmont and he surprised Retton with the completed home. Her parents and three brothers still live in Fairmont; her sister moved to Pennsylvania.

Three of their daughters participate in gymnastics, while Skyla prefers horseback riding. All four girls took turns wearing their mother's gold medal, though, while watching the 2004 Olympics.

CONTROVERSIES AND CRITICISMS

Retton has seldom been the target of criticism or the center of controversy, but there have been some who have voiced these two critiques: first, she won her gold medal in an Olympics where the powerhouse Soviet Union athletes did not compete. It is true that Retton did not compete against the Soviet athletes; it is also true that Americans won an embarrassment of riches at these

ATHLETES AND DIETS

People have criticized the strictness of diets that some gymnastics coaches, including Karolyi, have insisted upon for their athletes. Retton weighed about one hundred pounds when she arrived in Houston to work with Karolyi; he put her on a diet that slimmed her down to between ninety-two and ninety-four pounds. Even at that weight, during the 1984 Olympics one official told Retton the following: "You know, if I could, I'd take half a point off because of that fat hanging off your butt" (Putnam, 1999, 42). Retton laughed off the insult, but this exchange demonstrates how extremely gymnasts are expected to diet—and perhaps indicated that some officials had not, in 1984, adjusted to the increasingly muscular builds of many gymnasts, and that they still expected the long, lean look of previous eras of gymnastic athletes.

Olympic Games, winning 83 of the 223 gold medals awarded—and surely the lack of Soviet and other Eastern Bloc athletes contributed to America's overwhelming success in 1984. Supporters of Retton point out that she did, however, compete against excellent gymnasts from Romania and China.

The second criticism centers on the fact that she has called herself a pioneer of gymnastics. A scathing response to her statement appeared in *International Gymnast* in 2009: "Was Mary Lou Retton a Pioneer in Gymnastics?"

LEGACY

Bela Karolyi has said this about Retton: "I have been teaching gymnastics 25 years, and had many world and Olympic champions, but I have never coached anybody more positive and dedicated than this little girl" (Woolum, 1999, 206). "Of her 94 pounds," wrote one journalist, "65 are heart" (Retton, Karolyi, and Powers, 1986, xvii).

FURTHER READING

Associated Press. 2004. Hello Mary Lou: Twenty years later, America still smitten with Retton. *Charleston Gazette*, August 19: www.highbeam.com.

Heller, Dick. 1998. Retton Vaulted Her Way to History with Perfection. *The Washington Times*: 11.

Mary Lou Retton. http://www.marylouretton.com/.

Retton, Mary Lou, Bela Karolyi, and John Powers. 1986. *Creating an Olympic Champion*. New York: Dell Publishing Company, Inc.

Robinson, Julie. 2010. Mary Lou Retton makes another perfect landing: Champion gymnast takes a golden opportunity to return home. *Sunday Gazette-Mall*, August 8: www.highbeam.com.

Rusoff, Jane Wollman. 1996. New moves for a gold-medal mom. *Good Housekeeping*, June 1: www.highbeam.com.

Woolum, Janet. 1999. *Outstanding Women Athletes: Who They Are and How They Influenced Sports in America*. Phoenix, AZ: Oryx Press.

Manon Rheaume, 20 years old, listens to the National Anthem before her professional debut as the goaltender for the Tampa Lightning against the St. Louis Blues in 1992 in Tampa. (AP Photo/Chris O'Meara)

Manon Rheaume (1972–)

For Canadians, ice hockey is like American football, baseball, and basketball rolled into one; and unlike soccer, another popular sport north of the border, hockey is home-grown. No other public activity engages as many of the nation's inhabitants, whether they are athletes playing on indoor and outdoor rinks, or fans sitting in the bleachers or watching the game on television. For sports-minded Canadians, hockey is the national religion. More people attend hockey games than go to church, and church activities are rescheduled around playoff games. The enduring symbol of the sport's popularity is *Hockey Night in Canada*, a weekend broadcast ritual that started with radio in the early 1930s and then moved to television in the 1950s. *Hockey Night* on CBC Network remains the longest-running sports program still on the air. The nation's newspapers, not to be outdone, devote nearly half their column space in sports sections to action on the ice.

Despite the popularity of hockey, until recently a large segment of Canadians were relegated to the role of fans. Although women have been playing the game for more than a hundred years, they struggled to gain support for youth hockey programs and access to the rinks. The girls' and women's leagues had to fight for rink time, as male hockey players were given priority. When women did obtain entrée to the rinks, they often were mocked, harassed, and intimidated by male players and fans. Despite the sexism, girls' ice hockey teams grew in number. However, many girls preferred to play on boys' teams in order to get more ice time and receive superior coaching.

In 1955, eight-year-old Abby Hoffman registered with the all-male Toronto Hockey League and played for one season. The officials, coaches, and her teammates thought she was a boy. Neither Abby nor her parents corrected this impression, and she proved to be an exceptional player. When she made the all-star team, her gender was revealed. That revelation put an end to her playing hockey with the boys. The following year, Abby played on a girls' team, but the league ran into scheduling difficulties. The disillusioned young athlete switched to track and field. Three decades later, following a 1986 court ruling, the Ontario Hockey Association was directed to allow girls to play on boys' teams. The legal precedent had been established. By the 1990s, for better or worse, more Canadian girls were playing on boys' teams than in girls' leagues.

CHILDHOOD

Girls' hockey was slow to develop in Quebec, yet this French-speaking province would produce the most famous female hockey goalie in Canada. Like Abby Hoffman, she would learn the game playing on boys' teams. Manon Rheaume was born February 24, 1972, in the small town of Lac-Beauport, just north of Quebec City. Manon's father, Pierre, and his wife, Nicole, moved to Lac-Beauport just before Manon's older brother Martin was born. Manon was born two years later, followed by Pascal. The Rheaumes were an athletic family. Pierre enjoyed horseback riding and was an avid hockey fan. Nicole was a downhill skier and swimmer. The Rheaume home was cluttered with ski outfits and hockey gear. Manon and her brothers grew up playing improvised hockey in the basement.

A Canadian community without a hockey rink is like an American town without a baseball diamond. But Lac-Beauport was a ski resort; it had no rink. Pierre Rheaume decided to correct this oversight. The contractor persuaded the mayor to donate some land and boards, and Pierre built an outdoor rink for the town's youngsters. The novice hockey players needed a coach, so Pierre volunteered. The new coach believed in teaching the fundamentals and drilled the youngsters on skating skills. Only near the end of practice would he allow a puck on the ice so his charges could work on their passing and shooting. When the boys were ready for competition, Pierre appropriated some hockey sweaters and formed a team. Among the team's members were Martin Rheaume and his four-year-old brother Pascal.

Manon had been skating since she was three years old. Her brothers conscripted her to play goal so they could practice their shots during street hockey games. But when Martin and Pascal played league games, Manon was relegated to the stands with her mother. This arrangement proved to be short-lived, however, as her brothers' team had a serious deficiency. Her father, the coach, realized that he didn't have a capable goalie. After considerable debate, Manon was recruited for the position. She would change into her hockey uniform at home and made it a point to don her goaltender's mask upon entering the arena. Only the white figure skates hinted at her gender. Thus did Manon Rheaume begin her career as a hockey goalie at the tender age of five.

As the only girl in the family, Manon was never one to conform to French Canada's traditional gender roles. She was fiercely independent from the time she was a toddler. Her parents recall that she was a very active child. She preferred playing roller hockey in the basement with her brothers to playing with dolls. The youngster wouldn't let anyone hold her hand while she learned to skate. Manon's penchant for daredevil stunts resulted in a broken arm and a concussion before she reached school age. Even the casts on fractured limbs didn't seem to slow her down. The aspiring hockey player taught herself to endure bumps and bruises without crying. Manon's toughness worked to her advantage playing goal in boys' leagues, where she constantly had to prove that she could handle the action as well as the guys. When she broke her toe, she taped it to an adjoining digit and played through the pain.

Canada provides youth hockey programs (for boys) in virtually every city and province. Three- and four-year-olds are initiated into the game as Mites. They advance through graduated levels of competition in two-year intervals: Tyke (ages 5–6), Novice (ages 7–8), Atom (ages 9–10), Peewee (ages 11–12),

Bantam (ages 13–14), Midget (ages 15–17), and Juvenile (ages 18–20). Most areas of the country sponsor regional and provincial championships. The top players from the upper levels are recruited into the professional ranks. The competition for these limited positions is fierce. So it's not surprising that some of Manon's teammates and their parents resented her filling a position that would keep a talented boy from moving up through the leagues. Manon and her family learned to tune out the criticism.

When Manon Rheaume reached the Atom level, she persuaded her parents to send her to hockey camp. She recalls the official behind the registration table informing her she was in the wrong place; that she should be signing up for ringette—the hockey-like game for girls that utilizes rings instead of pucks. Rheaume reassured him that she was in fact a hockey player. She was allowed to enroll and held her own among the boys that summer. The young goalie began the 1980–81 season with much-improved skills. However, she lost her goaltending position to a boy and ended up playing defense, much to her chagrin. When the first-string goalie gave up nine goals in one game, Manon's teammates asked that she be placed back in the net. She played Atom AA hockey in 1983 on the team in the Quebec suburb of Charlesbourg. Games were held in an indoor arena filled with fans. This was a new experience that came with a lot of pressure on the youngsters. But Rheaume and her teammates played well. Charlesbourg dethroned the reigning champion. She gave up only one goal in the finals and was voted most valuable player of the game.

Ice hockey is a physical game, especially for goalies. Protecting the goal is like being a target in a shooting gallery. Manon's father improvised a fiberglass chest protector for his maturing daughter. Despite padding and a face mask, goalies routinely get injured. While playing in the Atom league, Rheaume suffered a concussion in a collision with another player and woke up in the hospital. It wouldn't be her last painful encounter with a player or the puck. The puck, made of hard rubber, comes flying at the goal as fast as a baseball thrown from the pitcher's mound. When it makes contact, it hurts. Former NHL goalie Ken Dryden observed that the pain from being hit by pucks is constant and cumulative over a season. He compared it to getting pummeled by a skilled boxer. Manon once complained to her father about being hurt. He responded pointedly, "Macramé isn't painful. Choose" (Preston, 1995, 72). The ultimatum was a reference to the popular hobby of fashioning decorative knots in fabrics. The confirmed tomboy wasn't about to give up hockey for handicraft. She learned to accept pain as part of the game she loved.

Manon Rheaume never allowed hockey to interfere with her studies. She was just as competitive when it came to school exams as she was when being tested in the net. She did so well in the early grades that her second grade teacher suggested she skip a grade. Nicole Rheaume deferred; she didn't want her daughter growing up too fast. While Rheaume made good grades in her academic subjects, physical education was her favorite class. The budding athlete was the first one in the gym and the last to leave. On weekends, the family headed to the nearby ski slopes, and then it was back to the hockey arena. Pierre and Nicole Reaume assumed the role of chauffeurs for their sports-minded youngsters. Whether karate, ballet, tennis or hockey, it seemed that someone always had a lesson or a game scheduled across town. More often than not, mom and dad were in the stands cheering on their prodigies.

When Manon turned eleven she moved up to Peewee league. Her aspiration was to play in the Quebec International Peewee Tournament. The tournament had previously been for boys only, but the gender provision was removed in 1980. Pierre, who was coaching the team, had been catching a lot of flak about playing his daughter at goal. It was decided that Manon would alternate in the net with a male teammate. The local newspapers picked up the story: a girl would play in the Peewee Tournament for the first time in its twenty-five-year history. The pre-teen goalie found herself being interviewed by newspaper reporters and TV film crews.

The international tournament is a major event, with teams coming all the way from Europe. Wayne Gretsky, the greatest hockey player in Quebec's history, had played in the Peewee Tournament. Young male hockey players viewed it as a crucial step toward professional careers. Manon's team made it to the semifinals. The crowd was with her. They jumped to their feet and cheered when she blocked shots.

During Manon's final season playing Peewee, she anticipated moving to Bantam for thirteen- and fourteen-year-olds. The Bantam leagues are divided into three levels, AA, BB and CC, ranked from high to low. Manon attended the Bantam AA camp and did well. Camp is where coaches look over the talent. Pierre Brind'Amour, a former Quebec Nordiques player, offered her a position on his team. Manon became the first girl to play Bantam AA hockey. Coach Brind'Amour gave her as much time on the ice as his other goalie, but there were repercussions. The other goalie's father was the league director, and he became increasingly spiteful about his son having to share the goal with a girl. Manon was used to being harassed for playing on boys' teams. During games, opposing players would take shots at her face trying to intimidate her, or run over her and drive her into the net. Her coach remained supportive, but she got less playing time than the other goalie. Manon finished her season under escalating pressure. Undeterred, she looked forward to playing in the Midget league.

Not surprisingly, no girls had ever played Midget AAA hockey, the highest level for fifteen-year-olds. Manon had to settle for Midget AA camp. Despite her proven ability, the directors of the AA teams had little intention of giving her a chance to play. She ended up playing on a Midget CC team, what was referred to as the "fun league." Half a dozen players might show up for practice. Manon's mother suggested that she give up ice hockey since they wouldn't allow her to advance any higher. A discouraged Manon did give up the game when she turned seventeen. She recalls this hiatus as a difficult time in her life. She resented the way she'd been treated and felt rebellious. The forlorn teenager had made few friends outside of hockey.

BEGINNING WITH A WOMEN'S HOCKEY TEAM; GOING ON TO THE MEN'S

Following graduation from high school, Rheaume enrolled in classes at Sainte-Foy Junior College near Quebec City. She thought about a career in communications or teaching. But soon she received word of an upcoming hockey camp *for women* to be held at Quebec's Laval University, and she signed up. Upon arrival, she realized that most of the camp attendees were playing at a level below what she experienced in the boys' leagues. Rheaume met two women at Laval who were playing for Sherbrooke, a town in southern Quebec. They invited her to try out for the team. Rheaume took them up on the offer. She was immediately impressed by the caliber of women playing for Sherbrooke, and she liked the coach. There was another reason for her to play hockey with a women's team. The International Olympic Committee was considering adding women's ice hockey as an Olympic sport.

Rheaume's pressing task was to get back in shape. Sherbrooke's team practiced once or twice a month and played weekly. It didn't sound like an exhausting schedule, but the two-and-a-half-hour drive to Sherbrooke and back, in addition to the road games, proved exhausting. She came down with mononucleosis, which compounded the fatigue The doctors suggested that Rheaume take a month off to rest, but she was playing again within a couple of weeks. Sherbrooke won the provincial tournament and placed second in the Canadian women's championships in Montreal. Rheaume received the trophy for best goaltender. She was looking forward to the 1992 women's world championships to be held in Finland.

At the end of the 1991 season, Rheaume received an unexpected invitation to attend the Junior A training camp for a new men's team, the Louiseville Jaguars. Louiseville is located an hour and a half west of Quebec. Her brother Pascal was also playing on the team. Rheaume was one of five goalies attending camp. She calculated that this was probably her last opportunity to play hockey with the men, if she could "make the cut." She had to play through a couple of nagging injuries and ended up on crutches for a couple of weeks, but she performed well. The judges appreciated that her techniques were superior to the four male goalies, and that she played the position intelligently. In the final draft, Rheaume made the Louiseville Jaguars squad as backup goalie. She would be the first woman to play at yet another level.

Rheaume continued to make contacts in the various men's leagues. At one of her brother's games, a hockey scout introduced her to Gaston Drapeau, coach of the Trois-Rivières Draveurs (Three Rivers Loggers). The Draveurs played in the Quebec Major Junior Hockey League, or QMJHL. Drapeau offered to let Rheaume train with his team and play at the Junior A level. This meant more time on the road, but Rheaume knew that playing with the men at this level would improve her game. It was an opportunity the aspiring goalie felt that she couldn't pass up. Rheaume moved into a studio apartment in Trois-Rivières and enrolled in the local junior college to complete her coursework toward a diploma in humanities.

Pascal Rheaume also was playing for the Draveurs and boarded at the home of teammate Claude Poirer. The three young hockey players had a lot in common. Manon and Claude began dating. A thigh injury kept Rheaume off the ice for a couple of months. The second week after her return, one of the Draveurs' goalies was injured, and Rheaume was instructed to suit up for a game. She came off the bench three games later after the other goalie gave up four goals to blow the lead. All eyes were on her. A shot in the third period broke the grill on her mask and cut her eyebrow. She had to be pulled from the game so the wound could be stitched. This turned out to be the extent of Rheaume's playing time. Notwithstanding her brief tenure as the first woman to play goalie in the QMJHL (one level below the National Hockey League), she received a huge amount of media attention. Rheaume and her coach were overwhelmed with requests for interviews. In the interim, Rheaume returned to her team in Louiseville. The struggling Jaguars had fired their coach. Their new coach didn't give her much playing time either.

Manon Rheaume played on the women's team in Sherbrooke during the 1992 season. Sherbrooke won the Quebec championships and placed third in the Canadian national tournament. She planned to attend training camp for the women's national team that was to compete in the world championships in Finland. Rheaume performed well in camp and was one of five Quebecers who made the team. In April, the women's squad flew to Finland. It was Rheaume's first trip to Europe. The newly assembled team stayed in a small village near Tempere, the tournament site, and got to know each other on and off the ice. They practiced twice daily for a week, and then headed to the arena for the tournament. Rheaume's mother and Aunt Mireille were there to welcome her. They weren't the only ones who showed up specifically to watch her play. Rheaume discovered that she was a something of a celebrity in Europe for having played men's ice hockey. The Canadian team played well and made it to the finals against the undefeated U.S. team. They shut out the Americans 8-0 before a huge crowd. Following a victory party that ran late into the evening, the women's team headed home.

THE TAMPA BAY LIGHTNING

The following summer Rheaume worked for RDS, the French-language sports network. That was when she learned that she might be invited to the NHL

Ottawa Senators training camp. Other professional teams were showing interest in her as well. A scout for the newest team in the NHL, the Tampa Bay Lightning, had sent owner Phil Esposito a video of Rheaume in action. At first, Esposito didn't realize that he was viewing a woman encased inside the goalie's mask and protective padding. He found the goalie to be somewhat small but quite talented, and suggested inviting *him* to camp. When Esposito was told he was watching a woman play goal, his response was to recruit her anyway and "see what she's got." Later that summer at the Montreal Forum, Rheaume was introduced to Esposito, who subsequently invited her to Tampa Bay's training camp. Rheaume would join the Florida-based men's professional hockey team on the twentieth anniversary of the signing of Title IX legislation that prohibited gender discrimination in school and college sports in the United States.

Professional ice hockey was new to Florida, but Phil Esposito was the consummate promoter. The Lightning had a brand new arena and recruiting a woman goalie was bound to draw wide media attention. News reporters from Quebec followed the story closely. Rheaume arrived in Florida in time for some of the promotional events and then headed to camp. She had trained hard all summer in preparation. The Rheaume family now had two of their offspring playing professional hockey in the United States. Manon's brother Pascal was at the New Jersey Devils training camp the same season. Pierre accompanied his younger son to New Jersey, and Manon's mother joined her in Florida. Nicole Rheaume roomed with her twenty-year-old daughter for a while and helped her adjust to living in a foreign country. It was a great opportunity for the Quebec native to practice her English, along with her goal-tending skills. However, her personal life was constrained during camp. Rheaume saw little other than the arena and her hotel room.

Rheaume was one of eight goalies arriving at the Tampa Bay camp. The first week was devoted to playing games. But first the athletes had to undergo a series of physical tests. Rheaume passed them all, and was one of the best at doing sit-ups. Then the recruits hit the ice. Once Rheaume successfully blocked a shot or two, all the tension seemed to dissolve. She was back in her element. In the first game, she held the opponents scoreless. Her teammates congratulated her. Rheaume finished camp with the third-best goals-against average (goals allowed per game). At times, the media blitz seemed more challenging than the assaults on goal. For the course of camp, she was besieged by requests for photo sessions and interviews, and for appearances on radio and television shows. The phone rang off the hook. Clearly, Rheaume was the media darling for the moment.

When camp ended, Rheaume had survived all the cuts. The next phase of the preseason agenda was a series of exhibition games with other NHL teams. Esposito told Rheaume that he was going to put her in for one period in the game against the Saint Louis Blues. She recalls being quite nervous going into the game. Her teammates rallied around her with encouragement during warm-ups. Rheaume's mother was in the crowd. When the first period ended, the game was tied 2-2. Rheaume had given up two goals in nine shots. She survived her initiation into the NHL. At the news conference following the game, the room was filled with reporters, photographers, and television cameras. The young goalie from Quebec had made professional hockey history. (The following year, she would play in one exhibition game with the Lightning against the Boston Bruins.)

Owner Phil Esposito realized that Rheaume wasn't ready to play full-time in the National Hockey League. His assessment wasn't a huge surprise, as there are very few twenty-one-year-old goal tenders in the NHL. Playing in goal at this level demands years of experience and maturity. What his female goalie did have going for her were intelligence, quickness, and agility. Esposito offered to send Rheaume to training camp for their farm club, the Atlanta Knights, who played in the International Hockey League. She would get the opportunity to play in Atlanta's 15,000-seat Omni Center if she made the team.

Manon Rheaume was confronted with a big decision. Playing for Atlanta meant remaining in the States and being separated from her steady boyfriend. Moreover, she had some attractive job offers in communications upon completing junior college. Rheaume returned to Quebec to consider her options. As the first woman offered a tryout with the International League, Rheaume received even more media attention when she arrived home. The Canadian reporters and photographers were waiting for her. All of the interest was gratifying, but she needed some personal time to plan her future. After conferring with her family and her public relations adviser Paul Wilson, she decided to attend training camp in Atlanta. The Knights organization informed her that if she played well during camp, they would keep her on as a third-string goalie.

Rheaume arrived in Atlanta dead tired after a couple of hectic weeks. The coaches were understanding and allowed her to skip the first game. Once back on the ice, the young goalie's performance was impressive. At the end of the first week, management decided to keep her on. Her agent, Steven Bartlett, worked out the contract with the Knights. The team put Rheaume on a physical fitness program to build her strength and endurance. The trainer handed her a workout program written in French for her benefit. The 1992–93 season would be one of learning techniques. When the team's first-string goalie was called up to Tampa, Rheaume got to dress for games. She was subjected to the customary initiation antics directed at rookies. In deference to her gender, the veteran players didn't make her shave her head. They settled for filling her shoes with mashed potatoes. Her life soon settled into the predictable routine: eat, sleep, practice, and show up for press conferences. The schedule could prove grueling at times, and she didn't have much of a social life in the big city at first. Despite living in a man's world, her closest companion was a girlfriend, Hilary, who showed her the sights of Atlanta.

Manon's boyfriend, Claude, decided to come to Atlanta with her at the beginning of the season, hoping to play in the American Hockey League. But he didn't get called up by any of the teams. The two grew apart, and Claude returned to Montreal. Rheaume realized that it's tough being in a relationship when both individuals are professional athletes. At the same time, she got along well with the guys on her team, was accepted as a member, and felt respected. The guys teased her like a little sister. Having grown up with two brothers, she could take it. Rheaume spent most of her time with the French-speaking team members while she was improving her English.

The second week of December, Rheaume was given the opportunity to "break the ice" with the Knights. They were playing a home game against the Salt Lake City Golden Eagles. Coach Gene Umbracio put her in at the start of the second period. She gave up one goal in four shots. She thus became the first woman to play in a regular season men's professional hockey game. The following April, she played an entire game against the Cincinnati Cyclones. A bevy of reporters showed up at the Omni Center that night from as far away as Montreal. Rheaume had a less-than-stellar game, giving up six goals. The season was indeed a learning experience. Coach Umbracio remained supportive. He refused to buy into the conventional wisdom that a five-foot-six-inch woman couldn't play goalie in professional hockey. Rheaume received more criticism from Canadians than from American fans. As she traveled the league circuit—Cleveland, Cincinnati, Salt Lake City, Phoenix, San Diego— she gradually adjusted to American culture. But she was never able to get much playing time.

THE FIRST WOMAN IN PROFESSIONAL HOCKEY

As the first woman in professional hockey, Rheaume was doing a lot of promotional activities. She met with various company executives who wanted her to endorse their products or use their sports equipment. She filmed ads and did numerous radio and television interviews. But most of her time was taken up by practice and games. Her day started at 7:00 AM. She had to be at the rink by 9:30 for the two-hour practice sessions. Afternoons would find her at the fitness center for hour-and-a-half workouts. The exhausted hockey player had the remainder of the day to take care of personal business. Life on the road could prove just as taxing. The team played a full schedule and tallied thousands of miles during the season. To travel with a professional sports team is to be constantly shuttled from hotels to arenas to airports and back. She did find time to collaborate with writer Chantal Gilbert on her autobiography, *Manon: Alone in Front of the Net.* One chapter was titled "All Alone in the Big City."

Manon Rheaume tended to be reserved and never desired to be a media celebrity, but the role came with the territory. She was repeatedly cast as the "first woman hockey player to . . ." The young goalie had been receiving national attention since she played for the Draveurs in Quebec in 1991. She recalls that it was as if everyone in the media wanted a piece of her. There wasn't enough time in the day to accept all the requests for interviews and photo sessions. All the pressure led to a bout of stomach ulcers. Rheaume realized that she had to make choices about which offers to accept. She made an appearance on the national television show *Late Night with David Letterman* that resulted in a good deal of publicity. She got mention in *USA Today* and *Time* magazine. *Playboy* magazine had offered Rheaume a sum rumored to be $50,000 to do an interview and photo shoot. Though some of her friends advised her to take advantage of the offer, she turned them down.

Manon Rheaume wasn't the first sportswoman to be exploited by the entertainment and news media. Images of female athletes have been manipulated by the media—and by the athletes themselves—going back to the era of French tennis star Suzanne Lenglen and swimmer Gertrude Ederle. The 1920s was the decade of flappers and bathing beauties. The press dubbed Lenglen, known for her avant-garde tennis outfits, "La Divine" ("the divine one"). Popular media

WOMEN ATHLETES ON PROFESSIONAL MEN'S TEAMS

Hockey goalie Manon Rheaume joined a select group of women athletes given the opportunity to play on men's professional sports teams. Baseball and basketball have provided most of the opportunities. Back in 1931, pitcher Jackie Mitchell signed a contract with the Chattanooga Lookouts, a Class AA minor league team. In an exhibition game against the New York Yankees, she struck out Babe Ruth and Lou Gehrig. Two decades later, five-foot-three-inch pitcher Mamie "Peanut" Johnson was one of three women signed to play in the Negro American League. Johnson pitched for the Indianapolis Clowns beginning in 1953, and she compiled a 33-8 win-loss record through 1955.

Olympic medalist Ann Meyers signed a contract with the NBA Indiana Pacers in 1980 and participated in the team tryouts, but didn't make the final squad. Meyers went on to play in the Women's Professional Basketball League. Point guard Nancy Lieberman, who starred at Old Dominion University, played two spring seasons in the men's United States Basketball League in the mid-1980s. Lieberman became the first woman to coach a professional men's basketball team, the Texas Legends in the NBA Developmental League.

Angela Ruggiero was the first woman to make more than a token appearance at a position other than goalie in a U.S. men's professional hockey game, when she played a period for the Tulsa Oilers in the Central Hockey League in January, 2005, a dozen years after Manon Rheaume's historic debut in men's pro hockey.

continue to focus on women's femininity and sexuality rather than their athleticism. Contemporary women athletes pose for provocative "cheesecake" photos, while male athletes appear in "beefcake" publicity shots. In today's celebrity culture, any type of publicity boosts athletes' name and image recognition, and, in turn, their commercial appeal. Sports stars of both sexes are induced to market themselves. Meanwhile, the conception of femininity has evolved to incorporate physicality. This generation of women athletes seems more comfortable blending sex appeal with athleticism. German figure skater and Olympic gold medalist Katarina Witt caused something of a sensation when she appeared nude in *Playboy* in 1998. Manon Rheaume, modest by nature and a devout Roman Catholic, wasn't comfortable with this type of exposure. Moreover, the attractive Canadian aspired to be recognized for what she accomplished "between the pipes" (in the goal), not for her physical appearance.

In 1993 Rheaume was traded to the Knoxville Cherokees. For the next couple of years she bounced around in minor league hockey playing for the Cherokees, the Nashville Knights, and Tallahassee Tiger Sharks in the East Coast Hockey League, and the Las Vegas Thunder in the IHL. She then was assigned to the semipro Las Vegas Aces in the Pacific South Hockey League. Overall, Rheaume played in a couple dozen games on the various men's teams. What she lacked in size and strength, she made up for in intelligence and effort. Coaches praised her work ethic. She got her first win as a professional with the Cherokees in a game she started at goal.

Beyond her career in the minor leagues, 1994 proved to be an eventful year for Rheaume. She appeared in a test match with VEU Feldkirch, thus becoming the first woman to play in the professional Austrian Hockey League. Rheaume played in goal as the Canadian women took the gold at the 1994 International Ice Hockey Federation (IIHF) Women's World Championship held in Lake Placid, New York in April. The Canadians went undefeated in the tournament, giving up only six goals, and beat the American 6-3 in the finals. This championship tournament, initiated in 1990, was a major event in the development of women's international ice hockey.

Rheaume had been playing roller hockey during the summers and in 1995 joined the New Jersey Rockin Rollers in the men's inline hockey league, Roller Hockey International. RHI had formed three years earlier in the wake of the inline skating boom in North America that first caught on in the 1980s. Inline, or roller, hockey is similar to ice hockey in that the players utilize a hockey stick to direct the puck into the opponents' goal. Roller hockey quickly gained popularity. It was a demonstration sport at the 1992 Barcelona Olympic Games. The first world championships for men were hosted in 1995 in Chicago. Rheaume played goal in four games with the Rollers. In 1996 she appeared in games with the Ottawa Loggers and the Sacramento River Rats, both in the RHI. Roller Hockey International gave way to Major League Roller Hockey in 1998. Rheaume proved to be a pioneer in this form of hockey as well. Women continue to play roller hockey with the men in Major League Roller Hockey's SLAMM league.

Rheaume was back on the ice for the 1996–97 season with the Reno Renegades in the West Coast Hockey League. She played in eleven games and had the best goals-allowed-per-game average among the team's three goalies on a team that had struggled defensively. Rheaume's career with various men's professional teams remained singular. Most women hockey players, at the time, played on college teams. The better players tried out for the women's national teams. Notably, the women's game is played at a much different pace. When Rheaume took a break from men's professional hockey to try out for the Canadian women's national team, she was cut from the squad and didn't play in the 1997 Women's World Championship. Playing with the men may have worked against her. She rejoined the national team that took the silver medal at the 1998 Winter Games in Nagano, Japan, as the backup goalie. This was the debut of women's ice hockey as an Olympic sport. Rheaume played in the championship game against the United States, giving up two goals, but was out of the game when the Americans scored the final goal in a 3-1 win.

In the spring of 1998, Manon and fiancé Gerry St. Cyr, a former minor league ice hockey player, teamed up as roller hockey instructors. Rheaume was instrumental in organizing women's inline hockey. The two athletes married in June of 1998 and had a son, Dylan. The coupled resided in Las Vegas, where Gary continued to play roller hockey for the Las Vegas Coyotes. Rheaume took the year off in 1999 to have the baby and didn't play on the women's national team. A one-hour documentary focusing on Rheaume's hockey career, *Manon Rheaume, Woman Behind the Mask*, was produced in conjunction with the National Film Board of Canada. The film was shown on the Canadian cable channel Women's Television Network (WTN) in 2000. The narrative centered on her formative years, and also included scenes with husband Gary and son Dylan. She and Gary later divorced.

THE HOCKEY COACH

Rheaume decided to retire after eight years with the women's national team. She played briefly at forward for the Montreal Wingstars in the recently formed National Women's Hockey League. The Wingstars finished with a record of 30-6-4 (wins, losses, ties) for the 2000–01 season. Rheaume then took a position with California-based Mission Hockey, a manufacturer of hockey equipment. She headed their campaign to market the Betty Flyweight hockey skate designed especially for women. She split her time between Irvine, California and Las Vegas, where she played on the women's roller hockey team. Rheaume coached the first all-girls' team to compete in the prestigious Quebec

International Peewee Tournament in 2002. The Mission Betty team of twelve- and thirteen-year-olds made it to the quarterfinals. They played before crowds of 12,000 fans during the tournament. Rheaume wanted to provide young girls with the same opportunities to play hockey that she had growing up. She explored the possibility of initiating an all-girl's division.

Rheaume relocated to Milwaukee in 2005, where she served as director of girls' hockey and marketing for the POWERade Iceport complex that operated rinks for ice hockey, figure skating, and roller hockey. She briefly served as goaltending coach for the women's team at the University of Minnesota–Duluth. Rheaume then moved to Michigan where she took a position as Director of Sales and Marketing with the Central Collegiate Hockey Association. CCHA, affiliated with the National Collegiate Athletic Association, includes several Michigan and neighboring state colleges competing in men's ice hockey.

The semiretired hockey star played forward on the Michigan-based Little Caesars Senior Women's A Hockey team during 2007–08. They won the first National Championship held at that level during her second season with the team. Rheaume also played for the Minnesota Whitecaps in the Western Women's Hockey League in 2008–09. The team made it to the Clarkson Cup Finals. She returned to play briefly with the men in the IHL during the 2008–09 season, on the home-state Port Huron Icehawks, and then suited up for one game with the Flint Generals. The thirty-six-year-old goalie had worked hard to get back in shape. She was inspired to come back by the example of forty-year-old swimmer Dara Torres, whose Olympic career spanned twenty-four years.

Rheaume continues to campaign in the interests of young sportswomen. The veteran hockey player formed the Manon Rheaume Foundation in 2008. The purpose of the foundation is to provide scholarships for young girls to help them realize their goals. In 2009 the Foundation partnered with Titan Sports to sponsor a teenage girls' hockey tournament in Farmington, Michigan. Rheaume remarried and gave birth to another son. She currently resides with her family in Northville, Michigan, near Detroit. Recently, she has been featured in sport training videos, appearing with ice skater Nancy Kerrigan and beach volleyball player Liz Masakayan. Rheaume still plays ice hockey with former NHL stars in charity games in the United States and Canada.

Manon grew up playing hockey with boys and then on men's teams for much of her professional career, although she also played on the Canadian national women's teams that competed in world championship tournaments and in the 1998 Winter Olympics. Her appearance on men's teams helped women ice hockey players to gain recognition. In the process, she became an international sports celebrity. Over her career, Rheaume has been interviewed on numerous national television programs in Canada and the United States, including *CBS This Morning*, *Good Morning America*, and *Entertainment*

Tonight, in addition to her appearance on David Letterman's show. She appeared as herself in the made-for-television movie *A Beachcomber's Christmas* in 2004.

Rheaume's accomplishments on the ice featured a progression of gender breakthroughs. Notably, she was the first girl to play in the International Pee Wee Hockey Tournament in Quebec and the first woman to play in the NHL. As of this writing, she's still the only woman to have signed a contract with a men's professional hockey team in North America. In 2008 Kim St.-Pierre played goal with the Montreal Canadiens during a practice session, becoming the second woman to play alongside NHL players. But no contract was offered her. Saskatchewan-born Hayley Wickenheiser, considered by many to be the best female player in the world, signed a one-year contract to play forward with a men's professional ice hockey team in Sweden for the 2008–09 season. Rheaume literally "broke the ice" for women like Kim and Hayley who aspire to play hockey at its most competitive levels.

Manon Rheaume's hockey career came with its share of controversy. As a young girl in Canada she intruded into the male bastion of youth hockey, causing predictable reactions by some of the players, their parents, and league officials. All athletes have to prove themselves, but Rheaume more than most as the only girl on the rink. By choosing to play goalie—arguably the most punishing position in hockey—she literally became a target. Rheaume found herself deflecting menacing pucks aimed at her head, as well as disparaging remarks within earshot from condescending fans and skeptical journalists. Notwithstanding, she always could count on the support of her teammates, her coaches and, most importantly, her family.

Rheaume's invitation to try out with the new NHL franchise in Tampa Bay was broadly characterized by hockey fans and reporters as a publicity stunt perpetrated by the team's savvy owner, Phil Esposito. Indeed, the twenty-year-old goalie was a marginal player competing with the best hockey talent in North America. But Rheaume had her own reasons for accepting the offer to play men's professional hockey. Quite simply, she craved the challenge to compete at the top level in her sport, regardless of the odds. She ventured to stand in the net against bigger, stronger, and more experienced players and absorb the impact of inevitable collisions and the shock of pucks fired at 90 mph. Herein lies the legacy of Manon Rheaume as a woman and athlete.

FURTHER READING

Etue, Elizabeth, and Megan K. Williams. 1996. *On the Edge: Women Making Hockey History.* Toronto: Second Story Press.

Kaufmann, Elizabeth. 1993. The Puck Stops Here. *Women's Sports & Fitness* 15:1: 48–53.

"Manon Rheaume." 2008. Greatest Hockey Legends.com. http://womenhockeylegends. Blogspot.com/2008/10/manon-rheaume.html.

"Manon Rheaume Biography." 2010. Jrank.org: Famous Sports Stars. http://sports .jrank.org/pages/3842/Rheaume-Manon.html.

Preston, Brian. 1995. Shots on Goal. *Saturday Night Magazine* (National Post) 110:1: 71–73.

Rheaume, Manon, with Chantal Gilbert. 1993. *Manon: Alone in Front of the Net.* Toronto: Harper Collins.

Theberge, Nancy. 1995. Playing with the Boys. Manon Rheaume, Women's Hockey and the Struggle for Legitimacy. *Canadian Woman Studies/Cahiers de la Femme* 15:4: 37–41.

The Women's Hockey Web. 2010. "Manon Rheaume, Team Canada." http://www .whockey.com/profile/canada/rheaume.html.

Dorothy Richardson reacts as she rounds second base after blasting a solo home run in the sixth inning against Puerto Rico at the Olympics in 1996, which USA won 10-0. (AP Photo/Elise Amendol)

Dot Richardson (1961–)

"Student-athlete" is the term we use to describe individuals who participate in school sports. It gained currency in the 1950s when the National Collegiate Athletic Association, or NCAA, instituted its new athletic scholarship policy. Today, the label is commonly applied to high school, as well as college, athletes. The hyphen connecting the two words implies that athletes are getting an education while honing their physical skills in the gym and on the practice fields. Unfortunately, this isn't always the case. Sports, in school and out, are demanding more and more time and energy. Student-athletes must attend classes and find time to study amidst a weekly regimen of grueling two-hour practices, early morning sessions in the weight room, late team meetings, and frequent road trips. The NCAA has limited college coaches to demanding no more than twenty hours a week of a student-athlete's time, but the rule isn't strictly enforced. Critics of the excesses of school sports suggest that "athlete-student" better reflects the reality.

College coaches have been known to advise promising recruits to take easy courses to maintain their eligibility. Few major sport athletes enroll in pre-med or make the honor role. Young athletes often put "all their eggs in one basket" with a singular focus on playing professional sport. Yet, the prospect of accomplishing that goal is remote. The odds of any high school athlete playing professionally are 10,000–1. Of the 50,000 young men playing college football each year, about 300 will end up on the rosters of NFL teams. Even then, they face a career that averages less than four years. The chances of competing professionally are more daunting for young women who play sports. The Women's National Basketball Association includes a dozen teams, each with about fifteen athletes under contract, totaling fewer than two hundred positions. The six-team National Pro Fast-Pitch softball league was struggling to survive as this was being written. A few hundred more women make their living playing professional golf and tennis. The message is clear. Athletes cannot afford to neglect their education.

Dr. Dorothy Richardson made it to the top in her sport without compromising her educational goals. She was a student-athlete in the best sense of the term. The talented softball player won two Olympic gold medals and earned a medical degree. It wasn't always easy for her to balance the demands of international competition with the rigors of medical school and residency. But she had grown up with an indomitable spirit and determination that led to success in the classroom and on the playing fields.

CHILDHOOD

Dorothy Gay Richardson, called "Dot," was born in Orlando, Florida, on September 22, 1961. Her father, Ken, was a mechanic in the U.S. Air Force, so the family moved around a lot. Growing up, Dot lived in the Midwest, the

Southwest, and in England and Guam. The Richardsons were a sports-minded family. Dot's father had been an athlete and her mother, Joyce, a cheerleader. Dot's older sisters, Kathy and Laurie, and her brothers, Kenny and Lonnie, all played sports. Ken and Joyce Richardson recall that Dot was a very active child. As a baby, she crawled more than most. When Dot reached school age, she wanted to play football and baseball like her older brother Kenny. She recalls watching the 1968 Olympic Games on television at age six and dreaming about standing on the Olympic podium with a gold medal around her neck.

The Richardsons lived in England when Ken was stationed there, giving Dot the opportunity to play goalie on a local soccer team. Later, while living in New Mexico, nine-year-old Dot wanted to play football on the boys' team. She thought they would allow her to be the punter. Despite her superior kicking ability, she was rejected. At that time, girls in the United States weren't allowed to play organized sports with boys. Ken Richardson then retired from the Air Force, and the family moved back to Orlando. Ken began coaching youth baseball. He made Dot the bat girl on her brother's team so she could practice with the boys and develop her skills. But she couldn't play in games. Girls had to wait until 1974 before Little League was required to allow them on teams.

Dot's talent on the baseball field caught the attention of a Little League coach who came up with a scheme for her to play. He would put her on his team if she would cut her hair and assume a boy's name. She told him no. A short time later, Dot was approached by another man who had been watching her play. He introduced her to the coach of a women's softball team. Dot didn't know anything about softball, nor had she heard of the Union Park Jets who played in the Class A fast-pitch league. The Jets' coach offered the talented preteen a position on the team. All the other players were in their twenties. Despite the age discrepancy, Dot's parents gave her permission to play and bought her an official softball glove. She had to adjust to hitting underhand pitches and throwing a twelve-inch ball. Otherwise, the game was much like baseball. Dot soon became the team's starting third baseman and leadoff hitter. Only an injury kept her from playing in the All-Star game at the end of the season. The inveterate tomboy had fallen out of a tree and sliced her foot on a rusty sickle.

While Dot was recovering from her injury, her mother signed her up the for the major league Orlando Rebels instructional league. The Rebels were a fast-pitch softball team affiliated with the Amateur Softball Association, the national governing body. Dot was a year shy of the qualifying age for the program, but coach Marge Ricker bent the rules and let her in. The experience exposed Dot to valuable instruction and began what became an enduring relationship with Ricker. Dot was invited to be the Rebels' bat girl, and then in 1975, Ricker offered her a position on the team. At age thirteen, Dot Richardson became the youngest player in the history of women's major-league softball. The Rebels played teams in the Atlanta Coast League and in national tournaments. Dot traveled with the team on their motor bus and competed against some of the great women softball players of the era. The Rebels traveled as far as New England to play nationally ranked teams like the Raybestos Brakettes.

Fast-pitch is a much different game from slow-pitch softball, where the pitcher releases the ball with an arc at a distance of fifty feet from home plate. The latter is a high-scoring game often played in recreational settings, with lots of base runners and fielding action. In fast-pitch, the pitcher's mound is just forty-three feet from the plate, and the top pitchers use a windmill delivery throw at speeds above 70 mph. This is the equivalent of a 100 mph fastball in baseball thrown from sixty feet, six inches. The batter has .4 of a second to react. Moreover, seasoned softball pitchers master a repertoire of off-speed pitches to fool the batters. Thus, fast-pitch is a low scoring game dominated by pitching. It's not unusual for half of all the outs to be strikeouts. Dot Richardson proved to be an exceptional hitter for her age. She had the ability to gauge the trajectory and speed of pitches and make contact with the ball. More significantly, she had the desire and work ethic to perfect her natural talent.

By the time Dot was in junior high school, Title IX legislation—prohibiting gender discrimination in education programs—had been signed into law by President Richard Nixon. Schools were now required to sponsor girls' sports teams or allow girls to play on boys' teams. Dot had gone out for the boys' track team at her school. This led to some teasing by her schoolmates about being a tomboy. The popular girls were the cheerleaders; so Dot decided to try out for the cheerleading squad. Her failure to make the squad was a blessing in disguise. The multitalented athlete devoted her time to the girls' volleyball, basketball, and softball teams. Dot was voted the most valuable player in each sport and became the school's first girl to win the Outstanding Athlete of the Year award. She continued to play several sports in high school, notably softball. She played on the school's slow-pitch team, batting right-handed, and played fast-pitch in summer leagues, batting left-handed. Dot not only excelled at school sports but also was elected to the National Honor Society, the prestigious organization that recognizes students for their scholarship and leadership. She recalls that it was during a sophomore-year biology class while dissecting a cat that she first thought about becoming a medical doctor.

COLLEGE SOFTBALL

During Dot's senior year of high school, she was recruited by several colleges that fielded slow-pitch and fast-pitch softball teams. She was quite interested in UCLA, even though it was three thousand miles from home. The California university had won national titles in several women's sports, including softball. However, Dot ended up enrolling at Western Illinois University, which had offered her a full scholarship to play fast-pitch. The summer following high school graduation, Dot had the opportunity to play in the Pan American Games in Puerto Rico. Softball was a new event at the 1979 quadrennial games, an indication of the sport's growing popularity. She was the youngest member of the U.S. team. The seventeen-year-old shortstop hit a home run in the championship game to give the Americans the victory. She had won her first gold medal in international competition.

In late summer, Richardson headed north to the small town of Macomb, Illinois, to begin her freshman year of college. She played basketball, field hockey—a new sport for her—and softball under WIU Coach Kathy Veroni who had recruited her and two of her Rebel teammates. Richardson had an outstanding year, finishing with the highest batting average in the nation. The freshman infielder was nominated for the prestigious Broderick Award, given to the best woman collegiate athlete. Her success on the athletic fields didn't go to her head. She realized that softball wasn't a vocation but an avocation. In her spare time, she worked with the college physical therapist and continued to contemplate a career in medicine.

Following her success at Western Illinois, Dot Richardson received overtures from the coach at UCLA. That was the school where she really wanted to play softball. At the time under rules of the Association for Intercollegiate Athletics for Women, transfer athletes didn't have to "sit out" a year. After talking it over with her family, Richardson transferred to UCLA and enrolled in their pre-med program. The determined sophomore realized she had her work cut out for her, managing the demands of a challenging science curriculum and a major sport—actually two sports, as she made the junior varsity basketball team. Richardson continued to excel in softball. She led the team in hitting and received the Most Valuable Player Award. UCLA played in the national collegiate championship tournament all three years Richardson was there, as women's collegiate sports came under the jurisdiction of the National Collegiate Athletic Association. In 1982, UCLA won the first NCAA softball championship that was held. ESPN Network covered the final game. The Lady Bruins missed repeating as champions the following year when several team members came down with food poisoning during the tournament. Richardson was one of the sickest of the UCLA players, but she played anyway. In a crucial game, she hit a double and then threw up on second base. It was a minor embarrassment for the four-time collegiate All American. That August, Richardson joined the national team in Caracas, Venezuela, where they took the silver medal at the Pan American Games.

While at UCLA, Richardson returned to Florida during summers to play with the local Orlando Rebels. In 1981 the Rebels traveled to Stratford, Connecticut to compete in the Amateur Softball Association National Championship. The tournament favorites were the hometown Raybestos Brakettes. The

Brakettes, sponsored by a local brake-lining company, were one of fast-pitch softball's legendary teams. A CBS film crew arrived at the tournament to record a segment for *60 Minutes*, the popular television program. The Rebels upset the favorites to win the championship before a crowd of four thousand spectators. This was the Orlando team's first national title. When the team arrived back in Florida, hundreds of fans were waiting to greet them. Richardson received the Erv Lind Award for her scintillating defensive play in the tournament. (She would win this award six more times.) Winning the ASA championship tournament meant that the Rebels would represent the United States at the fifth quadrennial International Softball Federation (ISF) World Championships. The event was held in Taipei, Taiwan, the summer of 1982. Softball was a popular sport in Taiwan, and some 30,000 fans showed up for the tournament. The Americans finished a disappointing fourth, but Richardson was named to the "All World" team as shortstop. She had led all hitters with a .560 batting average.

The talented shortstop excelled in the field and at the plate, playing on ASA, NCAA, and national teams. She also excelled in the classroom. Richardson graduated from UCLA in 1984 with a dual concentration in kinesiology and pre-med. Adelphi University, located on Long Island, offered her a graduate assistant coaching position. She moved to New York and enrolled in a master's degree program in exercise physiology at Adelphi. While there, she played ball for the nearby Brakettes. Under coach Ralph Raymond, the Brakettes had won seventeen national championships. Richardson played previously for Raymond on the U.S. teams that won medals at the Pan American Games in 1979 and 1983. The two would be together again on the team that won the gold medal at the 1987 Pan Am Games in Indianapolis.

MEDICAL SCHOOL, INTERNATIONAL COMPETITION, AND THE OLYMPICS

Richardson completed her master's degree in 1988. Her unbending goal was to become a doctor. She was accepted into the medical program at the University of Louisville. Remarkably, she continued to play softball on weekends with the Brakettes while in medical school. She would fly to the Northeast, jump into an awaiting car at the airport, change into her uniform, head to the softball field, and then rush back to the airport after the final game for her return flight to Kentucky. The toll of the hectic schedule finally caught up with her while playing in the 1990 World Championships. She failed an important exam. Richardson was given the option of taking the test again or repeating the year of school. She chose the latter. The following year, Richardson cut back on softball and devoted herself to academics. This time, she passed. The following year, Richardson tried out for the 1991 Pan American team. She flew to the Olympic Training Center, but the lack of training time was a factor in her not making the team. She took the disappointment in stride and accompanied the team to Cuba to cheer from the stands as the Americans again took the gold medal. All the while, Richardson retained her dream of playing in the Olympics.

In June of 1991 the International Olympic Committee, or IOC, voted to include women's fast-pitch softball as a medal event at the 1996 Summer Games in Atlanta. (Men's baseball was to be introduced as a medal sport at the 1992 Olympics.) Softball players in the United States and abroad were elated by the decision. Dot Richardson's two dreams—to play in the Olympics and to become a doctor—were again set to overlap. She was finishing her medical education when the IOC announcement was made. Upon graduation, she planned to enter an orthopedic residency program at a Los Angeles hospital. Medical residency is where new MDs learn clinical skills under the supervision of fully licensed physicians. It's an intense regimen. Richardson would have to train for the upcoming Olympic trials between double shifts at the hospital that sometimes extended to eighty-plus hours a week. The amateur ballplayer not only was training on borrowed time, but had to borrow more than $100,000 to pay for medical school. Unlike Major League Baseball, there were no "bonus babies" in women's softball. Professional softball didn't exist at the time. Richardson received her medical degree in 1993. That year marked the beginning of her medical career and the initial tryouts for the Olympic team.

The United States Olympic Committee, or USOC, designated the Amateur Softball Association (ASA) as the organization responsible for forming the U.S. Olympic fast-pitch team. The Association had been a major force behind women's softball since the 1930s. Women had been playing versions of the game since the turn of the century, but it was the ASA that sponsored the first fast-pitch championship tournament in Chicago in 1933 and organized the industrial teams during the 1950s. By the time that softball became an Olympic sport, thousands of ASA-sponsored teams were playing slow pitch and fast pitch in every state in the nation. The International Softball Federation governed international softball competition. The ISF was sanctioned by the International Olympic Committee, or IOC, to qualify teams for the 1996 Olympic Games. Thus, Olympic softball was to be governed by an "alphabet soup" of organizations.

The selection process for the Olympics allowed that anyone could show up for the Level One camps. There the players were screened, and the top prospects invited to Level Two Camps. Some six hundred softball players would try out for the Olympic team. Since Richardson had been named to the ASA All-American team the year before, she was allowed to bypass the first two levels. The two-year selection process took place in conjunction with the twelfth U.S. Olympic Festival, the off-Olympic-year event, held in July of 1993. The festival included a women's softball tournament that showcased the top players. The tournament was followed by a Women's National Team Camp at the ASA facility in Oklahoma City. More than one hundred top players were screened at this camp. The competition for positions on the team was intense. Richardson had decided to take a year off from her medical residency to devote all her time to achieving her dream of playing in the Olympics.

The 1994 ISF World Championships held in Newfoundland determined five of the eight teams that would participate in the 1996 Olympic Games. The United States was guaranteed a spot as the host country. Richardson played on the U.S. team that took their third ISF gold medal in a row in early August. The following March, Richardson was back as a member of the team that took their third straight gold medal at the 1995 Pan American Games in Argentina. The Olympic team selection process was completed later that year during the final U.S. Olympic Festival. The fifteen team members and five alternates were announced by the ASA on Labor Day weekend. Richardson was one of the lucky few. The thirty-three-year-old infielder would be the senior member of the team. Once more, she would be playing for Ralph Raymond who was selected as the Olympic coach. Richardson would be competing against a host of talented, younger players. She realized she had to get in top shape and stay healthy. The busy medical resident installed a batting tee and net in her bedroom, lifted weights, and ran on the treadmill in her limited spare time.

Softball isn't considered a high-risk sport, but players do get injured. Pitchers are susceptible to overuse injuries aggravated by the windmill delivery. Concussions occur rarely in softball as batting helmets are required while at the plate and on the bases. The most common injuries during games come from sliding into bases or colliding with other players. Muscle strains and ankle sprains are common, but usually not serious. As in most women's sports, knee joints are particularly vulnerable, but account for less than 10% of the injuries to softball players. Dot Richardson had experienced few serious, long-lasting injuries through her twenty-year career. She had suffered a severe hamstring tear as a teenager. During the tryouts for the 1996 Olympic Games, she hyper-extended her neck while batting. She played through the injury and even hit a homerun in her last at-bat at the trials. Then following the Olympic tryouts, Richardson ruptured a disc in her back, causing weakness in her right arm. She spent twelve days in traction and had to work with a trainer for several months before the arm completely healed. But she recovered in time for the pre-Olympic Tour.

Team USA went on a three-and-a-half-month, coast-to-coast tour with the goal of honing their skills and melding as a group. The tour also provided an opportunity to promote Olympic softball. The players made appearances at local shopping malls, meeting fans and signing autographs. Dot Richardson recalls that the schedule was exhausting at times. On the field, the Olympians dominated their opponents, winning fifty-nine of sixty exhibition games against regional all-star and college teams. The final game was played on the Fourth of July. The travel-weary women realized that the level of competition at the Atlanta Games would be much more challenging than what they had faced so far.

The U.S. softball team arrived in Atlanta in mid-July for the opening ceremony of the Olympics. Former heavyweight boxing champion Muhammad Ali had the honor of lighting the Olympic Torch. President Bill Clinton was among the crowd of spectators as the athletes from nearly two hundred nations paraded around the stadium. Olympic softball games weren't played in Atlanta but at Golden Park, a hundred miles to the southwest in Columbus, Georgia. The city of Columbus had spent some $2 million to renovate the historic ball park that had once been home to a minor league baseball team. Babe Ruth, Mickey Mantle, and Hank Aaron had played there. Now it was the women's turn to make history. NBC would be showing nightly highlights of their games. Because of the tournament location, the U.S. softball team didn't live in the Olympic Village but were housed at Fort Benning, an Army post fifteen minutes from the stadium. Following the opening ceremonies in Atlanta, Team USA headed for Columbus. The women arrived at 4 AM. They had less than twenty-four hours to prepare for their first official game.

Olympic softball tournaments use a round robin format in which the eight teams play each other in the qualifier round. The four teams coming out of this round with the best records move into the semifinals. The two teams losing in the semifinal round play for the bronze medal, followed by the gold-medal game between the two winners. The U.S. women beat Puerto Rico 10-0 in the opening game of the tournament. Richardson got the first hit and the first home run in Olympic softball history. The Americans went on to beat the Netherlands and Japan in the next two games. Richardson hit another home run against the Dutch. The following rain-delayed game against Canada lasted until 2:30 AM but the U.S. team came away with a victory. The fatigued U.S. women lost the following day against Australia in a disputed incident where a player didn't touch home plate after hitting a home run. But the U.S. team won their next game against China to finish the qualifier round with a 6-1 record. This was a big win for the Americans, as China was the last team to beat them in international competition prior to the Games.

The four teams going into the semifinals were the United States, Australia, China, and Japan. The Americans beat China 1-0, in a ten-inning semifinal match. Australia defeated Japan in the other semifinal game but then lost to China in the bronze medal game. This meant that the U.S. team and China were to play each other for the third time in the gold medal game. More than 8,700 fans filled the stands at Golden Park to watch the historic contest. Richardson hit a home run over the right-field fence in the bottom of the third with a runner on base. The Chinese coaches protested the call, claiming that the ball went foul; but the umpires' decision was upheld after a ten-minute argument. The U.S. team scored another run in the third and went on to win the game and the Olympic gold medal. Following the final strikeout, the victorious American women piled on top of one another in celebration, then gathered their composure for the ritual handshake with the Chinese players. Richardson's family and her former coach Marge Ricker were in the crowd to share in the victory.

The Olympic hero had scant time to celebrate. Following the medal ceremony and a late-night party with family and friends, Richardson boarded the next plane to Los Angeles to resume her duties at the USC medical center. When she walked through the metal detector at the airport at Atlanta her gold medal set off the alarm. She lifted up the medal and the crowd clapped and cheered. The L.A. hospital staff surprised her with another appreciation ceremony upon her return. The USC marching band was there along with eight hundred well-wishers. Richardson made time to tour the children's ward of the hospital, sharing her medal with the young patients. Things soon got back to the normal routine. Richardson completed her five-year residency in orthopedic surgery in 1997. She was now Dorothy Richardson, M.D., a certified bone and joint specialist with an interest in sports medicine. Her teammates began referring to her as "Dr. Dot."

BECOMING A DOCTOR WHILE PREPARING FOR THE 2000 OLYMPICS

Richardson teamed up with *Sports Illustrated* writer Don Yeager to tell her story in *Living the Dream* (1997). In the autobiography, she comments that one of her favorite Hollywood films was *Field of Dreams*, the nostalgic fantasy about early-twentieth-century baseball players. She identified with the character Archie "Moonlight" Graham, a real-life ballplayer who appeared in one major league game in 1905 before quitting baseball to enter medical school. Richardson could empathize with the ballplayer's agonizing decision to give up something he loved. Unlike Dr. Archibald Graham, Dot Richardson found a way to pursue both her dreams: softball and medicine.

Dot Richardson, the softball player, learned what it is like to be a well-recognized sports celebrity following the Olympics. She was invited to appear on late-night talk shows and to participate in a parade at Walt Disney World. In October, she threw out the first pitch at a World Series game. She was then invited to the White House by the First Family for a ceremony in the Rose Garden. For a while, Richardson wrote a column for *Sports Illustrated for Women*. The Olympic victory also opened opportunities for commercial endorsements. Richardson signed contracts with several sporting goods companies including Reebok and endorsed a soft drink. She hired Tom McCarthy, a former NHL hockey player, to serve as her agent.

LIFE AS A MEDICAL STUDENT

Dot Richardson somehow found time to compete in softball while attending medical school. This is an impressive accomplishment considering the rigors of medical education. Medical school in the United States typically consists of four years of study followed by three or more years of residency, during which time the novice M.D. undergoes more clinical training under the supervision of fully licensed physicians.

Most doctors comment that the first two years of medical school were the hardest. The hours of the day are long and jammed with responsibilities. Lectures begin as early as 7 AM. Attending classes, labs, and meetings make up much of the student's day. Evenings are spent in the library or at the study desk. Exams are frequent and challenging. Heavy academic assignments mean that bedtime often comes after midnight. Medical residents are required to make rounds and sit in on patient consultations, evaluate patients, interpret medical records, evaluate lab test results, and participate in medical team meetings. Residents may be on call nights or weekends.

It's common for medical students to feel physically and mentally exhausted. They find it helpful to schedule some relaxing recreation or exercise to cope with stress and maintain their health. Dr. Jordan Metzl, who later wrote a guide for parents of young athletes, competed in triathlons while in he was in medical school. He and Dot Richardson were exceptional. Most medical students have neither the time nor the energy to engage in highly competitive sports.

Other athletes have enjoyed successful medical careers. Famous pediatrician Benjamin Spock, author of *Baby and Child Care*, won a gold medal in rowing at the 1924 Olympics while a student at Yale University. He went on to graduate from Yale's medical school.

Softball gained in popularity following the Americans' gold medal performance at the Atlanta games. By 1998, some 7.5 million girls between the ages of seven and seventeen were playing the game. Richardson founded the Dot Richardson Softball Association whose purpose was to provide instruction for coaches and young players. The top adult softball teams were finally getting some corporate backing. A women's fast-pitch professional league formed with six teams playing in the Southeast. Richardson didn't play for a professional team, and she was dropped as a member of the national team in 1998. Instead, she played for the California Commotion in nearby Woodland Hills in 1997, 1998, and 1999. She led the team to three ASA National Championships and made the All America team at shortstop.

Dot Richardson now set her sights on playing in the 2000 Olympics. She was invited to attend the January training camp in San Diego. Coming off a scheduled twenty-four-hour shift at the hospital, she missed her flight and had to make the two-and-a-half-hour drive from Los Angeles. She had gone thirty hours without sleep. It was a familiar problem: trying to juggle a medical career and a softball career. She had the good luck to be on vacation from her medical duties during the important Women's National Team Festival that determined which players would travel with the U.S. national team to Japan that summer. Remarkably, Richardson was able to squeeze a social life into her packed schedule. She began dating future husband Bob Pinto, a softball instructor, whom she met in L.A. Richardson's finances were now on more secure ground. Her modest salary as resident physician was enhanced by a number of commercial endorsements reaching the six-figure range. Dot also found time to schedule some speaking engagements.

Richardson returned as a member of the national team. That July, the American women won the gold medal at the Pan American Games in Winnipeg, Canada. This was Richardson's fifth trip to the Pan Am Games. The 1999 Games featured the longest doubleheader in international softball history: a twelve-hour affair, interrupted by rain, in which the Americans prevailed. The U.S. team dominated the competition, outscoring opponents 83-1. They tallied their forty-second consecutive win dating back to the 1987 Games. Richardson also played in the sixth annual Canada Cup. The sixteen-team tournament included five Olympic qualifiers. Team USA won the gold, and Richardson was voted Most Inspirational Player.

A major development took place in 1999. The IOC changed the rule banning professional softball players from competing in the Olympics. This meant that Richardson would have to compete for a position on the 2000 Olympic team with Crystl Bustos, the power-hitting shortstop who played in the fledgling Women's Professional Softball League. The twenty-year-old Mexican American was voted the most valuable player on the WPSL Orlando Wahoos in 1998. Bustos was one of a bevy of talented young players who vied for positions on the team to represent the U.S. at the upcoming summer games in Sydney, Australia. As it turned out, both Crystl and Dot made the team with Dot shifting to second base. She had just a few months to get comfortable with her new fielding position. Richardson, who would celebrate her thirty-ninth birthday during the games, was the oldest member of the team and served as team captain.

The 2000 Olympics in Sydney kicked off in mid-September. The late opening date was to compensate for the climate in the Southern Hemisphere. September in Australia is considered early spring, a good time to begin playing baseball and softball by American standards. The U.S. softball team relished the opportunity to take on the Australians who had beaten them twice since the Atlanta Games when they won the bronze medal. Softball had become quite popular in Australia since they hosted, and won, the first ISF Women's World Championship in 1965. Softball was played in all the states and territories and at all levels of the Australian educational system. In the United States, Olympic softball had gained in popularity. Team USA's games in Sydney were to be televised by MSNBC and NBC networks.

The U.S. women won their first game in Sydney against Canada with Dot and Cristl both hitting home runs. Teammate Lori Harrigan pitched the first no-hitter in the sport's brief Olympic history. The Americans then lost an extra-inning game, 2-1, against Japan. The next day, the weak-hitting U.S. team lost another extra-inning game to China. Then in yet another long game, they lost to the Australians on a two-run home run in the bottom of the thirteenth. The favorites to win the 2000 Olympics had dug themselves into a hole. The American women had to win their next two games to advance to the medal round. They came through with consecutive victories over New Zealand and Italy. Richardson celebrated her birthday by driving in a run against the New Zealanders. The U.S. team finished the qualifying round with five wins and three losses, and faced the three teams who had beaten them: Japan, Australia, and China. They won against China in a semi-final game and then beat the Aussies to advance to the gold medal game. Richardson had the only RBI in the game against the host team.

Against all odds, the American women had made it to the championship game against the undefeated Japanese. Coach Raymond chose star pitcher Lisa Fernandez to pitch her second game in a row. The medal game turned into a pitchers' duel, tied 1-1 at the end of the regulation seven innings. The Americans scored the winning run in the eighth. Team USA had made an amazing comeback to win another Olympic gold. Dot Richardson had only five hits and three RBIs in twenty-eight appearances at the plate during the Olympics. It wasn't among her best performances, but she and her teammates arrived home as Olympic champions.

Following the close of the Olympic Games, Richardson returned to Los Angeles to begin a fellowship in sports medicine at the Kerlan-Jobe Orthopaedic Clinic. While there, she worked with athletes from the Los Angeles Dodgers and the Los Angeles Lakers. She had plans to open her own medical center in Florida. In the interim, she joined ESPN Network's broadcast team covering Women's Professional Softball League games. The struggling WPSL folded in 2001. There would be no more women's professional softball for three years until National Pro Fast-Pitch was initiated in 2004.

RETIRING FROM PROFESSIONAL SOFTBALL

Dot Richardson didn't play for the American team at the 2004 Olympic Games in Athens. Instead, she did play-by-play commentary for NBC. She retired from competitive softball in 2005. In July of that year, the International Olympic Committee voted to drop softball—and baseball—from the Olympic program for the 2012 London Games. The Eurocentric IOC argued that the women's sport was played competitively, by and large, only in the Americas and Asia. No European teams had medaled in the three previous Olympics. The U.S. domination of the sport—having taken three gold medals through the 2004 Games—may have worked against them in the end. Ironically, Team USA would lose the gold medal game to the Japanese at the 2008 Games in Beijing. Hope remains that softball will be reinstituted into the Olympics if the game can be successfully promoted globally. Currently, some forty European nations are playing softball as members of the International Softball Federation. The sport has spread to Africa where it is now played throughout the continent by ISF-affiliated teams from Tunisia in the north to the Republic of South Africa.

Dot Richardson responded to the IOC's decision to cancel softball by creating the ProFastpitch X-treme Tour which provides current and former college softball players in the United States an opportunity to showcase their talent. She continues to serve as Tour Commissioner. A year earlier, professional softball in the United States was reborn in the National Pro Fastpitch League with support from Major League Baseball. The women's league opened with six teams. NPF teams played each other in league competition as well as exhibition games against ASA "major-league" teams and foreign clubs from as far away as Australia. However, the NPF drew crowds of only a couple thousand per game and paid minuscule salaries to the players. Consequently, National Pro Fastpitch has struggled to survive. The league was completing its 2010 season as this was being written.

Richardson continues to pursue her dual interests in sports and medicine as Medical Director of the National Training Center in Clermont, Florida. The Center, founded in 2001, offers physical therapy and athletic training facilities, and conducts research into athletic performance. The medical staff specializes in shoulder injuries. The retired softball player and orthopedist continues to sponsor the Dot Richardson Softball Association, a non-profit organization that assists coaches and athletes in learning more about the game. In the summer of 2008, Dot traveled to Beijing, China to watch the U.S. team compete in what would be the concluding Olympic softball tournament.

Dot Richardson and Bob Pinto married in 2001. The couple currently resides in Clermont near Orlando, Florida. Bob, a local businessman, joins with Dot in promoting softball in the area. The couple also is active in World Vision, a children's relief agency. Richardson organizes softball clinics and does some public speaking in her spare time. She addressed the Republican National Convention in 1996. President George W. Bush appointed her Vice Chair of the President's Council on Physical Fitness and Sports.

Dot Richardson completed her three-decade-long softball career with an impressive record of accomplishments. She was the youngest player ever to compete in major league softball in the United States. In 1982, she played on the UCLA softball team that won the NCAA title. Richardson was a member of the gold medal team at the Pan American Games in 1979, 1987, 1995, and 1999, in addition to winning two Olympic gold medals. She also played on gold medal teams at the 1986, 1990, and 1994 ISF World Championships. Notably, several of these remarkable accomplishments were achieved while she was pursuing a medical degree.

The outstanding softball player has garnered a collection of honors and awards over the years. Richardson was selected an ASA All-American fifteen times and was a three-time NCAA All-American. She was inducted into the UCLA Hall of Fame in 1996. Richardson was named Most Valuable Player in the Major Fast Pitch National Championship four times and was voted Olympic Sportswoman of the Year on four occasions. In 1996, she was selected the USOC Athlete of the Year. The following year, she won the Babe Didrikson Zaharias Award as Female Athlete of the Year. She was inducted into the National Softball Hall of Fame in 2006. The Women's Sports Foundation bestowed the prestigious Flo Hyman Memorial Award on Dot Richardson for her commitment to excellence both on and off the field.

FURTHER READING

"About Dot." 2000. Dot Richardson.com. http://dotrichardson.co.2000olympics.html.

Babb, Ron. 1997. *Etched in Gold: The Story of America's First Ever Olympic Gold Medal Softball Team*. Indianapolis, IN: Masters Press.

Forkos, Heather. 2001. *Dorothy "Dot" Richardson* (Women Who Win). Philadelphia: Chelsea House.

Friedell, Nick. 2008. "Dot Richards discusses the future of softball." Yahoo Sports. Aug. 27: http://sports.yahoo.com/olympics/blog/fourth_place_medal/post/Dot-Richardson-discusses-the-future-of-softball?urn=oly-103786.

Louden, Susan. 2005. Sharing the Gold: Olympian & NTC's Dot Richardson. *Texture*, June: 10–11.

Murphy, Austin. 1994. Dot Richardson. *Sports Illustrated*, July 18: http:// sports illustrated.cnn.com/vault/article/magazine/MAG1005413/index.htm.

Richardson, Dot, with Don Yeager. 1997. *Living the Dream*. New York: Kensington Books.

Dawn Riley, when she was head of the America's Cup team, taken in Auckland, New Zealand. (AP Photo/Bob Grieser)

Dawn Riley (1964–)

Throughout most of history sailing remained an "all-boys club." Although men frequently named ships after women—eminently Christopher Columbus' flagship *Santa Maria*—and carved feminine figureheads on their prows, mariners nurtured the superstition that females on board brought bad luck. Women routinely were forbidden on military vessels. Merchant ship captains occasionally allowed officers' wives on board and women were accommodated as passengers on ships, but the actual craft of sailing was restricted to men. A few daring women disguised themselves as men to crew on ships, but sailing remained a male enclave. The culture of sailing ships is captured in the sea novels of Joseph Conrad. The author, who served in the merchant navy, portrays an insular world for the testing of honor, loyalty, and physical courage; a cauldron of initiation where men were men, and women were absent.

The reigning prejudice against women carried over to the sport of sailing. Yacht clubs customarily excluded women; the New York Yacht Club didn't admit women as full-fledged members until 1985. Notwithstanding fraternal chauvinism, a handful of adventurous women were sailing on racing yachts by the late nineteenth century. During the course of the next century, women would make their mark in the sport. In 1924, the progressive Boston Yacht Club sponsored the first American women's sailing championship, the Holder Cup (later the Adams Cup) that became an annual event. The Women's National Sailing Association was founded in Massachusetts in 1933. Across the Pacific, two women, Jenny Tate and Dagmar O'Brien, sailed with their husbands in the 1946 Sydney to Hobart Race. In 1975, an all-women crew competed in "the Hobart." Meanwhile, their American sisters were sailing more often and gaining recognition. The North American Yacht Racing Union established the Rolex Yachtswoman of the Year Award in 1961. Sailboat racing was becoming popular with women across hemispheres. The Modern Olympics initiated the 470 (dinghy) class for women at the 1988 Summer Games in Seoul, South Korea.

The most prestigious sailing competition for large boats is the America's Cup. The Cup Race dates back to 1851 when the schooner *America*, backed by a group of wealthy gambling men in the New York Yacht Club, took the Cup from the British. The two-foot-high silver pitcher endures as the oldest trophy in sport. The NYYC assumed the central role in staging the renamed America's Cup races. For over a century, the America's Cup endured as a sporting fraternity for blue bloods in blue blazers. Notable Cup racers included Harold Vanderbilt, great-grandson of railroad tycoon Cornelius Vanderbilt, and media mogul Ted Turner. Only a handful of women have competed in the Cup since American sportswoman Hope Goddard Iselin crewed on husband Oliver's yacht, defeating the British challenger *Shamrock* in the 1899 Cup Race. Nearly a century later, Dawn Riley joined the crew of the *America*[3] ("America cubed") in the 1992 America's Cup. She returned as captain of the first women's crew to compete in the Cup trials in 1995.

CHILDHOOD

Dawn Riley was born in Detroit on July 21, 1964. She was the eldest of three children of Chuck Riley, a computer executive, and his wife Prudence. Dawn grew up in the Detroit suburbs, sailing with her parents on nearby Lake St. Clair. She was introduced to the family sailboat the day she was baptized in the Catholic Church. Dawn underwent another baptism of sorts while in elementary school. Her father tossed her overboard into the frigid waters of Lake Huron with one oar and let her rescue herself. It was a lesson in self-reliance. Chuck Riley taught his daughter how to sail on the Great Lakes and during summer cruises to Canada. When Dawn was in the eighth grade, the Riley family took an extended cruise on their thirty-six-foot yacht across the Great Lakes, down the Atlantic coast, and on to the Caribbean Islands and back. Dawn, her sister Dana, and seven-year-old Todd were pulled out of school for a year and tutored on the boat. It was during this excursion that Dawn fell in love with sailing.

By age thirteen, Dawn was ready and eager to race sailboats. She took part in a regatta on Lake St. Clair aboard a thirty-five-foot cruiser, an experience that whetted her enthusiasm. The Rileys didn't belong to a yacht club, so Dawn joined the North Star Sail Club and became a commodore in the club's junior sailing program. She honed her skills with the Sea Scouts, a program sponsored by the Boy Scouts of America that provides opportunities for adolescents to sail. Dawn was an active teenager and all-around athlete. At L'Anse Creuse High School, she was involved in several extracurricular activities. She played tuba in the marching band, served as sports editor of the school newspaper, was a member of the swim team, and captain of the track team. She set a school record in the discus.

Dawn's parents divorced during her senior year of high school. This left less money for college. Dawn paid her way by working in boatyards, unloading trucks, and at other odd jobs. She moved into a basement apartment in Grosse Pointe, attended nearby Macomb Community College, and then enrolled in Michigan State University. At MSU she was captain of the coed sailing team. She graduated in 1987 with a degree in advertising. The twenty-three-year-old found it difficult to land a job in her major and turned to sailing as a prospective career. Dawn recalls never having held a nine-to-five job following college. She toured the East Coast Racing Circuit for a while and then worked on the Florida-based Southern Ocean Racing Circuit, grooming herself as a "jack-of-all trades." To break into the male-dominated vocation, Dawn learned everything from how to repair marine engines to public relations. She made sandwiches in the galley, cleaned winches, and did whatever it took to gain experience. The aspiring sailor was rewarded with a position on the crew of the fifty-footer *Gem* in the initial Key West Regatta in 1988. She dreamed of racing someday in the America's Cup.

AN ALL-WOMEN TEAM RACING ROUND THE WORLD

Dawn Riley heard about British yachter Tracy Edwards' plans to assemble an all-women crew for the 32,000-mile Whitbread Round the World Race (now the Volvo Ocean Race), and she faxed her résumé to England. The event, held every three years, typically starts in Europe with the first leg crossing the Equator to Africa or South America, and then around the southern tips of the three continents circling Antarctica, and back to the starting point. Riley was invited to join Edwards' crew and flew to Southampton the summer of 1989. It was a novel experience for her to crew with women. Riley had gotten used to being the only female on board. The *Maiden*'s crew worked with a physical trainer to get in shape for the grueling race. They also spent longs hours on the dock preparing the boat. Edwards sent Riley to diesel training school. Large sailboats rely on diesel engines to motor in and out of port, and in emergencies. The mechanical skills would look good on her résumé. Riley rejoined the crew in time to sail to Ireland, a rehearsal for the main event. They had come together as a team and were ready to race.

In September, a score of yachts ranging from fifty-one to eighty-four feet assembled in Southampton Bay for the start of the Whitbread. The first all-women entry generated a good deal of media interest. Skipper Tracy Edwards not only was an experienced sailor but a superb promoter. Through her acquaintance with the King of Jordan, she obtained £800,000 ($1,250,000) from Royal Jordanian Airlines to finance the project. The Duchess of York, wife of Prince Andrew, was invited to christen the *Maiden*. Following the ceremonies, the fleet sailed out of the harbor and headed south to the coast of Uruguay on the first of six legs.

Riley's assignment was to serve as watch captain on the *Maiden*. She relayed messages from the skipper and saw that each watch crew was on deck and in their assigned positions. The fifty-eight-foot sloop was smaller than many of the competitors. The women had their work cut out for them. The Whitbread exposes boats to pounding winds and towering waves for days on end. The consequences of raging seas and turbulent weather can shatter equipment, fray nerves, and endanger lives. The 1989 race would be remembered for a burial at sea. A sailor on the British yacht *Creighton's Naturally* was swept overboard in a storm in the Southern Ocean and expired from hypothermia.

The *Maiden*'s crew braved the elements without serious mishap, and completed the round-the-world race, winning two of the five legs and finishing second in their class overall. The women demonstrated that they could compete with men in the demanding trans-ocean marathon. Yacht racing wasn't a high profile sport in the United States, but the women's showing in the Whitbread caught the attention of the American news and entertainment media. Riley was invited to appear on David Letterman's late-night show in June to talk about her sailing adventures.

WORKING HARD AS CAPTAIN

The following January, Riley was offered a tryout with millionaire yachtsman Bill Koch's San Diego–based campaign to enter a boat in the 1992 America's Cup. The Cup Race is distinct from *point-to-point* races like the Whitbread and Sydney to Hobart. The America's Cup is held on a *closed course* laid out with legs marked by buoys a few miles apart. Another major distinction is the makeup of the competitors. Fleet races like the Whitbread include a number of boats of various sizes racing within classes. (The general rule is that a good big boat will beat a good little boat; thus, the class distinctions.) The America's Cup consists of a series of match races between paired yachts. Closed-course races rely on elaborate rules covering right-of-way. The sophisticated strategies employed rival those of a chess match. Races often are lost through tactical errors, as the boats and crews are evenly matched. Whether navigating oceans or circumnavigating buoys, sailboat racing is an all-consuming mental challenge.

The America's Cup, by tradition, is contested by yachts representing different nations. Both the defender (the previous winner) and the challengers hold a series of preliminary races that determine which yacht will race for the Cup. The 1992 America's Cup trials provided the occasion to breach the implacable gender barrier in yachting's most prestigious competition. Bill Koch, skipper and patron of the *America³*, recruited Dawn Riley to join the active crew in the Defender Series. She was assigned to the "pit," the center of activity on deck. This demanding position entails hauling halyards (the lines that hoist sails) and responsibility for trimming the headsail. As the lone woman on the *America³*, Riley received favorable media attention, but not all of the crew were accepting. A few of the men made uncomplimentary remarks, and one crew member resorted to underhanded tactics in an attempt to keep her off the boat. Following the competition, the spirited five-foot-six-inch blond walked up to her antagonist and threw a punch that landed. Riley wasn't selected to crew in the Cup finals to her disappointment, but she had made a lasting impression on Koch with her consummate skills, work ethic, and assertiveness. The *America³* went on to win the Cup. Dawn Riley had played an essential role in the boat's success.

Following the America's Cup, Riley competed in national and international races. She took first place in the Santa Maria Cup Race, a women's match race sponsored by the Eastport Yacht Club of Annapolis, and went on to win the 1992 Women's Cup race in Portofino, Italy. The peripatetic sailor spent the following years living out of a duffel bag, traveling from one race to another. She resided, now and then, in Michigan, California, and Auckland, New Zealand.

In 1993, Riley was presented with another opportunity to sail around the world; this time as skipper of an all-women's crew on the Whitbread yacht *U.S. Women's Challenge*. She was offered the position in a phone call to her home in Michigan from a representative of the firm that owned the boat. They asked her to take over as captain of the splintered crew whose previous skipper withdrew following a contentious first leg of the race. It is not unheard of for boats to change skippers during ocean races, but this had been a factious parting. Riley was given twenty-four hours to consider the offer, and decided to take it. She cancelled her plans to compete in the Steinlager Logan Cup in New Zealand, and flew to Uruguay to join the reshuffled crew preparing for the 7,500-mile leg to Australia. She arrived in the coastal town of Punta del Este at the eleventh hour with just enough time to take the vessel on a brief practice run before taking command. Normally, it takes several weeks of sailing to become familiar with a boat's idiosyncrasies. Riley wouldn't enjoy this luxury.

Some of the crew members on the *U.S. Women's Challenge* resented a fresh skipper being thrust upon them in mid-race. Three had resigned and were replaced. Literature conveys tales of mutiny, real and imagined, from Captain Bligh on the *Bounty* to Captain Queeg on the *Caine*. This crew had already run off one captain. Riley had to prove herself as the new team leader. Crewing on a yacht is a team sport in every sense. Operations on deck are precisely choreographed and have to be carried out under the most adverse conditions. Boat crews run through drills just like football teams. Everyone on board must execute their individual assignments with precision. During long races, crews are together in close quarters day and night. The crew on the Whitbread yacht was a diverse group representing half a dozen nationalities. They had to get along with each other and accept the skipper's authority without reservation. Riley gave serious thought to which command style she would employ with the reassembled crew. She opted for a laissez faire approach as she came on board, but by the time they approached Australia she freely exerted her authority.

The twelve crew members under Riley's command spent the few days before the restart of the race checking, refitting, and repairing the equipment on the sixty-four-foot boat. This would be the routine following each of the first five legs of the race. The women stuffed the limited allowance of clothing into their duffel bags, respectful of on-board weight limits, and loaded their all-weather gear. Riley packed her stuffed gremlin Gizmo into her bag for good luck, and took the last shower she would enjoy for a month. She received an encouraging fax from Tracy Edwards, her skipper in the 1989–90 Whitbread Race. Now it was Riley's turn to learn what it's like to captain a crew over several months on the high seas.

The skills required to command racing yachts are formidable. They encompass a general knowledge of seamanship as well as the mastery of racing strategy and tactics. Add to these a minimal competence in meteorology, mathematics, mechanics, and joinery (woodworking). Successful skippers must exhibit mental acuity, visual perception, leadership ability, opportunism, and determination. The stress of being at the helm for hours on end

THE PHYSICALITY OF YACHT RACING

Crewing on racing yachts can be as physically demanding as playing football or climbing mountains. All of these outdoor sports are pursued in extreme weather. While football players perform on level ground and climbers conquer a vertical plane, yacht racers perform their tasks on a surface that is rolling, pitching, and yawing—often violently during a squall. And in yacht racing unlike most sports, there are no timeouts. Ted Turner once "manned" the helm for thirteen hours straight during a race.

The entire crew of a racing yacht is engaged during every maneuver. The winch grinders have a particularly tough job. They repeatedly bend over the apparatus and rapidly crank the handles on each change of course to reset the sails. They do this until their shoulders ache with fatigue. Everyone on the boat takes a beating. At the end of a race, crew members' hands are swollen from hauling wet lines; fingers are chafed from handling the rough sails; elbows and knees are sorely bruised after scampering across the deck and tripping over objects and fellow crew members amidst the organized disorder.

Crew members must be tough-minded and stay physically fit. Women are equal to men in resilience and endurance, but are at a disadvantage when it comes to upper body strength. Dawn Riley trained intensely for the America's Cup trials. By race day, she could bench press 125 pounds, three sets of ten repetitions.

is unmatched in sport. A skipper has to be hyper-alert to the conditions of the sea, the weather, one's competitors, and any other boats in view—all the while staying attuned to conditions on the vessel one is sailing. An obsessed Ted Turner was known to remain at the helm for a dozen hours. During that interval, the helmsman makes hundreds of decisions. There's no latitude to allow one's mind to wander. The crew of the *U.S. Women's Challenge* took turns commanding the helm in more reasonable four-hour shifts.

Some of the problems facing the Whitbread yacht were beyond Riley's control. As the crew prepared to leave the east coast of South America, the boat still hadn't acquired a major sponsor, and the venture remained underfunded. U.S. corporations weren't sponsoring the sport of sailing in the mid-1990s as they were golf and tennis. The yacht's management team had to look elsewhere for corporate support. The fact that this was the only women's crew competing in the Whitbread was viewed as a marketing plus. The syndicate hoped to pick up a sponsor by the time the boat reached Australia. On November 13, the multinational fleet of ten Whitbread 60s and four Maxis (eighty footers) sailed out of Punta del Este harbor in the rain, and headed east toward the Australian port of Fremantle. The *U.S. Women's Challenge* was one of the older Whitbread 60s. Riley realized she wasn't skippering the fastest boat in their class.

During the long voyage to Australia, the new skipper corresponded with her boyfriend, New Zealand sailor and boat builder Barry McKay. Dawn and Barry had met during the previous Whitbread. The couple purchased a 140-year-old house on the North Island that they were refurbishing in their spare time, with plans for a future together. However, their busy racing schedules kept them apart for months at a time. Barry currently was preparing for his own round-the-world race on the crew of a ninety-two-foot catamaran, a multihulled boat. Their goal was to break the record for nonstop circumnavigation of the globe known as the Jules Verne Challenge (a reference to Verne's novel *Around the World in Eighty Days*). McKay was an experienced Whitbread sailor, familiar with the type of yacht that Riley was skippering. She needed a crash course and routinely picked his brain via shipboard communication. There was every expectation that the women's crew would encounter extreme conditions in the Southern Ocean. Communication was crucial in an emergency.

Modern racing yachts are fitted with an array of high-tech electronics. The essential navigation instruments are enhanced by onboard computers and state-of-the-art communication equipment. The *U.S. Women's Challenge* had a marine VHF radio and an SSB (single side-band) radio with a range of several thousand miles. It also had satellite communication capability. The navigation station on the boat received a variety of data including weather faxes and updates on their position and those of other boats in the race. Dawn and Barry would fax each other to stay in touch. The other crew members likewise corresponded with friends and family en route. The yacht might be isolated geographically hundreds of miles from the nearest shoreline, but it was connected to the outside world as long as the electronic equipment functioned and the batteries held out. On-board "engineer" Gloria Borrego, a former NASCAR pit crew member, had the responsibility of keeping the boat's mechanical equipment operating. The sophisticated electronics offered a more daunting challenge.

The crew settled into the assigned watch system of four hours on deck and four hours below. This meant no eight hours of uninterrupted sleep. Nor would there be much fresh food. The sailors subsisted on freeze-dried rations for the most part while at sea. Meals were served at watch changes. An onboard desalinator that converted salt water into fresh supplemented the thirty-gallon tank of drinking water on board.

As the yacht sailed south of forty degrees latitude, the weather turned freezing cold. The crew put on layers of underclothing and donned ski goggles in order to see through the icy spray. Occasionally, crew members were hurled across the deck by the violent motion of the boat in high seas. They worked the rigging tethered to safety harnesses to avoid being swept overboard into the frigid waters. The boom (horizontal spar) on the mainsail presented another hazard. Deckhands learn to duck when "coming about" or suffer bruises and fractures. The deck of a racing yacht can be a violent setting during gale-force winds. Fortunately, the boat's crew included a medical doctor.

The hopes of finishing first in their class (Whitbread 60s) on the second leg of the race were dashed when the mainsail toppled and ripped apart. This meant having to re-stitch the nearly impenetrable Kevlar sail cloth in the freezing cold while wearing rubber gloves. A few days later, the mainsail was torn again by a 40 mph gust of wind. It took the crew most of a day to sew it back together before they could rehoist it. The good news was that a new sponsor was coming "on board" when they reached Australia. After a month at sea, the crew sailed into the port of Fremantle in mid-December. They finished the leg a disappointing seventh place but had come together as a team.

Heineken, the Dutch brewing company, was the new sponsor. The *Women's Challenge* was hauled out of the water for refitting and re-branding. The boat was christened the *Heineken* and painted the sponsor's colors. In the interim, Dawn was flown to England by the management team to promote their campaign. Barry was there to meet her, and the couple enjoyed a brief time together over the holidays. He surprised Dawn by formally proposing to her at the jewelry counter at Harrods Department Store in London. Dawn, in high spirits, flew back to Fremantle the first of January to prepare for the next leg of the Whitbread.

On the ninth of January, the women boarded the rechristened yacht and headed around the southern coast of Australia into the stormy Tasman Sea, bound for Auckland on the northeast coast of New Zealand. A few days out, the *Heineken's* SatCom, the satellite communications device, temporarily stopped working; otherwise, the voyage was uneventful. They reached Auckland Bay at sunset, sixteen hours behind the lead boat. Once on shore, Riley retreated to the house that she and Barry had purchased; however, her short breather was again interrupted. The boat's new sponsor was eager to exploit the publicity value of the women's crew. They flew Riley to Washington, D.C., for a ten-day media tour during the layover. She found time to visit with friends and family between tour appearances before flying back to New Zealand.

Sailboat racing is a popular sport in the island nation of New Zealand. Over a hundred thousand people lined the shores to cheer the Whitbread yachts as they sailed out of Auckland's harbor on February 20. The bay was filled with small craft, while helicopters and private planes circled overhead. It was a heartwarming sendoff for the start of the six-thousand-mile leg across the South Pacific.

The weather turned frigid the ninth day out. A mixture of snow and sleet filled the air while water temperature dropped to near freezing. The crew of the *Heineken* fought off frostbite on exposed skin and tucked in their all-weather gear. The yacht skirted a monster iceberg that appeared off the bow one dark morning before sunrise, as they sailed the latitude that sailors dub the "Screaming 60s" for its high winds. In this part of the world, weather information is notoriously unreliable. But the elements cooperated, and the women made it across the Pacific with only a few minor setbacks. They lost a sail, had to repair a steering cable, and one crew member punctured her hand on a hook. They approached the west coast of South America in fairly good condition.

In early March, the *Heineken* reached Cape Horn, the southernmost point of the continent. The Horn had a reputation of its own when it came to stormy weather. The yacht had to sail around the Cape with a broken rudder blade. The crew shifted weight to the boat's stern to compensate as they entered the narrow Le Maire Strait. The steering was dicey, as thirty-five-foot waves relentlessly washed over the bow. The situation came to a climax as the tired skipper was easing into her sleeping bag below deck for a much-needed rest. Just then, a huge wave spun the boat around. Riley scampered back on deck to find the jib (foresail) torn to shreds. The crew cut it down, threw it overboard, and hoisted a smaller back-up jib. They rode out the storm, exhausted and bruised. The boat had lost three sails to violent weather since leaving Auckland. A dense fog set in as they sailed out of the Strait. The yacht headed north for Punta, four hundred miles away. The list of repairs for the stopover in Uruguay was growing by the day. The laminated rudder and fiberglass hull both had been damaged, and the SatCom needed to be repaired. All this had to be addressed, along with the usual wear and tear on the rigging.

The *Heineken* reached Punta mid-March, in seventh place. The crew spent their time on shore repairing the boat and relaxing, as time allowed. The women joined the men's crews for a night out at the local clubs. It felt good to go out following three weeks at sea on cold, cramped boats. Riley found time to play in a golf tournament before heading to Montevideo's shipyard to work on the yacht's keel. The sheared rudder was sent to Buenos Aires for mending. It took nearly two weeks to complete the repairs. While in Uruguay, Riley heard from her fiancé Barry. The catamaran *Enza* had completed their nonstop, around-the-world trip in less than seventy-five days, breaking the existing record. Riley still had some nine thousand nautical miles ahead of her. The *Heineken* returned from dry dock the end of March, and the crew prepared for the voyage to Fort Lauderdale, Florida, the next-to-last leg of the race.

The Whitbread fleet left Punta the day before Easter and headed north. The boats bunched tightly in the light winds, taking some two days to cover three hundred miles. Food had to be rationed during the lingering calm. A week out, the winds returned. Then the *Heineken* lost her wind instrument readings when the mast antenna broke, leaving the crew to guess at the wind speed. Despite the malfunction, the women were in the strongest position yet, running in fourth place among the Whitbread 60s. Rain poured as they crossed the equator, providing welcome relief from the unrelenting heat. Then the winds disappeared once again, and the boat inched northward at 2 to 3 knots

(1 knot = 1.15 mph). The rudder blade then sheared for a second time, knocking another knot off what little speed they were making.

The *Heineken* finally reached Fort Lauderdale in sixth place, sailing with a damaged rudder. The women got a big reception upon arrival. First Lady Hillary Clinton sent a congratulatory message to the *Heineken* crew. Riley's mother, stepfather, sister Dana, and various relatives were waiting to greet her. A list of repairs also awaited the crew's attention. The rudder was the major concern. While the *Heineken* was in the boatyard, the crew members enjoyed a brief holiday before preparing the boat for the final run. On the 21st of May, the Whitbread fleet assembled for the sixth time.

The starts of sailboat races are chaotic. Skippers maneuver their vessels back and forth behind the starting line—an unmarked demarcation between an officials' boat and a marker buoy—while attempting to maintain speed and gain a favorable position vis-à-vis the wind and the other boats. It's like a combination of musical chairs and a game of "chicken" with yachts bearing down on each other, and then veering off at the last second. At the sound of the gun, each skipper attempts to be the first across the line. Occasionally, yachts "jump the gun." The *Heineken*'s crew were assessed a thirteen-minute penalty at Fort Lauderdale for crossing the line prematurely. They would have to make up the time at sea.

The voyage across the Atlantic to England was less than four thousand nautical miles, but in some ways would prove the most difficult leg for the crew of the *Heineken*. Riley elected to ride the Gulf Stream up the North American coast to Nova Scotia and then head east to the British Isles. It was a calculated risk. A northerly wind against the current could turn the Gulf Stream into a washing machine. The boat's SSB radio stopped working, which limited their ability to communicate, but they progressed northward. With some three thousand miles to go, the women were running a disappointing eighth. They found a brisk breeze, raised the spinnaker (the huge foresail), and made good speed. The *Heineken* gained some 130 miles on the leaders. The boat sailed into a low pressure system on the first of June and zipped along at 25 knots. The crew was making record time.

The North Atlantic has a reputation for being cold and didn't disappoint. The crew of the *Heineken*, buried beneath layers of clothing, gulped cups of coffee, cocoa, and hot soup to stay warm. The winds picked up to forty knots. The boat plummeted off the crests of giant waves into the troughs and onto the next swell. Without warning, the vessel rolled precipitously with a loud bang. The lee side of the deck dipped into the sea. Riley, who had been sleeping, rushed on deck in time to observe the spinnaker shredding with a sense of déjà vu. The crew cut it free and hoisted a jib. Then the steering failed. They took down the sails, pointed the boat into the wind, and attempted to diagnose the problem. When daylight broke, they discovered that the rudder had sheared again. The crew had to jury-rig a provisional rudder.

It was a temporary fix and wouldn't get them to England. Riley contacted the maxi yacht *Uruguay Natural*, some forty miles away. She knew that they carried a spare rudder. The two boats rendezvoused and were able to transfer the rudder to the *Heineken*. By the time the crew completed the task of ret-rofitting the new rudder, most of the Whitbread boats had crossed the finish line in Southampton. Fortunately, the women got a break in the weather. But before they could sail into the stormy English Channel, the boat had to be fitted with a more suitable rudder. The *Heineken* shore crew sailed out to meet them with the replacement. The resolute crew of women completed the final leg on June 8. It was a frustrating finish to the long race, but they made it in one piece, of sorts. A large crowd was waiting on the Southampton dock to welcome them.

There's a maxim among sailors that races are won or lost by the "little things." It's equally true that races are lost due to "big things." During the *Challenge/Heineken's* nine-month journey of more than 30,000 miles, the crew survived a change in skippers, numerous shredded sails, erratic electronic equipment, a severed steering cable, several broken rudders, and one broken bone. It was a heroic endeavor by any standard. The summer of 1994, Dawn Riley was the highest-ranking woman on the racing circuit.

THE FIRST ALL-WOMEN CREW IN THE AMERICA'S CUP

Following the finish of the Whitbread, Riley flew to New Zealand for a brief reunion with Barry McKay before heading to San Diego for the next race on her busy schedule. She had decided to accept Bill Koch's invitation to join the first all-woman crew in the 140-year history of the America's Cup. Koch had announced his plans three months earlier while Riley was sailing in the South Pacific. Her decision to compete in the 1995 Cup Race put a strain on her relationship with Barry. The New Zealander wanted to spend more time with his fiancée. During her entire life, the thirty-year-old sailor had never formed the kind of attachments that tied her to one place. Riley didn't want to pass up the opportunity to take part in the historic America's Cup.

Back in the United States, Dawn enjoyed a brief visit with her family before heading to San Diego to join the *America³* team. The 1995 Cup race was to be held off the California coast. Five foreign syndicates entered yachts to challenge the American defender. Koch had won the 1992 America's Cup, but was required to compete in the round-robin prelims to determine who would defend the Cup in 1995. Bill Koch was something of an iconoclast. He was intent on defying tradition and entering the defender trials with an all-woman crew. The yachtsman had been impressed with Riley's rookie performance on the *America³* at the 1992 Cup trials, and invited her to skipper his new boat under construction. The state-of-the-art yacht, *Mighty Mary,* was named in honor of his athletic mother. A crew of women competing head-to-head with men would be a fitting tribute to her and a milestone in Cup history.

Tryouts were held in June of 1994, and the newly formed *America³* team assembled to begin training. The regimen consisted of morning weightlifting sessions followed by afternoons on the boat. The crew had a year to learn the necessary skills to race seventy-five-foot yachts with one-hundred-foot masts. The two dozen team members included several women with extensive sailing experience, along with a couple of Olympic rowers recruited to grind the winches that raised the huge sails. Dawn Riley was the only one with previous experience as a Cup racer. The women ran up against the same prejudice and intimidation that Riley had encountered in the 1992 Cup trials. The San Diego Yacht Club became the setting for sexist jokes and remarks about the "lesbo" crew. During the races, some of the men yelled obscenities and made crude gestures directed at the *America³*. Moreover, the male coaches and trainers hired by Koch seemed uncomfortable working with women.

Shortly after the trials commenced, Dawn Riley was removed as helmsman in favor of Jennifer "JJ" Isler, a world champion sailor and Olympic medalist. The management team designated Riley "crew boss" and moved her to the pit, the position she held in the 1992 Cup trials. From there, she orchestrated the functions of the sixteen on-board crew members. As a rule, Isler would be at a helm for the start of races and then turn the wheel over to Leslie Egnot, an Olympic silver medalist. This freed JJ to act as tactician. While Isler was intense, Egnot was reserved. Leadership styles and personality clashes became an issue. At a critical juncture in the competition, *America³* management assigned veteran yacht racer David Dellenbaugh to the position of tactician, replacing Isler. He would be the lone male among the crew of women. The confident, soft-spoken Dellenbaugh was generally liked and accepted by the other crew members. His presence reflected the growing concern over the crew's lack of experience. Notably, the Women's Sports Foundation publicly supported his addition to the previously all-woman crew.

The Defender Series featured some sixty match races held over four months to determine which boat would defend the Cup against the challenger. The course off the California coast was designed with a windward leg and a leeward (downwind) leg marked by two large orange buoys some three miles apart. The boats raced three times up and down the course for roughly 18 miles. The average race lasted nearly three hours. Koch's crew continued to sail the 1992 Cup winner *America³* while waiting for the *Mighty Mary* to be completed.

The 1995 Cup trials pitted the women's crew against two other American entries, former Cup winner Dennis Conner's *Stars & Stripes* and the Maine-based PACT 95 boat, *Young America*. As a warm-up for the Cup race, the women sailed *America³* to a second-place finish in the International World Championship in November, beating both Conner and PACT 95. The following January, the women's crew won the initial Defenders Series race by a margin of more than a minute. They were for real! When the *Mighty Mary* came online in March, the crew had to familiarize themselves with the new boat. Racing yachts are as temperamental as thoroughbred race horses. But once mastered, the state-of-the-art yacht would provide the crew with a competitive edge over the three-year-old *America³*. Speed is a major factor in winning, and all three yachts in the Cup trials were closely matched.

The Defenders Series came down to an unprecedented three-boat final. At mid-race, the *Mighty Mary* was leading Conner's *Stars & Stripes* by several minutes when tactician David Dellenbaugh made a crucial decision on the final leg that cost them the race. They were beaten by two boat lengths. The women had come close to pulling off a major upset. The *Mighty Mary* wouldn't have the honor of defending the Cup, but its crew had impressed everyone with their skill and determination. The 1995 America's Cup trials received unprecedented media attention. The crew of the *Mighty Mary* sent a message that women could compete as equals in the sport. Dennis Conner went on to lose five straight Cup races to the New Zealand challenger *Black Magic*. The America's Cup traveled to New Zealand, but Riley didn't.

During the Cup trials, Riley wore the engagement ring that Barry had given her, disregarding the cautionary rule about jewelry on racing yachts. Despite her attachment to the ring, she wasn't ready to settle down with Barry. She wanted to continue sailing. The betrothed sailors were performing yet another chorus of "My bonnie lies over the ocean." Their long-distance relationship didn't survive. Barry turned to another woman for companionship. Riley's passion for racing sailboats had once again bruised the male ego. On the other hand, her appearance in two America's Cups boosted the collective ego of women. She was nominated for the 1995 Team Sportswoman of the Year Award conferred by the Women's Sports Foundation. She would later serve on the Foundation's board, and then as president in 2003–04. The Women's Sports Foundation was created by tennis star Billie Jean King to promote girls' and women's sports. It was a goal Dawn Riley shared.

MORE PROFESSIONAL SAILING SUCCESS

The America's Cup veteran sailed in several world-class events over the next several years. She crewed on the *Morning Glory* in the 1996 Sydney to Hobart Race. The event proved to be both challenging and rewarding. The *Morning Glory* lost its mast during trials, and another mast had to be flown in at the last minute from New Zealand. The crew worked the entire night before the race to make the start. The refitted yacht went on to set a course record. Riley also competed in match races. Her team won the Santa Maria Cup in 1999. It was her second win at Annapolis. In recognition of Dawn's achievements, she was named Rolex Yachtswoman of the Year.

Dawn Riley went on to become the first woman to head an America's Cup syndicate. America True, based in San Francisco, was one of twelve syndicates sponsoring entries in the 2000 Cup competition held off the coast of New Zealand. Riley put up much of the $100,000 entry fee herself, while Chris Coffin, the COO of America True Foundation, underwrote the cost for entering the boat in Cup competition. Early success brought more than two dozen sponsors aboard the $20 million campaign including Gold's Gym, Qantas Airlines, Raytheon, the American defense contractor, and the National Aeronautics and Space Administration (NASA). Sailboat racing had become a very expensive sport. Modern yachts incorporate high-tech design and space-age technology. Riley took an active role in constructing the *America True*. NASA engineers contributed to the boat's design. The yacht raced in the Challenger Series with a coed crew. It was one of six competitors to make it to the semifinals. *America True* finished fifth among all challengers, and first among the U.S. entries. The winning Italian yacht *Prada Challenge* went on to challenge the New Zealand team for the 2000 Cup, but lost in five straight races.

Riley took some time off from her executive duties to compete on the world circuit. She raced in the IC45 one-design class (forty-five-foot yachts), winning the world championship and the One Ton Cup, one of the oldest trophies in sailing. She finished fifth in the 2002 ISAF Women's Match Racing World Championship held in Spain. Riley then took a position with the French-German K-Challenge racing team and won the 2002 Cassis Cup Race, held off the coast of France. K-Challenge became Areva Challenge in 2005 when Riley managed their $40 million campaign. The industrial conglomerate entered a yacht in the 2007 America's Cup Challenger Series, finishing eighth.

Dawn Riley remains active in the sport of sailing. Between races, she makes appearances at yacht club fundraisers, and does some coaching and consulting. In 2007, Riley took a position as spokesperson for ClearPoint, a high resolution weather information service. She represented ClearPoint at the Paris International Boat Show in December of that year. Riley served as a board member of the National Women's Sailing Association and is a founding member of the International Women's Match Racing Association. As CEO of America True, she directs the foundation's community sailing programs. Riley's interests transcended sailboat racing. She worked as a volunteer in Hillary Clinton's 2008 campaign for president. She also works with charitable foundations including the Aspen Institute's youth leadership programs. She is an active public speaker and has done some commentary for ESPN.

Dawn Riley maintains a home in Michigan and a boat in Sausalito, California, but is on the road a great deal. She recently accepted a position of executive director of the Oakcliff Sailing Center in Oyster Bay, New York.

The training center's Acorn Program grants scholarships to young adults who demonstrate potential as sailboat racers. Riley continues to race in regattas. The veteran sailor competed in a super-yacht regatta in Italy, the fall of 2009. Back home, she enjoys recreational sailing, skiing in the winter, cooking, and gardening.

Over three decades of sailing, Dawn Riley accumulated an impressive record of accomplishments. She was the first woman to sail in three America's Cups and two Whitbread Round the World Races, and the first woman to head a Cub racing team. Dawn Riley was the first two-time winner of the Santa Maria Cup, and she won the Women's World Cup in 1992. In 2000, she was awarded the Boating Industries Association (MIBA) Mayor's Cup. Michigan State University, her alma mater, named her Alumna of the Year in 1997. Riley serves on the Honorary Advisory Board of the National Sailing Hall of Fame. She has always found ways to stay active in her sport on land and sea. Her pioneering achievements at the helm of sailboats and in executive boardrooms are opening doors for women sailors, young and old.

FURTHER READING

Beech, Mark. 1999. She's the Boss. *Sports Illustrated* 90:24: http://sportsillustrated
    .cnn.com/vault/article/magazine/MAG1016138/index.htm.
Huntington, Anna Seaton. 1996. *Making Waves: The Inside Story of Managing and
    Motivating the First Women's Team to Compete for the America's Cup.* Arling-
    ton, TX: The Summit Publishing Group.
Lee, Janet. 1994. The Life of Riley. *Women's Sports & Fitness* 16: 622–25.
Riley, Dawn, with Cynthia Flanagan. 1995. *Taking the Helm.* Boston: Little, Brown
    & Co.
Streuli, Stuart. 2007. Riley Rises to the Areva Challenge. *Sailing World*, May 12:
    http://www.sailingworld.com/article/Riley-Rises-to-the-Areva-Challenge.
Whiteside, Kelly. 1995. A Whole New Tack. *Sports Illustrated* 82:7: http://sports
    illustrated.cnn.com/vault/article/magazine/MAG1006238/index.htm.
Whiting, Sam. 2007. Yachtswoman shows beginning sailors the ropes. *San Francisco
    Chronicle*, July 30: E1.

Wilma Rudolph wins the semi-final heat of the Women's 100-meter dash at the Summer Olympics in Rome, 1960. (AP Photo)

Wilma Rudolph
(1940–1994)

Wilma Rudolph was an American runner who became the first female in the United States to win three gold medals in one Olympics when she won gold for the 100-meter and 200-meter sprints, and the 400-meter relay race. She faced and overcame incredible challenges in her life, including significant poverty, serious health problems, a bout with polio that put her in a leg brace for several years and caused doctors to question whether or not she would ever walk unassisted again, and racial discrimination.

CHILDHOOD

Wilma Glodean Rudolph was born on June 23, 1940, in St. Bethlehem, Tennessee, to Edward and Blanche Rudolph; Edward had eleven children from a first marriage and Wilma was his ninth child out of what would be eleven children from his second marriage. Rudolph was born two months prematurely, weighing just four and a half pounds, after a fall by her mother. In 1940 only 50 percent of babies born under five pounds survived. To compound the difficulties faced by the Rudolph family, the local hospital served only white people (with the closest hospital for blacks nearly fifty miles away) and the town had only one black doctor to serve the approximately 10,000 black residents who comprised 25 percent of Clarksville, Tennessee.

The Rudolphs were impoverished, with Ed working as a railroad porter and handyman and Blanche taking in laundry and sewing, and occasionally serving as a maid for wealthier white families. Blanche sometimes cooked at a café in town that served only whites as well, from which she could take leftovers home to her family. Neither of Rudolph's parents completed elementary school. Her father never learned how to read nor write, and he relied upon his wife to do so for him.

Rudolph later estimated that her parents never made more than $2,500 per year, raising twenty-two children in a home that had no electricity or indoor bathroom. The family used an outhouse, relied upon kerosene lamps and candles for illumination, and wore clothing sewn from flour sacks. In Clarksville, only one restaurant existed for black patrons; separate public water fountains existed for blacks and whites; schools were segregated; and only seven percent of the black population in town finished high school.

Rudolph suffered from numerous illnesses within her first three years of life, including measles, mumps, and chickenpox. By age four, she had contracted scarlet fever, whooping cough, and double pneumonia; her left leg turned inward during an especially high fever and Dr. Coleman determined that she had also had polio. It was at least possible, the Rudolphs were told—and perhaps even likely—that she would never walk unassisted again.

Each year in that era, approximately 21,000 people in the United States contracted polio by becoming infected by the poliomyelitis virus. Polio affected people differently, depending upon where the infection attacked the body; some had trouble with breathing, while one in every two hundred people with polio suffered from paralysis. By 1955, when a vaccine was invented by Dr. Jonas Salk, more than 350,000 Americans had either been killed or disabled by the disease.

Rudolph needed to strengthen and straighten her weak leg, so she started wearing a heavy metal brace from her ankle to her knee, and she attempted exercises at home that the family hoped would strengthen her leg. A year later, little progress had been made and so she and her mother took a bus to the Meharry Medical Center in Nashville (the hospital associated with Fisk University) twice a week for physical therapy; they used heat and water therapy, putting her leg in a hot whirlpool and massaging the muscles.

During each of their trips, Rudolph and her mother needed to sit in the back of the bus, as Tennessee was still strongly segregated by race in that era. While in Nashville, they needed to be very careful about which restrooms they used, as those were also segregated by race; where they bought any food to supplement their bagged lunches; and otherwise ensure that they did not make a misstep and attempt to use anything intended only for white people.

Rudolph slowly improved. After two years of treatment, she only needed to go to the medical center once a week. Throughout her long recovery, the local black doctor, Dr. Coleman, visited Rudolph at home, trying to encourage her and her family. Her mother and her siblings that still lived at home took turns massaging her leg in the hopes that it would heal.

Because Rudolph could not walk well on her own, Cobb Elementary School officials would not let her attend. So, a tutor came to the Rudolph home to help educate Rudolph to supplement what her mother could teach her. It took Rudolph until second grade to heal sufficiently enough to be fitted with an orthopedic shoe and be admitted to the elementary school; although she was initially happy to attend the school, she hated how other children mocked her brace and how she needed to sit back and watch the others run and play.

Cobb Elementary School was segregated and taught black students only; they received fewer resources—meaning books, equipment and teachers—than white schools in the district. Although the groundbreaking Supreme Court decision, *Oliver L. Brown et al. v. the Board of Education of Topeka (KS)*, was reached while Rudolph was still in school, its ruling against the constitutionality of segregated schools did not have an impact on her. The schools where she lived remained segregated throughout her school years.

Rudolph, later on, talked about being keenly aware of the inequities in her town; knowing that her mother was a maid for whites in the town surely added to her resentment. Rudolph recalled observing, at around the age of six, that white people treated their horses better than they treated their black neighbors; any time she mentioned her observations to her mother, though, she was told to hold her tongue. Sometimes, people wondered why Rudolph—light-skinned, like her father—was walking with a black boy—her brother Wesley, who was dark like their mother. Two of Rudolph's older brothers fought in segregated military units in World War II and she overheard some of their bitter observations about being good enough to fight for the country, but not good enough to fight with white Americans.

On the plus side, Rudolph's health was slowly but surely being restored. When she was nine or ten years old, she felt strong enough one Sunday to attend church without the brace, which encouraged friends and family—and made Rudolph long, even more, to have a more normal childhood. About that time, she stopped needing to go to the medical center for treatments. Over the next two years, she wore the brace on bad days, but kept it off on days when she felt stronger. When she turned twelve, in 1952, she and her mother felt confident enough of her strength to mail the brace back to the medical center.

HIGH SCHOOL YEARS

During the years in which Rudolph could not participate in physical activities with the other students, she would intently watch basketball games, memorizing moves and strategies. Once she was able to move well without her brace, she began playing basketball games with other youth in the neighborhood, much to her mother's consternation and worry. Rudolph then tried out for the Burt High School basketball team; students at the school ranged from seventh graders through high school seniors.

Rudolph's older sister Yvonne played on the basketball team, and the tall and lanky Wilma Rudolph also made the team, although she spent her first year sitting on the bench. During the second season, the coach would put Rudolph in the game for a short time if they already held a commanding lead. During the third year, she also spent most of her time on the bench; her frustration was growing, because she felt that she was good as—if not better than—the first-string girls.

Shortly before her fourth year on the basketball team, she and a couple of other girls came up with a strategy. After school, the basketball coach, Clinton C. Gray, was supervising the practices of the school's annual show in the gym; so, the group of plotting girls would attempt to practice basketball at the same time. It never took him long to chase them out of the gym, but Rudolph hoped that this ploy would help him to recognize how seriously they were taking the sport of basketball.

Perhaps this plan worked. In any case, Rudolph made the starting lineup that year, and that is when she earned the nickname of "Skeeter"; the coach gave her that nickname, which followed her into adulthood, saying that she buzzed around like a mosquito. Her coach was also quoted as saying, "You're little, you're fast and you always get in my way" (Roberts, 2007).

Rudolph, by this time, was ready to play some serious basketball. She set a single-season scoring record, scoring 803 points in just twenty-five games, which averaged 32.12 points a game. She set a record number of points for a game at forty-nine, and became an All-State player. During the state championships, she and her teammates stayed at the house of Coach Gray's sister, Phyllis, who was married to a university professor.

During the first round of the state championships, Rudolph scored twenty-six points in a win for Burt High School, with her friend Nancy Bowen scoring thirty. In the second match, Rudolph's team lost, but a connection made during that game would, according to her recollections, change her life forever.

RUDOLPH'S PIVOTAL MOMENT: RUDOLPH'S VERSION

According to Rudolph's recollection, it was a meeting with the referee of the basketball game, Edward Temple, that changed her life. Temple also served as the Tennessee State University (TSU) track coach for women, the Lady Tigerbelles, and he sensed an extraordinary amount of ability in Rudolph. Temple, a black man, had grown up in Pennsylvania, attending racially integrated schools and competing in sporting events against both blacks and whites. He was shocked at the racial inequities that he faced when attending TSU.

Although Temple was a new coach when he first met Rudolph, he went on to lead more than forty athletes to Olympic competition, with those athletes winning twenty-three medals: thirteen gold, six silver, and four bronze. This made the Tigerbelles the most successful sports team in Tennessee's history. Moreover, he led his track teams to thirty-four national titles and his athletes won thirty medals from the Pan-American Games. When he first met Rudolph, though, he had yet to transform TSU into a track and field powerhouse; at this point, he had two athletes of some renown on his team: Heriwentha Mae Faggs and Barbara Jones.

Rudolph was not brand new to track; she had run for Burt High School the previous year, competing in informal meets against other black schools, which were known as playdays with the focus on socialization rather than competition. The track program, not surprisingly, received little attention or funding. Plus, Gray—who coached the team—was not in fact a track coach; he was a basketball coach who also oversaw the track program. Nevertheless, Rudolph participated to the fullest, winning every race during ninth grade.

Rudolph competed in her first Amateur Athletic Union (AAU) tournament at Alabama's Tuskegee Institute. The Tuskegee coach was Major Cleveland Abbott, and he built a track team that won the AAU championship every year from 1937 through 1956, except for 1952. Tuskegee was a black school that, during the regular season, could only compete against other black schools; the AAU championships, though, were integrated, proving that the Tuskegee program could build a true powerhouse team, year after year.

Coach Gray tried to prepare his team for the type of competition that they would face at Tuskegee, but it was hard for Rudolph and her teammates to put that into perspective. During the competition, Rudolph lost every race during that tournament. She later recalls having been completely crushed by her defeat, adding that it eventually caused to realize that her rudimentary training was not enough, even with the raw talent that she possessed. It was this experience, too, that made Rudolph want to become an outstanding runner. She returned to Burt High School, where she won every track meet for the rest of the season.

Temple, the referee of the state basketball championships, then reentered Rudolph's life. He clearly recognized the scope of her raw talent, requesting permission from Rudolph's parents to have her train with TSU during the summer. She would stay in a dormitory and have her expenses paid for by the college; her parents agreed to let her participate after Temple shared that Rudolph would have a curfew and a diligent chaperone in the person of Marian Armstrong-Perkins, who would later become Temple's assistant coach in 1958.

When it came time for Rudolph to leave for the summer to train with Temple, she hated to leave her boyfriend, Robert Eldridge, but she was persuaded to do so. The team—of which Rudolph was the youngest member—traveled to meets in Temple's car and he paid to have an oval-shaped area of dirt lined. He preached teamwork and insisted that athletes arrive to practice on time— or run extra laps. He insisted that training for track was a year-round proposition, not a seasonal commitment, and he had his runners practice certain moves, including the "Tennessee Lean," in which they leaned over the finish line over and over again.

According to Rudolph's recollections, the team ran every morning from 6 to 8 AM and then they ate breakfast. They ran six more miles at 10:30; ate lunch—and then would run six more miles at 3:00 PM. Whether or not this was the schedule adhered to, Temple definitely taught Rudolph techniques of running, something she knew nothing about previously. Her two biggest challenges were that she was slow in coming off the starting block, which meant that short races were difficult for her; and she needed to learn to relax before a race. Temple focused hard on overcoming those challenges.

In August, Rudolph competed in her second AAU meet, this time in Philadelphia, a city that seemed overwhelmingly large to her. After just a brief training stint with Temple, Rudolph had improved considerably in her running technique; she won both the 75-yard and 100-yard dash, and she anchored the winning 440-yard relay team. The junior girls' division of TSU, of which Rudolph was a part, won the national championship in their division, with only five girls on the team. The senior girls from TSU also won the national championship. Rudolph met baseball player Jackie Robinson there; Robinson had become the first black baseball player in modern times to play major league ball in 1947, and he encouraged Rudolph to pursue her dreams.

RUDOLPH'S PIVOTAL MOMENT: ALTERNATE EXPLANATIONS

Some people, including Maureen Smith, author of *Wilma Rudolph: A Biography*, question this timeline. Smith states that Rudolph's recollections put her initial training with Temple in the summer of 1956; she points out that this would be an extraordinarily short amount of time between when Rudolph first began receiving high-level training and when she qualified for the 1956 Olympics.

Temple himself remembers Rudolph first training with him in 1954, two years earlier than what she stated. Meanwhile, Smith points out that evidence exists that shares how Rudolph had participated in the 1955 AAU meet, held in Ponco City, Oklahoma, with the Tigerbelles (Smith, 2006, 17–18). At Ponco City, the TSU team overwhelmingly won their first AAU title, scoring 87.5 points; the Chicago Comets came in second place with 59 points. Mae Faggs served as the leader during this competition. The *New York Times* proclaimed that "The cathedral of women's track in this country is Tennessee A&I and Temple is its high priest" (Smith, 2006, 20). Rudolph competed in the junior girls' division; she placed fourth in the 75-yard dash and second in the 100-yard dash. Although the junior girls in 1955 did not perform as well as the touted senior girls, they improved significantly by 1956 and were closing in on the seniors.

This scenario raises a question: if Rudolph were training with Temple a year earlier than her memoirs state, how did the two meet? It is possible, although not a certainty, that Rudolph's basketball and track coach in high school, Coach Gray, had actually contacted Temple to share Rudolph's prowess before Rudolph had ever played in the state basketball tournament.

OLYMPIC DREAMS

Regardless of which version is true—or which sections of a merged version are true—accounts begin resembling one another again at the point when Temple invited Rudolph to travel to Seattle, Washington, to try out for the 1956 Olympic Games, which would be held in Melbourne, Australia. Rudolph did not have a conception of what the Olympics were and she did not know where Australia was located. Temple reassured her, though, that she was ready to try out.

Rudolph traveled to Washington in her coach's car, accompanied by Faggs who had competed in the 1948 Olympics and who had helped to set a world record in the relay event at the 1952 Olympics with a time of 45.9 seconds. Faggs counseled Rudolph, telling her to stop worrying about fitting in and to focus on becoming a successful individual, because that was the best way to help the entire track team. Before the qualifying heat of the 200-meter dash, Faggs encouraged Rudolph to put all thoughts, except crossing the finish line, out of her mind; Faggs told her that she intended to finish in the lead so to just stick with her—and the two women crossed the finish line together, qualifying for the United States Olympic team.

From a political standpoint, it was important that the six Tigerbelles that made the United States Olympic team perform well. The Soviet Union had just begun sending Olympic teams in 1952 and they believed that their athletic superiority in those Games proved their overall superiority as well; although the men's team from the United States had stacked up fairly well against their Soviet competitors, the women had not fared anywhere nearly as well in 1952.

Historian Susan Cahn was quoted as saying that "sport became a part of a Cold War international contest in which the United States and USSR vied not only for athletic laurels but to prove the superiority of capitalism or communism." Relevant to Rudolph and her teammates, Soviets had accused the United States of racial discrimination and the United States hoped that their black female athletes would disprove that assertion and show that black Americans had opportunities in sports. The history of legal segregation made it difficult to outright refute those accusations though, so U.S. officials "sheepishly" admitted that it was the "great American Negroes" that allowed them to rank second in the world in sport (Smith, 2006, 29–30). On the plus side for the United States, nine out of the seventeen female track and field athletes in 1956 were black, many of them among the stronger athletes on the team.

1956 OLYMPICS

Rudolph and her parents did not have money to purchase what she needed for her overseas trip, so local merchants and friends of the family donated clothing and luggage; Rudolph's father felt uncomfortable accepting what he saw as charity, but agreed to do so. Rudolph traveled to Los Angeles, California to train for the Olympics; this was her first airplane ride. During the trip, she turned down dinner, assuming that she would need to pay—and she did not have the money. Fortunately, Faggs informed her that she could eat for free. In California, Temple assisted the U.S. Olympic coach, Nel Jackson; having a familiar face in California comforted Rudolph, but he would not be able to accompany them to Australia.

Coach Jackson was an excellent athlete herself, competing in the 1948 Olympics in track and field and setting a world record of 24.2 seconds in the 200-meter event in 1949. She also became the first black woman to coach an Olympic track and field team for the United States. She did not provide any scouting reports about the athletes from other countries to her runners; instead, she focused only on training the U.S. team for competition.

When the team arrived in Australia, Rudolph was surprised but pleased when people asked her for her autograph. Overall, though, her nerves somewhat got to her. When she ran the qualifying heat for the 200-meter event, Rudolph was so nervous that she could not recall whom she ran against. She came in third place, securing a place in the semifinal heat; she also came in third in the semifinals, but only the top two advanced to the finals.

The winner of the 200-meter event—and the 100-meter and 400-meter event—was Betty Cuthbert of Australia, who befriended Rudolph and suggested that the American runner purchase a pair of the lightweight shoes used by Australian sprinters; they were crafted from kangaroo skin. Rudolph wanted the shoes, but turned down Faggs' offer to loan her the money, knowing that she had no way to pay her back.

Rudolph was to compete in the 100-meter relay event during the 1956 Olympics; in 1952, the American team had won the gold medal after the favored Australians had dropped the baton. In the 1956 event, Faggs ran the opening heat, and the Americans were tied for first place in the race when Faggs handed the baton off to Margaret Matthews; she had won the silver medal in both the 100-meter and 200-meter dashes, but lost ground to multiple teams in the relay event. After Matthews handed the baton off to Rudolph, the sixteen-year-old runner from Clarksville, Tennessee, boosted the team to third place; in the final heat, Isabelle Daniels almost passed the runner from

SEGREGATION IN THE OLYMPICS

In 1932, the first two African American women qualified for the U.S. track and field Olympic team. Their names were Louise Stokes and Tydia Pickett. Both women traveled to compete in Los Angeles, California, but the coach replaced them with white women, even though both Stokes and Pickett had clearly qualified to compete. In 1936, Stokes qualified for the 400-meter relay team, but she was once again replaced at the last minute by a white woman. It was not until 1948 that a black woman from the United States would win an Olympic medal; that is when Alice Coachman won the high jump in the London-based competition, receiving the gold. In 1956, American Mildred McDaniel competed in the Olympics held in Melbourne, Australia, where she also captured the gold in the high jump event.

Great Britain. The Australian team won the gold medal in 1956 with a world record time of 44.5 seconds; Great Britain, the silver, with a time of 44.7; and the Americans, the bronze, with a time of 44.9. Interesting enough, all three of the teams beat the previous world record. Two of the favored teams, the Soviet Union and West Germany, did not place. Of the six medals earned by the American women's track and field team, five of them came from TSU; the team wrote a letter to Temple sharing their triumphs, with Rudolph signing her name this way: Wilma "Skeeter" Rudolph (your future star).

POST-1956 OLYMPICS

Being part of an Olympic-medal team bolstered Rudolph's confidence and she wanted to return in 1960 to go after the gold. When she returned home, Burt High School closed so that everyone could attend a ceremony honoring Rudolph; giving a speech that day scared Rudolph even more than the Olympics had. That night, she played in their high school basketball game.

After Rudolph won in Rome, other basketball players and track team participants became intimidated by her, which frustrated her. Their nervousness and lack of confidence meant that they did not provide good competition for her.

That year, the girls' basketball team won every game of the season; scored a record-breaking average of more than one hundred points per game; and made the Tennessee High School Girls' Championships. Rudolph scored an average of thirty-five points a game that season, with her close friend Nancy Bowen scoring an average of thirty-eight.

Near the end of the very close state championship game, Rudolph lost the ball to an opponent. Although the other team did not capitalize on this opportunity—and even though Burt won the game—the coach screamed at Rudolph in front of numerous people, asking why she made such a stupid play; Rudolph was humiliated.

An even more devastating event happened after that. Rudolph and Eldridge—who was a star athlete in basketball and football—attended the prom, with Rudolph wearing a dark blue dress loaned to her by a friend from TSU. She also wore a white orchid corsage. After the prom, several cars full of students, including Rudolph and Eldridge, traveled to Hopkinsville, Kentucky to a nightclub that allowed high school students to drink.

The following morning, Rudolph was awakened by a panicked call from her basketball coach, asking her if she was okay. She was, but she soon learned that one carload of students did not return home safely, and her close friend, Nancy Bowen, had been killed.

Rudolph was devastated and she struggled to train with Temple that summer. Nevertheless, she set new girls' division records in the AAU championships, held in Cleveland, Ohio, in the 75-yard dash, the 100-yard dash, and the 300-yard relay.

To add to her distress, she discovered that she was pregnant and she feared telling her religious Baptist parents. She also dreaded telling church members who had supported her through her years with polio and she hated the thought of telling Temple, who had a policy against allowing mothers to run on his team. After talking with her parents, Rudolph decided to accept her older sister Yvonne's offer to help take care of the child. Rudolph's father prohibited her from seeing her boyfriend again; although that devastated her, Eldridge began dating someone else. Rudolph was graduated from Burt High School in May 1958, shortly before the time in which she gave birth to a baby girl named Yolanda in July.

Temple met with Rudolph—who had missed her entire senior year on the basketball team and the track team, due to her pregnancy—and her parents. He agreed to allow Rudolph to continue on his team. She had missed the opportunity to compete on a European tour with the Tigerbelles, but she was eager to train for future competitions. Ironically enough, one of the stigmas faced by serious female athletes of the day was the belief that a woman could not be feminine and a strong athlete; it was thought that too much training would prevent a woman from being able to conceive a baby.

COLLEGE YEARS

In September 1958, Rudolph left Clarksville to attend TSU, located in Nashville, on a full scholarship that required that Rudolph work, as well as study. Another one of the conditions stated that she needed to maintain a B average, and Rudolph struggled to study, train, work, and visit her baby. Eldridge proposed to Rudolph, but she refused, wanting to focus on her education and her running.

During her first two years at TSU, Rudolph's performances were inconsistent; a doctor eventually diagnosed a tonsil infection and, after her tonsils were removed, she regained her strength. Even with her health issues, she still won races, including the 50-yard dash in 6.2 seconds at the National Indoor AAU Track Championships during her freshman year. She also participated in the 440-yard relay, where TSU won second—which helped them to win first overall.

During the summer after her freshman year, she won the AAU championship in the 100-yard dash. During her sophomore year at TSU, she set two American records in the AAU indoor championships: she won the 50-yard dash; set a new record in the 100-yard dash (11.1 seconds); and set a record in the 220-yard dash (25.7 seconds). As she continued to train with Temple and the other Lady Tigerbelles, it was said that you could not blink around

Rudolph, or you'd miss her sprint. She also became known for slowing down during a race so that she could holler encouragement to a teammate.

In 1958 and 1959, Temple was selected as the women's track coach for competitions against the Soviet Union, along with the 1959 Pan American Games. At the AAU national competition, held in Corpus Christi, Texas, Rudolph once again won the 100-yard dash; her memory of that accomplishment was tainted by a bus driver who refused to drive the team because it partially consisted of black runners.

At the Olympic trials, Rudolph qualified for the 100-meter dash, the 200-meter dash, and the 400-meter relay; she set a world record in the 200-meter dash (22.9 seconds) although it took a year for the time to become official. With that win, she became the first American woman to hold a track and field world record.

1960 OLYMPICS

The 1960 Olympic track and field team consisted of eighteen athletes, eleven of whom were black and eight of whom were from TSU. Temple was selected as the U.S. Olympic coach, which added to Rudolph's confidence. This was the first Olympics to be televised worldwide, and Rudolph was one of the athletes to watch; these Games would appear on television in more than one hundred countries, including in the United States, albeit with a time delay. For many Americans, this served as the first opportunity to watch women compete in track and field; the increasing rivalry between the United States and Soviet Union boosted the level of interest in the Games.

Before the Games began, Temple shared a dream that he had, in which Rudolph won three gold medals. That inspired Rudolph, who had been frustrated because her name did not appear until page six of the track and field newsletter focusing on the Olympics.

Shortly after arriving in Rome, Italy, though, Rudolph injured her ankle. Since it was strained, rather than sprained or broken, Rudolph continued to prepare to compete, taping up her ankle and icing it when she could.

When the time came to run trial heats, which would determine who would run in the final Olympic races for a particular event, more than 80,000 people crowded into the stadium; many chanted Wilma's name when she entered and she later reported feeling a deep sense of calm and surety.

She qualified for the semi-final heat in the 100-meter dash, startling other athletes when she was so relaxed that she was able to take a nap on the grassy area by the track after qualifying. In the semi-final heat, she tied the current world record, held by Australian Shirley Strickland, with a time of 11.3. She won the third heat as well; in the fourth heat, she completed the race in an astonishing eleven seconds, which would have been a world record had the winds not been blowing faster than two meters—and she won her first Olympic gold medal in the finals with a time of eleven seconds; this was discounted as a world record because of what Rudolph called a mix-up by officials. Rudolph was the first American woman to win gold in that event since Helen Stephens in 1936.

Rumors suggested that she wanted to win that race in honor of Ray Norton, the male American athlete who did not win the 100-yard dash. After she won that race, the two left the stadium, arm in arm.

In the 200-meter event, she qualified for the finals with a time of 23.2 seconds, an Olympic record. In the finals, she ran a time of twenty-four seconds, easily beating Jutta Heine of West Germany—the silver medalist—and winning her second gold medal. Dorothy Hyman of Great Britain won the bronze. After achieving her second gold medal, Temple told newspaper reporters that "this girl has limitless potential. She has height (5-1), good legs, natural sped [*sic*], a dogged determination and, best of all, perfect relaxation" (Grimsley, 1960, 61). Rudolph was, in fact, five feet, eleven inches.

The final event for Rudolph in the 1960 Olympics was the 100-meter relay. To date, no American Olympic female athlete had won three gold medals in one competition, and Rudolph had the opportunity to accomplish that. It was nearly 100 degrees that day, which was the final day of track and field Olympic competition with an estimated 100 million people around the globe tuning in by television; Rudolph was keenly aware of how much attention she was receiving worldwide, but she could not know how televised coverage of women's athletic events would grow exponentially over the upcoming decades.

On September 7, 1960, the United States was not expected to win the 100-meter relay, although they did set a world record time of 44.4 seconds during the semi-final heat. Powerhouse teams included the Soviet Union, Great Britain, and West Germany. The entire United States team consisted of TSU students, with Rudolph serving as the anchor; other runners included Martha Hudson, Barbara Jones, and Lucinda Williams.

In the final race for the event, by the time that the first two American runners had competed, the team had a two-yard lead; as Jones passed the baton to Rudolph, it looked likely that the United States would win. Then, Rudolph nearly dropped the baton, losing the American advantage; plus, Rudolph needed to race against Irina Press of the Soviet Union and Jutte Heine of West Germany. At the beginning of the final stretch, Rudolph was a full two meters behind Press. Rudolph began racing with great intensity, crossing the finish line first with a time of 44.5 seconds. After the Star Spangled Banner played, Rudolph and her teammates were mobbed by joyous fans. As for her coach, Temple said, "I was so happy [for Wilma] I was bursting all the buttons from my shirt" (Lovett, 1997).

Altogether, members of the TSU track team captured nine gold medals. Rudolph was the only American in the 1960 Olympics, male or female, to bring home three gold medals.

As far as the competition between the Soviet Union and the United States, the former won 103 medals (43 gold) and the latter 71 medals (34 gold). One male American who won gold was eighteen-year-old Cassius Clay, the light heavyweight boxer who came to be known as Muhammad Ali and became famous for his ability to float like a butterfly and sting like a bee.

POST-1960 OLYMPICS

Rudolph received media attention around the globe, with Italians calling her "La Gazzella Nera," "The Black Gazelle"; the French nicknaming her "La Perle Noire," "The Black Pearl"; and Americans referring to her as the "Tennessee Tornado." After the Olympics, Rudolph raced in Athens, Greece; Amsterdam, Holland; London, England; and Cologne, Frankfurt, Wuppertal, and Berlin, Germany. She and her teammates also met Pope John XXIII.

All was not perfect, however. Rudolph's teammates began displaying signs of jealousy, feeling that Rudolph was receiving too much attention, given that some of them were also gold medal winners. After winning the 100-meter event in the British Empire Games, Rudolph was to attend a banquet, but her teammates hid her curlers; when she showed up at the banquet with untamed hair, Temple was upset and demanded to know why.

When Rudolph told him why, her teammates became even angrier and, during the next relay race, they decided to lose on purpose. By the time Rudolph received the baton to run the final leg of the race, she needed to make up forty yards. When she did, she received enormous cheers from the crowd as she crossed the finish line first. Temple, furious with the other relay runners, put the three of them on probation.

When she returned to the United States, a huge crowd awaited her, which included the governor of Tennessee, Buford Ellington; several mayors; television stations; and more. The town of Clarksville held a parade for Rudolph where she rode in an open convertible and waved at the cheering crowd; but, even more monumental, the parade and the banquet given in her honor were the first racially integrated events held in Clarksville. A white judge named Hudson spoke at the banquet, sharing that to play the piano well, both black keys and white keys were needed; it was clear that he was speaking symbolically. Rudolph made approximately one hundred appearances in the first few months after her Olympic triumph, receiving the key to the city of Chicago, appearing on the popular Ed Sullivan Show, and more.

In December 1960, European sportswriters chose Rudolph as the Sportswoman of the Year, the first time this award was granted to an American. The Associated Press named her the Female Athlete of the Year in 1960, only the second black American to win; tennis player Althea Gibson had been first. She also became the first American to win the Christopher Columbus Award from

Italy for the most outstanding international athlete, along with the Helms World Trophy for North America, which honored the best athlete on each continent.

Publications that honored Rudolph with awards included *Mademoiselle* and the *New York Times*. Yet other awards included the Sports Magazine Award for top performer in track and field, the Betty Crocker Award for outstanding achievement, and the National Newspaper Publishers Association's Russwurm Award.

After the excitement began dying down, Rudolph returned to TSU to complete her degree in elementary education; she also worked at a part-time job at the university's post office and joined a sorority, Delta Sigma Theta.

During the indoor track season in 1961, Rudolph received invitations to run in several prestigious races that were typically for males only; these included the New York Athletic Club races, the Millrose Games, the Los Angeles Times Games, the Penn Relays, and the Drake Relays. In a pre-feminist era when it was still believed by some that all female athletes looked and acted masculine, the media continued to point out that Rudolph looked feminine; *Newsweek* printed the following: "Unlike most American female sprinters, she wins; and, unlike many American female athletes, she looks feminine" (Smith, 2006, 68). Meanwhile, Temple appreciated that Rudolph knew better than to try to be better than men.

In January 1961, Rudolph ran the 60-yard dash at the Los Angeles Times Games in just 6.9 seconds, setting a new world record. In February 1961, at the New York Millrose Games, Rudolph again ran the 60-yard dash in 6.9 seconds, tying her world record for that event. Two weeks later, she ran 60 yards in 6.8 seconds; she also broke the world record for the 70-yard dash by almost half a second (7.8 seconds), a record that had been set by Stella Walsh and held for twenty-five years.

On April 14, 1961, Rudolph had the opportunity to meet President John F. Kennedy; she asked if her mother and coach could accompany her, and the answer was yes. When she first met the president, she was tongue-tied and nervous; when he tried to sit down, he missed his chair completely, landing on the ground. The Secret Service started to laugh, breaking the ice.

In July 1961, she won the 100-yard dash in the AAU nationals, her third consecutive title. The following year, she won the title again, with the same time as in 1961: 10.8 seconds. She then competed on a United States team that competed in multiple places in Europe, including West Germany, Ireland, London, England, and Moscow in the Soviet Union. In Moscow, she tied her world record time for the 100-meter dash at 11.2 seconds. That year, she won the James E. Sullivan Award for best amateur athlete, also winning the Associated Press Female Athlete of the Year award for the second consecutive year; she was the first track and field athlete to win this award twice.

On October 14, 1961, she married William Ward, a track and field athlete from TSU. She did not mention this marriage in her autobiography; in fact, she wrote that, after returning from Rome, she resumed dating her high school sweetheart and Yolanda's father, Robert Eldridge. Ward and Rudolph divorced one year later.

In 1962, she raced against a Soviet team at Stanford University in California. She won the 100-meter dash and anchored the relay; she was forty yards behind the Soviet team when she received the baton, but made up the difference and won the race. After that race ended, a young boy asked Rudolph for her autograph; she took off her track shoes, signed them, and gave them to the boy. That year, she won the Babe Didrikson Zaharias Award for the most outstanding female athlete in the world. She was also chosen for the 1962 All-American AAU women's track and field team.

Rudolph then retired from competition, instead serving as a goodwill ambassador at races. In May 1963, she represented the United States at the Games of Friendship in Africa. When she returned home, she got the news that her high school basketball coach, Clinton Gray, had been killed in a car accident. Two months later, after an Asian tour, Rudolph was offered his coaching position, plus a job as a second grade teacher at her old elementary school; as she had received her degree in elementary education on May 27, 1963, she accepted both. Shortly after that, Rudolph was photographed attempting to enter a segregated restaurant.

That summer, she married her high school sweetheart and the father of her daughter, Robert Eldridge. Temple, who did not approve of her retiring from running, did not attend; a former girlfriend of Eldridge's did attend, however, crying throughout. A photographer from *Jet* magazine snapped a shot of the crying woman and it was published in the next issue. The caption read, "Who was this woman crying at Wilma Rudolph's wedding?" (Harper, 2004, 175).

The following year, Rudolph gave birth to their second daughter, Djuana; the following year, in August 1965, to son Robert Jr. She then accepted a job in Evansville, Indiana, as the director of a community center—and then as the manager of a government-sponsored recreation program in Poland Springs, Maine.

In 1967 Vice President Hubert Humphrey asked Rudolph to accept a position in "Operation Champ," a program that trained athletes in sixteen of the country's poor urban areas. After that, she worked at the Job Corps Center in St. Louis, Missouri; she then taught at Pelham Junior High School in Detroit, Michigan—and then she worked for the Watts Community Action Committee in Los Angeles, California.

In March 1969, an Italian publisher who remembered her from the Olympics invited her to visit. She accepted, but was sick in bed for much of the trip. Rumors arose that she was being kept prisoner, and that she was extremely poor, so much so that she gave up custody of her three children and pawned her Olympic trophies. It was also said that she was in that position because Negroes were denied jobs in the United States. When she returned to the United States, she held a press conference, stating that she was jobless because of a car accident.

Rudolph then worked as an administrator at the Afro-American Studies program at UCLA. In the fall of 1970, she accepted a job at Sacramento State College as the women's track and field instructor. In 1971, she gave birth to their fourth child, a son named Xurry.

Rudolph served as a commentator for radio and television in West Germany, organized athletic programs for Mayor Daley's Youth Foundation in Chicago, provided public relations materials for banks, and occasionally modeled. In 1974, she was inducted into the National Track and Field Hall of Fame.

For hobbies, Rudolph jogged and played tennis. She also enjoyed watching her older daughter, Yolanda, run track and field events at her alma mater: TSU. Yolanda did not have her mother's speed, however, and she focused on the 400-meter event.

In the late 1970s, she formed her own company, Wilma Unlimited, and she spoke on the college lecture circuit about motivation. She wrote an autobiography in 1977, *Wilma: The Story of Wilma Rudolph*, which was made into a film, *Wilma,* and shown on NBC; the film starred Shirley Jo Finney, Cicely Tyson, and Denzel Washington. Rudolph acted as consultant on the film.

Although she received some attention from the autobiography and film, Rudolph was frustrated by the lack of compensation that she received. "I was besieged with money problems," she was quoted as saying. "People were always expecting me to be a star, but I wasn't making the money to live like one. I felt exploited both as a woman and as a black person."

In 1980, she divorced her husband, stating that he had wanted a housewife as a spouse and so the marriage never really worked. After her divorce, she began to paint, selling one painting for $10,000.

On December 2, 1980, TSU named its indoor track after Rudolph; that same year, the Black Sports Hall of Fame inducted her into their honorary organization. In 1981, she founded the Wilma Rudolph Foundation, a nonprofit organization for promising athletes in Indianapolis, Indiana; by the mid-1980s, there were more than one thousand participants and Rudolph provided free coaching. In 1983, she was inducted into the United States Olympic Hall of Fame and was awarded the Vitalis Cup for Sports Excellence. The following year, she won the Women's Sports Foundation Award.

She returned to Nashville in 1992, after accepting a job as the vice president of the Baptist hospital in the city. Just two years later, she received a double dose of bad news: her mother had died and, in July, doctors diagnosed her with both brain and throat cancer. Rudolph largely kept to herself after her cancer diagnosis, although she did walk around the TSU track with retired coach Temple.

Although she was frequently hospitalized over the next several months, she died at home on November 12, 1994, at the age of fifty-four. A memorial service was held at Kean Hall at TSU on November 17, with a funeral service at the First Baptist Church in Clarksville; that day, flags in Tennessee flew at half-mast in her honor.

Olympic track and field coach Bob Kersee (the husband of Olympic gold medalist Jackie Joyner-Kersee) was quoted in Rudolph's obituary as saying, "I don't think other people realise how big an influence Wilma Rudolph had on black female athletes. I hope Jackie and her generation will be able to influence young athletes, black and white, the way Wilma Rudolph did."

LEGACY

Rudolph was granted the National Women's Hall of Fame award, as well as two honorary degrees. A section of Highway 79 in Clarksville was renamed the Wilma Rudolph Boulevard. On August 11, 1995, TSU named their new dormitory the Wilma G. Rudolph Residence Center with her coach, Edward Temple, present for the ribbon cutting. On that occasion, the president of TSU Dr. James Hefner said that "Wilma Rudolph was an example to us not only in winning in sports, but . . . triumphing over the odds and winning at life."

On October 13, 2005, the annual Edward S. Temple Seminars in Society and Sport named their annual luncheon the Wilma Rudolph Memorial Luncheon. The Wilma Rudolph Memorial Commission honored Rudolph by putting a black marble marker at her grave, which was located in the Foster Memorial Garden Cemetery, on November 21, 1995. In April 1996, a life-sized bronze statue of Rudolph in motion was completed and then placed at the intersection of College Street and Riverside Drive in Clarksville. In 1997, Tennessee Governor Don Sundquist proclaimed June 23, her birthday, as Wilma Rudolph Day.

In 2004, Rudolph was honored on a postage stamp, as part of the U.S. Postal Services' Distinguished Americans stamp series. The stamp portrayed Rudolph as she looked after winning three gold medals in the 1960 Olympic Games.

FURTHER READING

Grimsley, Will. 1960. Wilma Rudolph Is Darling of Rome Olympics: First Double Winner for Women Since Babe. *Avalanche-Journal*, September 6.

Harper, Jo. 2004. *Wilma Rudolph: Olympic Runner*. New York: Aladdin Paperbacks.

Lovett, Bobby L. 1997. Leaders of Afro-American Nashville: Wilma Rudolph and the TSU Tigerbelles. *1997 Nashville Conference on Afro-American Culture and History*. http://ww2.tnstate.edu/library/digital/Rudolph.pdf.

Roberts, M. B. 2007. Rudolph ran and the world went wild. *ESPN*. http://espn.go.com/sportscentury/features/00016444.html.

Smith, Maureen. 2006. *Wilma Rudolph: A Biography*. Westport, CT: Greenwood Press.
YouTube. "Wilma Rudolph—An uphill battle." http://www.youtube.com/watch?v=igl8DmcKRhQ.
YouTube. "Women's 200 Final from Rome 1960." http://www.youtube.com/watch?v=FxWCZiNj5rM&feature=related.

Picabo Street passes a gate on her way to winning the gold medal in the Women's Super-G at the Olympic Winter Games in Nagano, February 11, 1998. (AP Photo/Diether Endlicher)

Picabo Street (1971–)

Central Idaho is a study in contrasts. A dozen miles down the road from Sun Valley Ski Resort, playground of the jet setters and country-club set, lies the working-class community of Triumph, population forty, a collection of modest tin-roofed houses and outbuildings. The unincorporated town has been on the economic downslope since the Triumph mine closed in the mid-1950s when the lodes of silver and lead ran out. It was an unlikely setting to produce a champion skier. But there on April 3, 1971, Picabo Street made a dramatic entrance into the world. Her mother Dee delivered her at home, miles from the nearest doctor. The newborn refused to breathe and began turning blue. Roland "Ron" Street picked up his daughter and breathed life into her. The Streets would later joke that this was Picabo's first temper tantrum.

CHILDHOOD

Picabo Street's early life was a study in contrast to the rich kids who vacationed at the nearby ski resorts. Dee and Ron Street had moved to Idaho seeking a simpler life during the tumultuous 1960s. Ron worked at the ski resorts and as a stone mason, while Dee taught music. The Streets raised rabbits and chickens and cultivated a large vegetable garden in order to put food on the table. They chopped their own wood for the cook stove and to heat their home during Idaho winters that arrived in October and lasted until early May. The family didn't own a TV until Picabo was fourteen. It took more than a little ingenuity to avoid cabin fever. While Ron Street worked at the nearby ski resort, Picabo's family had to settle for more down-to-earth recreation. They rode horses and camped in the nearby mountains. The Streets set aside enough money to take vacations during the cold winters. The family would pile into the pickup truck and head south to Arizona or Mexico.

Ron and Dee Street were not ordinary parents. They decided to give their children a say in choosing their names. Picabo's birth certificate read "Baby Girl Street" just as her older brother's read "Baby Boy." The name issue came to a head when the family planned to travel south of the U.S. border. Everyone needed a passport with a name on it. "Baby Boy" Street became Roland, after his father. For their three-year-old daughter whose favorite game was peek-a-boo, they settled on Picabo, an Indian word meaning "shining water." It also was the name of a nearby town and trout stream. The future Olympian's name was pronounced the same way as the children's game. It would routinely draw comment when she became a sports celebrity.

Picabo's childhood was unique in another sense. Only a handful of children lived in Triumph, and she was the only girl. The effect on her was predictable. Picabo didn't play with dolls; she had her own BB gun. She grew up riding bikes on the trails and playing tackle football with her brother, whom she called "Baba," and the other boys in the neighborhood. Dee Street recalls that her daughter wasn't afraid of anything. Picabo would put on boxing gloves and take on any kid in sight. She was a risk taker who suffered her first concussion when she lost her grip on the monkey bars at age ten. "Peek" and her brother were both athletic. Baba would set some school records playing linebacker in high school. The two Street children were allowed an unusual amount of freedom growing up, but they also were taught responsibility. They had chores to do before they could play. Picabo's jobs included sweeping the floor and making sure the kindling box was full. Despite their sense of independence, the Streets were a close family. The youngsters knew their parents would always be there if they needed them. As for temperament, Picabo was her father's daughter. She had inherited his obstinacy, and the two would often butt heads. This trait would prove both a curse and a blessing for the future world-class skier.

At age five, Picabo learned to ski chasing her father and brother down the slopes. When there was extra money, they skied on Dollar Mountain, Sun Valley's beginner hill. When money ran short, she and her mother would ski down the sloping road behind their house. Picabo won her first ski race at age six. By the time she turned seven she had her own skis, and could keep up with her father. As skiing became a passion, she quickly graduated from the beginner's run to Mount Baldy, the more challenging slope. That's when her father went into the rock business. During school vacations, Picabo and her brother worked in the quarry carrying rocks all day long. The experience did wonders for the developing skier's strength and coordination. She still had time during the summers to indulge her other passion, racing in bicycle motocross on the local BMX track. Picabo wasn't satisfied being the top girl rider; she wanted to beat all the boys too.

When winters came, Picabo would compete on the slopes as a member of the Sun Valley ski team. At age eleven, she won every Mountain Division age-group race she entered except one, finishing second on that occasion. The following winter, she left the Sun Valley team and joined the local team in Hailey. Her parents had been concerned about the lack of supervision at Sun Valley, as well as the mounting expenses. At age thirteen, Picabo qualified for the Western Regional Junior Olympics held in Alaska. In the winter of 1984, the youngster who grew up without television watched a neighbor's TV as five American skiers won medals at the Winter Olympics in Sarajevo, Yugoslavia. One of the medal winners was Christin Cooper from nearby Ketchum, the town where Picabo had attended elementary school. That's when she set her goal on becoming an Olympic Alpine skier. She was particularly attracted to the downhill race, the speed event. One key to winning this event is aerodynamics, and Picabo had an exceptional ability to compact her growing frame into a tight tuck.

Alpine and Nordic are two different classes of competitive skiing. The latter includes cross country and ski jumping. Alpine skiing consists of four events,

SUN VALLEY SKI RESORT

Sun Valley, Idaho was the first destination ski resort in the American West. It was built by the Union Pacific Railroad in 1936 under the direction of its chairman, Averill Harriman, who later became governor of New York and a presidential candidate. Sun Valley has long enjoyed a tradition as the ski resort of Hollywood celebrities. Clark Gable, Gary Cooper, and Ingrid Bergman vacationed there. More recently, Clint Eastwood and Arnold Schwarzenegger built homes in the area. Local legend has it that Ernest Hemingway worked on his novel *For Whom the Bell Tolls* while staying at Sun Valley Lodge. The book was made into a film starring Cooper and Bergman.

The resort attracted Olympic athletes along with film stars. In 1941, Hollywood released the film *Sun Valley Serenade*, shot on location and starring Olympic figure skater Sonja Henie. Alpine skier Dick Durrance, who competed in the 1936 Winter Olympic Games, helped cut the ski trails on Bald Mountain. Olympic silver medalist Christin Cooper, born in Ketchum, Idaho, learned to ski at Sun Valley. One of the ski runs on "Baldy" was renamed "Christin's Silver" in her honor. Another ski trail at Sun Valley carries the name Picabo's Street.

Sun Valley hosted World Cup ski races in the 1970s, and then served as a training site for the 2002 Winter Olympics in Salt Lake City. Today, Sun Valley features a vibrant arts community that sponsors exhibits, concerts, film festivals, and opera, to complement its popular ski resort.

or disciplines: downhill, slalom, giant slalom, and super giant slalom or Super G. Slalom is a Norwegian word meaning "sloping track." The downhill race is held on a long—up to a mile and a half—steep course with "gates" that mark the course. The gates consist of flexible poles with flags. The typical run features knolls and minor jumps. The slalom, unlike the downhill, requires skiers to zigzag down the slope. The basic slalom is held on a shorter course than the downhill with closely placed flags requiring a series of sharp turns. The giant slalom is held on a steeper, longer course, about a mile in length. The Super G event is longer yet and faster, more of a speed event.

Alpine skiing became an Olympic sport at the 1936 Winter Games in Bavaria. Men's and women's medals were awarded in the combined event. The "combined" consisted of the downhill run followed by two slalom races held the following day. When the Winter Games resumed in 1948 following the war, separate medals were awarded in downhill and slalom events. The giant slalom was added at the 1952 Olympic Games in Oslo. All Alpine events have one thing in common; skiers race against the clock. No one knows who the winner is until the last skier has completed the course. The finishers often are separated by hundredths of a second. In the slalom and Super G races, the finish is determined by a combined time in two runs.

There's a downside to Alpine skiing. It's been called "the NASCAR of winter sports." Skiers reach speeds in excess of 70 mph. When they crash and hit the frozen ground or a barrier, it's like bouncing off the wall of a race track—only there's no automobile surrounding the body to cushion the impact. Skiers get concussions despite wearing protective helmets. Broken bones are not uncommon. Fatalities have occurred during ski races. The key to competitive skiing is regaining one's confidence after a traumatic accident. Virtually all world-class skiers damage a knee ligament sooner or later. Most of them have undergone knee surgery. Picabo Street was no exception. She would carry the physical scars that follow serious spills, and she struggled with the demons that haunt an injured skier's mind. But she was tough-minded and intensely competitive.

The Europeans had always dominated the sport of skiing: both the men's and women's events. Gretchen Fraser was the first American to win an Olympic gold medal in Alpine skiing at the 1948 Games at St. Moritz. American women skiers would win very few Olympic medals over the following decades. Then in 1984, Debbie Armstrong and Christen Cooper finished first and second in the giant slalom at the Winter Games in Sarajevo. The summer following the Sarajevo Games, Picabo was invited by the U.S. Ski Team coaches to attend a training camp on Mount Hood in Oregon. Her family scraped together the money so that she could make the trip. This was an opportunity the Olympic hopeful couldn't pass up. She was the youngest skier at the camp.

Skiers who plan to compete at the international level hone their skills at training camps and at private ski academies. The academies combine academic programs with conditioning and training under the direction of professional ski coaches. Tuition at ski academies is high. Today, the top academies charge $20,000 to $30,000 a year plus room and board. At age fourteen, Picabo showed outstanding potential as a member of the local ski team. Her parents decided to move to Salt Lake City so she could enroll at the prestigious Rowmark Ski Academy. They packed their U-Haul and headed to Utah. The Academy skiers attended classes at the exclusive Rowland Hills–St. Mark's School. While Picabo's grades in school were marginal, her skiing performance at Rowmark was impressive. She acquired valuable racing skills and got the opportunity to compete in her first international event, the Topolino World Juvenile Championships in northern Italy. Competing against outstanding skiers from around the world, she finished sixteenth in the downhill. She then took her first serious spill at a meet in the United States, breaking four teeth and sustaining a hairline jaw fracture. Meanwhile, she was struggling from culture shock at the exclusive school, and the move had put a financial strain on her family. At the end of the year, the Streets returned to Idaho.

The Streets realized that skiing is an expensive sport, apart from ski academy tuition. Competitive skiers must pay for private coaching. The use of ski slopes requires purchasing tickets for ski lifts plus other sundry expenses. The ski lifts at Sun Valley currently run $40 per day and up. Then there's the cost of ski outfits and equipment: form-fitting suits, boots, gloves, helmets, goggles, ski poles, and several pairs of skis. The total can run over a thousand dollars. In addition, skiers incur travel expenses to compete at meets in the United States and abroad. Picabo's trip to the Junior Regionals in Alaska in 1985 cost almost two thousand dollars. She estimates that her parents, at some sacrifice, spent more than $15,000 a year to support her as a junior skier in her teen years. She relied on community support as well. Friends and neighbors often went door-to-door to solicit donations to help with expenses. Training and travel took an additional toll in terms of time and energy. Picabo's grades continued to suffer. She decided to drop out of high school and study on her own toward a general equivalency diploma, a G.E.D. She enrolled in a correspondence course, and the ski team coaches provided a tutor.

Picabo Street was skiing at Sun Valley when she caught the attention of U.S. Ski Team coach Paul Major, who put her on the U. S. Junior team. She accompanied the junior team to Argentina the summer of 1986 to train in the Andes Mountains with ski teams from all over the world. Street competed in the 1987 North American Ski Trophy Series at sites in the United States and Canada. The following season she was back racing in the Nor-Am events, and then traveled to Italy in January for the World Junior Alpine Championships. She finished sixth in the downhill, her best performance to date in an international event. She went on to win both the downhill and the Super G at the Junior Olympic Championships held in Oregon. Street's skiing so impressed her coaches that they moved her to the "C" team and sent her to her first World Cup event, the Aspen-Subaru Winternational. She skied all four events and finished in the top thirty, competing against older skiers. Meanwhile, the U.S. women's ski team got "shut out" at the 1988 Olympic Games in Calgary, not winning a single medal.

SERIOUS SKI TRAINING

The seventeen-year-old skier was on her own now. Picabo's parents had moved to Hawaii where her father had been offered a stone masonry job, and her brother was away at college. Picabo settled in a condo in Sun Valley to be close to the ski slopes, although she was on the road for half the year. The season normally ran from late November through March. During the summers, the ski team often flew to South America to practice on snow. Graduating from the junior team offered Street the opportunity to travel the world, but also meant training harder than ever. The Ski Team coaches put her on a program of wind sprints, weight training, and distance running between competitive events. Spending hours in the gym was not her idea of a good time while her teenaged friends were enjoying life. The young skier's failure to train diligently and maintain her fitness level would become a recurring issue with her coaches.

Skiing requires both physical and mental preparation. There's more to winning than the ability to zoom downhill at full speed. Skiers must master all of the strategic factors that determine the outcome of a race. They analyze the way that the gates are set on a course, looking for the "perfect line" to ski. They study snow conditions before the race. The surface of the course may be soft or hard; snow can range from powdery to icy. Skiers must decide on the type of wax to apply to the bases of their skis depending on the conditions of the course and the weather. Even the selection of the skis has become a science. In addition to the cognitive aspect of skiing, there's the fear factor. Skiers have to overcome their anxieties about falling and injuring themselves. A skier can't be too aggressive or too cautious. Street was confident that she had a high fear threshold and a high pain threshold. Both would be tested during the course of her career. Maturity presented a greater challenge.

Picabo competed in the Europa Cup during the 1988–89 season, where she faced some of the best skiers in the world. The prestigious World Alpine Ski Championships were held in Vail, Colorado. It was rare for the biennial event to take place in the United States. Four hundred top skiers arrived for the competition. Picabo Street attended as a member of the ski team, but didn't compete. She continued to race on the Nor-Am circuit. In February, she took a spill while skiing the Super G at a World Cup event in Steamboat Springs. She ruptured the anterior cruciate ligament, or ACL, that connects the tibia in the lower leg to the femur. It's a common injury among skiers. She underwent surgery on the knee and flew to Hawaii to stay with her parents while she recovered. She entered rehab on the Islands and then returned to the States in July. The doctors pronounced her fit to ski again. However, her fitness level had deteriorated, and she had trouble keeping up with teammates during the drills. Coach Paul Major admonished her for not getting in better shape. The following season was disappointing. Street won a couple minor races but finished fifth in the slalom at the World Junior Alpine Championships.

The responsibilities of being a ski team member proved trying for the free-spirited teenager. Competitive skiing requires intense discipline, and coaches expect the athletes to comply with their demands. There were required team meetings and training rules that included a curfew. Picabo had a tendency to rebel against rules. Being on a team also meant getting along with the other team members. Picabo not only neglected her training but routinely feuded with the other skiers. The small-town kid had a chip on her shoulder, and teammates found her intense competitiveness off-putting. It only made matters worse when Picabo threw public temper tantrums after skiing badly. There came a point when several of the coaches wanted her off the team. Paul

Major, however, stood up for her. He saw potential in the willful teenager, and felt he could turn her into a champion. The situation came to a head the summer of 1990 when Picabo showed up for training camp out of shape again. The coaches booted her off the team.

Picabo Street returned to Idaho with plans to stay with a friend. She told her parents that she was sick, but they soon found out the real reason why she had left the team. Her father instructed her to come to Hawaii. Picabo's brother put her on a plane to Maui. Ron Street decided to personally take charge of his daughter's training. He took Picabo to work with him, hauling rocks again. In addition, the ex-Marine enrolled her in his version of boot camp with a regimen of sit-ups, push-ups, and wind sprints. With stopwatch in hand, her father played the role of drill sergeant.

A CHANGE IN ATTITUDE

When the coaches accepted Street back on the junior team in September, they noted a significant change in her physical condition and attitude. The chastened young skier had begun to rein in her temper and unruliness. More importantly, she began to focus on the fun of skiing again. In 1991, Street won the North American Championship for junior skiers. The following year, she won it again. However, she nursed a jealousy toward Hilary Lindh, who had won the bronze medal at the 1992 Winter Olympic Games. Street didn't earn a position on the U.S. Olympic team. The next Winter Olympics would be held in two years, as the International Olympic Committee, or IOC, decided to stagger the Summer and Winter Games. Picabo and Hilary were both on the U.S. Ski Team preparing for the 1993 season. The team coaches had grown weary of tension between the two young women and insisted they start acting like teammates. Picabo had a tendency to ignore her female teammates and hang out with the guys. But this wasn't her old neighborhood.

Between Olympics Games, American skiers compete in the Nor-Am races sponsored by the United States Ski Association. The top skiers also compete on the World Cup circuit under the jurisdiction of the International Ski Federation, or FIS. World Cup competition included nine events during the 1990s. Points are awarded to the top thirty finishers at each event. The racer with the most points at the end of the season in March wins the Cup. There's also the Europa Cup, rated just below World Cup level. Street skied on both the Junior Nor-Am and Europa Cup circuits during the 1991 and 1992 seasons. Her skiing continued to improve. At the 1993 World Alpine Championships in Japan, Street surprised everyone by taking the silver medal in the combined. She then won three medals at the U.S. Championships, including a gold in the Super G. The young skier with the memorable name was beginning to receive public notice. She hired an agent Chris Hanna to handle the commercial offers that followed. Street signed endorsement contracts with companies that marketed ski equipment. She was paid a thousand dollars to wear a Ski USA logo on her headband. Her income exceeded $40,000 following the string of wins. The working-class skier bought herself a pickup truck.

THE 1994 OLYMPICS

The 1994 Olympics were to set to take place in the small town of Lillehammer, Norway. These were the first Winter Games held in an alternative year to the Summer Games. Twenty-two-year-old Picabo Street, who had watched the 1984 Winter Games on a friend's TV as a teenager, now had her opportunity to appear on international television. The exposure was seen as a mixed blessing by her coaches and teammates. Street had lost her temper again, on camera, after skiing badly at Aspen. Her language embarrassed the team. She was acquiring a reputation as skiing's "bad girl." But she also was the U.S. Ski Team's promising hope to medal in the downhill and the combined event at the Olympics. Her experience in the Super G had made her more versatile.

The prelim to the Winter Games was the World Cup race in March, 1993, in Lillehammer on the same ski slope that would be utilized for 1994 Winter Games. Street finished second, the best performance by an American woman in a World Cup downhill in seven years. She was on track for the upcoming Olympic Games. The skier to beat in the Olympics was Germany's Katja Seizinger, who had won the gold medal in the Super G at the 1993 FIS World Championships. Another skier's specter would haunt the 1994 Winter Games. At a World Cup event in January, 1994, Street watched as Austria's Ulrike Maier hit her head on a timing pole after catching a ski tip. Uli was pronounced dead at the hospital, the first woman skier ever to die at a World Cup event. This tragedy heightened the fear factor when the 1994 Lillehammer Games commenced on February 12.

When the U.S. Ski Team arrived in Lillehammer in early February, the weather was so cold they had to practice wearing face masks. Whenever Street felt cold, she reminded herself that she had made it to the Olympics and that her family would be there to watch her. Street did well during the training runs and finished first in the final downhill a day before the official skiing events commenced. On the day of the medal race, Street misplaced her favorite pair of skis. This only added to her nervousness when she arrived at the top of the slope. She was scheduled to start eighth, behind Katja and Hilary. When her turn came, she zipped down the frigid course and finished with a time that positioned her in second place. She waited anxiously for some forty-five minutes as the other skiers crossed the finish line. No one else beat her time. Street realized she'd won the silver medal in the downhill. Katja took the gold, and Hilary finished seventh. Street couldn't celebrate too long, as she had another race the following day. She skied poorly in the slalom and finished tenth, but she was thrilled to have won an Olympic medal.

Following the medal ceremony, Picabo Street held a press conference accompanied by her parents and brother. Her colorful father upstaged everyone in the family while at Lillehammer, sporting a beard and ponytail, and draped in the American flag. But it was Picabo who would have to deal with the public attention over the long term. Suddenly, she was an international sports celebrity. The Olympic silver medalist received the full red carpet treatment upon arriving back in the United States. There were autograph sessions, trade shows, and TV appearances that would include *Sesame Street* and *American Gladiators*. The governor of Idaho declared March 19 "Picabo Street Day," and the towns of Hailey and Ketchum each named a street after her. Sun Valley named one of its ski trails "Picabo's Street."

SKIING, ENDORSEMENTS, AND MAKING MONEY

When the celebrations came to an end, Street returned to the ski circuit. She skied at a World Cup event in Whistler, British Columbia, followed by the World Cup finals at Vail, where she finished fourth. The following spring while Street was at ski camp, her parents separated. The Olympic medalist went into the 1994–95 season with a good deal of pressure on her. The U.S. Ski Team had hired a new women's coach Herwig Demschar, who had previously coached the Austrians. Coach Demschar had a long talk with Street about her attitude and her relationships with teammates. After Hilary Lindh won the first World Cup downhill in Colorado, she went out of her way to console Street who had taken a tumble down the slope and tore a ligament in her hand. It was to be an eventful season filled with triumphs and near tragedy. Street recovered from her injury and went on to win six of nine downhill races, including five in a row. Then during the last meet of the season, Street was halfway through the Super G when she fell, landed on her back, and crashed into a pair of skis. The medics put her on a stretcher and took her to the hospital for a check-up. Fortunately, she incurred only minor injuries. The season had a happy ending. Street won the World Cup downhill title and was presented with the traditional crystal globe at the awards ceremony. She was the first non-European to win the title.

Street's success on the slopes translated into more commercial success. She signed an endorsement deal with Sprint, the telephone provider, and was approached by Sue Levin, head of the women's division at Nike. In late 1995, the skier signed a three-year endorsement deal with the sneaker company that extended through the 1998 Winter Olympics. At the time, Nike didn't make a single product for skiers. It was Picabo's charisma that made her attractive. She would join soccer's Mia Hamm, basketball's Sheryl Swoopes, and track star Jackie Joyner-Kersee in Nike's marketing campaign aimed at young women. Nike planned to sell a cross-training shoe endorsed by Picabo, called the "Air Skeet." Later, they would come out with a line of ski clothes.

The 1995–96 season kicked off at Vail in November then moved to Europe. Street won six downhills in a row before her streak was broken at a meet in Austria. At Sierra Nevada in Spain, she placed in the top three in the Super G. Then in mid-February, she took a spill that knocked her unconscious. But she recovered in time to claim her second consecutive World Cup downhill title in Norway. The following summer, Street underwent surgery for bone spurs, causing her to miss the off-season conditioning camps. While she was hobbling about on crutches, Rossignol, her ski sponsor, came out with a line of "Peak" skis. Street looked forward to exchanging her vertical stilts for the familiar horizontal "boards." Despite injuries, she had experienced two remarkable seasons in a row.

The young skier who grew up in modest circumstances was becoming affluent. Following her World Cup and Olympic success, Street was inundated with demands for personal appearances and commercial offers. She received numerous opportunities to endorse products including a soft drink and a lip balm, and she served as a spokesperson for a range of companies. Endorsement fees, added to the prize money, came to a half million dollars in 1996. All the personal obligations and business commitments could play havoc with a skier's training schedule. Her agent helped her sort through the offers.

Picabo Street went into the 1996–97 ski season with high hopes, shooting for her third downhill title in a row. However, she took a spill during a practice run at Vail in December and tore the ligament in her left knee. Following surgery on her ACL, she spent most of the year in rehab. She wasn't able to get back into serious competition until December of 1997. Street finished fourth in a downhill race the following January, but had another mishap on the slopes in Italy the last day of the month. She knocked herself unconscious and suffered whiplash and a slight concussion. On top of that, she had sprained an ankle playing volleyball while in Europe. Street reflected on her recent misfortunes and commented, "Ski racing is like football—you keep beating up on yourself until your body cries foul" (Street, 2002, 201). She didn't have long to recover. The 1998 Winter Olympics in Nagano were scheduled to open the first week of February.

A GOLD MEDAL, INJURIES, AND PERSEVERANCE

Street felt confident going into the Games. She was still nursing a stiff neck and swollen ankle, but the year of rehab and rigorous training had paid dividends. The skier put on ten pounds of muscle and felt in top shape. Street arrived in Japan on February 5th accompanied by her new agent Nadia and boyfriend

J. J., a former Stanford University football player. Her first event at Nagano was the Super G, the "rollercoaster of skiing." She had never won this event in international competition. The weather at Nagano was iffy. Races had to be postponed twice. Finally, the women's Super G was run. Street was scheduled second out of the gate. At the top of the run, technician Cookie Kairys handed Picabo her downhill skis—the ones she skied on to win the silver medal at Lillehammer—rather than her Super G skies. He convinced her that she didn't need the more compact boards. Picabo flew down the slope and made it to the finish line with a time of 1:18:02, two seconds faster than the first skier. Now she had to wait for the rest of the field to finish. One after another the skiers came down the mountain. Austrian skier Micki Dorfmeister finished .01 second slower. That's as close as anyone would get. Picabo won the gold medal by the narrowest of margins. Austria's Meisi Meissnitzer would take third with a time of 1:18:09. The three medalists had finished .07 of a second apart, the narrowest margin in Olympic skiing history. Picabo Street became the sixth American woman to win an Olympic gold medal in Alpine skiing.

This was the goal that Street had been training for all her life. Her father and brother were there to share her victory. After hugs all around, she called her mother in Hawaii to tell her the news. The awards ceremony was followed by a press conference and photo sessions. Finally, Street was able to head back to the ski lodge where she was staying and concentrate on her next event, the downhill race. The lodge, provided by the relative of a Nike employee, was within walking distance of the ski lifts: one of the perks of being a "Nike athlete." The retreat had accumulated a growing number of family, friends, and assistants over the course of the Games. The hubbub became a distraction. Ron Street's diabetes acted up, and then J. J. got into an altercation at a local club. In addition, Street was inundated with phone calls from the media and fans. President Bill Clinton called twice. Amidst all the commotion, she had to mentally prepare herself for the downhill in three days. To make matters worse, the weather didn't cooperate. Training sessions were interrupted, and the downhill was rescheduled from Thursday to Monday. On race day, the downhill course was something of a mess because of the rain. Picabo wasn't happy about starting in sixteenth position. She struggled through the first half of the course and attempted to make up speed at the bottom of the hill, but finished a disappointing sixth, .17 of a second slower than the bronze medal winner. However, she had won an Olympic Gold medal at Nagano.

Following the Olympic Games, Picabo flew to Hawaii to spend some time with her family before heading to Europe for three weeks. A hundred of the world's best skiers assembled in March for a World Cup event at Crans-Montana. Here in the Swiss Alps, the Olympic medalist took a tragic spill during the downhill race. Street lost her balance and crashed into the safety fence, ski tips first. Her legs crumpled under her, and she felt intense pain. Her left femur, the large bone in her upper leg, had snapped. She could feel the jagged end of the bone ripping into her quadriceps muscle. She lay in the snow, screaming in agony. Ski team physician Dr. Bob Scheinberg reached her within minutes and attempted to pull the bone back into place. The medics arrived, splinted her legs, placed her on a stretcher, and loaded her onto a waiting helicopter. At the local hospital, she was rushed to the emergency room. Street would learn that she also had torn the ligaments and cartilage in her right knee. Nadia, her agent, phoned her parents to tell them the bad news. The Swiss doctors bolted her femur together with a nine-inch steel plate, and the injured skier was put on a Medivac flight to Colorado.

Street was admitted to the Vail Medical Center where doctors diagnosed a ruptured ACL and torn meniscus cartilage in her right knee. She left Vail and headed to her new home in Portland, Oregon for a month to heal from the leg surgery before returning to have surgery on her knee. Street celebrated her twenty-seventh birthday with a stiff brace on her left leg. Lying in bed following knee surgery, she surveyed the long zipper-like ten-inch scar that ran the length of her left thigh. But she couldn't dwell on the negative. Her goal was to recover and win at the 1999 World Alpine Ski Championships to be held in Vail. Street went back into rehab. She realized that she had to be able to walk before she could ski again. She was down to one crutch by late summer. Then in October, as she was getting out of the car, the healing meniscus tore loose. She knew immediately from the painful sensation what had happened. The skier had to undergo surgery for the third time in less than a year. In November, she rejoined the U.S. Ski Team—as a spectator. The following month, Street attended the United States Olympic Committee, or USOC, Athlete of the Year Banquet in Indianapolis. She won the award and was able to walk to the podium and accept it without the aid of crutches.

Street took a job as director of skiing at Park City. Her responsibilities included promoting the Utah resort, which meant skiing with the vacationers. Meanwhile, she gradually resumed her training. The physical recovery would take a while, as her leg muscles had atrophied over the previous year. The former size-twelve skier was down to a size eight. Street set a long-term goal of skiing at the 2002 Winter Olympics to be held in Salt Lake City. She wasn't able to ski at the World Cup Championships, but did commentary for NBC Network. As it turned out, no one on the U.S. team skied very well in Vail. The Austrians dominated. While there, Street stopped by the local medical clinic for a check-up. The metal plate attached to the femur was causing some discomfort. In March, Dr. Steadman removed it—almost a year to the day from the accident. The operation put her back on crutches. Her prolonged recovery had other repercussions. One of her sponsors, Rossignal, the ski manufacturer, decided to exercise the injury clause in her contract and cancel their relationship. She sued the company and won a settlement, but the relationship ended. In December, she was involved in another lawsuit with Sun Valley Co. which had used her name without permission. Two months later, Street and long-time boyfriend J. J. ended their relationship. It had been an eventful year.

Street bought a house near Park City, close to the ski trails where she could observe the construction of the new highway to the Olympic site. She got back on her skis and began the road to recovery. The Winter Games were two years away. She alternated training with the "Ski with Picabo" sessions at Park City. Ski technology had advanced during her absence, and she had to adjust to the new shorter, hour-glass-shaped skis. Given her long absence from competition, it was like learning to ski again. Street rejoined the ski team at their May training camp and prepared for the World Cup opener in November at Park City. She stopped by the clinic in Vail for a routine checkup. Dr. Steadman had to draw fluid from her knee. A follow-up MRI indicated she had torn the meniscus once again. Street underwent arthroscopic surgery four days later. She would not be skiing at the World Cup event. She recovered from surgery and flew to France in December for her first international competition in nearly three years. Her old rival Kayja Seizinger was not there, having "blown out" both her knees in 1998. Street-skiing on sore knees, finished twenty-eighth in the Super G, her gold medal event. The next meet was in St. Moritz. Here too, she finished "out of the money." It had been a challenging tour, and she felt exhausted.

Picabo returned to the United States to spend Christmas in balmy Florida with new boyfriend John Mulligan, a ski technician. The couple took a brief fishing vacation on John's boat. In January, Street headed for Utah to train on the Olympic slopes. She realized she would have to fight for a place on the U.S. Olympic Ski Team, as a group of promising teenagers were making their presence felt. Street qualified in the downhill but failed to qualify in the Super G. She joined a group of young American skiers on the Europa Cup circuit. She did well in her two disciplines at Pra-Loop in France, and then missed the "cut" in the downhill competition in Lenzerheide, Switzerland. She and John then flew to Whistler, BC, for a Nor-Am race, a step down from Cup competition. Street won a couple of races on the Nor-Am circuit and felt she was ready for the Salt Lake City Olympics.

The 2002 Winter Olympic Games took place in the wake of a bribery scandal that resulted in the resignation of several IOC members. When the Games got underway in February, the U.S. ski team did not perform to expectations. The American men won two silver medals in Alpine skiing, while the American women were shut out by the Europeans. Street finished a disappointing sixteenth in the downhill. The realization began to set in that her skiing career was coming to an end. The string of injuries had taken a toll. The thirty-year-old skier decided to retire following the Olympics. She made it official at a World Cup event at Park City in November with a final ceremonial run down the familiar slope.

Picabo Street had enjoyed a remarkable career as an Alpine skier. In addition to her two Olympic medals, she won the 1996 World Championship in the downhill, and took the bronze in the Super G. Three years earlier, she had won the silver in the combined. Overall, she accumulated nine downhill titles and two season titles in the downhill: the first American ever to win a World Cup season title in a speed event. Street was named USOC Sportswoman of the Year in 1995 and 1998, and was inducted into the National Ski Hall of Fame in 2005. She remains one of the greatest downhill skiers in American history.

The working-class tomboy who grew up wearing her older brother's hand-me-downs went "from britches to riches." The Idaho teenager obliged to solicit donations to cover expenses at ski camp became a millionaire as a result of her skiing success. She never forgot her roots. The Olympic medalist created Picabo's Street of Dreams Foundation which provided financial assistance to help children fulfill their dreams. She also became a spokesperson for the National Children's Alliance, an advocacy group for abused children. In 2004, she organized a fund-raiser, The Picabo Ski Challenge, that takes place during the annual Sundance Film Festival in Utah, to raise money for the Alliance.

Retirement for Street hasn't meant slowing down. She worked as an analyst with CBS Sports and later as a correspondent for the NBC *Today Show* during the 2006 Winter Olympics in Turin. She also arranges ski clinics and is a motivational speaker. The skiing celebrity continues to do promotions for commercial products including ChapStick. For relaxation, Street keeps physically active through a variety of activities. In the winters, she snowmobiles and skis now for recreation. When the snow melts, she water skis and plays volleyball. She keeps several riding horses on her ten-acre spread in Park City.

In October 2008, Picabo and businessman John Reeser were married in a ceremony atop Prospect Mountain in Alabama. The couple splits their time between homes in Alabama and Utah. They have assembled a "yours, mine, and ours" family, raising John's son Eli, Picabo's son Treyjan James, and a third son Dax Meyer, born in August of 2009.

FURTHER READING

Anderson, Kelli. 2007. Full Speed Ahead. *Sports Illustrated*, 106:26: 108–11.

Anderson, Kelli. 2007. "Picabo Street." SI.com. http://sportsillustrated.cnn.com/2007/more/06/25/want.picabo/index.html.

Dippold, Joel. 1998. *Picabo Street: Downhill Dynamo*. Minneapolis, MN: Lerner Publications.

Farber, Michael. 1995. Playing Picabo. *Sports Illustrated*, Dec. 18: http://sportsillustrated. cnn.com/vault/article/magazine/MAG1007569/index.htm.

Phillips, Bob. 2010. "Injuries haven't stopped greatest U.S. skier." ESPN Classic. http://espn.go.com./classic/biography/s/Street_Picabo.html.

"Picabo Street Biography." 2010. Jrank.org: Famous Sports Stars. http://sports.jrank.org/ pages/4672/Street-Picabo.html.

Street, Picabo, with Dana White. 2002. *Picabo: Nothing to Hide*. Chicago: Contemporary Books.

Sheryl Swoopes points over to the Houston Comets bench after making a 3-point shot in the final minute of the game against the Sacramento Monarchs in 2003. The Comets won 74-71. (AP Photo/ Rich Pedroncelli)

Sheryl Swoopes (1971–)

Sheryl Swoopes is an American basketball player who became well known when she led Texas Tech University to a national championship. In the national championship, she scored forty-seven points, a National Collegiate Athletic Association (NCAA) record for men and women. After college graduation, she became one of the original members of the Women's National Basketball Association (WNBA), serving as a leader as the Houston Comets captured the first four league championships in a row. Only four other professional sports teams had ever done that before. Plus, she was the first player in the WNBA to get a playoff triple-double, meaning that she was the first person to get double-digit statistics in three different areas of play in one playoff game.

Moreover, Swoopes played on three Olympic gold-medal-winning basketball teams: 1996, 2000, and 2004. Swoopes could play all positions, but specialized in being a small forward. She was an excellent all-around player, able to lead in both offense and defense; she was incredibly quick as well.

CHILDHOOD

Sheryl Denise Swoopes was born on March 25, 1971, in Brownfield, Texas. When she was just a few months old, her father, Billy Ray Swoopes, left the family. Raised by her mother, Louise, Swoopes and her family lived in a three-room house (not three bedroom; three rooms, total), with Louise working multiple jobs, always short of money and sometimes on public assistance, Swoopes later recalled how they often literally did not know where their next meal would come from. They never owned a car. The family regularly attended church, though, and Louise's faith gave her strength.

As a young child, Swoopes wanted to be a nurse, a flight attendant or, with the most fervor, a cheerleader. She and her cousin would put on makeup and cheerleader costumes and root on her two older brothers, James and Earl, when they played basketball. (Swoopes also has a younger brother named Brandon.) The two girls also performed their cheerleading routines for their families.

Swoopes enjoyed playing basketball from about the age of seven; both her mother and her older brothers, though, discouraged her. Her mother would suggest that she come inside to play with dolls instead of roughhousing with the boys, while Swoopes' brothers would tell her that she was no good at the game and they refused to give her the ball when she was playing basketball with them. They would throw the ball at her head and play roughly enough that she would fall, scraping her knees and elbows.

Swoopes did not give up, though, joining the Little Dribbers, a recreational basketball league for girls, where she outplayed the other participants. In her third year in the league, her team qualified for the national championships; the trip to Beaumont, Texas was the family's first vacation. The team made it all the way to the finals, where they lost by a couple of points; the entire team cried.

Her brothers finally relented, allowing her to play basketball with them on the gravel in their backyard; at another location, they shot hoops into a rim made from an old bicycle wheel. Both of her brothers ended up playing basketball in high school, with James going on to play college ball; Swoopes could never beat them—until she came home from college, that is; that particular win on her "home court" was a huge victory for her.

HIGH SCHOOL BASKETBALL

Swoopes continued to play the sport in middle school. When the high school basketball coach stopped by, Swoopes tried hard to impress him and he encouraged her to keep playing. During the summer months, she played ball during open gym times—playing against the boys. At first, the boys would not choose her for a team; when she did play, they would mock her, handing her the ball and moving out of her way, suggesting that she could not otherwise make a basket.

By the time she reached Brownfield High School, though, she had earned a reputation as a top quality basketball player with the nickname of "Legs." After playing just one junior varsity game in ninth grade, the coach promoted her to the varsity team. She also ran track, setting a school record in the long jump.

In her sophomore year, Swoopes was named to the Texas All-State team. Swoopes served as the star of the Lady Cubs team during her junior year, when they qualified to play in the Texas Class 3A championship. They needed to play the Lady Hawks from Hardin-Jefferson to capture the state title; no one had beaten the Lady Hawks, though, that entire year, and the Lady Cubs' record was only 29-8.

At halftime, the score was 25-19 in favor of Hardin-Jefferson. After three quarters of play, Swoopes' team was losing, 31-27. At that point, Swoopes scored multiple baskets to put her team in the lead, 41-36. Near the end of the game, the Lady Cubs were losing again, 41-40, but then Swoopes made two free throws to put them back in the lead—and to firmly establish her reputation as a clutch player who made the big plays when they really counted. Swoopes had scored twenty-six points and made eighteen rebounds, and the Lady Cubs beat the Lady Hawks, 49-40, to win the title. Swoopes was the only player to reach double figures in rebounds and points scored.

College scouts attended her games. In her senior year, she was chosen as the Female High School Player of the Year statewide. She was also selected to participate on three All-American teams and was named the Most Valuable Player of the Texas High School Girls' Coaches Association North-South

All-Star Game. Her per-game high school averages were as follows: twenty-six points, fourteen rebounds, five assists, and five steals.

In 1989, Swoopes planned to participate in the U.S. Olympic Festival, which was like a mini-Olympic competition, but a knee injury prevented that from happening.

COLLEGE BASKETBALL

Swoopes received many scholarship offers and chose to attend the University of Texas in Austin; this school had an excellent basketball program, so her choice made sense. At the University of Texas, Swoopes would receive four years of free education and plenty of attention and exposure. But, upon reflection, Swoopes did not want to attend that college. As soon as she arrived in Austin, she was homesick, not wanting to live four hundred miles from her home. So, one week later, she left the University of Texas and all that they had offered her to attend a junior college, South Plains College, located close to her home.

The University of Texas coach, Jody Conradt, tried to change Swoopes' mind, but could not. Others warned Swoopes that, if she left this university behind, she was kissing her opportunity to play on a national championship team goodbye. Meanwhile, the South Plains basketball coach, Lyndon Hardin, was stunned at this turn of good fortune. At six feet tall, Swoopes was shorter than many of her opponents, but her speed put her ahead of them; her too-high dribble made it look as though it would be easy to steal the ball from her, but her quickness prevented that from happening very often. Meanwhile, she frequently stole the ball from the other team and her versatility allowed Hardin to use her as a center or forward.

During Swoopes' two years at South Plains, the team won fifty-two of sixty-four games and one regional championship. In 1991 she was selected as the National Junior College Player of the Year; both years in attendance, she won All-American recognition, meaning both NJCAA All-American and Kodak All-American. Also, each year she was named the Western Junior College Conference Most Valuable Player. At South Plains, Swoopes set 15 records, including: most points in a career (1,554); best career scoring average (25.4); most points in a game (45); most rebounds in a career (705); most rebounds in a game (22); and best career rebound average (11.5).

After completing two years at South Plains, Swoopes chose to play for Marsha Sharp's Red Raiders at Texas Tech, once again staying close to home. Texas Tech had advanced to the Southwest Conference (SWC) finals five times, losing to the University of Texas all five times. In the past fifteen years, Texas Tech had not beaten the University of Texas in Austin one single time—but now Sharp and the Raiders' fans hoped that Swoopes could change the tide and bring home the championship.

In January 1992, the largest crowd ever—5,600 spectators—filled the gym, hoping to see Swoopes dominate the court. Every time she had possession of the ball, the crowd screamed her name (which rhymed with "hoops"), drawing out the double "O" into a long sound. Swoopes did not let the fans down. Instead, she fulfilled their dreams by scoring thirty-two points as the Red Raiders beat their rival, 78-65. These two teams met up again in the SWC Tournament Finals when Swoopes—the SWC Player of the Year—once again led her team to victory, 76-74, clinching the state title. They attempted to compete for the national title, but lost to Stanford—who eventually won the national championship—in the NCAA regional semifinals. After the season ended, Swoopes' name was included on multiple major college All-American teams.

Swoopes tried out for the 1992 U.S. Olympic basketball team, but did not make the squad after she twisted her ankle. When she returned home, disappointed, she struggled to regain her momentum. She was thinking about quitting and was praying for guidance while at a mall; just then, she shared in her autobiography *Sheryl Swoopes: Bounce Back* (written with Greg Brown in 1996), a young girl approached her to tell her that she and her mother prayed for Swoopes every single night—and that God assured them that she would be okay. Swoopes said that she felt chills all over her body at that message.

At the beginning of the 1992–93 season, Texas Tech was ranked fifteenth in the country. During the opening game against Stanford, Swoopes scored thirty-five points, a career record for her. Although the Lady Raiders lost that game, they won a significant portion of the other games that they played. On January 2, 1993, Swoopes scored an astonishing forty-eight points against Washington, which was both a school record and a conference record. During that season, South Plains College decided to retire Swoopes' number, 22, an honor that no other junior college had given to an athlete.

Late in the season, the Raiders beat the University of Texas, the first time that Texas Tech had beaten its rival in Austin in fifteen years; in that game, Swoopes scored thirty-seven points. The two teams met up again in the state finals, with Swoopes uncharacteristically struggling on the court, missing her first six of seven shots; her team was losing, 26-11. In a bold show of confidence, her teammates kept throwing her the ball—and Swoopes ended up scoring fifty-three points, with Texas Tech winning the state championship, 78-71. Swoopes was named the National Player of the Year and the SWC Player of the Year.

This victory meant that Texas Tech would go on to compete for the national championship. First, they played Washington to a sellout-plus crowd, with Swoopes scoring thirty points and the Lady Raiders winning the game. Next, they played against Southern California, with Swoopes scoring thirty-three points; this victory put them in the top eight teams of the nation, a feat never before accomplished by this school.

Texas Tech played Colorado next, with their coach admitting that no one could be effectively matched up against Swoopes; she scored thirty-six points, boosting her team to the final four and causing even more people to call her the Michael Jordan of women's basketball. Next on the list was a game against the Vanderbilt Commodores, a college with a six-foot, ten-inch tall center, Heidi Gillingham. Moreover, the Commodores ranked number one in the nation. That was not enough to stop Texas Tech; Swoopes played well, and the Raiders won the game, 60-46.

In the final match for the national title, Texas Tech faced Ohio State University, a school that had just beaten Iowa State University to earn its spot in the finals. Like Texas Tech, Ohio State was new to the finals. On a personal level, Swoopes needed to score just five points in that game to break the five-game point-scoring tournament record (134 points) set by Bridgette Gordon in 1989. On a team level, a win against Ohio State would truly make this a Cinderella season for Texas Tech. The game was televised nationally while sixteen thousand people packed the Atlanta, Georgia gymnasium to watch the game live. One of them drove nineteen hours to see the game: Louise Swoopes.

During the first half, Swoopes scored twenty-three points, with Texas Tech winning at halftime, 40-31. Three times during the second half, though, Ohio State took a one-point lead. As the time wound down during the second half, Ohio State frequently was only two points behind the Texas powerhouse team. With just 2:16 remaining, the score was 75-73 in favor of Texas. Swoopes then made two free throws, making the score 77-73; she was fouled while making a shot, made a free throw, and brought the score to 80-73. The final score was Texas Tech 84, Ohio State 82.

Swoopes scored an incredible forty-seven points during that game. Prior to that, the women's NCAA record for points scored in a title game was twenty-eight, shared by Dawn Staley of Virginia and Dena Head of Tennessee. The men's record was forty-four, scored by Bill Walton for UCLA in 1973. Swoopes had just topped both of those accomplishments. She also scored the most points ever in an NCAA tournament, with 177, breaking the old record of 134 points by 43 points. Swoopes also broke the record for the most field goals (56) and free throws (57). When she and her mother returned home after the game, a huge crowd greeted them at the airport; then, President Bill Clinton invited them to the White House. When she stopped by a local store, so many people asked for her autograph that she spent four hours at the shop.

Not surprisingly, Swoopes received the Outstanding Player Award for tournament play. She also was named the Player of the Year by *USA Today* and *Sports Illustrated*, and was chosen as the Associated Press Female Athlete of the Year. She received the Naismith Award as National Player of the Year and Texas Tech retired her number.

POST-COLLEGE

After Swoopes' magnificent performance in the NCAA finals, basketball legend Michael Jordan invited her to a one-on-one match up at his basketball camp during the summer of 1993. She accepted, with Jordan winning, 7-5. After the game, Jordan expressed his admiration of her by saying, "Girl, you can play" (Rappoport, 2002, 49). Later, parts of this match aired on television.

Nike offered her a shoe contract in 1995, debuting the "Air Swoopes." This was the first pair of shoes manufactured that honored a female basketball player. Swoopes then traveled to Italy, where she played ten games for a professional team called Basket Bari. When she returned home, the United States National Team invited her to participate in USA Basketball. As part of a USA Basketball team, Swoopes helped the team to win the bronze medal in the world championship. She then played on the 1994 USA Goodwill Games team, where they captured the gold medal. Afterwards, she began lifting weights to bulk herself up for international play. In 1995, Swoopes married Eric Jackson, whom she had first met in high school.

ROAD TO THE OLYMPICS

In April 1995, Tara VanDerveer from Stanford University was named the coach of a national women's basketball team; the goal was to provide the best basketball players in the United States an opportunity to compete in high-level games in their own country. The formation of this team would prepare the players for the upcoming Olympics, to be held in Atlanta, Georgia. VanDerveer would also serve as the Olympic head coach for the United States in 1996.

The following month, the player selection committee invited 27 candidates to try out for the team, held at the U.S. Olympic Training Center in Colorado Springs, Colorado. Swoopes received an invitation—and made the team. The national tour began in November 1995 and consisted of twenty games against top collegiate teams. In January 1996, the tour became international, with trips to the Ukraine, China, Cuba, South Korea, Canada, and Australia. After playing fifty-two games, the national team from the United States remained undefeated. Moreover, they won each game by an average of 30.8 points.

Women's basketball received plenty of attention at that time, with the national team appearing on the cover of *Sports Illustrated*. Swoopes herself appeared on David Letterman's show and *The Tonight Show*.

After the completion of the international tour, the United States chose the members of the team as the 1996 Olympic team for women's basketball: Jennifer Azzi, Ruthie Bolton, Teresa Edwards, Lisa Leslie, Rebecca Lobo, Katrina McClain, Nikki McCray, Carla McGhee, Dawn Staley, Katy Steding, and Swoopes. Venus Lacey also made the Olympic team, with alternates of this dream team being Shanda Berry, Edna Campbell, Sylvia Crawley, Katie Smith, Teresa Weatherspoon, and Kara Wolters.

1996 OLYMPICS

The U.S. team was captained by Teresa Edwards, who was competing in her fourth Olympics; the team played well, beating Cuba (101-84) after trailing at the beginning of the game, 20-13; they also beat the Ukrainian team (98-65), with Swoopes scoring eleven points, having seven assists and six rebounds, as well as Zaire (107-47), which was the most lopsided win in Olympic history.

Tragedy then struck, as a pipe bomb went off in Centennial Olympic Park, where crowds of people listened to a rock concert; the bomb killed two and wounded 111 people. Police had received a call specifying when and where the bomb would go off, but they did not have enough time to clear the park.

After that horrifying incident, the International Olympics Committee (IOC) received more bomb threats, including one specifying the Georgia Dome, which is where the women's basketball games were being played. The IOC debated on whether or not to cancel the rest of the games, but decided on heightened security instead. When basketball play resumed, everyone in the building observed a moment of silence for the bombing victims.

The United States team played Australia next, albeit to a more subdued audience. On more than one occasion during the first half, Australia led the United States by as much as six points; when about sixteen minutes were left in the game, the United States only led by two points—but then Swoopes scored a three-point shot followed by two successful free throws, with the United States winning the game, 96-79.

The American team then beat South Korea (105-64) and Japan (108-93), before advancing to the semifinals; after beating Australia a second time, 93-71, they advanced to the finals. All that now stood between the United States team and the gold medal was the Brazilian team. In the most recent world championships, Brazil had beaten the Americans, 110-97, and then celebrated their win by dancing on the court; this only increased the desire of the U.S. team to beat Brazil at the Olympics. The U.S. team led at the half, 57-46, and then they clinched the gold medal after winning the game, 111-87.

The United States won each of the Olympic Games by an average of 28.6 points; they had an average of 15.1 more rebounds than their opponents as well. Swoopes averaged 13 points a game, the third highest for the United States team, with an average of 3.5 rebounds per game. Her field-goal percentage was .547.

Because of the huge success of this basketball team, interest skyrocketed in the sport, to the degree that two professional basketball leagues formed in the United States for women: the American Basketball League (ABL) and the

Women's National Basketball Association (WNBA). The WNBA would go on to be the more successful of the two leagues; on October 23, 1996, officials announced the first two player signings: that of Sheryl Swoopes and Rebecca Lobo. Next on the list were Ruthie Bolton, Lisa Leslie, Cynthia Cooper, and Michele Timms, the latter of whom was the first international player.

Initially, there were eight teams established in two conferences; in the Eastern Conference, there were the Charlotte Sting, the Cleveland Rockers, the Houston Comets, and the New York Liberty; in the Western Conference, there were the Los Angeles Sparks, the Phoenix Mercury, the Sacramento Monarchs, and the Utah Starzz. Both Swoopes and Cooper would play for the Houston Comets.

PROFESSIONAL BASKETBALL: 1997–98 SEASON

When the initial season began for the Comets, Swoopes was not on the court. Instead, she was working hard to get back into shape after giving birth to a son, Jordan Eric, in June 1997. Swoopes and her husband named their son after Michael Jordan, with the superstar's blessing.

It was important to the league that Swoopes participate in game play as soon as possible. The WNBA marketing campaign had focused heavily on Swoopes, with "Swoopes—as in hoops" becoming a familiar phrase. While she was out with her newborn son, Cynthia Cooper took over the leadership of the Houston Comets, a team that remained in second place in the Eastern Conference behind the New York Liberty team. Late in the season, Swoopes joined the Comets, struggling through her first three games, scoring no points. Over the next two games, though, she scored a total of thirty-eight points before heading to New York to tackle the first-place team on their home court.

When the Comets arrived, more than 17,000 people filled the arena as Swoopes and her team challenged Rebecca Lobo (an Olympic teammate of Swoopes) and her winning team. At the half, the Comets led, 28-22. In the second half, the score became tied at 32—but then the Comets scored ten straight points, and then won the game, 70-55. One week later, the Comets were the conference champions with a season record of 18-10. In the playoffs, the Comets beat Charlotte and then New York to capture the first-ever WNBA championship.

PROFESSIONAL BASKETBALL: 1998–99 SEASON

On opening night, the Comets beat the Liberty team, 74-62. Twenty-four of the first twenty-five points came from either Swoopes or Cooper. The season went well, with the Comets winning the first fourteen out of fifteen games,

CAREER OF A FELLOW COMET: CYNTHIA COOPER

Cynthia Cooper played on two college national championship teams, as well as the first three WNBA championship teams; she was named the MVP for the playoffs all three of those seasons and the league MVP for two of them. Cooper got a late start in basketball. Born on April 14, 1963, she grew up in the poor Watts region of Los Angeles; she did not begin playing basketball until she was sixteen years old, but quickly excelled. Earning a scholarship to the University of Southern California, she helped them to win national championships in 1983 and 1984, but did not receive huge amounts of attention, which went to Cheryl Miller instead. Cooper then played professional basketball in Europe. She also competed in the Olympics for the United States in 1988, bringing home a gold medal from Seoul. Cooper then joined with Swoopes on the Houston Comets team until 2000, when she became the head coach for the Phoenix Mercury of the WNBA. She briefly returned to playing in 2003, retiring in 2004 with the following career per-game averages: 21 points scored; 4.9 assists; 3.3 rebounds; and 1.56 steals. In 2005, Prairie View A&M University named Cooper their head coach for women; in 2010, she was inducted into the Naismith Memorial Basketball Hall of Fame.

beating the Liberty in a second engagement by twenty-five points. In this 1998 season, the Comets switched from the Eastern Conference to the Western Conference, owing to expansion of the league that saw new teams forming in Detroit and Washington. Swoopes was down to her pre-baby weight of 148 pounds, which seemed perfect for her rangy, athletic six-foot frame.

Swoopes collapsed from dehydration at one point during the season, but was determined to play in the upcoming tough game against the Utah Starzz, with its seven-foot, two-inch center, Margo Dydek. The Starzz played well, with a 51-40 lead early in the second half. The Comets then burst into life, with a nineteen-point run, ten of which were scored by Swoopes. She ended up scoring 18 points total in this 72-68 victory.

The Comets ended the season with the best record overall at 27-3. Cooper had scored the highest average number of points that season: 22.7; Swoopes scored an average of 15.6 per game the sixth best average in the league. She averaged 2.48 steals per game, as well, the third best in the league.

In the playoffs, the Comets faced the Charlotte Sting in the opening round. The Comets won, 85-71, with Cooper scoring twenty-seven points; Swoopes had seventeen points and eight rebounds. After the game, both Swoopes and Cooper needed to ice their knees, while Kim Perrot needed to treat her sprained ankle. In the second game of this series, the Comets won, 77-61, with Swoopes boasting a career high of thirteen rebounds.

The Comets faced the Phoenix Mercury next; they had lost to Phoenix earlier in the season, and they lost again to them, 54-51. The second game of the three-game series took place in Houston, where the Comets were outplayed again for most of the game. With less than eight minutes to go, the Mercury had a twelve-point lead. Then, Cooper and Swoopes both sprang to life at the same time, with a run of 13-2 in favor of the Comets. At the end of regulation play, the score was tied at 66. Swoopes and Cooper once again took command of the court, winning the game, 74-69.

Swoopes had this to say about their thrilling victory: "When we got down about 10 points, the only people who believed we could come back were our fans and us. We always believed we could win this game. It never crossed my mind that we weren't going to win" (Rappoport, 2002, 81).

In the tie-breaking game that would determine which team would capture the championship, the Comets had a one point lead with less than eight minutes to go. Swoopes played especially well, both offensively and defensively, and the game had a final score of 80-71, in favor of the Comets. Swoopes and her team had just won their second consecutive national title.

PROFESSIONAL BASKETBALL: 1999–2000 SEASON

In the third season of the WNBA, Swoopes' playing went up yet another notch. She had recently divorced from Jackson, so it was challenging for her to balance motherhood with her career, but her mother helped out considerably and it was not unusual to see Jordan and Louise Swoopes in the stands in Texas, with the little boy wearing his mother's number 22. They often accompanied Swoopes on road trips as well. The competition during this season was especially tough, as the ABL had folded, causing its talented players to flock to the WNBA to obtain positions on the teams.

At the midpoint of this season, the WNBA added an All-Star Game, with both Swoopes and Cooper playing for the Western Conference; their team won, 79-61. All was not going as smoothly for the Comets overall, though. The Houston team struggled with the tougher competition, losing six games during the regular season. The team struggled with something else as well: the lung cancer diagnosis of their point guard, Kim Perrot, in February—and then her death from the disease in August after the cancer had spread to her brain. The WNBA described Perrot as the heart and soul of the Comets, which made her loss especially devastating.

Under these tough circumstances, the Comets also lost the first game of the playoffs against the Los Angeles Sparks. Determined to win the championship in Perrot's honor, the Comets played fiercely in game two of the three-game series; when Cooper made a free throw, she held up an index finger on one hand, and made a fist with her other hand, to represent the number 10,

Perrot's number. The Comets won that game, and the decisive game three of the series, with Swoopes and Cooper scoring twenty-three points each in the third game.

During the finals, the Comets were matched up against the New York Liberty team once again. Swoopes and her teammates notched the first victory, 73-60, and needed just one more win to clinch their third title in a row. The second game did not go as well for the Comets, though; although they had an 18-point lead in the first half, the Liberty team chipped away at the lead, with a last second three-point shot by Teresa Witherspoon securing a win for New York, 68-67.

When the Comets arrived at the Compaq Center for the final game of the playoffs, fans waved signs of support, including one that read "3 for 10," encouraging the Comets to win their third straight championship, this time for number 10, Kim Perrot. As the clock ticked down, with the Comets in the lead, fans chanted, "Three for Kim . . . three for Kim . . ." The Comets ultimately pleased their fans with a 59-47 victory.

Cooper won her third straight scoring honor. Meanwhile, Swoopes shone in multiple areas that season, ranking first in playoff points per game (20.7), first in steals per game (2.81), fifth in minutes per game (35.2), eighth in assists per game (3.8), eighth in field goal percentage (.506), and ninth in blocks per game (1.06). Swoopes also won the 2000 WNBA Most Valuable Player Award.

2000 OLYMPICS: MILLENNIUM GAMES

Sheryl Swoopes once again played for the U.S. women's basketball team. Also on the team were Ruthie Bolton-Holifield, Teresa Edwards, Yolanda Griffith, Chamique Holdsclaw, Lisa Leslie, Nikki McCray, DeLisha Milton, Katie Smith, Dawn Staley, Natalie Williams, and Kara Wolters. This powerhouse team successfully defended their gold medal in Sydney, Australia. The host team received the silver medal, and Brazil the bronze.

PROFESSIONAL BASKETBALL: 2000–01 SEASON

During the opening match in the season, the Comets beat the rival Liberty team, 84-68, with Swoopes the leading scorer with twenty-seven points. She accomplished this even though she needed to sit out five minutes with leg cramps. When in double overtime with the Portland Fire that season, Swoopes scored eight of her twenty-nine points to secure that victory. That season, she received the most votes in All-Star balloting.

Once again, the Comets qualified for playoff play. If they won a fourth championship in a row, they would join the ranks of just four other professional sports teams with that accomplishment: the basketball team, the Boston

Celtics (with seven consecutive wins from 1960–66); the baseball team, the New York Yankees (five straight from 1949-1953); the ice hockey team, the Montreal Canadiens (five straight from 1956–60); and another hockey team, the New York Islanders (four straight from 1979–83).

With Swoopes serving as the leader of the Comets, the team swept the Sacramento Monarchs and the Los Angeles Sparks to meet the New York Liberty team in the finals. The first game went to Houston but, during the second game, Swoopes injured her foot; she returned to the game, however, scoring thirty-one points, a record for the finals. The Comets won, 79-73, securing their fourth consecutive title. That year, Swoopes was the league's leading scorer with 20.7 points. She was named the Most Valuable Player and the Defensive Player of the Year.

PROFESSIONAL BASKETBALL: THROUGH 2009

A knee injury kept Swoopes on the sidelines for the entire 2001 season. Without her contributions, the Comets made it to the playoffs, but could not secure the post-season victories that they needed to win a fifth title. Instead, the Los Angeles Sparks won the championship.

In 2002, the Comets earned their best record in two years, at 24-8. They finished second in the Western Conference, behind the Los Angeles Sparks. Although they made it to post-season play, they lost in the first round to the Utah Starzz. Swoopes was named the Most Valuable Player that year, as well as the Defensive Player of the Year.

In the 2003 season, Cooper—who had retired—came out of retirement to play four games with the Comets. Their record for the season was 20-14; they were once against second in the Western Conference, behind the Los Angeles Sparks. In post-season play, they lost in the first round to Sacramento. During that season, Swoopes discovered that her father, who had abandoned the family when she was a baby, had been coming to watch some of her games. The two talked and Swoopes reported that seeing him in the stands made her feel good. As another piece of positive news, Swoopes once more was named the Defensive Player of the Year.

For the first time ever, the Comets played poorly during the 2004 season. They ended up sixth out of seven teams in their division, with a losing record of 13-21. More troubles piled upon Swoopes that year, as she filed for bankruptcy, saying that she mismanaged her money (Robbins, 2005).

2004 OLYMPICS AND 2005 WNBA SEASON

Swoopes participated in her third gold-medal-earning basketball competition at the Olympics, held in Athens, Greece. Australia repeated its silver-medal-winning performance, while Russia captured the bronze. The U.S. fans were stunned, though, when the men's basketball team did not win gold, losing to Puerto Rico, 92-73. This was the first time since National Basketball Association (NBA) players could participate in the Olympics that the United States did not capture the gold.

Swoopes began the 2005 season as a three-time Olympic gold medal winner, and she played that way, too. In 2005, she averaged 18.6 points per game, with 85 percent accuracy in her free throws. She averaged 4.3 assists per game, plus 2.65 steals and 37.1 minutes of playing time. That year, she was named the Most Valuable Player. In playoffs, the Comets won the first round against the defending champions, the Seattle Storm, but lost in the second round against the Sacramento Monarchs.

COMING OUT

Although Swoopes played quite well in 2005, it was a challenging time of life for her. In October 2005 Swoopes announced to ESPN that she was gay, saying that she was tired of living a lie (Robbins, 2005). She also shared that she was in a romantic relationship with Alisa Scott, known as "Scotty," who had served as an assistant coach for the Comets from 1998 through 2004. The relationship began as a friendship and deepened as time passed; the two had been in a relationship for several years by this time. Swoopes said that she had never told the head coach of the Comets about their relationship, adding that the players either knew about it or deliberately chose not to know. She recognized that some might see ethical issues with a player having an affair with her coach.

"I'm content with who I am and who I'm with," Swoopes later told the *Seattle PI*. "Whether people think that's right, whether they think it's wrong, I don't care. We shouldn't and can't judge each other. I am a Christian, and my biggest dilemma is when people start throwing in the whole religion thing— you're going to hell for this or that" (Moore, 2008).

The *New York Times* pointed out that this announcement came at the same time that Swoopes accepted a six-figure endorsement deal with Olivia Cruises and Resorts, a cruise line that catered to lesbians (Robbins, 2005). Her salary at the time was approximately $90,000; she also earned money from playing in a southern Italy basketball team and from her Nike sponsorship. But, more funds were needed, as she still owed $711,050 from her bankruptcy, including $275,000 to the Internal Revenue Service.

Swoopes was not the first WNBA player to live openly as a gay woman, although she was definitely the most famous. Michele Van Gorp, who had played for the Minnesota Lynx, and Sue Wicks, who had played for the New York Liberty, preceded her. Swoopes' mother initially struggled with her daughter's lifestyle, still does not like it, but is "dealing with it" (Seattle PI, 2005).

FINAL DAYS OF WNBA PLAY

In 2006 the WNBA and its fans chose the best ten players to celebrate the league's ten-year anniversary, with Swoopes included in its list. The Comets finished third that season, with an 18-16 record, behind the Los Angeles Sparks and the Sacramento Monarchs. They made it to post-season play, but lost in round one against Sacramento.

Swoopes had back surgery in 2007, after first playing three games for Houston with a ruptured disk. After her surgery, she had injections and therapy on her back, with a Dallas specialist telling her he could not believe that she could still walk with all the problems she was having. Some mornings, she did struggle to walk and her toes would feel numb. The Comets struggled that season as well, losing their first ten games and finishing 13-21 overall. They did not make the playoffs.

While Swoopes was rehabilitating from her surgery, she signed a one-year contract with the Seattle Storm for 2008, leaving behind the Houston Comets; her contract contained an option for a second year. Seattle had high hopes for the 2008 season with the addition of Swoopes; the team did finish with their best season ever, with a record of 22-12, but lost during the first round of playoffs against the Los Angeles Sparks. In the twenty-nine games that she played, Swoopes, who suffered from multiple injuries that season, scored only 7.1 points per game with only 4.3 rebounds per game, her lowest ever. Seattle released Swoopes at the end of January 2009, right before her contract would have been guaranteed for the second season.

After retiring from the WNBA, Swoopes had reached the following milestones: two thousand career points, five hundred career rebounds, three hundred career assists, and two hundred career steals. She went on to play in a basketball league in Greece in 2009, playing for the Esperides team. Her agent then contacted all twelve teams in the WNBA, offering Swoopes' services at the minimum salary for veteran players; none were interested. Swoopes was most upset with Tulsa, who rejected her but who did take on Marion Jones, the track star who had had her Olympic medals taken away because of her steroid use. In January 2008, Jones had been sentenced in a federal court to six months in prison for lying about her use of performance-enhancing drugs. More relevant to Swoopes' point of view, Jones had not played competitive basketball in thirteen years, yet Tulsa chose Jones over Swoopes.

In 2010, Swoopes played a basketball game in a rural area of Kansas to raise funds for cancer screenings for women in the region. The event was called Hoops for Hope. While in Kansas, she spoke to ESPN, saying that she felt hurt, angry, and rejected because the WNBA did not provide her with a fond farewell when she left (Voepel, 2010).

Swoopes told ESPN that the only contact she has had with the WNBA was when the league's chief of basketball operations called about Cynthia Cooper being inducted into the Naismith Hall of Fame.

"I have respect for the game, the league, the players," Swoopes told ESPN. "But when I get frustrated is when I start thinking and talking about how it ended. I feel like it's time to move on to things that are going to positively affect my life and others, maybe more than basketball ever did. But I am hurt. I know what I've given to the league, to the fans, to the game. It doesn't hurt me now that I'm not playing in the WNBA. It hurts me to not feel appreciated" (Voepel 2010). The Houston Comets, which would have been the most likely organization to honor and recognize Swoopes, had disbanded after eleven years.

In February 2011, Swoopes gave a presentation at Colgate University, talking about goal setting and sharing tips for overcoming adversity. Students who attended the talk came away saying that they felt inspired and motivated.

FURTHER READING

Moore, Jim. 2008. Sheryl Swoopes speaks from the soul. *Seattle PI*, April 28: http://www.seattlepi.com/moore/360040_moore22.html.

Rappoport, Ken. 2002. *Sheryl Swoopes: Star Forward*. Berkeley Heights, NJ: Enslow Publishers, Inc.

Robbins, Liz. 2005. Swoopes Says She Is Gay, and Exhales. *New York Times*, October 27: http://www.nytimes.com/2005/10/27/sports/basketball/27swoopes.html.

Swoopes, Sheryl, and Greg Brown. 1996. *Sheryl Swoopes: Bounce Back*. Dallas, Texas: Taylor Publishing Company.

Voepel, Mechelle. 2010. Sheryl Swoopes still waiting for farewell. ESPN, October 21: http://sports.espn.go.com/wnba/columns/story?columnist=voepel_mechelle&id=5749137.

Woolum, Janet. 1998. *Outstanding Women Athletes: Who They Are and How They Influenced Sports in America*. Phoenix, AZ: Oryx Press.

Dara Torres waves to the crowd after swimming to victory in the women's 100-meter freestyle final at the U.S. Olympic swimming trials in Omaha in 2008. Her finish qualified her for her fifth Olympic games. (AP Photo/Mark J. Terrill)

Dara Torres (1967–)

Some two thousand athletes from twenty-two countries assembled in London for the 1908 Olympics. Only three dozen women competed, none of them from the United States. The American Olympic Committee opposed allowing women to participate in activities in which the women didn't wear long skirts. The prudish Americans didn't have to concern themselves with the length of swimsuits, as women's swimming was not yet an Olympic event. Among the male swimmers at the Games was forty-two-year-old Bartholemeus Roodenburch from the Netherlands. Competing against opponents half his age, he failed to qualify in his event, the 100-meter backstroke. He would remain the only swimmer on the far side of forty to compete in the Olympics for a century. Exactly one hundred years later at the 2008 Olympics, Dara Torres swam for the American team three months after her forty-first birthday, making her the oldest female swimmer in Olympic history. The mother of a toddler won three silver medals. Eight years earlier at the Games in Sydney she had become the oldest swimmer to win an Olympic medal. At Beijing, she raised the ante for middle-aged medalists.

Swimming, like gymnastics, is one of the so-called youth sports where the typical competitor is a teenager. World-class swimmers are known to retire in their early twenties. The first American woman to win an Olympic gold medal in swimming at the 1920 Games was only fourteen. American swimmer Amanda Beard was three months shy of her fifteenth birthday when she won three medals at the 1996 Olympics in Atlanta. So it's understandable that when a retired Olympic swimmer talks about making a comeback in her late thirties, after giving birth, she might find it difficult to persuade coaches and trainers to take her seriously. But Dara Torres made her case convincingly. After all, she had been swimming almost daily through her eighth month of pregnancy.

CHILDHOOD

Dara Grace Torres was born April 15, 1967, and grew up in Los Angeles. Her mother, Marylu, had been a professional model. Edward Torres, her father, was a real estate magnate descended from Spanish Jews. He purchased the Freemont Hotel, the first high-rise in Las Vegas, that opened in 1956. He later ran the Riviera and then bought the Aladdin Hotel in partnership with entertainer Wayne Newton. Torres was a workaholic who spent most of his time in Las Vegas. He was fifty when Dara was born. Dara had two half-brothers Michael and Kirk, from her mother's previous marriage and two older brothers, Rick and Brad, and a younger sister, Lara. The Torres children enjoyed a privileged upbringing. They lived in a nine-bedroom Beverly Hills mansion with their mother. As a teenager, Dara often drove the family's Mercedes station wagon to swim practice.

Edward and Marylu Torres divorced when Dara was eight. She missed her father, who now was even more distant. However, her parents stayed in close touch following the breakup. Her mother would take the children and spend summers at their father's house on Long Island across from the beach. The Torres kids would swim in the bay and go sailing. They were a sporting family. Back home, Marylu drove the children to practices and meets all over the L.A. area, and she swam and skied with them. New York and California were two different worlds. While Dara's mother was easygoing, her father was demanding. He made it clear what the rules and expectations were for his children. Despite the geographic distance between father and daughter, Dara would remain close to him over the years.

Dara Torres describes herself as a tomboy. She had no interest in dresses or dolls. She recalls that she was either on the basketball and tennis courts, or racing the neighbor kids on her bike. Torres was the kid who always had to win whether it was table tennis, pinball, or finishing dinner first. She was constantly competing with her brothers, her sister, and her friends to the point it became annoying. Dara's best friend quit playing golf with her because of the hyper-competitiveness. She was physically aggressive and got into trouble for fighting with the boys. On one occasion, she was suspended from her Beverly Hills elementary school for rebellious behavior.

The Torres family had their own swimming pool. Dara's mother taught her how to swim at an early age. When she was eight, she began age-group swimming at the Beverly Hills YMCA, following her brothers' example. She later quit the Y team and began training with Tandem Swim Club in Culver City. By age twelve she was swimming six days a week. She quickly emerged as the best swimmer in the family, outpacing her brothers who moved on to other sports.

Marylu Torres married Ed Kauder in 1977 when Dara was ten. Kauder was a former ranked tournament tennis player who held the record for most aces (fifty-nine) in a match. Dara's stepfather encouraged her athletic interests. He would drive her to practice and attend her swim meets. Despite the support from her mother and stepfather, Dara missed the attention of her father. She grew up with a need to be noticed and appreciated. Her characteristic brashness at the club swimming pool belied an underlying fragility. She often revealed signs of nervous tension at swim meets and occasionally choked under pressure. However, this vulnerability didn't deter her equally strong desire to achieve at sports.

While swimming at the Beverly Hills Y under coach Karen Moe Thornton, a former Olympian, she developed into a swimming phenomenon. She competed in the YMCA Nationals, and then began swimming under coach Terry Palma for the Tandem Swim Club in Culver City. Palma had her swimming 4,000–5,000 meters (two to three miles) during practices on a five-day schedule. He also changed her stance on the blocks to a "track start," with one leg extended behind the other. Dara had an extraordinarily fast reaction time at the gun. At age twelve, she set a national age-group record for 50 yards. The following year Coach Palma took her to the Nationals held at Harvard University. She felt awed being in the company of the nation's best swimmers, including Rowdy Gaines and Tracy Caulkins. In the women's locker room, she observed a pre-race practice she'd never seen: swimmers shaving their bodies to reduce drag. Whether the advantage gained was real or merely psychological, shaving would become one of the obligatory rituals of competitive swimming. Dara made the finals in the 50-meter freestyle and tied for sixth place with Tracy Caulkins' sister, Amy. Her first Nationals had been encouraging.

The 50-meter freestyle that features the crawl stroke was Dara's specialty. Early on, she struggled with longer races. She was a natural sprinter. In 1982, she swam in the U.S. Nationals in Gainesville, Florida. The young Californian bested twenty-year-old Olympian Jill Sterkel in the 50m. Prior to that race, she had never finished better than sixth at a national meet. It was a big thrill to make the national team for the first time. Being a member meant that she could accompany the team to Europe. The following February, Torres broke Sterkel's world record in the finals of the 50-meter freestyle at the meet in Amersfoort, Holland. The fifteen-year-old had developed a crush on handsome teammate Rowdy Gaines. She received a kiss on the cheek from the world-record holder following her own record-breaking performance. The French sports journal *L'Equipe* ran a photo of the two swimmers. They were the celebrity couple of the moment.

HIGH SCHOOL AND THE 1984 OLYMPICS

Dara returned to California, and life got back to normal. She attended Westlake School for Girls, a private prep school in Los Angeles. As a sophomore, she played volleyball and basketball and was a member of the school's swim team. She did well in the state interscholastic finals, but it was a step down from international competition. Moreover, she was not happy with her progress. Her coach at Culver City advised her to train with a more competitive team. In the June of 1983, Torres joined the Mission Viejo Nadadores, one of the premier swim clubs in the area. Her father didn't like the idea of her relocating, but the Nadadores' young coach Mark Schubert convinced him that it was the best thing for Dara's future. She moved to Mission Viejo fifty miles south of Los Angeles, enrolled in public high school there, and lived with the family of teammate Heather Stutzman. It had become common for promising young swimmers to leave home in order to obtain the necessary training under the best coaches. The practice goes back to the era of Olympic gold medalist Don Schollander, who set three world records at the 1964 Games. At age fifteen, Don moved from his parents' home in Oregon to California to advance his swimming career. The Nadadores' new member was a bit closer to home.

Torres was a sprinter on a team known for developing distance swimmers, but she looked forward to training under the club's highly-successful coach. Schubert told her that he wanted to focus more on sprinters. He had a reputation for demanding discipline and hard work, and that's what she needed at this point in her career. His swimmers were expected to do five hundred sit-ups a day, in addition to weight training and laps in the pool. Dara thrived under this regimen. She was selected as one of ten team members to represent the Nadadores at the 1983 Senior Nationals that year in Clovis, California. She clocked a world record performance in the 50-meter freestyle. The sixteen-year-old was the fastest woman in the world at 50m. Schubert also had her training for the 100-meter freestyle. Torres realized that she'd have to master the 100-meter race if she wanted to swim in the Olympics, as the individual 50-meter freestyle wasn't an Olympic event. Torres accompanied the American team to the 1983 Pan Am Games in Caracas, Venezuela and swam in the 100-meter relay. Then in January of 1984, she swam her personal best in the individual 100-meter freestyle with a time of 56.65 seconds.

Dara Torres had the classic features of a competitive swimmer, extremely tall at five feet, ten inches, with the characteristic musculature, plus the pain tolerance of a champion. She exemplified the temperamental sprinter who gave coaches headaches and could generate resentment among team members. She was known to hedge on her training routine, climbing out of the pool before completing her sets. She also rebelled against the team's strict dietary rules and would eat ice cream or Twinkies on the sly. These minor transgressions said more about her independence than her lack of desire. Torres admits to climbing over swimming pool fences at night to log some extra laps. As for temperament, she was conspicuously high-strung, always chewing on things: gum, towels, anything within reach. She was gregarious, but her competitiveness could be off-putting to others. She described herself as having a Type A personality, a recognition of her impatience. She had a need to tune out all the commotion. Teammates rarely saw her on deck without her Sony Walkman. She found the *Chariots of Fire* theme inspirational, but her favorite musical group was Men at Work.

Torres trained hard for the 1984 Olympic Games. The Olympic Trials were held in the newly-built natatorium in Indianapolis, Indiana. Torres set her sights on the 100-meter freestyle. She would have to finish in the top two to make the Olympic team in this individual event. The top four swimmers in the 100m would make up the 100-meter relay team. Torres finished fourth in the 100 with a time of 56.36 seconds. She had qualified for the relay. Her hometown of Los Angeles was hosting the Olympics. More than 7,000 athletes from 140 countries gathered in the Olympic Village. The 1984 Games were the first to be held in the United States since the 1932 Los Angeles Games. It had been eight years since the American swimmers had competed in the Summer Games, because President Jimmy Carter ordered a boycott of the 1980 Moscow Olympics. The American women came back from the eight-year hiatus to win the gold medal in the 100-meter freestyle relay. Torres's time for the 100-meter split at 55.92 seconds was her fastest ever.

Torres returned to school in Los Angeles following the Games, now a local celebrity. She was asked by the headmaster to stand up in front of the student body at an assembly and display her gold medal. She felt a bit embarrassed by all the attention. She continued to play sports in school and was elected a team captain. That fall semester, she didn't swim but instead went out for the volleyball and basketball teams, the two other sports she most enjoyed. She relished going out with friends on weekends and living a normal life free of training with her face in the water for hours on end. For the last several years, life had been little else but eat, sleep and swim.

COLLEGE, COMPETITION, AND THE 1988 OLYMPICS

In the spring of her senior year, Torres began looking at colleges. She was interested in majoring in journalism and in swimming competitively. She considered several schools and eventually chose the University of Florida, reputed to have one of the best swim programs in the nation under coach Randy Reese. She enrolled at Florida on an athletic scholarship. Reese, like Schubert, had a reputation for being demanding. He might require his swimmers to do 7,000 meters during a practice session (140 lengths in the university's 50-meter pool) and schedule eleven workouts a week. The Gators swim team also lifted weights and pulled football sleds on the practice field. Reese set rigorous body weight standards for his swimmers. Torres, now five feet eleven inches, was expected to keep her muscled body below 152 pounds. Desperate to please her coach, she over-exercised and developed an eating disorder. She would run an extra four miles a week on her own and force herself to throw up after meals. Torres would struggle with bulimia for some five years. But she thrived in the pool under Reese, despite the training overkill. By her sophomore year, she had improved significantly in the 100-meter freestyle. While at Florida, she would win nine conference championships, nine NCAA championships, and accumulate twenty-eight collegiate swimming awards, the maximum possible. Torres looked back at her college years as a positive chapter in her swimming career but a troubling episode in her personal life.

In the summer of 1987, Torres won the individual 100-meter freestyle at the Long Course Nationals. She then won three gold medals at the Pan Pacific Games in Brisbane, swimming her personal best time in the 100-meter freestyle. She also swam on the winning freestyle and medley relay teams in

Australia, carrying home three gold medals. She began training for the 1988 Olympic Games during her junior year of college. That year she won the 50- and 100-yard freestyle and the 100-yard butterfly at the NCAA championship meet, and was named College Swimmer of the Year. Torres looked forward to the Olympic Games in Seoul where the 50-meter freestyle would be on the program for the first time. She didn't swim well in the Olympic Trials and failed to qualify for this event. Torres went into the Games ranked number one in the world in the 100-meter freestyle, but again swam poorly in the individual 100m at Seoul. She and her teammates finished in the top three in the 100-meter freestyle relay and 4x100 medley. She brought home a silver and a bronze medal.

THE 1992 OLYMPICS

Following the Olympics, Dara Torres took a break from swimming and returned to Florida to complete her degree. The university provided her an athletic scholarship in volleyball. She graduated in 1990 with a major in broadcast journalism. Torres accepted an internship with NBC in New York City. She began as a runner at NBC Sports and soon was promoted to production assistant. She found that she missed swimming competitively and decided to train for the 1992 Olympics. She still held the record in the 50-meter freestyle.

Torres contacted University of Florida coach Mitch Ivey, who had coached her sister Lara. Ivey had some concerns about her making a comeback. He questioned her on whether she'd dealt with the eating disorder. She had sought professional help after graduating, but she continued to struggle with her eating. She found a psychotherapist in Florida to deal with the bulimia and convinced Ivey to work with her in the pool. Torres headed to Gainesville to begin training with the Gators' team. The twenty-four-year-old was back into the familiar routine of swimming laps for hours on end with just enough energy left to watch TV. In 1992, Dara met Jeff Gowen, a sports producer eight years older than she, while he was filming the Florida Gators football team. They began dating, but saw little of each other owing to Dara's intensive training schedule.

At the Olympic Trials, Torres finished fourth in the 100-meter freestyle, earning her a place on the 100-meter team. She was disappointed with her eighth place finish in the 50-meter freestyle. At the 1992 Olympics, Torres swam the second leg of the 100-meter relay, her only event. The American women took the gold. Boyfriend Jeff was in Barcelona to watch her receive her gold medal. She went through the familiar post-Olympic letdown. After the Barcelona Games, she had little interest in swimming competitively but continued to exercise regularly. Staying in shape had become a habit. While jogging with a surgeon friend in Florida, Torres began to wheeze. She had experienced this previously while working out, but thought nothing of it. The physician told her it sounded like asthma. A check-up confirmed the diagnosis. Torres began taking asthma medication. She realized that she had been suffering unnecessarily from shortness of breath for some time.

Dara moved back to New York and did some modeling with Wilhelmina Models for a while. She and Jeff married in May of 1993, but the marriage would last only a couple of years. In 1994, she got a call from *Sports Illustrated*. The magazine wanted her to be the first athlete to appear in their annual swimsuit issue. Following her appearance in *SI* she became a TV personality. She worked for ESPN2 and the Discovery Channel, hosting sports lifestyle shows. She also picked up more modeling work including photo shoots for *Glamour* and *SELF*. Torres continued to run in Central Park to stay in shape. She spent the weekends with her father on Long Island. The retired Olympian attended the 1996 Summer Games in Atlanta, but didn't watch any of the swimming events.

COMPETING IN SWIMMING AFTER THE AGE OF THIRTY

Dara Torres was invited to present the awards at the 1998 U.S. Nationals but expressed no desire to return to swimming. She commented that she didn't miss the smell of chlorine in her hair. The following year, however, she began to think about competing again, although she hadn't swum since the Barcelona Games. She was enjoying successful careers in modeling and television, but lacked a sense of fulfillment and still harbored a need to be recognized as an athlete. She was sitting in the crowd at a swim meet in California when she decided to attempt a comeback. At this point, no American woman over thirty had competed in swimming at the national level.

In her seven years away from competitive swimming, Torres had overcome her long struggle with bulimia, but she continued to be exceedingly diet-conscious. She consumed an array of nutritional supplements. She also maintained a vigorous exercise regimen: lifting weights, riding the exercise bicycle, and running up to twenty miles a week. But she missed the water. The former Olympian seemed to have a love/hate relationship with swimming. Torres once commented that swimming in an outdoor pool alone is the most peaceful place in the world. She felt connected to the water in the same way some people feel connected to nature. At the same time, she realized that training in the pool could be brutal and boring. She described the endless hours of swimming laps as an exercise in sensory deprivation: you can't hear anything, your vision is blurred, the dominant smell of chlorine overpowers the olfactory senses. At the same time, swimming gave her a sense of focus and meaning that she struggled to find elsewhere in her life.

Dara visited her mother in Sun Valley, Idaho, to inform her that she was going to make a comeback. She dreaded informing her father. Ed Torres tended to be highly practical about career decisions. Now in his eighties, he divided his time between Long Island and Florida. Torres headed south for a visit. She convinced herself that he wouldn't approve of her attempting a comeback at her age. It was a pleasant surprise for her when he did support her decision. The dutiful daughter had the approval she needed. She phoned U.S. Olympic swim coach Richard Quick, whom she had known for some time, for his advice. Quick told her to fly to California where he was coaching college and club swimmers at Palo Alto. He wanted her to observe the talented, young swimmers on the Santa Clara Swim Club team that included gold medalist Jenny Thompson, before making a decision. After visiting with Quick and gaining his support, Torres decided to train with him. While in California, she shot a couple of infomercials for Tae Bo, the trendy exercise program, and then flew back to New York to take care of lingering commitments there.

In July, Torres began training in the Stanford University pool and working out in the gym. The Olympic Games were a year away. Quick refined her stroke, getting her to swim lower in the water. The early results were dramatic. At a World Cup meet in Maryland in November, her first competition since returning, she swam her personal best times and medaled in four events. She cut some more off her times at a meet in San Antonio in December, where she broke her own record, set fifteen years earlier, in the 50-meter freestyle. After some twenty weeks of training she beat Jenny Thompson, the world's top woman's swimmer. Torres now ranked number three in the world.

The mounting rivalry between Torres and Thompson, both highly competitive athletes, created mounting tension on the swim club. Their coach wasn't oblivious to what was occurring. While at Colorado Springs Olympic Center training camp, Quick made the decision that Torres would no longer practice with the women's team. He would continue to work with her one-on-one in the mornings, and she could train with the Santa Clara men. Torres was taken aback by the decision but had to comply. She refocused and brought new energy to the men's practice sessions. On occasion, she posted times as good as some of the guys.

Quick told Torres that he wanted her to swim fewer laps than the younger swimmers. Torres had a history of overtraining, putting in five hours a day and then going on a weekend run or heading to the gym for another session. She appreciated that it took longer to recover at her age. She often felt exhausted at the end of practice sessions. With a life-long inclination to be hyperactive, she had to force herself to rest on weekends. As a result, she returned for Monday practice sessions with more energy. At the same time, Quick put her on an aggressive weight training program. Torres put on fifteen-plus pounds of muscle. The two, coach and swimmer, were exploring new territory. There weren't any established guidelines for training sprinters who were in their thirties.

THE 2000 OLYMPICS

The impact of Dara Torres' training regimen became evident at the Olympic Trials, again held in Indianapolis in July. She set a new American record in the 100-meter butterfly. She and Thompson both made the Olympic team in this event. Torres touched second to Jenny in the 100-meter freestyle at the Trials and won the 50-meter freestyle. She would swim in five events in the Olympics, three individual races and the 100-meter relay and medley relays. An aging Ed Torres was in the crowd at Indianapolis, relishing his daughter's success.

At the 2000 Sydney Games, Dutch swimmer Inge de Bruijn, holder of eight world records, dominated the sprinting events. Torres took a bronze medal to Inge's gold in the 100-meter butterfly and tied with Jenny Thompson for the bronze medal in the 100-meter freestyle, as Inge again took the gold. Torres won her third bronze medal in the individual 50-meter freestyle. The American women won two gold medals in the 100-meter relay and medley. Torres returned from Sydney with five medals. The thirty-three-year-old had topped her performances at the three previous Olympics. She became the oldest swimmer to win a medal in Olympic history. Back home in the States, she was a sports celebrity. *Women's Wear Daily*, the fashion industry trade journal, invited Torres, along with gymnast Nadia Comaneci and track star Jackie Joyner-Kersee, to take part in a salute to women athletes at Madison Square Garden.

In 2002, Torres moved in with her father at his Palm Beach house. He had been diagnosed with colon cancer. Her mother came to Florida to nurse her former husband. Dara married her father's Israeli doctor, Itzhak Shasha, in June of 2003, and converted to Judaism. Shasha was nineteen years older than Dara. At age thirty-five, she was trying to get pregnant. She underwent in vitro fertilization but without success. Her frustration with infertility was one of several problems in the relationship. The couple divorced in December 2004. Torres moved to a condo near her father's beach house. Her professional career was going well. She had lucrative contracts with Toyota and USA Network. The high profile swimmer was drawing a six-figure salary from commercial endorsements and television work.

Dara began dating David Hoffman, an endocrinologist who was her former physician. They had become friends through his nurse. He was going through a divorce, as was she. Hoffman, fifteen years older than Torres, had been a college swimmer and became the father of her first child. The couple resided in Parkland, Florida, where he had a medical practice. Torres didn't allow pregnancy to curtail her swimming regimen. There was a Masters' swim club at nearby Coral Springs. Masters swimmers compete within age groups. The thirty-eight-year-old former Olympian continued to swim at the Coral Springs pool into the ninth month of her pregnancy. She remarked that it felt good to exercise, even though she had gained thirty-five pounds by the time she delivered. Torres was aware that doctors had changed their views of how much exercise is allowable during pregnancy, although she was pushing the limits by swimming five days a week for two hours. She also was training in the gym four days a week. She gave birth to daughter Tessa in April of 2006. Ed Torres got to hold his granddaughter before he died in October, after having battled cancer for five years.

Dara Torres was back in the pool and the gym a week and a half after having the baby. She continued to swim at Coral Springs, driving over from Parkland and leaving Tessa with a sitter. David also began swimming again. Dara soon was competing in Masters' swim meets. She would nurse Tessa in the restroom between races. As she got back up to competitive speed, people approached her and asked her about making another comeback. She mulled over the idea. David was supportive.

Torres began training with Chris Jackson, who ran the Masters' program in Coral Springs. He had her swimming 4,000 meters three times a week. Jackson worked with Dara's former coach, Michael Lohberg. He would come by the pool, watch her swim, and give her some tips on her stroke. She convinced him that she was serious about making another comeback, and he agreed to help with her training. Lohberg would prove to be a valuable mentor. He had gone through the German sports training system. Over his career, he had coached swimmers who held more than sixty national records. That fall Torres contacted Andy O'Brien, the strength coach with the Florida Panthers professional ice hockey team. He agreed to work with her when time allowed. O'Brien put her on a more suitable weight training program for sprinters that included stretching. Torres slimmed down some twelve pounds and increased her flexibility. The veteran swimmer was pulling together her team of advisors to make an unprecedented comeback.

Throughout her athletic career, Torres seemed to be constantly on the lookout for anyone or anything to give her an edge and assuage her doubts about performing well. She occasionally consulted a psychic to build up her confidence before swimming in major events. She took an array of diet supplements including ten tablespoons of amino acid daily and drank a Living Fuel shake every day for breakfast. Torres scheduled sessions with chiropractors when her muscles and joints ached. She hired personal masseuses to travel with her to meets around the world. She explored personal training programs, everything from Pilates to Tae Bo. Torres reputedly spent as much as $100,000 a year on training.

Torres accompanied Lohberg and his club swimmers to a training camp in Saint Croix. Her mother, stepfather, and Tessa accompanied her to the Virgin Islands, making it something of a family vacation. She stayed in a hotel with her family rather than boarding with the much younger swimmers. Torres had no illusions about making the U.S. Olympic team at her age. Her strategy

ATHLETES AS MOTHERS

Dara Torres wasn't the first or the last mother to compete as a world-class athlete. Fanny Blankers-Koen, known as "The Flying Housewife," was the mother of two when she won four gold medals in track & field at the 1948 Olympics. In 1982, Canadian Debbie Brill set the world indoor high jump record five months after giving birth. A total of fifteen mothers competed at the 2010 Winter Olympics in Vancouver. Women have had to learn how to manage their dual identities of athlete and mother, and not to feel guilty about continuing their sports careers while raising a child. Golfer Nancy Lopez won twenty-one LPGA tournaments after becoming a mom. Joy Fawcett interspersed seventeen years on the U.S. National Soccer Team with giving birth to three daughters. She convinced the United States Soccer Federation to provide a nanny.

Most athletes appreciate that there are prudent tradeoffs between motherhood and sports. Women must follow their physician's advice as to how hard and how long to train during pregnancy and when to resume competition following delivery. Dara Torres had a reputation for pushing the limits. Stacy Allison, the first American woman to scale Mt. Everest, quit climbing mountains and took up less risky forms of outdoor recreation when she became a mother. A fellow climber had died on the slopes leaving her two children without a mother.

was to concentrate on the 100-meter freestyle with the goal of qualifying for the 100-meter relay. Again, the top six swimmers at the Olympic Trials would qualify for a spot on the four-member relay team, while only the two fastest qualified for individual events.

Over the past several months, Torres had been swimming in Master events. She realized she needed to move to a higher level of competition. In June of 2007, she traveled to Rome to swim in the European Mare Nostrum tour, and then on to Monte Carlo. Lohberg and her two personal trainers made the trip with her. It had been seven years since she competed in an international event. The Olympic Trials were a year off. In Rome, Torres qualified for the finals in the 50-meter freestyle. She finished second in the 50-meter race and then won the 100-meter freestyle with a time close to her personal best. This performance convinced her that she had a good chance of making a successful comeback.

In July, Dara Torres headed to Indianapolis for the U.S. National Swimming Championships. The Nationals are the premier American swim meet in non-Olympic years. It was a familiar pool, the site of previous Olympic Trials and Nationals. She'd swum there in 1982 when the facility opened and on more than a dozen occasions during her career. Entering the natatorium, she saw a huge poster of her much younger face hanging in the rafters among a select array of Olympic swimmers. Her mother, David, and Tessa were there to watch her compete on the twenty-fifth anniversary of the opening of the Indiana University facility. She won the 50-meter freestyle, setting the American record, and then won the 100-meter freestyle. Torres, who turned forty in April, held daughter Tessa while being awarded her gold medal on the podium. She had bested swimmers young enough to be her daughters. As for Tessa, she would get used to the smell of chlorine; her mother had her splashing in the pool in Florida at three months.

Torres swam in a meet in Germany in November, breaking the short course (25-meter pool) records in the 50- and 100-meter freestyle, but her shoulder was giving her problems. She scheduled an appointment with an orthopedic surgeon upon returning to the States. He operated on the shoulder, shaving off bone spurs and repairing a torn rotator cuff, the group of muscles and tendons that stabilize the shoulder. Following surgery, she was back in the water on a training regimen that emphasized kicking drills to strengthen her legs and pamper the recovering shoulder. The intense training was having an adverse effect on more than one of her joints. An old knee injury began acting up, and Torres was soon back in the hospital for more surgery. With the knee repaired, she began thinking about qualifying for more than a spot on the 4x1,000 relay team. She felt she had a chance in the individual 50- and 100-meter freestyle.

Torres trained through the fall of 2007 and into 2008. Lohberg had her swimming 5,000 meters, five days a week. She was up early on practice days, arriving at the pool at 8:00 AM. It was like the old days when she was a teenager. Lohberg felt that Torres needed more competition, so he included her in the group of swimmers who competed in the Missouri Grand Prix in early 2008. This large meet would feature several Olympic aspirants. The scheduling of events imitated those in the upcoming Olympic Games, with preliminaries scheduled in the evening and finals in the morning. NBC Network had requested this arrangement to facilitate prime-time coverage of swimming events in Beijing. Saving one's best effort for the early morning was a major adjustment for the swimmers. Torres had her own concerns. She had to test her rebuilt shoulder and knee while swimming against the top competitors in the nation.

The swimmers at the Missouri Grand Prix had to undergo another major adjustment. Speedo, the swimwear manufacturer, chose this meet to introduce its revolutionary high-tech LZR racing suit. The radical design that encased the swimmer's legs and torso was meant to compress the body for a streamlined effect. It proved to be a major undertaking to squeeze into the super tight body suits. Torres ripped three of the $500 suits trying to get one on. She ended up swimming in her old racing suit. She also had her old pair of goggles that her youth coach had duct taped to discourage her from looking for the competition in mid-race. For both swimmer and accessories, it was a contest of the old versus the new. Torres finished second in the 50-meter freestyle against formidable competition. She wasn't exactly elated. She hated finishing second. Following the awards ceremony, she handed her silver medal to an admirer. She recalled what her tennis-playing stepfather said to her years ago, "You'll always feel like a loser if you don't win" (Torres, 2009, 146).

The public *was* elated by Dara Torres' performance in Missouri. The forty-year-old's comeback caught the attention of the national news and entertainment media. All the attention was gratifying, but it raised expectations and caused her some apprehension. Amidst the comeback clamor, Torres's coach Michael Lohberg was diagnosed with a herniated disc and hospitalized. She missed his presence and was quite concerned about his prognosis. If this worry wasn't enough, she had to deal with growing speculation that she was taking performance-enhancing drugs. Partisan fans were unwilling to accept that she could swim competitively at her age unaided by drugs. To stifle the allegations, Torres volunteered to participate in the United States Anti-Doping Agency's enhanced testing program. The agency would test her a dozen times during the run-up to the 2008 Olympic Games. The only drug she took was her asthma medication which was approved by the USADA.

THE OLDEST SWIMMER TO MAKE AN OLYMPIC TEAM: THE 2008 OLYMPICS

The Olympic Trials in Omaha were held in June, five weeks before the Games. Torres was scheduled to swim in six events at 50 and 100 meters in just four days. She hadn't competed in the 100-meter freestyle since the 2007 Nationals. Up to this point, Rowdy Gaines, at age thirty-five, had been the oldest swimmer to qualify at the Trials. Torres, at forty-one, had six years on him. She'd recovered from her recent shoulder surgery and the several knee surgeries, but seemed to be developing arthritis in her shoulder. Such was the accumulated wear and tear on joints from swimming thousands of laps over the years—what doctors refer to as overuse injuries. Dara's entire family flew to Nebraska to watch her compete. Some of her brothers hadn't seen her swim since she was a teenager. A record crowd showed up at the Trials to watch Torres along with twenty-three-year-old "phenom" Michael Phelps. Torres broke fifty-four seconds for the first time in the 100-meter freestyle semifinals and went on to win the finals. It was her first win at this distance in an Olympic Trials. In the 50-meter freestyle, she took back the American record with a personal best time. Remarkably, she had won both the 50 and 100. Dara Torres would swim in Beijing, the first female swimmer over forty in Olympic history.

The Trials were followed by training camp in California. From there, the team would head to China. They planned to arrive early to acclimate to the time change and the weather. Torres planned to take her personal trainers with her to China to keep her relaxed and loose. Mark Schubert, her old Nadadores coach, was now coaching the U.S. swim team. It was a young team with several swimmers competing in their first Olympics. They didn't quite know what to make of a teammate old enough to be their mother. They elected Dara Torres co-captain. The other co-captain, Amanda Beard, would be swimming in her fourth Olympics; Dara, in her fifth. While in California, Torres flew to Los Angeles to appear on *The Tonight Show with Jay Leno*. The mom who made the Olympic swimming team was a TV celebrity. After appearing with Leno, it was back to Palo Alto for team meetings and training.

The 2008 Olympics were the first to be held in China. The Chinese government had constructed a modern, stylistic Olympic site. Swimming events took place in the National Aquatics Center, a cube-shaped structure dubbed fittingly the Water Cube. The natatorium was light and airy, and accommodated 17,000 fans. The crowd wouldn't be disappointed by the state-of-the-art facility or the competition. They would watch the world's best swimmers in their high-tech suits set twenty-five world records.

The U.S. swimming team arrived in Beijing in early August, five days before swimming competition began. Torres would be swimming in three events on another tight schedule. The medley relay (butterfly, backstroke, breaststroke, and freestyle) on which she swam anchor was scheduled thirty minutes after the finals of the 50-meter freestyle. The latter race was especially important to her, as she had never won an Olympic gold medal in an individual event. She had decided not to swim in the individual 100-meter freestyle so she could focus on the 50. Torres' initial race was the 100-meter relay. Again, she would swim the last leg. The Germans and Dutch were the main competition. The Australians also had a good team. She swam her relay split in a remarkable 52.4 seconds, the fastest in the history of women's relay swimming and nearly a full second faster than her personal best; but she couldn't catch Dutch anchor Marlene Veldhuis. The American women took the silver medal.

Dara had a few days between events to show David and her mother around the Olympic site before she swam in the medley and individual 50-meter freestyle. Meanwhile, twenty-three-year-old Michael Phelps, a veteran himself by Olympic swimming standards, was accumulating eight gold medals. Dara was content to share the limelight with him. She made it through the prelims in the 50m, but her shoulder was bothering her by the time she squeezed into her LZR suit for the semifinals. She would be swimming against Sweden's Therese Alshammar, whom she had never bested in the long course. In the tension-filled locker room before the start of the race, Dara felt a tap on her shoulder. It was Therese, who seemed quite upset. Her LZR suit had split down the back. In a display of unusual sportsmanship, Dara persuaded the meet officials to delay the start so her competitor wouldn't have to scratch in the event. Olympic officials rarely grant delays, but they allowed enough time for Therese to put on another suit. Torres appreciated that what she did was consistent with the Olympic spirit: all the world's best swimmers would be competing. With everyone suited up, the swimmers mounted the starting blocks. Dara's old friend Rowdy Gaines was doing the commentary for NBC. The starting gun fired and the swimmers sliced into the water. Upon touching the wall at the far end of the pool Torres looked up at the clock and saw that she had swum the 50m just .02 seconds off her personal best. She had a shot at the gold medal.

On the day of the finals in the 50m, Torres was up early. She read emails from well-wishers to calm her nerves. As race time approached and the arena filled with fans, she recognized NBA stars Jason Kidd and LeBron James in the crowd. This time the race went off without a hitch. When Torres hit the wall at the opposite end of the pool, the clock registered 24.27 seconds. She had swum her fastest ever 50m at age forty-one. But again, it wasn't fast enough. She finished behind Britta Steffen of Germany by .01 second, the narrowest of margins. Steffen had set a new Olympic record in the 50m. Four minutes after the award ceremony, Torres was back on the blocks for her next event, the medley. When she entered the water on the anchor leg, her team was trailing the Australians by almost a second. Torres gave it all she had. She hit the wall so hard she tore a thumb ligament. She had swum the fastest 100m in the history of women's relays, but she couldn't make up the distance they trailed the Aussies. The American women had to settle for the silver medal in the 4×100 medley as well.

Dara Torres didn't win a gold medal in Beijing, but it proved to be the most rewarding Olympics in a career that spanned three decades. The veteran had broken her own records—as well as her thumb—in the process, and brought home three silver medals. The nomadic mother couldn't wait to arrive back in Florida and rejoin daughter Tessa after seven weeks on the road. Following the homecoming, she was back in the orthopedist's office for treatment of her thumb injury and then underwent more surgery to remove bone spurs in her shoulder. A month later, she was in the Coral Springs pool working out and nursing her shoulder back into shape. Torres took it easy through the end of the year, but had her sights on the FINA World Championships in Rome. She clocked 24.42 in the 50-meter freestyle at the U.S. National Championships at Indianapolis in July, but finished a disappointing eighth in the 50 meters in Rome. Her knee was still bothering her. Despite advancing age and mounting infirmities, Torres wasn't ready to retire. Swim fans speculated on whether she would compete in the 2012 Olympic Games in London. Most forty-five-year-old swimmers would be content to compete in Master's events. But Dara Torres isn't most swimmers.

The semiretired swimmer continued to do public relations work for companies offering a variety of products and services. She was one of four athletes approached by BP, the global oil and gas company, to be a spokesperson for their advertising campaign billed as "Team Invigorate," promoting a new blend of gasoline. She also did promotions for NXT Nutritionals, a marketer of artificial sweetener. She served as a fitness spokesperson for *Self* magazine and Turner Sports. Torres collaborated with fitness writer Billie Fitzpatrick on *Gold Medal Fitness*, a work-out program. The book became a *New York Times* Bestseller. Following surgery to repair arthritis on her knee, she took part in the "Everything Possible" campaign sponsored by Brigham and Women's Hospital in Boston, where she had the operation performed.

She still is on the road a lot, giving inspirational speeches and attending promotional events. Torres is a veteran celebrity swimmer for Swim Across America, a charitable group that raises money for cancer research. When home, she spends time with daughter Tessa. They reside in Parkland, Florida, and she keeps an apartment in Manhattan. In her leisure, Torres watches television and reads sports and gossip magazines. She continues to work out five days a week.

Dara Torres's legacy is captured in the title of her autobiography, *Age Is Just a Number*. She redefined the upper age limit for competitive swimmers. Olympic medalist Don Schollander joked about being considered an old man at twenty-two, the age at which he retired. If Torres makes it to the London Games in 2012, she'll be twice that old. She's added a new dimension to the Olympic motto, *Citius, Altius, Fortius*, "Swifter, Higher, Stronger." Appended, it would proclaim, *Citius, Altius, Fortius, Grandior*, "Swifter, Higher, Stronger, Older." At the 2000 Sydney Games, she became the oldest U.S. gold medalist in swimming history. She remains the oldest swimmer to make an Olympic team at age forty-one, and the first American to swim in five Olympics. She has collected twelve Olympic medals over twenty-four years of competition.

LEGACY

The veteran swimmer has accrued a long list of accomplishments and received numerous honors over her career, beyond the Olympics. She held age-group and California interscholastic swimming titles, and then won nine NCAA championships while at the University of Florida. She claimed sixteen U.S. National titles beginning in 1982. She held several American records and set a world record (long course) in the 50-meter freestyle in 1983 and again in 1984.

In 1999, Torres was inducted into the University of Florida Hall of Fame as a "Gator Great." She was invited to be part of President George W. Bush's inaugural ceremonies. Torres was elected to the International Jewish Sports Hall of Fame in 2005. She received the Best Comeback Award at the 17th Annual ESPY Awards ceremony. In 2009, she was recognized by the International

Committee for Fair Play for her act of sportsmanship during the Beijing Olympics that enabled Therese Alshammar to compete.

Women have come a long way since the days when Victorian prudery restrained their scope of physical activities, and male prejudice impugned their potential to compete as athletes. Yet modern America's obsession with youth culture has relegated mature women to the role of spectators when it comes to national and international athletic competition. Dara Torres stands out as the contemporary sports icon who redefined the parameters of middle age, pregnancy, and motherhood. Regardless of whether she swims in the 2012 Olympic Games, the torch has been passed to her daughter's generation to accept the Olympic challenge of "swifter, higher, stronger" even after they have become the over-thirty generation.

FURTHER READING

Anderson, Kelli. 2008. The Mother of All Comebacks. *Sports Illustrated,* July 14: http://sportsillustrated.cnn.com/2008/olympics/2008/07/08/torres0714/.index/htm.

Carswell, Sue. 2007. Interview with Olympic Swimmer Dara Torres. *Women's Health Magazine*, Nov: http://www.womenshealthmag.com/life/meet-dara-torres?page=3/htm.

Levin, Dan. 1984. She's Set Her Sights on L.A. *Sports Illustrated*, June 18: http://sports illustrated.cnn.com/vault/article/magazine/MAG1122191/index.htm.

Michaelis, Vicki. 2011. Dara Torres, 43, to race in preparation of 2012 Olympics. *USA Today*, Feb. 17: http://www.usatoday.com/sports/olympics/2011-02-17-dara -torres-compete-missouri_N.htm.

Park, Alice. 2008. Faster than Ever at 41. *Time*, Aug. 4, 172:5: 46–48.

Torres, Dara, with Elizabeth Weil. 2009. *Age Is Just a Number*. New York: Broadway Books.

Ulmansky, Diane. 2010. Making Waves. *Healthy Living*, Spring issue: 28–30.

Venus and Serena Williams at the 1999 TIG Tennis Classic, Carlsbad, California. (Shutterstock)

Venus Williams (1980–) and Serena Williams (1981–)

Venus and Serena Williams are American athletes—and sisters—who play professional tennis. They became pros in 1994 and 1995, consecutively, and were still winning major tennis tournaments in 2010.

Serena Williams has won titles in each of the four Grand Slam tournaments (Australian Open, French Open, Wimbledon, and the U.S. Open), including wins in singles, doubles, and mixed doubles. After a win in Australia in early 2003, Serena was the reigning champion for all four Grand Slam tournaments, only the fifth female tennis player to ever attain that accomplishment. She is also a two-time Olympic gold medalist. As of May 1, 2011, ESPN has recorded her career earnings to date as $32,773,004, the highest amount ever won by a female tennis athlete. She has captured thirty-seven singles titles and eighteen doubles titles, with a singles win-loss record, overall, of 474-101.

To date, Venus Williams has won Grand Slam titles in singles, doubles, and in mixed doubles, also winning titles in each of the four Grand Slam tournaments. She has earned three Olympic gold medals, one in singles and two in doubles; this is the largest number of tennis gold medals won by a female tennis player. As of May 1, 2011, ESPN records her career earnings as $27,734,852, the second highest amount ever won by a female tennis professional. She has snagged forty-three singles titles and eighteen doubles titles, with a singles win-loss record, overall, of 592-145.

When the sisters started playing professional tennis, no black player had dominated the sport since 1975—and that was a man, Arthur Ashe, who won Wimbledon in 1975. The last time that a black woman had won a major tennis tournament was in 1957 and 1958, when Althea Gibson won the U.S. Open and Wimbledon.

CHILDHOOD

Venus Ebony Starr Williams was born on June 17, 1980, in Lynwood, California, and Serena Jameka Williams was born on September 26, 1981, in Saginaw, Michigan. Their parents are Richard Williams and Oracene "Brandi" Price Williams; Price was previously married to Yusef A. K. Rasheed and they had three daughters: Lyndrea, Isha, and Yetunde. Meanwhile, Williams had previously been married to Betty Johnson, with whom he had two daughters and three sons; these children were not raised by Williams and Price, as her children from her first marriage had been. Two sons of Williams have spent time in prison. Richard Williams and Brandi Price married in 1980, after the birth of Venus.

The Williams family—including Lyn, Isha, Yetunde, Venus, and Serena—was raised in the Jehovah's Witness religion, the religion of their mother.

When Venus and Serena were children, Richard owned his own security firm, Samson Security, working at night, while Price worked as a nurse.

Venus and Serena were raised in the Los Angeles suburb of Compton; there, crime rates were high, in large part because of significant drug peddling and use, and violent gang activity. In the 1980s, when the Williams sisters were children, rappers wrote songs about the roughness of Compton, including "Straight Outta Compton," a song recorded by the hip-hop group N.W.A. on Eazy-E's record label. (The album helped to pioneer the anti-authority form of music now known as gangsta rap.) By 2005, Compton was ranked as America's second most dangerous city (in the category for populations under 100,000) and, in its ten square miles, fifty-seven gangs actively flourished.

Richard Williams has said that he deliberately moved his family to Compton, where he believed his daughters would gain a competitive edge. "I'd done research on athletes from the ghetto. A ghetto makes you want to fight. A ghetto makes you want to be the best just to get out of the damn ghetto" (Intini, 2009). He said that nearly everyone on their street took drugs, adding that there was a dead body in the middle of the street nearly every day.

Richard Williams has also said that he had planned to have two daughters who could play professional tennis before Venus and Serena were even born. Referring to that time, Williams said, "I didn't know nothing about tennis. I hadn't even watched a tennis match" (Intini, 2009).

What he did know is that tennis commentator Bud Collins had just stated to Romanian tennis player Virginia Ruzici that $40,000 was not bad money for four days' work. At first, Williams thought that was a joke but, when he realized that it was true, he said to himself, "'I'm going to have me two kids and put them in tennis.' To this day, I don't know anything a child could do to make that kind of money in one week" (Intini, 2009). Williams and his wife therefore began to teach themselves how to play tennis so that they could in turn teach their children.

The three older daughters did not show much interest in tennis, but both Venus and Serena did; and the family had a photo wherein Venus was pushing Serena around a tennis court in a stroller, with other photos showing Serena lugging a tennis racquet around as she was just learning to walk. The family would never throw away a tennis ball, with even old, flat balls somehow used in a drill that would teach the girls something new about the game. As for Venus, she started to play tennis when she was four years old, returning hundreds of her father's volleys. At one point, her father took away her tennis racquet, fearing that perhaps she loved the sport too much. Meanwhile, Serena began playing tennis when she was five years old.

For the first couple of years, the Williams sisters practiced for a couple of hours per day, four or five times a week, and then they began practicing three or four hours a day—every day of the week. Some days, there were two practices scheduled, one at 6:00 AM and the other after school. Richard Williams would write encouraging messages on pieces of paper and hang them up on the court; as a treat, he would sometimes allow them to take a break to play in the sandbox or to turn cartwheels.

Williams, who also taught other neighborhood children how to play tennis, recalled filling a shopping cart with 550 tennis balls; it took three teenagers a significant amount of time to hit all of those balls, and they needed to take breaks. He said that he first knew that Venus would be a good tennis player when, at age four, she cried until she was allowed to try to swing at all 550 of those balls. She missed quite a few, but she swung at every one of them.

When Williams returned home that day, he told his wife that Venus would be a champion. Price laughed and said that he was acting like a proud father. In turn, Williams remembered telling her, "No matter what age, all champions are able to demonstrate that they are rough, they are tough, they are strong, and they are mentally sound. You cannot teach that. That is a God-given quality, and Venus demonstrated that on the first day" (Chappell, 2000).

Later, newspaper reports shared how Williams needed to clean the broken glass off the public tennis courts before allowing his daughters to practice on them; how they couldn't afford new tennis balls so they would search for old ones that had been abandoned; and how the girls needed to learn how to dodge bullets while practicing. Because of the roughness of the area where the Williams sisters learned to play tennis, their father referred to them as ghetto Cinderellas.

When Serena was seven and Venus was eight, the girls participated in a workshop where Billie Jean King facilitated; by that time, both girls had already played matches in tennis leagues and competitions. Serena ultimately won forty-six of the forty-nine tournaments that she entered as a child, becoming the number-one player in the Southern California rankings for players aged twelve and under. Venus excelled in other sports as well as tennis; when she was eight years old, she won nineteen straight track meets, finishing the mile in 5:29. She also participated in gymnastics and dance.

Richard Williams has received a significant amount of criticism for multiple reasons, including his offbeat training regimes for his daughters, for continuing to train his daughters when professional coaches were better suited for the job, for what was perceived as arrogance, and for his comments about racism and stuffiness in the sport of tennis.

Most painful of all, though, was when people criticized Williams' daughters. He once overheard someone saying that Venus did not belong at a Southern California tournament because she was both black and poor. At this same tournament, he heard it said that, because she came from Compton (called "the worst ghetto in the world" by Williams), she could not play tennis well. "People would pick at us all the time," Williams was quoted as saying. "They should be glad that I am a good man because if I wasn't a good man, I would have picked up a stick and knocked the hell out of somebody. There comes a time when you get tired of people picking on you. . . . You don't have to be brought up in the country club to do this. You can actually come out of the ghetto and play tennis" (Chappell, 2000). Williams also noted that his family became stronger because of the challenges that they faced together.

By the time his girls were ten years old, William was interviewing them on a camcorder, in preparation for what he envisioned would come. Sports agents soon wanted to represent them and manufacturers gifted them with free clothes and shoes. By this time, Venus was serving the ball at close to 100 miles per hour; by the time that she was 12, her record on the USTA junior tour was 63-0.

FLORIDA YEARS

In 1991, Williams withdrew his daughters from the junior tournament circuit after seeing the damage done to so many other young players who were pushed too hard on the circuit. He also worried about their safety as people in the area knew about the prizes that they were winning and might be thinking about stealing from them; so he sold his security business, and the family moved to Florida. At this time, Venus was ranked number one in the twelve-and-under division and Serena was ranked number one in the ten-and-under division of the junior circuit of California.

He sent them to train in Palm Beach Gardens, Florida, where they began to be coached by Rick Macci, the former coach of tennis pros Jennifer Capriati and Mary Pierce. Venus and Serena were homeschooled by their mother, a nurse, until they entered Driftwood Academy, which was a private high school that educated thirty students in Lake Park, Florida.

In 1995, Venus and Serena left Macci's tennis academy, and Williams began coaching and promoting his daughters again and finding a variety of trainers to also work with them. During these years, the girls would often walk to the tennis courts with their dogs following behind them. Richard would frequently supervise them from a golf cart that he drove around. He would also post inspirational notes and reminders around the court, just as he did when they were younger. He also continued to receive criticism for his offbeat methods of training his daughters, with tennis professional Tracy Austin being especially vocal.

That year, Venus received the Sports Image Foundation Award for offering tennis clinics in low-income areas. This was one of the first awards of significance that she would receive, but it was far from the last.

PROFESSIONAL TENNIS

Venus turned professional on October 31, 1994, shortly before the World Tennis Association (WTA) banned fourteen-year-olds from competing in an unlimited number of events. Her father professed reluctance over this move, citing Jennifer Capriati's experiences. Capriati had turned pro in 1990, at the age of thirteen, becoming the youngest player to reach the finals of a professional tennis tournament. In 1992, she captured Olympic gold. By 1993, she had already placed in the quarterfinals of three Grand Slam tournaments. In the fall of 1993, after finding high levels of success, she left competitive play to complete high school; that December, she received a citation for shoplifting a ring from a mall. As a minor, this news should have remained confidential but the press found out about it and the story appeared in multiple newspapers.

Capriati moved out of her parents' home after turning eighteen. In May 1994, she was arrested for possession of marijuana, and the two friends accompanying her were charged with possession of heroin and suspicion of having crack cocaine. Eventually, Capriati entered a drug rehabilitation program (Reed, 1994).

Richard Williams did not want burnout to affect his daughters in the way that it had apparently affected Capriati. Despite his reservations, Williams allowed Venus, who had remained unbeaten in the twelve-and-under division, to turn pro—in theory, for only one tournament, which was the Bank of the West Classic, held in Oakland, California.

Only nine hundred fans watched Venus play in her opening professional match; the press, however, showed up in quantity, hoping to report on a potential star. She beat Shaun Stafford in two sets: 6-3, 6-4. In her second matchup, she played against Arantxa Sanchez-Vicario from Spain, who was ranked second in the world; Sanchez-Vicario won.

Serena began playing professionally in October 1995, when she competed in the Bell Challenge in Vanier, Quebec, a tournament that was not sanctioned by the WTA. Early in her career, she was clearly outshone by Venus, who quickly became ranked in the top ten, relatively speaking, while Serena was not even listed in the top five hundred by the end of 1996.

1997 TENNIS

Serena's rankings began to climb in 1997, when she went from number 453 to number 304; she then beat both Mary Pierce (ranked number seven) and Monica Seles (ranked number four) at the Ameritech Cup, which boosted her rankings to one hundredth in the world. These wins made Serena the lowest ranked player to ever beat two top ten players in a tournament, and she finished the year with a ranking of number ninety-nine. Although she planned to play in the doubles tournament in the Ameritech Cup with Venus, an injury caused Serena to withdraw from the event.

That year, Venus graduated from the Driftwood Academy, after taking a mixture of high school and college courses, as well as spending some time being homeschooled. That same year, she competed in her first major tournament, the French Open. In the 1997 U.S. Open, she became the first unseeded (unranked and not expected to place well) player to ever reach the finals in this event. Venus was also the first black woman to reach the U.S. Open finals since Althea Gibson won in 1957 and 1958. Although Venus lost to Martina Hingis from Switzerland, 6-0, 6-4, her excellent performance caused her own ranking to go up from number sixty-six to number twenty-five in just one day. Because of her outstanding play, Venus was named the WTA Newcomer of the Year; she was also chosen as September's Olympic Committee Female Athlete.

1998 TENNIS

In 1998, Venus played against Hingis in the Australian Open. Hingis had also become a professional tennis player at the age of fourteen and, at the age of sixteen, she had won the 1997 Australian Open; with that win, she became the youngest Grand Slam champion since fifteen-year-old Lottie Dodd won at Wimbledon in 1887. So, when Venus played Hingis in the Australian Open in 1998, she was competing against the reigning champion; Venus beat Hingis (and Serena) in the Australian Open, reaching the quarterfinals. At the same tournament, Venus and Justin Gimelstob won the mixed doubles tournament. Venus also beat her sister in a match during the Italian Open that year.

In March, Venus won her first WTA singles title at the IGA Tennis Classic; she also won the Lipton International, which placed Venus in the top ten female tennis players worldwide. To win the latter tournament, she beat her sister in the finals, the first time in more than a century that two sisters played in the final match of a tennis tournament. The other time was during the first-ever Wimbledon match for women, in 1884, when nineteen-year-old Maud Watson beat her sister Lillian, age twenty-six; those sisters won silver flower baskets, silver glass mirrors, and silver-backed brushes for placing in the finals. Venus finished the season by reaching the quarterfinals in two of the Grand Slam tournaments—the French Open and Wimbledon—and the semifinals in a third Grand Slam tournament, the U.S. Open. The Williams sisters also won the doubles title at the French Open—and Venus was awarded *Tennis Magazine*'s Most Improved Player. Venus's serve was clocked at an astonishing 127 mph, a world record.

That same year, Serena won her first Wimbledon title—mixed doubles with Max Mirnyi of Belarus; the duo beat Mahesh Bhupathi from India and Mirjana Lucic from West Germany, 6-4, 6-4. By August, Serena was ranked number twenty-one worldwide. The sisters then won the doubles title at the U.S. Open, the first black team to ever do so. Serena was named the WTA Most Impressive Newcomer of the Year and the winner of *Tennis Magazine*'s Rolex Rookie of the Year. Serena signed a $12 million deal with sponsor Puma; by this time, Venus was already sponsored by Reebok, a deal that would earn her an incredible $40 million (in addition to money made winning tennis tournaments).

1999 TENNIS

In October 1999, Venus lost her first professional match to her sister during the finals of the Grand Slam Cup, held in Munich, Germany. At the end of the 1999 season, Venus was ranked number three in the world, earning the second-most amount of prize money; by this point, she had earned almost $4.6 million by playing tennis.

Serena won the singles competition at the Open Gaz de France, held in Paris; she beat Amelie Mauresmo of France, becoming the first American to win that event. She went on to win five singles titles that year, including the U.S. Open against Martina Hingis and a win over Steffi Graf in the Evert Cup tournament. The two sisters also won the U.S. Open tournament in women's doubles, beating Chanda Rubin from the United States and Sandrine Testud from France in three sets: 4-6, 6-1, 6-4. Awards won by Serena in 1999 include the WTA Most Improved Player of the Year and *Tennis Magazine*'s Player of the Year.

That year, both of the Williamses attended the Art Institute of Florida, where they studied fashion design. Venus earned a certificate in interior design from Palm Beach Community College as well.

2000 TENNIS

In 2000, Venus was suffering from injuries and her father announced that she might retire, something that he supposedly looked forward to happening. That was not what happened with Venus, however. Instead, she won the Wimbledon singles event, after beating her sister in the semifinals, and then she beat the reigning champion, Lindsay Davenport from the United States, in the finals: 6-4, 7-5. Serena left the tournament in tears, with Venus comforting her. The next day, the Williams sisters won the doubles event at Wimbledon, beating Julie Halard-Decugis from France and Ai Sugiyama from Japan, the first time this event had ever been won by sisters. As a wild card entry, the Williams sisters were not expected to win this event and it gave them significant attention when they did.

Both of the sisters made the 2000 Olympic tennis team, where they would be coached by tennis legend Billie Jean King in Sydney, Australia. Venus won the gold in the women's singles event; Elena Dementieva from Russia captured the silver; and Monica Seles, now a U.S. citizen, won the bronze.

The Williams sisters then competed in doubles, capturing the gold medal in what was their twenty-second straight doubles win. In the finals, they beat the Dutch team of Miriam Oremans and Kristie Boogert. Els Callens and Dominique van Roost from Belgium won the bronze. With that win, Venus became one of only two women with Olympic gold in both singles and doubles; the other was Helen Wills Moody, who had accomplished that feat in 1924. In large part because of their Olympic win, the Williams sisters won the WTA Doubles Team of the Year Award.

On September 9, 2000, Williams and Davenport met in another Grand Slam final—in the U.S. Open; Venus won, making that her twenty-sixth straight win; this was the first time since 1997 that a woman had won two Grand Slam singles titles in one year.

In 2000, Venus was selected as the WTA Player of the Year; she was also named the *Sports Illustrated for Women*'s Sportswoman of the Year, and given the Teen Awards Achievement Award and the Women's Sports Foundation's Athlete of the Year Award.

ACTING BUG

The sisters made a guest performance on the animated television show *The Simpsons* in 2001. Serena then signed with the William Morris Agency and she made a cameo appearance in *Black Knight*, a movie starring Martin Lawrence. She then appeared in *My Wife and Kids*, a program starring Damon Wayans; a year later, she appeared in an episode of *Street Time*. In 2003, she was also chosen for a role in *Beauty Shop*, a movie starring Queen Latifah.

That summer, Serena was supposed to compete in the Rogers AT & T Cup in Toronto and fans bought tickets to see her play. She backed out just weeks before the tournament, citing scheduling conflicts; when it was discovered that she did not play in the competition so that she could film *Street Time*, she received criticism. In 2004, she began dating Hollywood director Brett Ratner. Many expected Richard Williams to be upset, as he had been quite vocal about the inappropriateness of interracial dating in the past, but the two men seemed cordial with one another when seen together at the U.S. Open.

2001 TENNIS

In 2001, Serena made it to the quarterfinals of the Australian Open, but lost to Martina Hingis; Venus also lost to Hingis, after that, but the sister team successfully defeated another duo from the United States (Lindsay Davenport and Corina Morarui) in doubles, 6-2, 2-6, 6-4.

Serena made it to the quarterfinals in the French Open and Wimbledon in singles, while Venus won the Wimbledon singles title again, beating Justine Henin from Belgium. In the U.S. Open, she beat Jennifer Capriati to play her sister in the finals match; Venus won in two sets, 6-2, 6-4. Venus was given the ESPY Awards for Best Female Athlete and Best Female Tennis Player.

In 2002, Richard and Brandi Williams divorced. The reason given was irreconcilable differences, and financial details were kept quiet. The *Watchtower*, a publication of the Jehovah's Witnesses, published a statement about the divorce, stating that Venus and Serena were raised to be Jehovah's Witnesses by their mother, adding, "The father is as far as I know not a Witness and is only interested in their tennis careers" (*Watchtower*, 2002). Brandi was quoted as saying that she and Richard would continue to work together with their daughters, and that she planned to take back her maiden name of Price.

JEHOVAH'S WITNESSES

Venus and Serena Williams are members of Jehovah's Witnesses, a religion that traces its origins back to the late nineteenth century when a small group of people gathered together for Bible study near Pittsburgh, Pennsylvania. They became known as the International Bible Students, a name they used until 1931, when the modern-day name of Jehovah's Witnesses came into use. They first published their journal, *The Watchtower*, in 1879. Membership statistics provided by the Jehovah's Witnesses show 7.5 million members worldwide, a figure that includes the Williams sisters. Although they do not talk about their religion publicly in any great detail, Serena did discuss one aspect of her faith with reporters in June 2008, admitting that she was excited by Barack Obama's run for president, but because Jehovah's Witnesses do not get involved in politics, she could not vote for him. Information provided about the religion suggests that, although voting is not expressly prohibited for its members, it is discouraged. When Venus was asked about her views about the Obama candidacy, she refused to comment. As a side note, in July 2009, Serena was invited to the White House, where she met the president and his family, including his pet dog. President Obama complimented Serena on her choice of shoes that day, which were five-inch heels.

2002 TENNIS

In 2002, Serena missed the Australian Open because of a sprained ankle, but she then won seven of her next twelve events. She was to beat her sister in multiple matches, including the finals of the French Open, Wimbledon, and the U.S. Open; Serena won Wimbledon in straight sets. When it was time for Serena to receive her Wimbledon trophy, it was older sister Venus who reminded her to curtsy. The sisters then paired up to win doubles at Wimbledon. At the U.S. Open, Serena received extra attention when she wore a sleek black cat suit.

Throughout 2002, Venus had captured—and then lost—the coveted number one ranking in the world more than once. After these series of wins, Serena took over the number-one spot, something that she maintained for fifty-seven weeks. WTA named Serena the 2002 Player of the Year and she was named the ITF Women's Singles World Champion, as well as the Associated Press Female Athlete of the Year.

2003 TENNIS

Serena won the 2003 Australian Open, which meant that she had won four Grand Slam competitions in a row: the 2002 French Open, the 2002 Wimbledon competition, the U.S. Open, and now the 2003 Australian Open, wherein she beat her sister. The Williamses then paired up to capture the doubles title in Australia, beating Virginia Ruano Pascual from Spain and Paola Suarez from Argentina, 4-6, 6-4, 6-3.

Serena was one of two women to be named the International Tennis Federation world champion in 2003, along with Lleyton Hewitt of Australia. That year, Serena won multiple awards, including the thirty-fourth NAACP Image Awards President's Award; the ESPY Award for Best Female Athlete; the ESPY Award for Best Female Tennis Player; the Laureus World Sportswoman of the Year; the Avon Foundation Celebrity Role Model Award; and BET's Best Female Athlete of the Year. As for Venus, who struggled in 2003, she was awarded the thirty-fourth NAACP Image Awards President's Award.

FAMILY TRAGEDY

In 2003, Yetunde Price, Venus and Serena's oldest sister who had been working as their personal assistant, was killed. When the Williams family had moved to Florida, Yetunde had decided to stay in Compton. She had fallen in love with Jeffrey Johnson, a member of the notorious Bloods gang, known for its intense and violent rivalry with the Crips. She and Johnson had a son whom they named Jeffrey Jr. Johnson was arrested for car theft and assaulting a police officer and he went to jail. Yetunde then met Byron Bobbitt, and the two married. Yetunde finished earning a vocational nursing degree and she opened a beauty salon with a friend, called Headed Your Way.

By the time that she had three children, one with Johnson and two with Bobbitt, Yetunde decided to move away from Compton, to Corona, where she felt that the neighborhood was safer. She and Bobbitt then divorced in 2002, with Yetunde claiming that he was violent towards her, a charge that he denied. Yetunde continued to visit friends in Compton, meeting a man named Rolland Wormley in April 2003. Wormley had a criminal record, including petty theft, possession of unlawful firearms, and selling marijuana. On probation at the time, Wormley has said he was open about his criminal past to Yetunde and that the two fell in love.

On September 14, 2003, in the early morning hours, Yetunde sat in a car with Wormley. While in that car, she was shot by an AK-47. Wormley drove Yetunde to his mother's house in Long Beach, where he called police. He then took her to the Long Beach Memorial Hospital, where she died at the age of thirty-one.

"I was sharing a room with Lyn [one of the five Williams sisters] in Toronto when I found out," Serena Williams told Matthew Syed in *The Sunday Times*. "We just couldn't take it in. I had been talking to Tunde on the phone earlier that day and she had been real excited about what was going on in her life, and mine. I just couldn't make sense of it. It was like something out of a dream" (Syed, 2009).

On January 20, 2004, two members of the Crips gang, Robert Edward Maxwell and Aaron Michael Hammer, were charged with her murder. Maxwell was also charged with the attempted murder of Wormley, while Wormley himself was charged with parole violation and assault with a deadly weapon.

Oracene Williams wanted custody of her three grandchildren—Jeffrey Jr., Jair, and Justus—and Jeffrey's father agreed with this arrangement; Byron Bobbitt, the father of the younger two children, did not. On November 5, 2004, a judge declared a mistrial for Hammer, who had been accused of murdering Yetunde; a few days later, Maxwell's prosecution also ended in a mistrial.

2004 TENNIS

Serena had planned to compete in the 2004 Olympics, speaking about how much another gold medal would mean to her as she appeared on a series of television shows the day before her plane was set to leave for Greece. A few hours after her television appearances, Serena consulted with a doctor about her knee, which had been operated on a year earlier. The doctor confirmed what other medical professionals had been telling her—that her knee needed more time to heal and that, if she played on it, she risked damaging it even further. Although Serena had needed to withdraw from other tournaments that year because of her injury, this was the most disappointing for her. Although Venus did compete in the Olympics in women's doubles without her sister, she brought home no medals. In fact, she and partner Chanda Rubin, also from the United States, lost in the very first round to the eventual winners, Sun Tiantian from China and Li Ting, also from China.

In women's singles, Justine Henin from Belgium won gold; Amelie Mauresmo from France, the silver; and Alicia Molik from Australia, the bronze. In women's doubles, Tin and Tiantian captured the gold; Conchita Martinez and Virginia Ruano Pascual from Spain, the silver; and Paola Suarez and Patricia Tarabini from Argentina, the bronze.

Serena was able to play at Wimbledon, losing to Maria Sharapova from Russia in the finals, 6-1, 6-4. In the U.S. Open, Serena appeared in a startling outfit: a denim skirt, a black studded tank top, a denim jacket with "SERENA" in rhinestones on the back, and a pair of black knee-high "boots" that were really removable Lycra leggings. Media around the world reported on this outfit, as well as a micro-mini that she wore during another match. In the quarterfinal match, she played against Jennifer Capriati, whose career had rebounded after the controversies and challenges that had plagued her earlier years. Serena beat Capriati in the first set, 6-2, but she then began making errors and arguing calls against her, and she lost to Capriati.

WTA nevertheless named Serena, who struggled after the shooting death of her sister, as the WTA Comeback Player of the Year; she also was given the Family Circle/Prudential Financial Player Who Makes a Difference Award and was named the ESPY Best Female Tennis Player. Serena was also named the BET Female Athlete of the Year. Venus also struggled in 2004; she was nevertheless named the Harris Poll Most Favorite Female Sports Star.

During this time frame, the sisters published two books: *How to Play Tennis: Learn How to Play the Williams Sisters' Way* (DK Children, 2004) and *Serving From the Hip: 10 Rules for Living, Loving and Winning* (Sandpiper, 2005).

2005 TENNIS

Venus won Wimbledon singles, beating Davenport in the longest finals match in Wimbledon history; that year, she received *Glamour* magazine's Women of the Year Award. Meanwhile, seventh-seeded Serena—who had beaten first-seeded Lindsay Davenport to win the Australian Open—was named BET's Female Athlete of the Year.

2006 TENNIS

Injuries prevented Venus from any prestigious wins in 2006, although she and Bob Bryan from the United States made it to the finals of Wimbledon, mixed doubles, losing to Andy Ram from Israel and Vera Zvonareva from Russia, 6-3, 6-2.

In November, Serena traveled to Ghana, where she helped in the efforts to get young children immunized and to distribute free mosquito nets to help protect families against malaria. In 2006, UNESCO and the WTA Tour chose Serena as the first Promoter of Gender Equality in their effort to promote women's leadership. Serena was honored as ESPY's Best Female Tennis Player and BET's Best Female Athlete of the Year; she was also Harris Poll's Most Favorite Female Sports Star. Venus was given the Gitanjali Diamond Award.

2007 TENNIS

While in Africa, Serena gained weight, with some newspapers mocking her new shape, one even calling her a "fat cow." She nevertheless decided to compete in the Australian Open, capturing the singles title by beating Maria Sharapova from Russia, 6-1, 6-2. When she received her trophy, she dedicated it to her sister Yetunde, who had been murdered in 2003. Meanwhile, Venus won women's singles at Wimbledon, beating Marion Bartoli from France, 6-4, 6-1.

This was also the year that Venus's clothing line, EleVen, debuted at Steve & Barry's retail stores. The collection consisted of sportswear, lounge wear, accessories, and footwear, with shoes being named after tennis terms: *Ace*, *Deuce*, and *Swing*.

That year, Serena was named BET's Best Female Athlete of the Year, the Laureus World Comeback of the Year, and Harris Poll's Most Favorite Female Sports Star.

2008 TENNIS

The sisters met up in the finals for women's singles in Wimbledon, with Venus coming up on top, 7-5, 6-4; that year, Venus won Wimbledon in straight sets. Venus and Serena then captured the doubles title at Wimbledon.

That year, Venus and Serena competed in another Olympics, this time held in Beijing, China. The duo recaptured the gold that they had won in Sydney in 2000, with Anabel Medina Garrigues and Virginia Ruano Pascual from Spain earning the silver; and Yan Zi and Zheng Jie from China, the bronze. Serena also won the U.S. Open that year in women's singles, beating Serbian Jelena

Jankovic, 6-4, 7-5. Serena was named the WTA Player of the Year and she was, for a brief period, ranking number one in the world again, while Venus was given the Whirlpool Sixth Sense Player of the Year Award.

2009 TENNIS

Serena added another Australian Open win to her resume, beating Dinara Safina from Russia, 6-0, 6-3. She and her sister then beat Daniela Hantuchova from Slovakia and Ali Sugiyama from Japan to win the Australian Open women's doubles title, 6-3, 6-3.

Then, just as the previous year, the two sisters competed against one another in Wimbledon finals for singles; this time, it was Serena who captured the title. The sisters then won yet another Wimbledon doubles title. They also won doubles at the U.S. Open.

Serena was considered one of the favorites to win singles at the 2009 U.S. Open in 2009, after winning thirty out of the past thirty-one matches from major tournaments. In the semi-finals, Serena was playing against unseeded Kim Clijsters, who had not competed in the U.S. Open since 2005 and who entered the tournament by being a wild card choice. After losing the first set to Clijsters, Serena was losing the second. She then faulted on her first serve; when a line judge called a foot fault on her second serve, Serena had a double-fault called against her, something that rarely happens—and certainly not to a top-level athlete. That call put Clijsters one point away from a victory in the semi-finals.

Instead of serving again, Serena walked over to the line judge, shouting and cursing, and shaking the tennis ball at her; she also threatened to shove the ball down the judge's throat. At this point, the tournament referee became involved and, because Serena had already received a warning when she broke her racquet after losing the first set, the chair umpire gave Clijsters a penalty point, which meant that she had won the match. Serena was fined $10,500 for her actions.

In better news for Serena, she was named the BET Best Female Athlete of the Year and the Harris Poll Most Favorite Female Sports Star. She also received the following awards: the ESPY Award for Best Female Tennis Player; the *Glamour Magazine* Woman of the Year Award; the SI.com Best Female Athlete of the Decade; the AP Female Athlete of the Year Award; the ITF Women's Singles World Champion; the Second Best Tennis Player of the Decade by ESPN (with Roger Federer receiving the top ranking); and the WTA Player of the Year. For eleven weeks that year—and then, later in the year for two weeks—she once again was ranked number one in the world. She then recaptured that status on November 2, 2009, maintaining that until October 10, 2010.

In 2009, Venus and Serena bought a minority stake in the football franchise the Miami Dolphins. They continued to be showered with awards, with

Venus winning the Anti-Defamation League Americanism Award; the Whirl-pool Sixth Sense Player of the Year Award; the ITF Women's Doubles World Champion (with her sister); the WTA Doubles Team of the Year Award (with her sister); and the WTA Fan Favorite Doubles Team of the Year Award (with her sister). The sisters also won the Outstanding Leadership Award as part of the Doha Twenty-First Century Leaders Awards.

2010 TENNIS

Serena successfully defended her Australian Open title, beating Justine Henin from Belgium, 6-4, 3-6, 6-2. She and Venus also defended their doubles title, beating Cara Black and Liezel Huber, 6-4, 6-3. During the competition, Venus attracted significant attention for a yellow outfit of hers that appeared to have a deeply plunging neckline and that appeared to reveal the completely bare bottom of the tennis player. In fact, Venus's chest and buttocks were covered with a sheer panel that very closely matched her skin tone. This outfit was designed by Venus herself and drew even more attention because, in 2009, the Australian Open created a ban on revealing outfits after Alize Comet from France wore a see-through top.

At the French Open, the Williams sisters beat Czechoslovakian Kveta Pe-schke and Slovenian Katarina Srebotnik to capture the doubles trophy. Because of this win, Serena became only the sixth woman to hold the number one ranking in both singles and doubles. The sisters were now 12-0 in their Grand Slam doubles finals.

At Wimbledon, Serena successfully defended another title, beating Vera Zvonareva from Russia in the finals, 6-3, 6-2. Serena captured this title in straight sets, with this win meaning that either she or her sister had won nine out of the past 11 Wimbledon singles titles. Because of a foot injury, after a waitress in Germany dropped a glass that shattered and sliced her tendon, Serena withdrew from doubles competition. The injury required two surgeries.

In 2010, Serena was chosen as the Laureus World Sportswoman of the Year. *Time* magazine selected her as one of the World's 100 Most Influential People. Meanwhile, Jon Wertheim from SI.com declared Serena as his choice as the best female tennis player ever; this statement was the source of significant debate, both online and in print.

2011 TENNIS

Because of her foot injury sustained in 2010, Serena did not compete in the 2011 Australian Open, in either singles or doubles competition. What is more, in March 2011, she underwent emergency treatment for a blood embolism in her lungs, a potentially life-threatening condition, perhaps an effect from her foot surgeries.

Meanwhile, Venus drew significant attention at the Australian Open, but not for her tennis playing. Instead, it was for her outfit, which consisted of a criss-crossing yellow top with many diamond-shaped cutouts; the skirt was short and psychedelic, a look that Venus has said was inspired by Alice in Wonderland. A hip injury caused her to withdraw during the third round of competition.

After the Australian Open, Serena—who had been ranked number one on the tour in the previous year before her injury and was ranked number four right before the Australian Open—was projected to have her rankings fall to about number thirteen, a three-year low for her. Venus, who was ranked number five going into the Australian competition, was also expected to have falling rankings after she needed to drop out of the tournament.

In late March 2011, a commercial that had been filmed by Serena for a tennis video game, *Top Spin 4*, was determined to be too sexy for television. Part of the issue was the tight, skimpy leotard worn by Serena; the other part was the grunting sounds that she made while playing the game, which some claimed sounded more sexual in nature than athletic.

In mid-April 2011, Serena returned to tennis practice, wearing a tight, hot pink bodysuit that was designed to provide compression that would aid in her recovery. That month, it was speculated that she was also beginning work on a rap album. On April 28, 2011, both sisters offered tennis training at the Southeast Tennis and Learning Center in Washington, D.C., to youth who would not otherwise have this opportunity. Neither sister would comment on when they would be able to return to competitive play but indicated that was the goal. In 2011 Venus was diagnosed with Sjogren's Syndrome, a little-known autoimmune disorder.

FURTHER READING

Chappell, Kevin. 2000. Richard Williams: Venus and Serena's Father Whips the Pros and Makes His Family No. 1 in Tennis. *Ebony*, June. http://findarticles.com/.

Edmonson, Jacqueline. 2005. *Venus and Serena Williams: A Biography*. Westport, CT: Greenwood Press.

Intini, John. 2009. Q & A with Richard Williams, Venus and Serena's Famous Father. *Macleans*, September 1. http://www2.macleans.ca/2009/09/01/richard-williams-venus-and-serena%E2%80%99s-famous-father-on-creating-champions-his-critics-parenting-and-the-problem-with-tennis/.

Serena Williams website. http://www.serenawilliams.com/.

Reed, Susan. 1994. "Losing Her Grip." *People*, May 30: http://www.people.com/people/archive/article/0,20108234,00.

Syed, Matthew. 2009. Serena Williams: How I emerged from pit of despair after my sister's death. *The Sunday Times*, October 27. http://www.timesonline.co.uk/tol/sport/tennis/article6891173.ece.

Venus Williams website. http://www.venuswilliams.com/.

Williams, Serena, and Daniel Paisner. 2009. *On the Line*. New York: Grand Central Publishing.

YouTube. Serena Williams outburst (HQ) close up video at US Open semi-finals. http://www.youtube.com/watch?v=DO_jlXjgxN8.

Babe Didrickson Zaharias shattered female stereotyples by achieving great success in golf, basketball, and track and field during the 1940s and 1950s. (AP Photo)

Babe Didrikson Zaharias (1911–1956)

1911 was an eventful year; the Mexican Revolution was raging, Ray Harroun won the first Indianapolis 500 auto race, and the citizens of Boston broke ground on a new baseball stadium to be named Fenway Park. In late June of that year, a couple hundred miles north of the Mexican border in Port Arthur, Texas, Hannah Didricksen delivered a daughter Mildred, called "Baby" and then "Babe." Babe would always claim that the nickname came from her girl-hood ability to hit home runs like the iconic slugger Babe Ruth who made his major league debut at Fenway. The nickname story is apocryphal, but the young Babe from Texas was destined to generate a revolution in women's sport and become an icon in her own right.

CHILDHOOD

Babe's father Ole, a ship's carpenter, immigrated to Port Arthur from Norway in 1905. Three years later, he sent for his wife Hannah and their three children. The enterprising Ole took up cabinet making and furniture refinishing in his adopted country. These trades allowed him to make a modest living to support a family that would grow to seven children. Babe was the sixth, born June 26, 1911. The family moved inland to Beaumont, Texas, when Babe was four years old. It was here that Babe spent the formative years of her life. Beaumont had been a small Texas cattle town and farming community that became a boomtown when oil was discovered at nearby Spindletop in 1901. The Didriksens lived in a wood-frame house in the working-class South End of town, near the railroad tracks and close enough to the Magnolia Oil Refinery to smell the fumes.

Ole Didriksen was a hard worker and a good provider. He made adequate wages when he was employed, but it took a lot to support his growing brood. At times, the family struggled to make ends meet. Hannah took in laundry to supplement the family income. The older children held jobs at one point or another. A teenaged Babe worked briefly in a fig-packing plant and later at a gunnysack factory. But it wasn't all work and no play. The Didriksens were a musical family; Ole played the violin, and the girls, Esther and Dora, played the piano. Babe was a self-taught harmonica player who would later perform in public. The children describe a close, loving home. Babe didn't have it easy, but it was a good life for a young girl growing up in a working-class family in the American South.

Mildred "Babe" Didriksen got her athletic ability from her mother Hannah, who had been an accomplished skier and ice skater in Norway. If heredity is vital in creating a future sports champion, so is environment. Babe had plenty of outlets for her athletic inclinations. Ole built a home-made gymnasium with a trapeze in the backyard on Doucette Avenue. The woman who lived across the street had actually been a trapeze artist. She took the Didriksen children to see the circus. Babe was the tomboy in the family. In addition to climbing on the backyard gym, she roller-skated and played touch football and baseball with the neighbor kids. Babe preferred playing with the boys. When they showed up on the sandlots on Saturdays, she would be there. Typically she was the best at everything, the first to be picked when choosing sides. In second grade, she beat all the boys at marbles and won the school championship. Babe was combative and had a temper. If a boy made an objectionable remark, she knocked him to the floor. The young spitfire routinely showed up at school with bruised knuckles, cuts, and lumps on her face from getting into fights.

Babe's rough and tumble behavior carried into her adolescence. She yearned to play on the Beaumont High School football team, and easily convinced the coach that she could kick extra points better than the boys. The coach was ready to put Babe on the team, but the Texas League rules wouldn't allow girls to play football. Undeterred, Babe devoted her efforts to sports she was allowed to play. She was on all the girls' teams: volleyball, tennis, swimming, and the star of the basketball team. She showed less interest in her studies or in the school's social events. Beaumont P.E. teacher Bea Lyle recalled that the only book Babe was interested in reading was a sports rule book. Nor was Babe particularly popular with the other students. She avoided most of the girls, and they returned the favor. The boys didn't quite know what to make of her. She lacked the social graces and was a "put down" to all things feminine. But no one questioned her athletic ability. Articles on Babe began appearing in the local *Beaumont Journal* her junior year of high school. The following year, the nineteen-year-old high school senior was recruited to play basketball with the Employers Casualty Insurance Company's semi-pro basketball team in Dallas.

CAREER BEGINNINGS: BASKETBALL, SOFTBALL, AND TRACK AND FIELD

Babe Didriksen had never been more than a few miles from home when she and her father made the 275-mile train trip to Dallas, launching an athletic career that would extend to three continents. Babe was "discovered" by Col. M. J. McCombs, manager of the insurance company's women's teams. The "Colonel" had been scouting a Houston-area basketball star when he first saw her play. McCombs forgot about the original prospect and signed Babe to a $900-a-year contract as a typist—when the average typist's salary was $600—and to play on the company team. Such arrangements were common among companies fielding "semipro" teams, as it allowed the athletes to maintain their amateur status. Basketball was the premier women's sport in Texas and throughout much of the American heartland. The EC team, outfitted in their audacious (for the time) sleeveless blouses and blue and white shorts, drew over a thousand fans for home games. Babe had entered a world where athletic women not only were accepted but applauded. She was no longer an aberration.

As Babe Didrikson (she changed the spelling of her surname) the budding athlete rapidly became the star of the Golden Cyclones. She led the team to a national championship in 1931 and made All-American. Corporate recruiters from other teams tried to entice her with offers to leave Employers Casualty. Babe realized that she had value as an athletic commodity. Indeed, she was an all-around athlete. She played on the company's baseball team and in the Dallas city softball league, where she pitched and batted over .400. However, it was her accomplishments as a track and field athlete that would lead to national recognition.

Babe had never pursued track and field seriously before joining the insurance company's team. McCombs had her throwing the javelin, putting the shot, and competing in the high jump and long jump. Babe trained relentlessly and quickly became the team's best performer. She soon held the national record in the javelin. At the national AAU meet in New Jersey, Babe personally accounted for fifteen of the Cyclones' nineteen points in their second-place finish. The *Dallas Daily News* ran a half-page photo of her. This was a lot of attention paid to a young woman raised in the South End of Beaumont, Texas. Some of the fame went to her head. Babe could be arrogant and coarse. Many of her teammates found her swaggering attitude to be off-putting. She came across as less a team player than a *prima donna*, intent on personal glory. There was no doubt that she was the star, and she knew it.

At the 1932 AAU track and field championship meet in Evanston, Illinois, Babe put on another dominating performance. She competed in eight events, won six of them, and broke the world records for the javelin, 80-meter hurdles, high jump, and baseball throw. She set an American record in the shot put. The Illinois Women's Athletic Club with its two dozen athletes was the favorite, but Babe outperformed the entire field to win first place for Employers Casualty. She single-handedly accumulated thirty points, while second-place IWAC scored twenty-two. It was an unparalleled display of athletic ability. Babe had won six firsts and broken four world records in a single day!

1932 OLYMPICS

The 1932 Olympic tryouts also were held in Evanston. Didrikson qualified for five events; however, the rules prohibited athletes from competing in more than three. At the Los Angeles Games, she set world records in all three events but was deprived of her gold medal in the high jump by a judges' ruling that she dived over the bar head first. She was awarded a silver medal in the high jump and gold medals in the javelin and 80-meter hurdles. Her very first throw of the javelin broke the world's record by an amazing eleven feet. Babe became the darling of the sports media. When a *New York Times* reporter heard about the number of sports that Babe competed in, he asked, "Is there anything you don't play?" "Yeah," she responded, "Dolls" (Cayleff, 1996, 23).

The Associated Press voted Babe Female Athlete of the Year. All the attention only encouraged the young Texan's cockiness. Babe's Olympic teammates resented her constant attention-grabbing antics. Jean Shiley, the team captain, had to room with Babe because no one else would.

Babe returned from the Olympics to Dallas where she was greeted enthusiastically by local dignitaries and feted with a parade. Two days later, Babe flew to Beaumont. Thousands cheered the home-town girl. She was given the keys to the city by the mayor. Babe knew she could always count on local support. Over the years she had kept a running correspondence with William "Tiny" Scurlock, the 300-pound editor of the *Beaumont Journal*. Tiny was Babe's unofficial publicist in Texas, and not averse to propagating "puffed up" stories about her athletic feats. Babe, for her part, was a willing partner in creating her own legend. Her personal story was replete with myths and disputed facts, including claims about her name and birth date. Babe's sport career took off at a time when newspaper sports pages had become standard fare, and radio was coming into its own. She was a publicity hound who pursued the press relentlessly. However, the image crafted by the national media wasn't always a positive one.

QUESTIONS ABOUT FEMINITY AND AMATEUR STATUS

Many sportswriters of the time, invariably men, were uncomfortable even with the more conventional women athletes, and Babe certainly wasn't conventional. As a young woman, she was garrulous, full of fun, a prankster, jokester, hustler, and sometimes a huckster. An outward toughness eclipsed her gentleness and generosity. Though not physically imposing, Babe Didrikson was surprisingly strong and knew how to exploit her strength. Short hair gave her a boyish look, and she showed an indifference to clothes and makeup. Moreover, she carried herself with a masculine swagger. The twenty-year-old Olympic champion was described as lean-built and flat-chested at 128 pounds and five feet, five inches tall. Babe's long jaw, Roman nose, and wide smile were subject to comments, not all of them complimentary. Journalists portrayed Babe as something of a freak. One referred to her as a "Muscle Moll." She often was insulted and laughed at, but rarely ignored. Clearly, Babe challenged the reigning perceptions of women's role in society.

Didrikson would gradually feminize herself over the course of her life, often appearing in dresses, donning jewelry and make-up. She filled out to a full-figured 140 pounds at the peak of her golf career. The news media always seemed more interested in Babe's appearance and mannerisms than her athletic performance. A characteristic *New York Times* headline read: "Miss Didrikson Buys First Hat for Trip to U.S. Title Games." The article that follows devotes paragraphs to the referenced shopping spree; one final sentence mentions Babe's athletic feats. A 1947 *Saturday Evening Post* article features side-by-side photos of Babe on the "links" in slacks, and in the kitchen in an apron, frying trout for her "amiable husband."

Didrikson's femininity wasn't the only thing in dispute. In 1932, the Amateur Athletic Union challenged her amateur status. The object of contention was a Dodge automobile that Babe was driving. The alleged violation involved her photograph and name appearing in a Dodge advertisement. The AAU suspended her indefinitely, squelching her plans to play basketball with the Golden Cyclones. However, Dodge Division of Chrysler was able to convince AAU that Babe wasn't paid for her appearance in the ad, and didn't even know her image was being appropriated. AAU relented, and Didrikson regained her right to compete. She hired an agent George Emerson to explore opportunities to capitalize on her fame that wouldn't compromise her amateur standing. Emerson booked her for a stint on the vaudeville circuit, where she sang, played the harmonica, and ran on a treadmill in her track outfit. After a week or so of stage performances, Babe decided she would rather play golf. She returned to Beaumont to work on her game under the tutelage of local pros.

By the fall of 1933, Didrikson felt she was ready for her golf debut. She hopped in her car and headed for a tournament in Arkansas. Babe loved sporty cars and had a reputation for driving fast. On the way to the tournament, she was involved in a fatal accident. In Louisiana, near the Texas state line, she hit and killed an elderly man backing out of his driveway. The records indicate that there was subsequent litigation, but her lawyers got her off. The incident wasn't picked up in the press, and Babe mentions it briefly in her autobiography only to say that Employers Casualty took care of the insurance and paid the damages. Her rather dismissive recollection of the tragic event suggests a young woman on the fast track who disregarded anything that got in her way. It was a side of Babe Didrikson that escaped the perception of an adoring public, but it was tangible to the women who competed against her.

In the 1930s, there were virtually no professional sports for talented women athletes: no professional basketball, no professional tennis or golf tours. The athletes had little choice but to compete as amateurs. The only way to make money was on exhibition tours or to join one of the barnstorming ball clubs. In 1934, promoter Ray Doan arranged for Didrikson to play with a traveling basketball team of four men and two women, called "Babe Didrikson's All Americans." They toured Middle America competing against local men's teams. Didrikson was paid a salary of $1,000 a month, an incredible sum for the Depression era. In March of 1934, Didrikson signed a deal to pitch an inning against major leaguers in spring training games for a fee of a couple hundred dollars per appearance. Doan then booked her to play with the House of David's exhibition baseball team that toured the country playing local semi-pro teams to support their religious community in Michigan. Babe would pitch a few innings prior to the regular pitcher coming in—what was little more than a publicity generating stunt. It was an odd arrangement all around. She didn't travel with her bearded teammates but had her own automobile. She would arrive at the local ballpark, pitch one or two innings, and then head to the next venue.

Babe Didrikson was still employed part-time at Employers Casualty, but her touring career brought in extra money. She might be paid up to $500 for an appearance. It wasn't an easy life on the road, but estimates are that Babe may have made over $40,000 in three and a half years. The ingenuous young athlete insisted on being paid in one-dollar bills. She spent money on herself and acquired a taste for expensive things, but she also stuffed cash into an envelope and mailed it to her family in Texas. Her generosity was noteworthy, given her public image as a hustler.

GOLF CAREER

The ball-playing exhibition tours proved lucrative, but Babe Didrikson wanted to pursue golf as a career. She had dabbled at it, but the exacting sport required precise skills honed through long hours of practice. As with so many other things Didrikson attempted, it quickly became evident that she had an unusual aptitude for golf. The novice was able to hit 250-yard drives despite flaws in her form and technique. No one in women's golf could hit longer. But she realized that her natural ability would carry her only so far. Didrikson headed to sunny Los Angeles to take lessons from Stan Kertes, a driving range pro who mentored Hollywood celebrities like Al Jolson and Harpo Marx. Babe, the devoted student, would hit balls from early morning until closing time, until her hands bled. In November of 1934, she entered the Fort Worth Women's Invitational, her first big tournament. She lost in the first round, returned to Dallas, and prepared for the Texas Women's Amateur Championship the following spring.

Didrikson ran into unexpected opposition upon entering the Texas Amateur tournament. Members of the prestigious Texas Women's Golf Association, or TWGA, were offended by her lack of social status (not to mention social graces). However, they couldn't forbid her to play as she was a member in good standing with the Beaumont Country Club. Several of the affronted women actually dropped out of the driving contest that Didrikson entered, and won. The following tournament involved match play among the top thirty-two qualifiers. Didrikson won the tournament as well, beating out Texas champion Peggy Chandler, a socialite who condescendingly referred to

Babe as the "truck driver's daughter." The campaign to ostracize Babe wasn't over. The day after she won the tournament, a member of the TWGA complained to the United States Golf Association that Didrikson was in fact a professional, citing her barnstorming career. The USGA ruled that if an athlete had been a pro in *any* sport, she shouldn't be allowed to play golf as an amateur. A committee of the Association barred Didrikson from all future amateur tournaments. This left one tournament: the Western Open that invited both amateur and professional golfers. Didrikson entered as a pro, held a press conference, and announced she had signed a contract with the Wilson Sporting Goods Company to represent their product line. She made it to the quarter finals of the Western. There was nothing left for the professional golfer to do but wait for the next infrequent open tournament.

In the summer of 1935, Didrikson began a two-month exhibition tour with PGA champion Gene Sarazen. She was to be paid a few hundred dollars for each match, an amount enhanced by a $2,500 offer from a sporting goods company to play with their clubs and balls. Babe jumped at the opportunity to exploit her reputation and make some money. The tour improved her game, as she learned the finer points of golf by studying the techniques of the seasoned U.S. Open winner. She and Sarazen finished the tour in time for the initial Texas Open. On this occasion, Didrikson would have some local support. During the previous year's Fort Worth Invitational, Babe had been introduced to R. L. and Bertha Bowen, a wealthy, socially connected couple who were part of the Texas golfing scene. They had been taken with Babe's stirring play during the previous women's tournament. The Bowens "adopted" Babe, guided her budding career, and exposed her to Southern gentility. Bertha's advice on personal appearance and etiquette would help guide the twenty-six-year-old tomboy into womanhood.

BABE DIDRIKSON BECOMES BABE ZAHARIAS

As for Babe's romantic life, she never had much use for boys in high school except as rivals on the sandlots. Later, when working for the insurance company in Dallas, she had a few casual dates but no lasting love interest. All this would change with a chance pairing at the 1938 Los Angeles Open. Didrikson's game had improved enough to qualify for the men's tournament. She had no chance of winning, but entered to enhance her status. Didrikson was teamed with George Zaharias, a robust and attractive professional wrestler. Like Babe, he was outgoing and exuded self-confidence. In her eyes, he was a Greek god. It was love at first sight for both of them. The two made a date for the evening following the second round. They continued dating, lived together for a short time, announced their engagement in November, and married in December of that year.

The following spring, George promoted an Australian golf tour for Babe that would double as the couple's honeymoon. The grueling tournament schedule was preview to their hectic married life, traveling from venue to venue. The Zahariases would own several homes during the following years, but most of their life was spent on the road. As a businessman, George had a tendency to plunge into risky money-making schemes. He would invest in golf courses and other properties, making and losing money in bundles. The couple's relationship had its ups and downs. Babe wanted children—apparently she had at least one miscarriage—but George was ambivalent, and both of them were always on the move. It was no life to start a family. On the up side, George was willing to balance his wrestling enterprises with promoting Babe's career.

Babe Zaharias wanted to continue playing golf, but there were scant opportunities for women to make money. Early in 1940, Babe petitioned the United States Golf Association to reinstate her amateur status. The USGA rules allowed this accord if a recent professional agreed not to accept prize money for three years. During this interim, Babe and George took up residence in their

GEORGE ZAHARIAS, PROFESSIONAL WRESTLER

George Zaharias, his ring name, was born Theodore Vetoyanis in Pueblo, Colorado, in 1908. He was a great showman with an avid following among wrestling fans. Zaharias made his fame and fortune as a three-hundred-pound ring villain billed as the "Crying Greek from Cripple Creek," a reference to his ethnicity and hometown. The colorful giant earned $100,000 at the peak of his career in the 1930s. His most celebrated bout was a 1932 match against the popular Jim Londos, "The Golden Greek," at Maple Leaf Gardens in Toronto. The sellout crowd of 14,500 was the largest wrestling audience of any North American event that year. Of course, George lost the match according to script.

Wrestling generally had been legitimate through the 1920s, but the sport was losing spectator appeal. In response, the promoters implemented a choreographed scenario of ring action buttressed by a cast of heroes and villains and assorted gimmicks. The fans didn't care if it was mostly pretense. It was great entertainment. They loved the ring acrobatics and the larger-than-life characters.

The business of wrestling in the decade of the 1930s proved to be just as wild. It had its own version of gangland-style rivalries—without the Tommy guns. Syndicates like the (Jack) Curley-Londos faction would employ cutthroat business practices in a scramble for fans and profit during the Great Depression. Zaharias retired as a ring performer in 1939 to become a successful wrestling promoter. He also managed Babe's career.

Los Angeles duplex. Babe, the all-around athlete with her golf career on hold, decided to pursue a new sport. She began tennis lessons with Eleanor Tennant, the well-known coach who had mentored 1939 Wimbledon champion Alice Marble. Like everything Babe attempted, she immersed herself in the game, playing dozens of sets a day. She developed a powerful, if inconsistent game, hitting for fun with movie celebrities at the Hollywood Country Club and more seriously against some of the better women players on the circuit. After a year and a half of training, Babe attempted to enter the USLTA-sponsored Southwest championships, but was informed by the tennis association that she was ineligible because she had been a professional athlete. Babe had been through this before. The disappointed neophyte tossed her tennis racket into the closet for good.

GOLFING EXCELLENCE

Babe Zaharias's next foray was into the sport of bowling. She and George had discussed buying a bowling alley in the L.A. area, as the sport was booming in popularity. They ultimately changed their minds about investing in the alley, but bowling became Babe's next challenge. She took lessons, gave up her natural power ball for an effective hook, and became one of Southern California's premier women bowlers, carrying a 170 average. True to character, Babe arranged exhibition matches against some of the leading men on the tour including the legendary Andy Varipapa. Meanwhile, Babe kept up her golf game. She shot a spectacular 64 at Brentwood Country Club and then entered the Western Open and the Texas Open tournaments. According to the agreement with USGA, she competed as an amateur. (George was making plenty of money as a wrestling promoter.) Babe won both tournaments, her first victories in five years.

In late 1941 with the bombing of Pearl Harbor and the U.S. entry into the war, sporting events were cancelled and many athletes enlisted in the armed services. The overweight George was rated 4-F by his draft board, so he put his efforts into arranging wrestling exhibitions for the soldiers at military posts. Babe scheduled golf exhibitions with celebrities like Bob Hope to help sell defense bonds. She had the opportunity to play with Babe Ruth at one tournament. She referred to him as "The Big Babe" and herself as the "Little Babe." The crowd-pleasing golfer developed a repertoire of tricks and stunts to entertain the gallery. One of her favorites was setting two balls on top of each other, and hitting one down the fairway while the other popped into her pocket. The tour was an opportunity to be patriotic and, at the same time, keep her skills honed.

Although Babe Zaharias had been declared an amateur in good standing by the USGA, there still weren't many tournaments during the ongoing war.

Zaharias competed in a few celebrity events, then won the Western Open in 1944. This was a noteworthy feat for an amateur. When the war ended in August, the major tournaments recommenced. Now, Zaharias could play golf full time. In the fall of that year, she won the Texas Women's Open and then defeated U.S. Women's Amateur Golf champion Betty Jameson in a series of matches. The Associated Press voted Babe Zaharias the Outstanding Woman Athlete of the Year. Her initial success as an amateur was a preview of things to come. Beginning in the summer of 1946, Babe put together an unprecedented string of seventeen straight tournament wins. Among these was the British Women's Amateur. No American had won this tournament since 1893. Babe proved just as popular with the fans in Scotland as in the U.S. Crowds followed her around the course. She bantered with them and performed her repertoire of trick shots. Babe played several of Scotland's historic courses and then headed home, a trans-Atlantic celebrity.

Babe received several offers to turn professional. The prospect was tempting, as it cost some $15,000 a year for her to compete on the amateur tour. She and George made the decision and hired noted sports agent Fred Corcoran to manage Babe's professional career. Corcoran's clients included baseball player Ted Williams and golfer Bobby Jones. Babe held a press conference at Toots Shor's restaurant in Manhattan where she announced she was turning pro and that she planned to enter the U.S. Open Championship, a men's tournament. At the time, no provision barred women from competing in the Open. The very next day, the austere USGA implemented a rule disallowing women entrants. Once again, Babe made the headlines.

The stymied golfer found other diversion to fill her summer. Corcoran signed Babe to a tour of ballparks where she would play third base during batting practice and then hit golf balls into the outfield. She would pull gags and occasionally play her harmonica for the fans. Again, the crowds loved her. Babe was back playing golf in October. She entered the Texas Open in Fort Worth and finished second to Betty Mims White, thus ending her string of tournaments victories at seventeen. Babe went on to win her next tournament in Little Rock, and again was named Woman Athlete of the Year. As the leading money winner in 1948, Babe made $3,400. She would make "big money" at golf exhibitions, personal appearances, and through her commercial contract with Wilson Sporting Goods. Meanwhile, the fledgling Women's Professional Women's Golf Association, which had struggled for three years, disbanded in March of 1947. Corcoran and Babe decided it was time to expand the women's tour and talked L. B. Icely, the president of Wilson, into providing the money.

In January of 1948, Babe and Fred Corcoran met with five other women golfers in Miami to form a Ladies Professional Golf Association. Icely agreed to put up prize money of $15,000 over nine tournaments, and Patty Berg agreed to serve as president. The LPGA was inaugurated in 1950 and quickly became a success, drawing new members and additional financing. By the association's fifth year, the total prize money had grown to $225,000. Most golfers still found it necessary to supplement their incomes with exhibitions, endorsements, or part-time jobs. The most money Babe Zaharias won in a single LPGA tournament was a little over $2,000. She led a hectic life keeping up with George's and Fred's bookings. Babe recalls one month when she spent seventeen nights on an airplane. Thus, when she was offered a job as the resident professional at Chicago's Sky Crest Country Club at $20,000 a year, she took it. Babe was the first woman to fill a position of club pro. It turned out to be a poor match. Babe left the position in the summer of 1951 amidst complaints by some of the club members that she was hustling money from them. If true, it wouldn't have been out of character.

Among new golfers on the LPGA tour was Louise Suggs, winner of the 1948 British Women's Amateur tournament. Louise became Babe's foremost rival. The two women were opposite personality types, and the rivalry became personal. Suggs resented Babe's showboating and felt upstaged by her. Indeed, the headlines frequently read, "Babe Loses," rather than "Suggs Wins." Babe was an overpowering golfer whose behavior on the links hadn't mellowed over the years. She could be overbearing when she won and ungracious upon losing. Babe may have been the first woman athlete to employ "trash talk" to intimidate opponents. She would come into the locker room before a tournament and jibe, "Well, you girls going to stick around and see who finishes second?" Not surprisingly, she had few close friends among women golfers (Cayleff, 1996, 125).

Babe didn't always add dignity to the game but she was its main drawing card, and she took advantage of her gate appeal. She would demand appearance money to enter tournaments and usually found sponsors willing to advance it. No one disputed the fact that her presence on the links sold tickets. In short, Babe changed the very nature of women's golf. Her power game, competitiveness, and showmanship transformed what had been a refined, country club sport into a form of entertainment. It seemed her name was always in the sports page headlines. In 1947–48, Babe won twenty-one straight tournaments. She became the first woman to earn a six-figure salary from combined prize money and endorsements. Babe's success also proved beneficial to the LPGA. It was the most financially successful women's sports organization of the post-war era.

In 1950, Fred Corcoran arranged for the six best golfers in the LPGA to play a series of matches against Britain's best women. Amateur women golfers from the States had been playing the British since 1932. But this time it was a professional team that made the trip. Corcoran added another wrinkle to the trans-Atlantic competition. He proposed a match against any British men's team willing to take on the American women. Britain's Walker Cup

Team accepted the challenge. The match ended with the professional women trouncing the amateur men 6-0. True to form, Babe livened up the tour with her antics. Before the match-up with Leonard Crawley, Babe suggested that the former Walker Cup captain shave off his mustache if she beat him. Babe shot a triumphant 74; the embarrassed Crawley left the tournament early with his mustache intact.

Back home, the Zaharias marriage was struggling. George had played a less active role in managing Babe's career. When they were together, she found his voracious eating habits repulsive. He had become so obese he couldn't fit into Babe's Ford convertible. George couldn't control his drinking any more than his eating, and when under the influence, was guilty of boorish behavior. He ignored Babe's requests that he have cosmetic surgery on his cauliflower ears, a legacy from his wrestling days. George had become an embarrassment. There were arguments, brief separations, and talk of divorce. Babe looked elsewhere for companionship. In 1950, she met golfer Betty Dodd, a tall, thin 19-year-old, two decades her junior. Betty was introduced to Babe at a Miami golf tournament, then visited the Zahariases in Tampa the following year. The two women became constant companions, routinely traveling to golf tournaments together. They also had music in common. Betty would play guitar to accompany Babe's harmonica. The duo regularly entertained friends and even cut a record. Rumors began to circulate that they were lesbians. Whatever their level of intimacy, Betty was Babe's primary partner at this point. George resented the liaison between the two, while Betty envisioned that Babe would leave George. It was an odd threesome that would endure until Babe's death.

HEALTH ISSUES

In late 1952, Babe began complaining of unusual fatigue and discomfort. She put off seeing a doctor until she arrived in Beaumont the following spring for the Babe Zaharias Open. Doctors diagnosed colon cancer and informed her that they would have to operate to remove the malignancy. Babe also had to undergo a colostomy, a procedure to reroute solid waste through an incision in the side of her stomach. This meant wearing a collection pouch underneath her clothing. For a woman as active as Babe Zaharias this was a major adjustment, but she came to accept it. The champion golfer was one of the first public figures to come out publicly and announce that she was fighting cancer. Letters poured in from sympathetic fans. The cancer spread to Babe's lymph nodes, but this development was kept from her at first. Betty provided constant support during Babe's surgery and recovery. George, on the other hand, remained in denial. He would become highly emotional and insist that Babe didn't really have cancer. Babe left the hospital in April following surgery, and she and Betty went to live with Babe's brother Louis in Texas. They stayed until June when Babe began feeling better. She returned to Tampa to train and play golf again.

Fourteen weeks after surgery Babe entered the All American Tournament in Chicago, defying her doctors' prognosis that she would never play golf again. She refused the golf cart that was offered, but the tournament director paired Betty with her for support. Babe finished fifteenth in the tournament, shooting in the 80s. It was a Herculean feat considering what she had been through. Babe then finished third in the World Golf Championship. She completed the tour, winning over $6,000 in prize money. The USGA honored her with the Ben Hogan Trophy for the greatest comeback of the year. The following season she won five tournaments including the U.S. Women's Open. Babe was living up to her reputation as the greatest woman athlete of the era.

Early in 1954, Babe was invited to the White House by President Eisenhower and the First Lady for an American Cancer Society event. She was presented with the Society's Sword of Hope award. Babe and "Ike" talked golf, their mutual passion. That same year, she began dictating her life story into a magnetic tape recorder—a new invention—for an autobiography, *This Life I've Led*, to be written by sports journalist Harry Paxton. As it turned out, 1954 would be her final year of glory. The cancer returned. During an outing on Padre Island in Texas in the spring of 1955, she suffered terrible back pain and had to go back into the hospital. Doctors first diagnosed a disc problem and operated, but the pain got worse. She was put on potent pain killers. Finally, a radiologist identified a malignancy in her lower spine. It was inoperable. All they could do was try to make her comfortable.

Babe returned to Tampa with Betty and George in late July. She would play a little golf that summer when the pain abated, but it would always come back. In October, an old friend Peggy Kirk Bell visited, and they played what would be Babe's last round of golf. Babe had to use the cart this time. She returned to the hospital in Galveston in December, got out briefly for Christmas, and then in February of 1956 went back to Florida. She was able to watch Betty compete in a tournament at Sarasota from her car seat. But the pain became chronic, and she was back in the hospital in March. She realized she was going to die. Babe kept her golf clubs in the room with her to the end. The once robust, muscular, 140-pound athlete had shrunk to 70 pounds. Babe died early in the morning on September 26, 1956, three months after her forty-fifth birthday.

Babe Didrikson Zaharias became a sport icon at a time when virtually all sports heroes were men. She first captured the nation's attention with her performance at the 1932 Olympics in front of 100,000 fans. Her triumph at the Los Angeles Games would reify the status of women Olympians.

Babe achieved her greatest fame, however, at venues that drew much smaller crowds. The galleries at women's golf tournaments were modest in comparison. Moreover, Babe's career preceded television coverage of women's sports. The print news media made her into a national celebrity. Among women of the era, her fame rivaled that of aviator Amelia Earhart and First Lady Eleanor Roosevelt.

Over her career, Babe won eighty-two amateur and professional golf tournaments. She occasionally shot in the 60s on courses longer than those at today's LPGA tournaments. No woman golfer has dominated the game as she did. Yet in her best year, she collected only $15,000 in tournament prizes. Notably, she would draw a six-figure annual income through endorsements, exhibitions, and public appearances. This was a singular accomplishment at a time when very few athletes, men or women, were offered lucrative commercial endorsements. Babe further enhanced the opportunities for women golfers through her role in founding the Ladies Professional Golf Association, the longest enduring professional sports organization for women in the United States.

Babe wasn't a feminist in the conventional sense, but she cultivated a public persona that altered the perception of women athletes. She also opened doors for young women interested in sports. In 1941, a women's intercollegiate golf tournament was organized, the first college championship event for women in any sport. Babe's achievements surely played a role in this breakthrough. While Babe's focus was on her own career, in her unique way she fought for the right of all women athletes to be treated equally.

Rarely has the nation produced such a consummate athlete. Babe's feats weren't limited to basketball, baseball, track & field, and golf. She was an excellent bowler, had won a couple of tennis tournaments in Texas, could punt a football as well as the men, and was an outstanding swimmer at short distances. She also was an accomplished dancer. Given the current focus on specialization, few contemporary athletes have been able to excel in as many sports as she did. In her autobiography, Babe wrote, "I was always determined to be the greatest athlete who ever lived." The honors and awards that she received confirm her attainment of that goal.

Associated Press voted Babe Woman Athlete of the Year six times from 1932 through 1954. In 1999, the AP voted her Woman Athlete of the 20th Century. *Sports Illustrated* magazine named her second on its list of the Greatest Female Athletes of All Time behind Jackie Joyner-Kersee, and she is the highest ranked woman on ESPN's list of the fifty top athletes of the twentieth century. Babe was inducted into the World Golf Hall of Fame in 1951. Hollywood released a film of her life in 1975 with Susan Clark playing Babe and former pro football player Alex Karras cast as George. The following year her home town of Beaumont opened the Babe Didrikson Zaharias Museum where her admirers still converge to celebrate her life.

FURTHER READING

Cayleff, Susan E. 1996. *Babe: The Life and Legend of Babe Didrikson Zaharias*. Urbana: University of Illinois Press.

Freedman, Russell. 1999. *Babe Didrikson Zaharias: The Making of a Champion*. New York: Clarion Books.

Gallico, Paul. 1956. Farewell to the Babe. *Sports Illustrated*. Oct. 8: http://sports illustrated.cnn.com/vault/article/magazine/MAG1131617/index.htm.

Johnson, William O., and Nancy P. Williamson. 1977. *Whatta-Gal: The Babe Didrikson Story*. Boston: Little Brown & Co.

Postman, Andrew. 2000. Athlete of the Century: Babe Didrikson. *Women's Sports & Fitness* 3:2: 110–15, 130–31.

Van Natta, Don. 2011. *Wonder Girl: The Magnificent Sporting Life of Babe Didrikson Zaharias*. Boston: Little, Brown & Co.

Zaharias, Babe Didrikson, with Harry Paxton. 1955. *This Life I've Led*. New York: A. S. Barnes.

Selected Bibliography

Aaseng, Nathan. 1989. *Florence Griffith Joyner: Dazzling Olympian.* Minneapolis: Lerner Publications Company.

Aaseng, Nathan. 2001. *Women Olympics Champions.* San Francisco, California: Lucent Books, Inc.

Ackerman, Martha. Women Baseball Players of the Negro League. www.scrippscollege.edu.

Allison, Stacy. (Web site). http://www.beyondthelimits.com/.

Allison, Stacy. 1999. *Many Mountains to Climb.* Wilsonville, OR: Book Partners.

Andrews, David L., & Steven J. Jackson, eds. 2001. *Sport Stars: The Cultural Politics of Sporting Celebrity.* London: Routledge.

Badenhausen, Kurt. August 18, 2010. The World's Highest-Paid Female Athletes. *Forbes.* www.forbes.com.

Bale, John, & Mette Krogh Christenson, eds. 2004. *Post-Olympism? Questioning Sport in the Twenty-First Century.* Oxford, England: Berg.

Beecham, Justin. 1974. *Olga.* New York: Paddington Press.

Benoit, Joan, with Sally Baker. 1987. *Running Tide.* New York: Alfred A. Knopf.

Brake, Deborah. 2010. *Getting in the Game: Title IX and the Women's Sports Revolution.* New York: NYU Press.

Budd, Zola, and Hugh Eley. 1989. *Zola.* London: Transworld Publishers.

Cahn, Susan K. 1994. *Coming On Strong: Gender and Sexuality in Twentieth-Century Women's Sport.* New York: The Free Press.

Carty, Victoria. 2005. Textual Portrayals of Female Athletes: Liberation or Nuanced Forms of Patriarchy? *Frontiers: A Journal of Women's Studies* 26(2).

Chapman, Deborah. November 2007. Celebrate Title IX and Know It's Not Only about Athletics. *The Register-Guard,* A11.

Christensen, Karen, Allen Guttman, and Gertrud Pfister, eds. 2000. *International Encyclopedia of Women and Sports.* New York: Macmillan.

Comaneci, Nadia. 2004. *Letters to a Young Gymnast*. Cambridge, Massachusetts: Perseus Book Group.

Comaneci, Nadia. 1983. *Nadia: The Autobiography of Nadia Comaneci*. New York: Proteus Publishing Company, Inc.

Daddario, Gina. 1998. *Women's Sport and Spectacle: Gendered Television Coverage and the Olympic Games*. Westport, CT: Praeger.

Daly, Wendy. 1996. *Bonnie Blair: Power on Ice*. New York: Random House.

Davidson, Scooter T., & Valerie Athoney, eds. 1999. *Sport of Kings: America's Top Women Jockeys Tell Their Stories*. Syracuse, NY: Syracuse University Press.

Dickson, Mike. June 12, 2009. Exclusive: Steffi Graf at 40 . . . Still Striving for Perfection. *Daily Mail*. www.dailymail.co.uk.

Edmonson, Jacqueline. 2005. *Venus and Serena Williams: A Biography*. Westport, CT: Greenwood Press.

Festle, Mary Jo. 1996. *Playing Nice: Politics and Apologies in Women's Sports*. New York: Columbia University Press.

Fleming, Peggy. (Web site). http://www.peggyfleming.com/.

Fleming, Peggy, & Peter Kaminsky. 1999. *The Long Program: Skating Towards Life's Victories*. New York: Pocket Books.

Fraser, Dawn. (Web site). http://www.dawnfraser.com.au/.

Fraser, Dawn. 2001. *Dawn: One Hell of a Life*. Sydney: Hodder Headline Australia Pty Limited.

Freedman, Russell. 1999. *Babe Didrikson Zaharias: The Making of a Champion*. New York: Clarion Books.

Friedman, Steve. October 2009. After the Fall. *Runner's World*. www.runnersworld.com.

Gavora, Jessica. 2003. *Tilting the Playing Fields: Schools, Sports, Sex, and Title IX*. San Francisco: Encounter Books.

Gibson, Althea. (Web site). http://www.altheagibson.com/.

Gibson, Althea, & Ed Fitzgerald. 1958. *I Always Wanted to Be Someone*. New York: Harper & Brothers.

Goff, Karen Goldberg. March 15, 1999. Despite Sensitive Testing, Athletes Still Dope to Win. *Insight on the News* 15(10): 42.

Graff, Steffi. (Web site). http://www.steffi-graf.net/.

Gray, Frances Clayton, & Yanick Rice Lamb. 2004. *Born to Win*. Hoboken, New Jersey: John Wiley & Sons, Inc.

Green, Michelle Y. 2002. *A Strong Right Arm*. New York: Scholastic, Inc.

Grundy, Pamela, & Susan Shackelford. 2007. *Shattering the Glass: The Remarkable History of Women's Basketball*. Chapel Hill, NC: The University of North Carolina Press.

Hall, M. Ann. 2002. *The Girl and the Game: A History of Women's Sport in Canada*. Toronto: University of Toronto Press.

Hamill, Dorothy. (Web site). http://www.dorothyhamill.com.

Hamill, Dorothy. 1983. *On & Off The Ice*. New York: Knopf.

Hamill, Dorothy, & Deborah Amelon. 2007. *A Skating Life: My Story*. New York: Hyperion.

Hamm, Mia, with Aaron Heifetz. 2000. *Go for the Goal*. New York: Harper Collins.

Hargreaves, Jennifer. 1994. *Sporting Females: Critical Issues in the History and Sociology of Women's Sports*. London: Routledge.

Hargreaves, Jennifer. 2000. *Heroines of Sport. The Politics of Difference and Identity*. London/New York: Routledge.

Harper, Jo. 2004. *Wilma Rudolph: Olympic Runner*. New York: Aladdin Paperbacks.

Hartmann-Tews, Ilse, & Gertrud Pfister, eds. 2003. *Sport and Women: Social Issues in International Perspective*. New York: Routledge.

Hastings Ardell, Jean. 2001. Mamie 'Peanut' Johnson: The Last Female Voice of the Negro Leagues. *Nine* 10(1).

Hawthorne, Peter, & Kenny Moore. April 19, 1984. A Flight to a Stormy Haven. *Sports Illustrated*. http://sportsillustrated.cnn.com.

Heller, Dick. 1998. Retton Vaulted Her Way to History with Perfection. *Washington Times*, 11.

Heywood, Leslie. November 1998. After the Northern Lights: Florence Griffith Joyner and the Making of Contemporary Women's Sport. *Mesomorphosis*. www.mesomorphosis.com.

Heywood, Leslie, & Shari L. Dworkin. 2003. *Built to Win: The Female Athlete as Cultural Icon*. Minneapolis: University of Minnesota Press.

Hill, Christopher R. January 1999. The Cold War and the Olympic Movement. *History Today* 49(1): 19.

Hogshead-Makar, Nancy. 2003. The Ongoing Battle over Title IX. *USA Today* 132(2698).

Howard, Johnette. 2005. *The Rivals: Chris Evert vs. Martina Navratilova: Their Epic Duels and Extraordinary Friendship*. New York: Broadway Books.

Hulme, Derick L., Jr. 1990. *The Political Olympics: Moscow, Afghanistan, and the 1980 U.S. Boycott*. New York: Praeger.

Joyner-Kersee, Jackie, & Sonja Steptoe. 1997. *A Kind of Grace: The Autobiography of the World's Greatest Female Athlete*. New York: Warner Books, Inc.

King, Billie Jean, & Christine Brennan. 2008. *Pressure Is a Privilege: Lessons I've Learned from Life and the Battle of the Sexes*. New York: LifeTime Media, Inc.

King, Billie Jean, & Frank Deford. 1982. *Billie Jean*. New York: The Viking Press.

Kirby, Michael. 2000. *Figure Skating to Fancy Skating: Memoirs of the Life of Sonja Henie*. North Carolina: Pentland Press.

Korbut, Olga. (Web site). http://www.olgakorbut.com/.

Lapchick, Richard E., ed. 1995. *Sport in Society: Equal Opportunity or Business as Usual*. Thousand Oaks, CA: Sage Publications.

Leder, Jane. 1996. *Grace and Glory: A Century of Women in the Olympics*. Chicago: Triumph Books.

Leslie, Lisa, with Larry Burnett. 2008. *Don't Let the Lipstick Fool You*. New York: Kensington Books.

Levinson, David, & Karen Christensen, eds. 1999. *Encyclopedia of World Sport*. New York: Oxford University.

The Lincoln Library of Sports Champions, seventh edition, volume 6. 2004. Cleveland, Ohio: The Lincoln Library Press.

Longman, Jere. June 23, 1996. How the Women Won. *New York Times*. www.nytimes.com.

Lopez, Nancy. (Web site). http://www.nancylopezgolf.com/.

Maier, Timothy W. November 12, 2001. Olympic Tragedy: 1972 Revisited; The Shadow of Terrorism Still Haunts the Olympics Almost 30 Years After Israeli Athletes Were Massacred in Munich. *Insight on the News* 17(42).

Mamie "Peanut" Johnson: A League of Their Own. *National Visionary Leadership Project*. http://www.youtube.com/watch?v=iw-ACi9TPBc&feature=related.

Mamie "Peanut" Johnson: Leaving Baseball. *National Visionary Leadership Project*. http://www.youtube.com/watch?v=MYQaclQrcU4.

Mamie "Peanut" Johnson: Negro Leagues Ending. *National Visionary Leadership Project*. http://www.youtube.com/watch?v=FQ2_yv4d0HA&feature=related.

Mamie "Peanut" Johnson: Seeing Jackie Robinson Play on TV. *National Visionary Leadership Project*. http://www.youtube.com/watch?v=0910AyG5Cts&feature=related.

Mamie "Peanut" Johnson: Women in Major League Baseball. *National Visionary Leadership Project*. http://www.youtube.com/watch?v=xoZjfA2_s04&feature=related.

Manon Rheaume Foundation. (Website). http://www.manonrheaumefoundation.org/.

Matthews, George R. 2005. *America's First Olympics: The St. Louis Games of 1904*. Columbia, MO: University of Missouri Press.

McDonagh, Eileen, & Laura Pappano. 2009. *Playing with the Boys: Why Separate is Not Equal in Sports*. New York: Oxford University Press USA.

Messner, Michael A. 2002. *Taking the Field: Women, Men, and Sports*. Minneapolis: University of Minnesota.

Mia Hamm Foundation. (Web site). http://www.miafoundation.org/.

Miller, Ernestine. 2002. *Making Her Mark: Firsts and Milestones in Women's Sports*. New York: McGraw-Hill.

Miller, Patrick B., & David K. Wiggins, eds. 2004. *Sport and the Color Line: Black Athletes and Race Relations in Twentieth-Century America*. New York: Routledge.

Mitten, Matthew J. November 2005. Is Drug Testing of Athletes Necessary? *USA Today* 134(2725).

Mottram, David R., ed. 2003. *Drugs in Sport*. London: Routledge.

Muldowney, Shirley. (Web site). http://www.muldowney.com/.

Muldowney, Shirley, with Bill Stevens. 2005. *Shirley Muldowney's Tales from the Track*. Champaign, IL: Sports Publishing.

Navarro, Mireya. February 13, 2001. Claiming Their Share: A Special Report; Women in Sports Cultivating New Playing Fields. *New York Times*. http://www.nytimes.com.

Navratilova, Martina. (Web site). http://www.martinanavratilova.com/.

Oglesby, Carole A., Doreen L. Greenberg, Ruth Louise Hall et al., eds. 1998. *Encyclopedia of Women and Sport in America*. Phoenix, AZ: Oryx Press.

O'Reilly, Jean, & Susan K. Cahn, eds. 2007. *Women and Sports in the United States: A Documentary Reader*. Lebanon, NH: University Press of New England.

Patrick, Danica. (Web site). http://www.danicaracing.com/.

Patrick, Danica, with Laura Morton. 2006. *Danica—Crossing the Line*. New York: Simon & Schuster.

Poliakoff, Michael B. July/August 2004. The Nature of the Game: The Olympic Legacy. *Humanities* 25(4). http://www.neh.gov/news/humanities/2004-07/natureofgame.html.

Rapoport, Ron. 1994. *A Kind of Grace: A Treasury of Sportswriting by Women*. Berkeley, CA: Zenobia Books.

Rappoport, Ken. 2002. *Sheryl Swoopes: Star Forward*. Berkeley Heights, NJ: Enslow Publishers, Inc.

Retton, Mary Lou. (Web site). http://www.marylouretton.com/.

Retton, Mary Lou, Bela Karolyi, and John Powers. 1986. *Creating an Olympic Champion*. New York: Dell Publishing Company, Inc.

Rheaume, Manon, with Chantal Gilbert. 1993. *Manon: Alone in Front of the Net*. Toronto: Harper Collins.

Richardson, Dot. (Web site). http://www.dotrichardson.com/.

Richardson, Dot, with Don Yeager. 1997. *Living the Dream*. New York: Kensington Books.

Riley, Dawn. (Web site). http://www.dawnriley.com/.

Riley, Dawn, with Cynthia Flanagan. 1995. *Taking the Helm*. Boston: Little, Brown & Co.

Sagert, Kelly Boyer. 2009. *Encyclopedia of Extreme Sports*. Westport, CT: Greenwood Publishing.

Salter, David. 1996. *Crashing the Old Boys' Network: The Tragedies and Triumphs of Girls and Women in Sports*. Westport, CT: Praeger Publishers.

Sandoz, Joli, & Joby Winans, eds. 1999. *Whatever It Takes: Women on Women's Sport*. New York: Farrar, Straus & Giroux.

Scherman, Tony. November 28, 1983. Sports History: How Games Tell Us Who We Are. *New York Times*. www.nytimes.com.

Sharp, Anne Wallace. 2008. *Nancy Lopez: Golf Hall of Famer*. Farmington Hills, MI: Lucent Books.

Smith, Lissa, ed. 1999. *Nike Is a Goddess: The History of Women in Sports*. New York: Atlantic Monthly Press.

Smith, Maureen. 2006. *Wilma Rudolph: A Biography*. Westport, CT: Greenwood Press.

Stout, Glenn. 2009. *Young Woman and the Sea: How Trudy Ederle Conquered the Channel and Inspired the World*. Boston: Houghton Mifflin.

Strait, Raymond, & Leif Henie. 1990. *Queen of Ice, Queen of Shadows: The Unsuspected Life of Sonja Henie*. Chelsea, Michigan: Scarborough House.

Street, Picabo, with Dana White. 2002. *Picabo: Nothing to Hide*. Chicago: Contemporary Books.

Struggling to Sustain Stardom: Few Olympic Athletes Maintain Marketability after Games. August 6, 2008. *Washington Times*, C01.

Study Uses Title IX to Show Effect of Athletic Participation on Educational Attainment. December 16, 2009. *Title IX Blog*, http://title-ix.blogspot .com/2009/12/study-uses-title-ix-to-show-effect-of.html.

Suponev, Michael. 1976. *Olga Korbut: A Biographical Portrait*. Moscow: Novosti Press Agency Publishing House.

Swoopes, Sheryl, & Greg Brown. 1996. *Sheryl Swoopes: Bounce Back*. Dallas, Texas: Taylor Publishing Company.

10 Top Olympic Moments. July 1996. *Ebony* 51(9).

Top 20 Female Athletes of the Decade. December 22, 2009. http://m.si.com.

Torres, Dara. (Web site). http://daratorres.com/.

Torres, Dara, with Elizabeth Weil. 2009. *Age Is Just a Number*. New York: Broadway Books.

Vinokur, Martin Barry. 1988. *More Than a Game: Sports and Politics*. Westport, CT: Greenwood Press.

Wiggins, David K. 1997. *Glory Bound: Black Athletes in a White America*. Syracuse, NY: Syracuse University Press.

Williams, Serena. (Web site). http://www.serenawilliams.com/.

Williams, Serena, & Daniel Paisner. 2009. *On the Line*. New York: Grand Central Publishing.

Williams, Venus. (Web site). http://www.venuswilliams.com/.

Woolum, Janet. 1998. *Outstanding Women Athletes: Who They Are and How They Influenced Sports in America*. Phoenix, AZ: The Oryx Press.

YOUTUBE VIDEOS

"Althea Gibson." YouTube. http://www.youtube.com/watch?v=YmbLdCJN pR8.

"Althea Gibson." YouTube. http://www.youtube.com/watch?v=wrpNlpu6ix0.

"Babe Didrickson, 50 Greatest Athletes, ESPN SportsCentury." YouTube. http://www.youtube.com/watch?v=GUKNj_tpi14&feature=related.

"Billie Jean King, Tennis Pioneer (Greatest Sports Legends)." YouTube. http://www.youtube.com/watch?v=lbW9E1Hwnp8.

"Cara Beth Burnside Interview." YouTube. http://www.youtube.com/watch?v=OBMKdmwvI-E.

"Cara Beth Burnside Protec Pool Party 2010." YouTube. http://www.youtube.com/watch?v=iz7i_42EBSo.

"Danica Patrick Wins at Twin Ring Motegi." YouTube. http://www.youtube.com/watch?v=t0xw6qoe6zw&feature=related.

"Danica Patrick Wins Indy Japan 300." YouTube. http://www.youtube.com/watch?v=kjFPIubBNwQ&feature=related.

"Dawn Fraser." YouTube. http://www.youtube.com/watch?v=4yvQbjpCHt0.

"Dorothy Hamil [*sic*] 1986 Worlds Short Program." YouTube. http://www.youtube.com/watch?v=8r42MTdTTCc.

"Dorothy Hamill Interview in NYC." YouTube. http://www.youtube.com/watch?v=U2XeVxhkcHk.

"Dot Richardson's Big UCLA Moment." YouTube. http://www.youtube.com/watch?v=4dLfo5xyQF8.

"Florence Griffith Joyner." YouTube. http://www.youtube.com/watch?v=6q9_N8YzZ6U.

"41-Year-Old Swimmer Makes Olympic History." YouTube. http://www.youtube.com/watch?v=V5bR2d7VKhg.

"Gertrude Ederle Swims the English Channel 1926." YouTube. http://www.youtube.com/watch?v=B7-rE-DflDA.

"Gertrude Ederle." YouTube. http://www.youtube.com/watch?v=2jfGy3pzKvc.

"Henie Career Highlights." YouTube. http://www.youtube.com/watch?v=uaMq_6qOwvY.

"Holmsey & Flan Interview Dawn Fraser." YouTube. http://www.youtube.com/watch?v=8SIdLFrb1es.

"Jockey Julie Krone with Dave Johnson ESPN 1990." YouTube. http://www.youtube.com/watch?v=u5MDCEkKESs&feature=related.

"Julie Krone Wins the Belmont Stakes." YouTube. http://www.youtube.com/watch?v=lAk8-4GZJd4&feature=related.

"Life After Sports; Winning in Life." YouTube. http://www.youtube.com/watch?v=LvEkCHCzd6A&feature=fvwrel.

"Lisa Leslie—First Women's Dunk." YouTube. http://www.youtube.com/ watch?v=-xjMFRfX4MY&feature=related.

"Lisa Leslie Career Look Back." YouTube. http://www.youtube.com/watch?v =b9akMzVMzB0&feature=related.

"Manon Rheaume Becomes the First Woman to Play in IHL." YouTube. http:// www.youtube.com/watch?v=UG9XgD9NeR4.

"Manon Rheaume: Making Hockey History." YouTube. http://www.youtube .com/watch?v=TiGXbq2NSWE.

"Martina Navratilova Chats with Jim Clash, Calls Henin Best." YouTube. http://www.youtube.com/watch?v=Z5gHfwjYu80&feature=related.

"Mia Hamm Hall of Fame Induction Speech—1 of 2." YouTube. http://www .youtube.com/watch?v=7qdwmhidOL0&feature=related.

"Mia Hamm Hall of Fame Induction Speech—2 of 2." http://www.youtube .com/watch?v=49XPYmcbYyg&feature=related.

"Mia Hamm." YouTube. http://www.youtube.com/watch?v=kNvIGlmD xHY.

"Mildred Didrikson: Voted Best Female Athlete of the Millennium." YouTube. http://www.youtube.com/watch?v=X26_8jeehbQ.

"Monica Seles Stabbing: Full Footage." YouTube. http://www.youtube.com/ watch?v=vl-2uVhNLJI&feature=related.

"Nadia Comaneci: 1976 Olympic Gold Balance Beam Routine." YouTube. http://www.youtube.com/watch?v=odTtfnWdfGU&feature=related.

"Nadia Comaneci: Montreal 1976 TEN!!!: YouTube. http://www.youtube .com/watch?v=1Tl0kE7Oels.

"Nancy Lopez Swing." YouTube. http://www.youtube.com/watch?v=6VeRj7 WaJCg.

"1988 Olympic Women's 100m Final—Florence Griffith Joyner." YouTube. http://www.youtube.com/watch?v=QWzAaydIJcA.

"1988 Seoul Olympics Jackie Joyner Kersee 7 40." YouTube. http://www.you tube.com/watch?v=0vOBvpK09YU.

"1984 Olympic Women's 3000m Final—Maricica Puica." YouTube. http:// www.youtube.com/watch?v=JziXi_NS3YY.

"1992 Mary Decker & Zola Budd Interview." YouTube. http://www.youtube .com/watch?v=BOwJGay1sxM.

"Olga Korbut—1976 Olympic Uneven Bar Routine." YouTube. http://www .youtube.com/watch?v=YsiLsguqXBU.

"Olga Korbut 1972 Olympics EF BB." YouTube. http://www.youtube.com/ watch?v=a2gNQcbicsA.

"Olympic Women's Marathon Gold Medal Joan Benoit Samuelson." You-Tube. http://www.youtube.com/watch?v=GIztjAZJHmQ.

"Peggy Fleming—1968 Olympics LP." YouTube. http://www.youtube.com/ watch?v=Pw9XZAA72lw.

"Peggy Fleming 68 US Nat." YouTube. http://www.youtube.com/watch?v=
    SdPKgg8SGys.

"Picabo Street—Olympic Dreams." YouTube. http://www.youtube.com/watch
    ?v=2Gx1Nnf9K94.

"Picabo Street." YouTube. http://www.youtube.com/watch?v=Y3_xrZqmy4Y
    &feature=related.

"Rosie Casals vs Billie Jean King, 1971 US Open Final." YouTube. http://www
    .youtube.com/watch?v=XhwlK6hdzUM.

"Sheryl Swoopes Recorded a Triple-double." YouTube. http://www.youtube
    .com/watch?v=12GLkdzwxW8.

"Sheryl Swoopes Speaking at 2007 HRC National Dinner." YouTube. http://
    www.youtube.com/watch?v=bXd266CUIec.

"Shirley Muldowney and the Last Pass." YouTube. http://www.youtube.com/
    watch?v=9US7OCXyu_Q.

"Shirley Muldowney Scores First Professional NHRA Win for Female Driver."
    YouTube. http://www.youtube.com/watch?v=VjPVDyzmWBw.

"Signature Shot: Serena Williams." YouTube. http://www.youtube.com/watch
    ?v=Em9uuA03hi8&feature=related.

"16 Days of Glory—Mary Lou Retton—Part 1." YouTube. http://www.you
    tube.com/watch?v=T3uzIe0uFFQ.

"16 Days of Glory—Mary Lou Retton—Part 2." YouTube. http://www.you
    tube.com/watch?v=klLc_i_HaXg&feature=related.

"Sonja Henie." YouTube. http://www.youtube.com/watch?v=vx4CREppX8c.

"Stacy Allison—First American Woman to Climb Mt. Everest, Inspirational
    Keynote Speaker." YouTube. http://www.youtube.com/watch?v=fPxu
    _VOjq4M.

"Stacy Allison Inspirational Speaker." YouTube. http://www.youtube.com/
    watch?v=ZumSQA4ryyY.

"Steffi Graf: The Golden Slam 1988." YouTube. http://www.youtube.com/
    watch?v=gY3NTXhMLD8.

"Title IX, Women's Sports and Social Change—Donna Lopiano." YouTube.
    http://www.youtube.com/watch?v=y-CbrIIhAi8.

"A Tribute to Dr. Donna Lopiano." YouTube. http://www.youtube.com/watch
    ?v=91EpmSMat4g.

"2008 Women's Olympic Marathon Trials—Joan Benoit-Samuelson." You-
    Tube. http://www.youtube.com/watch?v=5KlCePEPSMY.

"Venus Williams Signature Shot." YouTube. http://www.youtube.com/watch?
    v=4_pd7pETnIE.

"What Does Title IX Mean to You, Dot Richardson?" YouTube. http://www
    .youtube.com/watch?v=6oDRzjBflHU.

"Wilma Rudolph—An Uphill Battle." YouTube. http://www.youtube.com/
    watch?v=igl8DmcKRhQ.

"Wimbledon History: Martina Navratilova." YouTube. http://www.youtube
    .com/watch?v=qqyuAEmxBhI.

"Wimbledon History: Steffi Graf." YouTube. http://www.youtube.com/watch
    ?v=hC1WdHNHc3M&feature=related.

"Women's 200 Final from Rome 1960." YouTube. http://www.youtube.com/
    watch?v=FxWCZiNj5rM&feature=related.

Index

About the Authors

Steven J. Overman, a retired college professor, has spent most of his professional life writing about various aspects of sport and physical activity. He has published some three dozen articles and reviews in academic journals, including a coauthored study of professional women's childhood play experience for the journal *Sex Roles*, and an article on black women athletes in *Journal of Sport Behavior*. His books include *The Protestant Ethic and the Spirit of Sport* (2011) and *Living Out of Bounds: The Everyday Life of Male Athletes* (2010). He currently is researching a book on children's sport.

Kelly Boyer Sagert has written extensively on athletic pursuits, including three books: *About Boomerangs: America's Silent Sport* (1996); *Joe Jackson: A Biography* (ABC-CLIO/Greenwood, 2004), and the *Encyclopedia of Extreme Sports* (ABC-CLIO/Greenwood, 2008). She also has published six other books. She has contributed material to numerous sports-themed encyclopedias as well, including the *International Encyclopedia of Women and Sports* (2001) and the *Berkshire Encyclopedia of World Sport* (2005). Boyer Sagert also coauthored a biography of baseball player Charles "Swede" Risberg that appeared in the book *Deadball Stars of the American League* (2006), and she wrote a biography of baseball player Lee May for *The Encyclopedia of the African and African-American Experience* (2005).